Theistic Evolution

In this book, Mariusz Tabaczek develops a contemporary, reimagined proposal of an Aristotelian–Thomistic perspective on theistic evolution. Deeply rooted in classical philosophy and theology, the volume combines careful textual analysis of ancient, medieval, and contemporary literature with innovative, original, and constructive argumentation and modelling. Tabaczek offers a wide-ranging set of arguments on behalf of those who advocate for the relevance of classical philosophical and theological thought in the context of contemporary science and the dialogue between science and religion. Avoiding simplistic answers to complex questions concerning the origin of species, including the human species, his book inspires critical thinking and a systematic approach to all major philosophical presuppositions and both philosophical and theological repercussions of the theory of evolution. Without contradicting or abandoning the letter of the tradition, Tabaczek echoes the spirit of Aristotle's and Aquinas's philosophy and theology, moving them forward to embrace the evolutionary aspect of the contemporary view of reality.

Mariusz Tabaczek, O.P., is a friar preacher, professor of theology, and member of the Thomistic Institute at the Pontifical University of Saint Thomas Aquinas in Rome. He is the author of *Emergence: Towards a New Metaphysics and Philosophy of Science* (2019) and *Divine Action and Emergence: An Alternative to Panentheism* (2021).

Theistic Evolution

A Contemporary Aristotelian-Thomistic Perspective

MARIUSZ TABACZEK

Pontifical University of St. Thomas Aquinas, Rome

Shaftesbury Road, Cambridge CB2 8EA, United Kingdom

One Liberty Plaza, 20th Floor, New York, NY 10006, USA

477 Williamstown Road, Port Melbourne, VIC 3207, Australia

314–321, 3rd Floor, Plot 3, Splendor Forum, Jasola District Centre, New Delhi – 110025, India

103 Penang Road, #05–06/07, Visioncrest Commercial, Singapore 238467

Cambridge University Press is part of Cambridge University Press & Assessment, a department of the University of Cambridge.

We share the University's mission to contribute to society through the pursuit of education, learning and research at the highest international levels of excellence.

www.cambridge.org
Information on this title: www.cambridge.org/9781009367011

DOI: 10.1017/9781009367028

© Mariusz Tabaczek 2024

This publication is in copyright. Subject to statutory exception and to the provisions of relevant collective licensing agreements, no reproduction of any part may take place without the written permission of Cambridge University Press & Assessment.

First published 2024

A catalogue record for this publication is available from the British Library

A Cataloging-in-Publication data record for this book is available from the Library of Congress

ISBN 978-1-009-36701-1 Hardback

Łukasz Wiśniewski, O.P., Provincial, Province of Poland

Cambridge University Press & Assessment has no responsibility for the persistence or accuracy of URLs for external or third-party internet websites referred to in this publication and does not guarantee that any content on such websites is, or will remain, accurate or appropriate.

To my family

You must let me thank you for the pleasure which the Introduction to the Aristotle book [*Parts of Animals*] has given me. I have rarely read anything which has interested me more, though I have not read as yet more than a quarter of the book proper. From quotations which I had seen, I had a high notion of Aristotle's merits, but I had not the most remote notion what a wonderful man he was. Linnaeus and Cuvier have been my two gods, though in very different ways, but they were mere schoolboys to old Aristotle.

Charles Darwin, "C. Darwin to W. Ogle" (letter from Feb. 22, 1882) in *The Life and Letters of Charles Darwin: vol. 3*, edited by Francis Darwin (London: John Murray, 1887), 251–52.

Throughout all our efforts, in every dramatic struggle between old and new views, we recognize the eternal longing for understanding: the ever-firm belief in the harmony of our world, continuously strengthened by increasing obstacles to comprehension.

Albert Einstein and L. Infeld, *The Evolution of Physics*

Contents

List of Figures		*page* x
List of Tables		xi
Acknowledgments		xii
List of Abbreviations		xv
Introduction		1
	Evolutionary Biology	2
	Aristotelian–Thomistic Metaphysics	8
	Thomistic Theology of Creation	12
	The Plan of the Project	14
1	**Metaphysics of Evolutionary Transitions**	18
	Hylomorphic Notion of a Living Being	19
	Substantial Unity of a Living Being and Virtual Presence of Its Parts	26
	Disposition of Matter and Levels of Potentiality	28
	Matter as Striving for Perfection – *Scala Naturae*	31
	Metaphysics of Evolutionary Transitions	34
	The Principle of Proportionate Causation and Evolution	42
	Conclusion	55
2	**Essentialist and Hylomorphic Notion of Species and Species Transformation**	57
	Nominalism *versus* Realism about Species	58
	Debate over Species Concepts	61
	Relational Species Concepts	62
	Intrinsic Species Concepts	71
	Classifying Species under Higher Taxa	88
	Conclusion	91

viii   *Contents*

3   Natural Selection, Teleology, and Chance in Evolution   92
    Classical Notion of Teleology   95
    Aristotle on Teleology and Chance   99
    Aquinas on Teleology and Chance   104
    Natural Selection in Aristotle and Aquinas   105
    Contemporary Debate on Teleology   107
    Evolution and the Interplay of Teleology and Chance   123
    Conclusion   125

4   Aquinas's Account of Creation   127
    Augustine's Notion of Creation   128
    The Meaning of *Rationes Seminales*   131
    Augustine's Creation Theology as Evolutionary   135
    Aquinas's Philosophical Theology of Creation   137
    Aquinas on the Three Stages of the Work of the Six Days   147
    Aquinas's Use of Augustine's Notion of *Rationes Seminales*   149
    Evolutionary Redefinition of the Concept of *Rationes Seminales*   154
    Conclusion   155

5   Aquinas and Evolution   156
    Aquinas on the Emergence of New Species   157
    Thomistic Version of Theistic Evolutionism   166
    A Response to an Objection   169
    Conclusion   176

6   Evolution and Creation   178
    The Meaning of Theistic Evolutionism   179
    God as Creating through Evolution   180
    Thomistic Notion of God Creating through Evolution   185
    "Theistic Evolutionism" *versus* "Evolutionary Creationism"   187
    Distinctiveness of Creation   189
    Creation and Evolution   198
    Conclusion   200

7   Concurrence of Divine and Created Causes in Evolutionary
    Transitions   201
    Divine Action   202
    Secondary Causation in Theistic Evolution Outside of
        Thomistic Circles   204
    Secondary Causation in Theistic Evolution within
        Thomistic Circles   207
    Concurrence of Divine and Natural Causes in Begetting
        Offspring   212
    Concurrence of Divine and Natural Causes in an Evolutionary
        Transformation   216
    The Question of Unity of Immanent Cause(s) in an Evolutionary
        Transformation   219
    Conclusion   220

8 Theological Anthropogenesis and Evolution	222
Aristotelian–Thomistic Notion of Human Nature	223
Thomistic View of the Evolutionary Origin of the Human Species	231
Other Views on the Origin of the Human Species	236
Monogenism *versus* Polygenism	244
Conclusion	277
General Conclusion	278
Bibliography	281
Index	308

Figures

1.1	Two levels of potentiality and the flexibility of the dynamic processes in nature	*page* 31
1.2	Hylomorphic metaphysics of an evolutionary transition	35
2.1	Classification of species concepts	62
2.2	Depiction of evolutionary processes	89
2.3	Classification of domestic cat (*Felis catus*) under two different schools of taxonomy	90
3.1	Two divisions of events in Aristotle	100
3.2	The distinction between chance and luck (fortune)	101
4.1	Graphic depiction of the sequence of the work of the six days in the account of Genesis 1	149
7.1	Concurrence of divine and natural causes in begetting offspring of the same species	213
7.2	Concurrence of divine and natural causes in an evolutionary transition	217
8.1	Concurrence of divine and natural causes in the evolution of man	233

Tables

5.1 Selection of the passages from the works of Aquinas showing the complexity of the debate on the possibility of the emergence of new species through biological evolution in reference to his theology of creation   *page* 158

5.2 Categories used in the proposed model of theistic evolutionism   172

Acknowledgments

The material presented in this volume originates from several years of my reflecting, teaching, researching, and writing on the topic of evolution – shared between the Thomistic Institute in the Dominican priory of St. Joseph in Warsaw (Poland) and the Thomistic Institute at the Angelicum in Rome (Italy). I would like to thank my brothers assigned to the priory of St. Joseph in the years 2017–2020, the director of the Thomistic Institute in Warsaw, Fr. Mateusz Przanowski, O.P., and the regent of studies from the Polish Dominican Province in those years, Fr. Maciej Roszkowski, O.P., for their fraternal support. After my transition to the Pontifical University of Saint Thomas Aquinas in Rome (Italy), my further research conducted under the auspices of Thomistic Institute at the Angelicum was generously supported by the benefactors of the Institute to whom I am deeply grateful. Many thanks to my students both in Rome and in Poland for their curiosity and challenging questions. I also thank the Dominican community at the priory of saints Dominic and Sixtus in Rome for shared experience of the Dominican life. I am forever grateful to my family and friends and all who support me and show appreciation of my work. Last but not least, I would like to thank my teacher and mentor, Michael Dodds, O.P. He taught me the principles of the Aristotelian–Thomistic system, which I have applied in this volume to the theory of biological evolution.

Part of my research on species, covered in Chapter 2, was sponsored by the Templeton Foundation (Grant ID 61360, *Thomistic Evolution and the Defense of Faith and Reason: Engaging Catholic Families, Philosophers, and Theologians*). I wish to express my gratitude for this support.

Parts of the material presented in this volume have previously appeared in print. They have been rethought, extended in various degrees, and

Acknowledgments   xiii

organized into a coherent whole. I wish to thank the following publishers for their permission to reproduce my previously published works:

(1) Mariusz Tabaczek, "An Aristotelian Account of Evolution and the Contemporary Philosophy of Biology," in *The 1st Virtual International Conference on the Dialogue between Science and Theology. Dialogo Conf 2014: Cosmology, Life & Anthropology*, ed. Cosmin Tudor Ciocan and Anton Lieskovský (Zilina: Publishing Institution of the University of Zilina, 2014), 57–69, www.academia.edu/9636884/An_Aristotelian_Account_of_Evolution_and_the_Contemporary_Philosophy_of_Biology. My thanks to Cosmin Tudor Ciocan and Anton Lieskovský.

(2) Mariusz Tabaczek, "Thomistic Response to the Theory of Evolution: Aquinas on Natural Selection and the Perfection of the Universe," *Theology and Science* 13, no. 3 (2015): 325–44. My thanks to Taylor & Francis.

(3) Mariusz Tabaczek, "What Do God and Creatures Really Do in an Evolutionary Change? Divine Concurrence and Transformism from the Thomistic Perspective," *American Catholic Philosophical Quarterly* 93, no. 3 (2019): 445–82. My thanks to George Leaman at Philosophy Documentation Center.

(4) Mariusz Tabaczek, "The Metaphysics of Evolution: From Aquinas's Interpretation of Augustine's Concept of Rationes Seminales to the Contemporary Thomistic Account of Species Transformism," *Nova et Vetera* 18, no. 3 (2020): 945–72. My thanks to Matthew Levering, Thomas Joseph White, O.P., and Emmaus Academic Press.

(5) Mariusz Tabaczek, "Does God Create Through Evolution? A Thomistic Perspective," *Theology and Science* 20, no. 1 (January 2, 2022): 46–68. My thanks to Taylor & Francis.

(6) Mariusz Tabaczek, "Essentialist and Hylomorphic Notion of Species and Species Transformation," in *A Catholic View on Evolution: New Perspectives in Thomistic Philosophy and Theology*, ed. by Nicanor Austriaco (Washington, DC: Catholic University of America Press, 2023). My thanks to Nicanor Austriaco, O.P.

(7) Mariusz Tabaczek, "Contemporary Version of the Monogenetic Model of Anthropogenesis: Some Critical Remarks from the Thomistic Perspective," *Religions* (2023), https://doi.org/10.3390/rel14040528. My thanks to editors of *Religions*.

xiv   *Acknowledgments*

I also want to express my gratitude to all the reviewers of these articles, members of the philosophy and theology teams on the aforementioned Templeton grant project on the Thomistic view of evolution, and a number of my colleagues in philosophy and theology for their valuable comments and critical evaluation of my ideas. Thanks to audiences at conferences and public lectures at which I presented various parts of the research gathered in this volume.

Abbreviations

ABBREVIATIONS FOR THE WORKS OF ARISTOTLE

De an.	*De anima* (*On the Soul*)
De gen. an.	*De generatione animalium* (*On the Generation of Animals*)
De gen. et corr.	*De generatione et corruptione* (*On Generation and Corruption*)
De part. an.	*De partibus animalium* (*On the Parts of Animals*)
Hist. an.	*Historia animalium* (*The History of Animals*)
Meta.	*Metaphysica* (*The Metaphysics*)
Meteo.	*Meteorologica* (*The Meteorology*)
Phys.	*Physica* (*The Physics*)

ABBREVIATIONS FOR THE WORKS OF ST. THOMAS AQUINAS

Comp. theo.	*Compendium Theologiae* (*Compendium of Theology*)
De ente	*De ente et essentia* (*On Being and Essence*)
De mixt. elem.	*De mixtione elementorum ad magistrum Philippum de Castro Caeli* (*On the Mixture of the Elements, to Master Philip of Castrocaeli*)
De prin. nat.	*De principiis naturae* (*The Principles of Nature*)
De Trin.	*Super Boethium De Trinitate* (*On Boethius's De Trinitate*)
De vir.	*Quaestiones disputatae de virtutibus* (*Disputed Questons on the Virtues*)

xvi   *List of Abbreviations*

In De an.	*Sententia libri De anima* (*Commentary on Aristotle's* De anima)
In Meta.	*In Metaphysicam Aristotelis commentaria* (*Commentary on Aristotle's* Metaphysics)
In Phys.	*In octo libros Physicorum Aristotelis expositio* (*Commentary on Aristotle's* Physics)
Super Sent.	*Scriptum super libros Sententiarum* (*Commentary on* Sentences)
Q. de an.	*Quaestiones disputatae de anima* (*Disputed Questions on the Soul*)
Q. de malo	*Quaestiones disputatae de malo* (*Disputed Questions on Evil*)
Q. de pot.	*Quaestiones disputatae de potentia* (*Disputed questions on the Power of God*)
Q. de ver.	*Quaestiones disputatae de veritate* (*Disputed questions on Truth*)
Quod.	*Quaestiones quodlibetales* (*Miscellaneous Questions*)
SCG	*Summa contra gentiles* (*On the Truth of the Catholic Faith*)
ST	*Summa theologiae* (*The Summa Theologica*)
Super De causis	*Super librum De causis expositio* (*Commentary on the* Liber de causis)

ABBREVIATIONS FOR OTHER BIBLIOGRAPHICAL REFERENCES

De Gen. ad litt.	*De Genesi ad litteram libri duodecim* (*The Literal Meaning of Genesis*)
NABRE	*New American Bible Revised Edition*

OTHER ABBREVIATIONS

AF	accidental form
AAFF	accidental forms
BSC	biological species concept
ESC	ecological species concept
EssSC	essentialist species concept
EST	evolutionary school of taxonomy
EvoSC	evolutionary species concept
HPCSC	homeostatic property cluster species concept

List of Abbreviations

ID	intelligent design
ISCs	intrinsic species concepts
MSC	morphology species concept
MT	monophyletic taxon
NIODA	non-interventionist objective divine action
P-CSC	phylogenetic-cladistic species concept
PM	primary matter
PorST	Porphyrian school of taxonomy
PPC	principle of proportionate causation
PSC	phenetic species concept
PSSC	"population structure" species concept
PST	phenetic school of taxonomy
PT	paraphyletic taxon
RSCs	relational species concepts
SF	substantial form
SSFF	substantial forms
TVTE	Thomistic version of theistic evolution

Introduction

The main objective of this book is to contribute to and further develop the contemporary Aristotelian–Thomistic account of the theory of evolution, in both its philosophical and theological dimensions. It thus builds on the thought of a number of thinkers, coming from and continuing the classical tradition, who commented on more speculative – philosophical and theological – repercussions of Darwin's view of nature.[1] What motivates the research presented in this volume is the current status of the conversation engaging evolutionary biology, philosophy of biology and metaphysics, and Christian theology of creation. Past strongly reductionist, antiteleological, and antiessentialist views of species transformism – on the one hand – and theological interpretations of evolutionary theory leaning toward panpsychism and pantheism – on the other hand – we seem to face an opportunity for developing a multidimensional, open-minded, and comprehensive account of evolutionary theory. One that remains in line with and benefits from a reference to the categories of classical metaphysics and Aquinas's notion of God and divine action in the universe – which makes it attractive also to readers who do not have any prior commitment to Thomism. To see this opening, one needs to investigate the inner dynamics of each partner of this interdisciplinary endeavor.

---

[1] Among more significant contributors who will be referenced in this volume, we should mention Mortimer J. Adler, Nicanor Pier Giorgio Austriaco, F. F. Centore, William E. Carroll, John N. Deely, Charles DeKoninck, Joseph Donceel, Ryan Fáinche, Étienne Gilson, James R. Hofmann, Norbert Luyten, Jacques Maritain, Ernan McMullin, Antonio Moreno, Raymond J. Nogar, Fran O'Rourke, Edward T. Oakes, and Gerard M. Verschuuren.

EVOLUTIONARY BIOLOGY

We should begin with evolutionary theory. As commonly known, Darwin's original idea of the common descent with modification of all living organisms from one ancestor – through spontaneous changes subject to the mechanism of natural selection – has itself undergone a considerable transformation. The neo-Darwinian contribution, grounding evolutionary theory in the newly established notion of "independent" hereditary units – called "genes" – served as a transition to the contemporary evolutionary synthesis.[2] The first step of its development was marked by the implementation of mathematics, statistics, and modeling in the new branch of theoretical biology known as population genetics, which formally defines evolution as changes in the genetic composition of populations (i.e., changes in the frequencies of genetic variants). It was established by Sir Ronald A. Fisher. The second phase of the advancement of the current evolutionary synthesis came with the discovery of the structure of DNA, which "transformed" genes from mathematical abstractions into actual entities. Helpful in better understanding of the mechanisms of evolutionary transitions and mindful of factors other than DNA mutations that effect evolutionary changes (including genetic recombination, gene transfer, and genetic drift), the molecular approach to biology did not avoid some more extreme reductionist philosophical interpretations. Many philosophers and biologists alike saw it as foundational for an antiteleological notion of evolution perceived as an effect of pure chance. Despite a much more moderate approach to the metaphysics of evolution expressed by the fathers of the late twentieth-century version of the evolutionary synthesis – solidified in writings of the Russian-American geneticist Theodosius Dobzhansky, German-American geneticist Ernst Mayr,

---

[2] Darwin basically followed the classical version of inheritance theory, going back to Hippocrates. It suggested the existence of inheritance molecules, manufactured by parental organisms' body parts and tissues, and transmitted in gametes. Darwin called them "gemmules" and speculated that they direct the development of a new organism (forming a tissue or organ which produced them). As commonly known, a revolutionary improvement in biological knowledge of hereditary mechanism and embryology came with the rediscovery, in early twentieth century, of the research of Darwin's contemporary, Gregor Mendel, an Augustinian friar from the priory of St. Thomas in Brno (in Bohemia). His science was brought to light by Hugo de Vries, and further developed by Thomas Hunt Morgan who discovered the location of genes on chromosomes and realized – based on the experiments he conducted of fruit flies (*Drosophila melanogaster*) – that the number of small mutations that may occur in a genome is considerably high. It proved that evolution might progress in a gradual manner and that it could be described within the framework of Mendelian genetics.

Evolutionary Biology

and Spanish-American biologist and philosopher (former Dominican) Francisco J. Ayala – many began to treat genes as completely independent, primary units of evolutionary transitions, ignoring possible nonlinear interactions among them. This promoted even more radical agnostic and atheistic views grounded in evolutionary theory, shared by Richard Dawkins, Sam Harris, and others.

However, that the twentieth-century notion of evolutionary synthesis – both in its reductionist and nonreductionist versions – is not a conclusive one becomes obvious to all those who patiently follow the developments of evolutionary biology and the philosophical reflection it inspires. Among early protagonists of a renewed assessment of Darwinism, we find several thinkers, whose diverse ideas are often summarized and labeled as meta-Darwinian. The movement began over 50 years ago, with the theory of punctuated equilibrium, which accepts evolutionary mechanism proposed by the contemporary synthesis while challenging the conviction with regards to its pace. Steven J. Gould and Niles Eldredge suggested that evolution happens through rapid bursts or spurts, taking place in lineages that most of the time remain in stable equilibrium. Their theory suggested a radically different view of a species. Rather than an infinitely fluid unit, implied by the proponents of Neo-Darwinism and the current evolutionary synthesis, they saw it as a stable entity resistant to change.[3] Moreover, the same theory of punctuated equilibrium, in virtue of its argument in favor of the stability of species, suggests species or even groups of species – and not only organisms and populations (or genes as want ultra-Darwinists) – as possible units subject to evolutionary transformations.[4] That this claim challenges one of the basic presuppositions of extrapolation from micro- to macroevolution becomes obvious.

---

[3] "If we view a species as a set of subpopulations, all ready and able to differentiate but held in check only by the rein of gene flow, then the stability of species is a tenuous thing indeed. But if that stability is an inherent property both of individual development and the genetic structure of populations, then its power is immeasurably enhanced, for the basic property of homeostatic systems, or steady states, is that they resist change by self-regulation. That local populations do not differentiate into new species, even though no external bar prevents it, stands as strong testimony to the inherent stability of species" (Niles Eldredge and Stephen Jay Gould, "Punctuated Equilibria: An Alternative to Phyletic Gradualism," in *Models in Paleobiology*, ed. T. J. M. Schopf [San Francisco: Freeman, Cooper & Co., 1972], 114–15).

[4] "I believe that the traditional Darwinian focus on individual bodies, and the attendant reductionist account of macroevolution, will be supplanted by a hierarchical approach recognizing legitimate Darwinian individuals at several levels of structural hierarchy, including genes, bodies, demes, species, and clades" (Stephen Jay Gould, "Darwinism and the Expansion of Evolutionary Theory," *Science* 216, no. 4544 [1982], 384).

4   *Introduction*

Another set of fresh and challenging ideas came once again from Gould, this time working with Richard Lewontin. They put in question the Darwinian concentration on the directly adaptive character of traits "favored" by natural selection. They claimed it is possible to argue that many traits originate as nonadaptive chance by-products, having initially no selective advantage. Gould coined for his theory the term "exaptation," describing transmission of traits with no usage or function (or a different usage or function), which are later "coopted" for the role they play in organisms that succeed in the struggle for existence. If true, this mechanism provides yet another pool of variations for natural selection to "choose" from.[5] Related to Gould and Lewontin's suggestion is Motoo Kimura's neutral theory of evolution, which builds on his emphasis on the role of DNA mutations that are initially neutral, having no effect on the protein's ability to perform its function and rarely spread throughout the population. Putting a greater emphasis on genetic drift, Kimura suggests that such neutral changes, hidden at the molecular level, may become advantageous over extended periods of time, due to the changing conditions of the environment.[6]

Whether these theories are correct and subject to experimental verification, and whether they offer new and viable mechanisms by which evolution might proceed, remains an open question. However, and most importantly, they challenge the received pan-selectionist and adaptationist view of evolutionary theory as unambiguously defined within the lines of the contemporary synthesis and unanimously received and agreed upon by all biologists, once and for all. Quite to the contrary, taken as a Lakatosian research program, the theory of evolution should be treated as a "work in progress," less dogmatic than we usually tend to think of it.

The accuracy of this approach finds confirmation in the more recent emphasis on the causal and explanatory interconnectedness between evolutionary and developmental biology (evo-devo), as well as the changes described as epigenetic and the niche construction theory.

---

[5] See S. J. Gould and R. C. Lewontin, "The Spandrels of San Marco and the Panglossian Paradigm: A Critique of the Adaptationist Programme," *Proceedings of the Royal Society of London. Series B. Biological Sciences* 205, no. 1161 (September 21, 1979): 581–98.

[6] "We should not overlook the possibility that some of the 'neutral' alleles may become advantageous under an appropriate environmental condition or a different genetic background; thus, neutral mutants have a latent potential for selection ... [They] can be the raw material for future adaptive evolution" (Motoo Kimura, *The Neutral Theory of Molecular Evolution* [Cambridge: Cambridge University Press, 1983], xiii).

Evolutionary Biology

Concerning evo-devo, biologists now realize that differences in genetic makeup can lead to differences in development and *vice versa*, that is, differences in development (such as changes in expression of the same genes due to various environmental conditions) can lead to genetic difference.[7] Biological observation and analysis show how vastly different organisms "use" the same genes in various ways effecting different phenotypes. Hence, Robert Lickliter goes so far as to say that "[u]nlike the gene-centered emphasis of the Modern Synthesis, evo-devo views evolution as changes in developmental processes rather than simply changes in gene frequencies."[8] In the same vein, Kostas Kampourakis and Alessandro Minelli suggest that central to evo-devo is "the idea that it is not adult phenotypes that evolve but their developmental trajectories. The question then is not how adult form A evolved into form B but, rather, how the developmental processes that produced form A evolved into those that produced form B."[9] What is more, the same theory seems to offer a feasible explanation of rapid, saltational evolutionary transitions, suggested already by Gould. Today, we know that minor genetic mutations of developmental (homeotic) genes (e.g., a group of genes called Hox genes) may have large effects on the structural organization of organisms. Consequently, going against the claim on which Darwin staked the entire edifice of his theory, a number of contemporary biologists claim that rapid evolutionary leaps that make evolution "skip ahead" are indeed possible.[10]

---

[7] See Jason Scott Robert, "Evo-Devo," in *The Oxford Handbook of Philosophy of Biology*, ed. Michael Ruse (Oxford, New York: Oxford University Press, 2008), 291–309; Jan Baedke and Scott F. Gilbert, "Evolution and Development," in *The Stanford Encyclopedia of Philosophy*, ed. Edward N. Zalta, Fall 2021 (Metaphysics Research Lab, Stanford University, 2021), https://plato.stanford.edu/archives/fall2021/entries/evolution-development/ (retrieved 20 July 2022).

[8] Robert Lickliter, "Developmental Evolution," *Wiley Interdisciplinary Reviews. Cognitive Science* 8, no. 1–2 (2017), 3.

[9] Kostas Kampourakis and Alessandro Minelli, "Understanding Evolution: Why Evo-Devo Matters," *BioScience* 64, no. 5 (May 1, 2014), 382. In other words, whereas "very few evo-devo practitioners doubt that natural selection within populations is responsible for the changes that occur within species," they also "believe that additional mechanisms, mechanisms involved with ontogeny rather than population genetics, must contribute to a full understanding of evolution" (Ron Amundson, *The Changing Role of the Embryo in Evolutionary Thought: Roots of Evo-Devo*, Cambridge Studies in Philosophy and Biology [Cambridge: Cambridge University Press, 2005], 3).

[10] See *ibid.*, 382; Elizabeth Pennisi, "Evo-Devo Enthusiasts Get Down to Details," *Science* 298, no. 5595 (November 1, 2002), 953. In correspondence with the theory of evo-devo, a developmental biologist Brian Goodwin offers an intriguing, albeit controversial theory of "morphogenetic fields." He sees development as the process of breaking

Introduction

The science of epigenetics, on its part, explores evolutionary changes that do not occur due to changes in gene frequency. Epigenetic inheritance is thus the inheritance of specific ways of expression of the raw genetic material. Eva Jablonka and Mary Lamb speak about mechanisms that can maintain cellular identity and heredity through (1) self-sustaining feedback loops (such as in metabolic networks), (2) copying of structural templates (such as prion proteins), (3) silencing of genes with chromatin markers (such as DNA methylation, phosphorylation, or acetylation), or (4) transmission of small RNAs, which can function as a source of immunity against viral infection or adaptively regulate nutrition-related genes protecting against starvation. Most importantly, we seem to have now a robust evidence that epigenetic traits are stably transmitted across generations and ubiquitous in a wide range of taxa, determining phenotype expression, developmental processes, and the generation of new variations.[11]

Another important development in evolutionary studies puts an emphasis on the phenomenon known as "niche construction," that is, an active influence of organisms on their environment. Or rather, as note Jeremy Kendal et al. "the defining characteristics of niche construction is not the modification of environments per se, but rather the organism-induced changes in selection pressures in environments."[12] Celia Deane-Drummond comments on this important paradigm shift in our understanding of biological evolution and says that while the

standard evolution theory is "externalist," inasmuch as the environment is viewed as external factors that are acting in order to select those internal properties that are most adapted to that environment ... [in the new approach] niche construction works *with* natural selection in the evolutionary process in a dynamic interchange. Niches are themselves part of the inheritance process, so that an

---

symmetries of cells that leads to their specialization. He defines "morphogenetic fields" as areas where symmetries get broken, governed by the laws of organization that make certain developmental paths more robust and stable. See Brian Goodwin, *How the Leopard Changed Its Spots: The Evolution of Complexity* (New York: Charles Scribner's Sons, 1994), 66.

[11] See Eva Jablonka and Marion J. Lamb, *Evolution in Four Dimensions: Genetic, Epigenetic, Behavioral, and Symbolic Variation in the History of Life* (Cambridge, MA: MIT Press, 2014). Apart from genetic and epigenetic inheritance systems, Jablonka and Lamb suggest introducing the categories of behavioral and symbolic inheritance systems. See also Renato Paro et al., *Introduction to Epigenetics* (Berlin: Springer, 2021); C. David Allis et al., eds., *Epigenetics, Second Edition* (Cold Spring Harbor, New York: Cold Spring Harbor Laboratory Press, 2015).

[12] Jeremy Kendal, Jamshid J. Tehrani, and John Odling-Smee, "Human Niche Construction in Interdisciplinary Focus," *Philosophical Transactions of the Royal Society B: Biological Sciences* 366, no. 1566 (2011), 785.

interactionist evolutionary theory replaces an *externalist* theory. Niche construction emphasizes not just genetic and cultural inheritance, but also ecological inheritance in dynamic interaction with the first two.[13]

Finally, we must not ignore the contribution of the theories of complexity and self-organizing systems, which assume that Darwinian mechanisms are not sufficient to explain the complexity of living systems. Rather, they see such spectacular organization as spontaneously emerging in an instant within systems remaining far from thermodynamic equilibrium. Standing at the forefront of this movement – that takes its origin in the famous Belousow-Zhabotinsky (BZ) reaction, which generated spontaneous ordered patterns that change over time – Stuart Kauffman suggests that complexity theory may explain the origin of life.[14] Note that on this view natural selection's role is limited to fine-tuning of what is built by an entirely different mechanism.[15]

In light of these developments, many join the "growing constituency among biologists and other evolutionary theorists these days" that the current synthesis is becoming outdated and that "biology now goes far beyond and sometimes even contradicts" that synthesis.[16] In other words, notes David O. Brown, "If the twentieth century has come to be seen as something of a 'victory lap' for Darwin's theory of evolution through

---

[13] Celia Deane-Drummond, "In Adam All Die?: Questions at the Boundary of Niche Construction, Community Evolution, and Original Sin," in *Evolution and the Fall*, ed. William T. Cavanaugh and James K. A. Smith (Grand Rapids, Michigan: Wm. B. Eerdmans Publishing, 2017), 33–34.

[14] See Stuart Kauffman, *At Home in the Universe: The Search for the Laws of Self-Organization and Complexity* (New York: Oxford University Press, 1995), 45 where he, not without controversies that followed his daring claim, states that "There are compelling reasons to believe that whenever a collection of chemicals contains enough different kinds of molecules, a metabolism will crystalize from the broth. If this argument is correct, metabolic networks need not be built one component at a time, they can spring full-grown from a primordial soup."

[15] This comment is made by Thomas B. Fowler and Daniel Kuebler, who in their book *The Evolution Controversy: A Survey of Competing Theories* (Grand Rapids: Baker Academic, 2007) analyze a number of theories that fall under the umbrella of the meta-Darwinian school of evolutionary theory (see *ibid.*, 277–326).

[16] Peter A. Corning, "Beyond the Modern Synthesis: A Framework for a More Inclusive Biological Synthesis," *Progress in Biophysics and Molecular Biology* 153 (July 1, 2020), 5. As notes James Grieemer, "Darwin's vision no longer seems grand enough … in the face of our vastly greater knowledge of chemistry, biochemistry, molecular developmental biology, phylogenetic systematics, evo-devo, epigenetics, genomics, proteomics, and metabolomics, in addition to paleobiology, geophysics, geochemistry, mineralogy, climatology, and astrobiology" (James Griesemer, "Origins of Life Studies," in *The Oxford Handbook of Philosophy of Biology*, ed. Michael Ruse [Oxford, New York: Oxford University Press, 2008], 266).

8 *Introduction*

natural selection, then the twenty-first century has seen the emergence of respected biologists who question whether that victory was declared too hastily."[17] This tells us that we need a new, extended synthesis which most likely is on the way. According to its main principles:

Genetic evolution (defined as changes in gene frequencies) is a special case situated within a diverse range of evolutionary modes. ... Inheritable phenotypic variation arises not just from genetic variation, but from the dynamics of gene regulatory networks and the interaction with biophysical processes and tissue mechanics as well as the microbial and larger environment. Natural selection can arise from environmental selection but also from the relationship between organisms and their social, cultural, and physical environments as they construct and alter the selective environment.[18]

ARISTOTELIAN–THOMISTIC METAPHYSICS

The second partner of the dialogue is the philosophy of biology and metaphysics. What becomes crucial for a philosopher of the Aristotelian–Thomistic orientation is that the new developments in evolutionary biology described above provide a new opportunity for the retrieval of some of the crucial categories of classical metaphysics. First, we should emphasize the way in which contemporary biology puts in question the overemphasis of the twentieth-century evolutionary synthesis on the

---

[17] David O. Brown, "St. George Jackson Mivart: Evo-Devo, Epigenetics and Thomism," *Theology and Science* 20, no. 4 (2022), 479. See also David J. Depew and Bruce H. Weber, "The Fate of Darwinism: Evolution After the Modern Synthesis," *Biological Theory* 6, no. 1 (December 1, 2011): 89–102; David J. Depew and Bruce H. Weber, "Challenging Darwinism: Expanding, Extending, Replacing," in *The Cambridge Encyclopedia of Darwin and Evolutionary Thought*, ed. Michael Ruse (Cambridge England; New York: Cambridge University Press, 2013), 405–11.

[18] Lynn Chiu, *Extended Evolutionary Synthesis: A Review of the Latest Scientific Research*, www.templeton.org/wp-content/uploads/2022/08/EES_Review_FINAL_.pdf, 38 (retrieved 12 January 2023). In other words, "The EES [Extended Evolutionary Synthesis] seeks to overcome the predominant idea that development is the passive unfolding of a predetermined, inherited genetic program. ... Instead, development is continuously and actively shaped by interactions and adaptive responses driven by the organism with itself, others, and the environment. Developmental processes are constructed throughout the lifetime of an organism from diverse resources across multiple levels of organization (e.g., genetic, molecular, cellular, organismal, environmental, etc. ...). These heterogeneous resources are inherited across generations, some facilitated by the organism's actions" (*ibid.*, 44). Once again, "Standard evolutionary theory is a gene-centric theory that defines evolution as the micro-changes of genetic frequencies in a population, pushed around by the four forces of evolution. ... The EES, on the other hand, is an organism-centric theory of evolution that redefines evolution as '*transgenerational change in the distribution of heritable traits of a population*'" (*ibid.*, 46).

Aristotelian–Thomistic Metaphysics

role of chance, requiring a closer analysis of its intrinsic dependence on order (the interplay of chance and order). As we shall see down the road (in Chapter 3), Aristotle and Aquinas help us develop a metaphysical account of chance perceived as ontologically real yet not causal in the strict meaning of the term but dependent on causal features that are foundational for the order of things (both inanimate and animate matter). I will argue that their position is significant in the context of the current reflection on the nature of evolutionary transitions.

The category of order, in turn, opens a way back to formal causation and essentialism, which should not be perceived as hostile and opposite to the evolutionary concept of species. Quite to the contrary, as I will argue in Chapter 2, the historical and relational approach in defining species must be complemented with the alternative, classical view – the one that acknowledges the reality of essences of particular organisms. Moreover, hylomorphism may also contribute to the further development of the philosophical interpretation of the theories of complexity and self-organization. In particular, the category of formal cause – defined as a metaphysical principle providing for the identity and the active and passive dispositions of a given entity – may be seen as grounding the unique potential of inanimate matter to spontaneously and instantaneously emerge into a primitive living system.[19] Finally, the notion of incessant changeability and evolvability of living systems is not necessarily opposite to Aristotelian–Thomistic hylomorphism and essentialism. Contrary to the opinion of those who reject classical metaphysics as presenting too static an explanation of nature and suggest replacing it with the metaphysics of process – which sees change as the foundation for the entire edifice of nature – I will argue in this volume that what Aristotle and Aquinas offer is in fact a moderate position that gives a proper account of both stability and change in nature.[20] I believe their ontology is worth

---

[19] Although the topic of the origin of life is closely related to evolutionary theory – in particular to chemical and biochemical evolution – it will not be treated in detail in this book which concentrates mainly on biological evolution. This is due to the limited space and the complexity of subject matter.

[20] Apart from the foundational development of the general account of process metaphysics, offered by Alfred North Whitehead, and its more recent explications in the writings of Nicholas Rescher and Johanna Seibt, we find applied versions of process framework in both philosophy of biology (John Dupré, Daniel J. Nicholson, and others) and in the metaphysics of emergence theory developed by Richard Campbell. See respectively Alfred North Whitehead, *Process and Reality* (New York: Free Press, 1979); Nicholas Rescher, *Process Metaphysics: An Introduction to Process Philosophy* (Albany: State University of New York Press, 1996); Johanna Seibt, ed., *Process Theories: Crossdisciplinary Studies in*

considering as meaningful and flexible enough to be applied in contemporary philosophical reflection inspired by evolutionary biology, where it enables us to develop a suitable and much needed metaphysical foundation for the current model of evolutionary transitions. Naturally, this is not to say that Aristotle or Aquinas developed or supported a theory of evolution.[21] And yet, some of the categories introduced in their philosophy not only leave room for such a possibility but even suggest it. We must not ignore this fact.

One more important point of convergence between classical metaphysics and the most recent developments in biology is the notion of teleology or goal-directedness. Both the general departure from reductionist genocentrism in biology and the development of evo-devo studies bring back the notions of teleology and functionality. Goal-directedness must be taken into account in the study of the ordered nature of organisms, as well as their adaptiveness and phenotypic plasticity, manifested in self-organizing goal-directedness and capacity to make compensatory changes to their structure or physiology during their lifetime (e.g., acclimatization or immune response). Even more importantly, teleology cannot be ignored in the analysis of developmental processes. Due to the interrelatedness of these processes with evolutionary mechanisms, it also becomes indispensable for our understanding of evolution. This confirms the early intuition of Dobzhansky and Ayala with regard to the role of teleology in evolutionary transitions and answers to the objection concerning its nature raised by Mayr. (I will say more about their debate over teleology in Chapter 3).

Most importantly, the suggested return to the classical categories of hylomorphism, essentialism, and formal and final causation is not an isolated postulate on my part, limited to my reference to the framework of contemporary developments in philosophy of evolutionary biology. On the contrary, it subscribes to the general revival of Aristotelianism

---

Dynamic Categories (Dordrecht/Boston/London: Kluwer Academic, 2003); John Dupré, *Processes of Life: Essays in the Philosophy of Biology* (Oxford: Oxford University Press, 2012); Daniel J. Nicholson and John Dupré, *Everything Flows: Towards a Processual Philosophy of Biology* (Oxford: Oxford University Press, 2018); Richard Campbell, *The Metaphysics of Emergence* (New York: Palgrave Macmillan, 2015). See also my response to Campbell in Mariusz Tabaczek, *Emergence: Towards A New Metaphysics and Philosophy of Science* (Notre Dame, IN: University of Notre Dame Press, 2019), Appendix 2, 279–284.

[21] Still, as I shall prove in Chapter 3, their speculation did anticipate the concept of natural selection.

Aristotelian–Thomistic Metaphysics

observed in most recent analytic philosophy, particularly in analytic metaphysics. The dynamic aspects of Aristotle's view of reality – framed within his notion of intertwined categories of potentiality and actuality – are rediscovered in the contemporary metaphysics of dispositions and their manifestations, which also offer an important (dispositional) view of causation that both challenges and contributes to the number of post-Humean notions of causation discussed in analytic metaphysics.[22] Moreover, the recognition of dispositions as "pointing" or being "directed" toward their characteristic manifestations brings back the notion of teleology. Hence, the proponents of dispositionalism talk about "physical" and "natural intentionality," characteristic of inanimate objects as well as nonsentient, sentient, and conscious forms of living organisms.[23] Finally, an important and heated debate is ongoing with regard to various contemporary analytic notions of hylomorphism. This definitely proves the renewed interest in this crucial conceptual tool of Aristotle, which further translates into the contemporary retrieval of essentialism and the debate over natural kinds.[24]

The framework of the renewed interest in Aristotelianism in analytic metaphysics and its possible application in the philosophical analysis of evolutionary biology inspire my research developed in this volume. I will present and defend a more classical account of Aristotle's metaphysics, with some crucial elements of its interpretation provided by Aquinas, as a necessary basis for my own constructive proposal of the metaphysics of evolutionary transitions and the account of the role that chance and teleology play in their occurrence.

---

[22] See my critical introduction to dispositionalism and dispositional view of causation in *Emergence*, Chapters 5 and 6, on pages 181–245.

[23] David Oderberg speaks about the return of the idea of natural (inorganic and organic) teleology, which "fell by the wayside under the anti-Aristotelian assaults of empiricism and materialism and has not yet recovered" (David S. Oderberg, *Real Essentialism* [New York: Routledge, 2007], 137).

[24] See my critical evaluation of contemporary versions of hylomorphism in *Metaphysics*, 216–241. Concerning the current retrieval of essentialism and the debate on natural kinds see Oderberg, *Real Essentialism*, Brian D. Ellis, *Scientific Essentialism* (Cambridge and New York: Cambridge University Press, 2001); and Brian D. Ellis, *The Philosophy of Nature: A Guide to the New Essentialism* (Montreal and Ithaca, NY: McGill-Queen's University Press, 2002); Helen Beebee and Nigel Sabbarton-Leary, eds., *The Semantics and Metaphysics of Natural Kinds* (New York: Routledge, 2010); Joseph Keim Campbell, Michael O'Rourke, and Matthew H. Slater, eds., *Carving Nature at Its Joints: Natural Kinds in Metaphysics and Science* (Cambridge (Mass.): Bradford Books, 2011); Joseph LaPorte, *Natural Kinds and Conceptual Change* (Cambridge, U.K.; New York: Cambridge University Press, 2003).

12   *Introduction*

THOMISTIC THEOLOGY OF CREATION

The third partner of the interdisciplinary research project that will be developed in this volume is the Thomistic theology of creation. As commonly known, the theory of evolution was and still is perceived by many as challenging the more literal interpretation of the Bible and the creation story found in Genesis. The more than 160 years that have passed since the publication of Darwin's book *On the Origin of Species by Means of Natural Selection* abound in both supportive theological interpretations as well as fierce theologically motivated refutations of his theory, which has risen to the status of one of the major intellectual accomplishments of the Western thought.[25] The main area of theology engaged in this

---

[25] Ted Peters and Martinez Hewlett offer a map of various theological responses to evolutionary theory in *Evolution from Creation to New Creation: Conflict, Conversation, and Convergence* (Nashville: Abingdon Press, 2003). Another overview can be found in Fowler and Kuebler, *The Evolution Controversy*.

For the historical account of the debate on evolution see Peter J. Bowler, *Evolution: The History of an Idea, 25th Anniversary Edition, With a New Preface* (Berkeley, CA: University of California Press, 2009); Peter J. Bowler and John Henry, "Evolution," in *Science and Religion: A Historical Introduction*, ed. Gary B. Ferngren, 2nd ed. (Baltimore: Johns Hopkins University Press, 2017), 204–19; Richard G. Olson, *Science and Religion, 1450–1900: From Copernicus to Darwin* (Westport, Conn: Greenwood Press, 2004), 167–221. Don O'Leary, *Roman Catholicism and Modern Science: A History* (New York: Continuum, 2006); Mariano Artigas, Thomas F. Glick, and Rafael A. Martínez, *Negotiating Darwin: The Vatican Confronts Evolution, 1877–1902* (Baltimore: JHU Press, 2006); Louis Caruana, ed., *Darwin and Catholicism: The Past and Present Dynamics of a Cultural Encounter* (London and New York: T&T Clark, 2009); David N. Livingstone, *Adam's Ancestors: Race, Religion, and the Politics of Human Origins* (Baltimore: Johns Hopkins University Press, 2011); and David N. Livingstone, *Dealing with Darwin: Place, Politics, and Rhetoric in Religious Engagements with Evolution* (Baltimore: Johns Hopkins University Press, 2014).

For a general introduction to the encounter of theology and evolutionary biology see Christopher Southgate, ed., *God, Humanity and the Cosmos – 3rd Edition: A Textbook in Science and Religion* (London and New York: T & T Clark, 2011), Chapter 6, 162–203; Denis Alexander, *Creation or Evolution: Do We Have to Choose?* (Oxford: Monarch Books, 2008); Robin Attfield, *Creation, Evolution and Meaning* (Aldershot, England; Burlington, VT: Ashgate, 2006); William Joseph Levada et al., eds., *Biological Evolution: Facts and Theories: A Critical Appraisal 150 Years after "The Origin of Species,"* Analecta Gregoriana 312 (Roma: Gregorian & Biblical Press, 2011).

An introduction to the debate on the theory of Intelligent Design can be found in William A. Dembski and Michael Ruse, eds., *Debating Design: From Darwin to DNA* (Cambridge University Press, 2004); William A. Dembski and Jonathan Witt, *Intelligent Design Uncensored: An Easy-to-Understand Guide to the Controversy* (Downers Grove, Ill: IVP Books, 2010); and Robert T. Pennock, *Intelligent Design Creationism and Its Critics: Philosophical, Theological, and Scientific Perspectives* (Cambridge, Mass: A Bradford Book, 2001).

Thomistic Theology of Creation

debate explores, among many other topics, the concept of God bringing everything into existence from nothing (*ex nihilo*) as well as the notion of his relation to the already-existing and ever-changing universe and all creatures that fill it. In addition, the notion of divine action, divine providence, and divine governance of things finds a particular and unique exemplification in the analysis of the origin of the human species, which undoubtedly became the most controversial point of contention in the encounter of theology with the theory of evolution. The second part of this volume will actively engage in the analysis of some crucial theological repercussions of evolutionary biology.

Except for several contextualizing references to more contemporary theologians outside of the Thomistic circle, the theological investigation presented in this volume will be strictly grounded in and limited to Aquinas and the Thomistic framework of theology of creation. This strategy results from the objective aim of the present research: the elaboration of a constructive model of the most up-to-date Thomistic version of theistic evolution. It will be built upon a renewed interest in Aquinas's philosophy of God and his metaphysical notion of creation and divine action, developed more recently in close reference to contemporary science.[26] It is precisely this context that makes Aquinas an intriguing and timely partner in the debate on the theological repercussions of the theory of evolution. The emphasis his theology puts on philosophy (including philosophy of nature) and philosophical categories as indispensable for logically meaningful, convincing, and communicative theological argumentation, makes the Thomistic school of theology competent to successfully engage in an interdisciplinary dialogue.[27]

My hope is that the research presented in this book will succeed in contributing to the ongoing conversation of science, philosophy, and theology – in search for truth about the universe we live in and of which we are an integral part. A truth in all its breadth that takes into account both the material and immaterial, the contingent and necessary, the changing and unchanging, the limited and unlimited, the natural and divine, the immanent and transcendent.

---

[26] Among the most significant contributors to this movement, whose works will be referenced in this volume, we should mention William E. Carroll, Michael Dodds, Ignacio Silva, William R. Stoeger, and John F. Wippel.

[27] Consequently, theological reflection presented in this project will, inevitably, abound in references to various philosophical categories that are valued and respected in the classical tradition of Aristotelianism and Thomism. At the same time, its strongly metaphysical overtones will be balanced by the analysis of Augustine's and Aquinas's theological commentaries on the work of the six days in Genesis.

THE PLAN OF THE PROJECT

Assuming a general understanding of the key aspects of the theory of evolution on the side of the reader, I will begin the entire project in Chapter 1 by delineating a constructive proposal incorporating the Aristotelian–Thomistic model of the metaphysics of evolutionary transitions. The necessary background for such an endeavor requires providing a meaningful defense of hylomorphism and a metaphysically robust interpretation of the categories of matter and form, with the emphasis on the substantial unity of living beings that consist of parts that are not merely aggregated to them but substantially transformed and virtually present in them. Crucial in this context is also a proper understanding of the Aristotelian–Thomistic notions of the disposition of matter and levels of potentiality. Hence, it is only after discussing all these themes that I will proceed with my proposal of the metaphysical interpretation of evolutionary transitions. The remaining part of the chapter will be dedicated to the complex debate concerning the classical principle of proportionate causation – allegedly supported and implemented by both Aristotle and Aquinas – and the question of whether the proposed metaphysical model of evolutionary changes contradicts it. I will analyze several interpretations of the principle as well as the most important and promising responses to the challenge of its violation.

Chapter 2 will be entirely dedicated to the complicated contemporary debate on the notion of biological species. Beginning with an allusion to the old controversy concerning nominalism *versus* realism about the category of species as universal, I will next introduce and critically analyze all major definitions of species that are taken into account in most recent philosophy of biology, dividing them into the two camps of relational and intrinsic species concepts. Among the members of the latter group, special attention will be paid to the essentialist species concept, both in its several contemporary variants and in the context of the classical Aristotelian–Thomistic version of essentialism, which grounds the notion of species in the category of substantial form and in the intrinsic teleology proper for a given type of a living being. The adequacy of intrinsic species concepts – and of the essentialist species concept in particular – will then be tested against the two major arguments denying their compatibility with evolutionary biology. Needless to say, the success of the entire project presented in this volume depends on the outcome of this test. The chapter will close with a short analysis of the four strategies of classifying species under higher taxa.

The Plan of the Project

15

The following Chapter 3 engages in the investigation of the meaning and role of natural selection, teleology, and chance in evolutionary processes. It will begin with the presentation of the classical notion of teleology, followed by a more detailed analysis of Aristotle's and Aquinas's understanding of chance and its interplay with teleology and order in nature. The transitional section will refer to an intriguing philosophical observation made by Aristotle and commented on by Aquinas, which might be interpreted as a preliminary formulation of the principle of natural selection. The central part of Chapter 3 will address the contemporary debate on teleology. Beginning with an argument portraying Darwin as reinventing teleology, I will next trace the fate of goal-directedness in the origins of the twentieth-century evolutionary synthesis, as well as its status in the most current philosophy of evolutionary biology. It is in this context that a critical question will be asked of whether natural selection should be regarded as teleological. The remaining part of Chapter 3 will refer once again to the idea of the interplay between teleology and chance, this time in reference to the proposed metaphysical account of evolution, delineated in this and the previous chapters. This account will conclude the philosophical part of the project.

The theological component of the argument presented in this volume will depart from a close analysis of Aquinas's understanding of creation, which is undeniably crucial for any attempt of constructing and evaluating a Thomistic version of theistic evolutionism. The exposition of Aquinas's original theology of creation will be preceded by the investigation of Augustine's reading of the Hexameron and the meaning of the concept of *rationes seminales* introduced in his commentary – as it proves crucial in Thomas's own interpretation of the account of the work of the six days in Genesis. The first part of Chapter 4, dedicated to this topic, will conclude with a short comment on historical attempts of interpreting Augustine's theology of creation as evolutionary. In the central part of the same chapter, I will offer a detailed account of Aquinas's philosophical theology of creation, paying attention not only to his emphasis on the importance of creatures' dependence on God in their *esse* but also in their *essentia* (i.e., in both "that" and "what" they are). Moving back to the biblical account of creation, I will analyze Aquinas's commentary on this crucial text, emphasizing his distinction among the three stages of the work of the six days in Genesis and carefully analyzing his use and interpretation of Augustine's notion of *rationes seminales*. Finally, I will suggest a new Aristotelian and more "evolutionary friendly" redefinition of this term that opens a way to develop a contemporary Thomistic version of theistic evolution.

16 *Introduction*

In Chapter 5, I move forward, asking a question about the hypothetical reaction of Aquinas to evolutionary biology. Aware of the fallacy of trying to confront a medieval author with the scientific and philosophical framework that did not exist in his time, I will first carefully trace and discuss various textual arguments in Aquinas's corpus, relevant to the topic of emergence of new species. I believe it will reveal the complexity of the debate on whether there is a "space" for evolution in his theology, as well as the openness for reinterpretation and further development of his ideas on this matter in reference to contemporary metaphysical analysis of speciation, developed in the first part of this project. Mindful of this complexity, I will nonetheless take the next step and offer a constructive proposal of the contemporary Thomistic account of theistic evolution. I will strive to keep it grounded in Aquinas's theology, while openly naming necessary changes that need to be introduced for it to be relevant with respect to the current version of evolutionary theory. In the concluding part of the chapter, I will share some comments on the objection against the proposed version of theistic evolution raised by Michael Chaberek.

Turning toward the next Chapter 6, I will speak in it against the popular and commonly accepted image of God as creating within and through evolutionary processes. Building upon Aquinas's distinction between the three stages of the work of the 6 days, investigated in Chapter 4, and mindful of his precise distinction between *creatio ex nihilo, conservatio rerum*, and divine providential governance of the continually changing universe of already existing creatures, I will argue that the category of "evolutionary creation" is not only unacceptable for Thomists but generally speaking theologically ambiguous, if not entirely wrong. Moreover, I will also criticize as equally confusing the accompanying notion of contingent creatures that causally contribute to the emergence of new species, as co-creating with God, who shares with them his divine power to create, taking thus yet another step on the way of his divine act of kenosis. Critical of this theological image, popular within the circles of the contemporary advocates of theistic evolutionism, I shall insist that we should classify evolutionary changes and newly emerged species as an integral aspect of divine governance rather than divine creation, which for Aquinas means but one thing or action – that is, bringing things into existence *ex nihilo*, and not through transformation of already existing matter.

The strong argument against evolutionary creation, developed in Chapter 6, does not question or negate God's presence and involvement

The Plan of the Project

in evolutionary transitions. To the contrary, their classification as an integral aspect of God's providential governance of creation makes us think that God must be immanently present in their instantiation. At the same time, theological interpretation of evolutionary biology faces the difficulty of delineating a precise account of the concurrence of divine and contingent causes engaged in speciation. Invoking Aquinas's famous distinction between primary and principal causation of God and secondary and instrumental causation of creatures, I will present in Chapter 7 my constructive model of the concurrence of divine and natural causes in evolutionary transformations.

Finally, in Chapter 8, I will address some crucial questions concerning the encounter between biological and theological anthropogenesis, which inspired the most emotional reactions to evolutionary theory and posed a considerable challenge to several fundamental presuppositions of systematic and philosophical theology. Aware of the complexity of the debate on hominization, I will strive to present and defend the contemporary Thomistic approach to the question of the origin of our species as theologically more accurate and precise than the most prevalent semi-naturalistic position that is favored and repeated by many theologians and presented in the official statements of the Magisterium of the Catholic Church. I shall also argue that it is preferable from the biological point of view. Lastly, after presenting an adjusted version of the model of the concurrence of divine and natural causes in evolutionary transitions (developed in Chapter 7) – this time depicting their cooperation in the evolutionary emergence of the first human – I will turn to the account of the complexity of the debate concerning the mono- *versus* polygenetic character of human speciation. I will conclude by sharing my conviction that the theological debate on this topic remains open.

I

Metaphysics of Evolutionary Transitions

The main thrust of Aristotle's philosophy of nature is to provide a proper account and description of the causes and mechanisms of the processes of generation, change, corruption, and decay in nature, and to posit the plausible characteristics of both the changing and persistent aspects therein. So, although the idea of juxtaposing Aristotle and Darwin may appear counterintuitive at first (as the latter is commonly believed to have ultimately proven the inadequacy of the biology of the former), it is still quite reasonable, given Aristotle's method, to search his philosophy, as well as its further development in Aquinas, for the metaphysical principles that may help us to better understand and philosophically ground evolutionary processes.

The aim of this chapter is to develop a constructive proposal of the Aristotelian–Thomistic metaphysics of evolutionary transitions. In order to accomplish this goal, I will proceed in the following way. First, I will present the hylomorphic notion of a living being, paying attention to and defending a metaphysically robust interpretation of the categories of matter and form. In the next step, I will address the notion of substantial unity of a living being in classical philosophy. Special attention will be paid to the need and relevance of the contemporary interpretation of the concept of virtual presence of parts in a whole. Next, preparing ground for the metaphysical analysis of speciation, I will present and discuss the concepts of the disposition of matter and levels of potentiality, as well as Aristotle's and Aquinas's suggestion that matter strives for greater perfection. The following and central section of this chapter will delineate my constructive proposal of the metaphysical analysis of evolutionary transitions. In the next step, I will address the challenging question of

Hylomorphic Notion of a Living Being

whether the proposed model goes against the classical principle of proportionate causation. Various aspects and interpretations of this principle, as well as several possible responses to the challenge of its violation, will be discussed. A short conclusion will close the entire chapter.

HYLOMORPHIC NOTION OF A LIVING BEING

The first and crucial aspect of Aristotle's philosophy that grounds the interpretation of the theory of evolution I am about to propose can be found in his most basic metaphysical rule: the concept of hylomorphism (from Greek ὕλη [*hylē*] = matter, and μορφή [*morphē*] = form). The idea seems to be quite simple. Things consist of matter and form, and the process of change is explained in terms of imposing a new form on a given chunk of matter. Yet, hylomorphism is a much deeper metaphysical concept.

Primary Matter

In order to understand the depth and philosophical acumen of hylomorphism, we must first realize that, when introducing the category of "matter," Aristotle refers not only to empirically verifiable things (such as elements) out of which more complex objects are made but also – and predominantly – to a principle from which they become. He introduces the concept of "primary matter" (PM) (πρώτη ὕλη – *prōtē hulē*), which is best understood and defined as a metaphysical principle of pure potentiality, something that persists through all the changes to which a given substance may be exposed. In other words, PM constitutes the very possibility of being a substance at all and should be distinguished from secondary (proximate) matter, which is perceptible to our senses and quantifiable.

In his most cited, preliminary account of four causes, Aristotle defines material cause in terms of empirically traceable things:

[T]hat out of which a thing comes to be and which persists, is called 'cause', e.g. the bronze of the statue, the silver of the bowl, and the genera of which the bronze and the silver are species (*Phys.* II, 3 [194b 24–25]).[1]

Nevertheless, he makes it clear through a number of further assertions that what he has in mind is ultimately PM.

---

[1] See also *Meta.* V, 2 (1013a 24–25).

Metaphysics of Evolutionary Transitions

The underlying nature [ὑποκείμενον φύσις, *hypokeimenon physis*] is an object of scientific knowledge, by an analogy. For as the bronze is to the statue, the wood to the bed, or the matter and the formless before receiving form to any thing which has form, so is the underlying nature to substance, that is, the "this" or existent (*Phys.* I, 7 [191a 8–12]).

The matter comes to be and ceases to be in one sense, while in another it does not. As that which contains the privation, it ceases to be in its own nature, for what ceases to be – the privation – is contained within it. But as potentiality it does not cease to be in its own nature, but is necessarily outside the sphere of becoming and ceasing to be. (...) For my definition of matter is just this – the primary substratum [πρῶτον ὑποκείμενον] of each thing, from which it comes to be without qualification, and which persists in the result (*Phys.* I, 9 [192a 25–33]).

By matter I mean that which in itself is neither a particular thing nor of a certain quantity nor assigned to any other of the categories by which being is determined. ... The ultimate substratum is of itself neither a particular thing nor of a particular quantity nor otherwise positively characterized; nor yet is it the negations of these, for negations also will belong to it only by accident (*Meta.* VII, 3 [1029a 20–21, 24–25]).

And if there is a first thing, which is no longer, in reference to something else, called "thaten," this is prime matter (*Meta.* IX, 7 [1049a 24]).[2]

Building on Aristotle's metaphysics, Aquinas states in *De principiis naturae*:

[13] Only that matter which is understood without any form or privation, but which is subject to form and privation, is called prime matter, inasmuch as there is no other matter prior to it. It is also called "hyle." ... [14] We know prime matter as that which is related to all forms and privations, as bronze is related to the form of a statue and to the privation of some shape. It is called primary without qualification. ... [16] We should note also that prime matter is said to be numerically one in all things.[3]

In addition, in *In Meta.* VII, lect. 2 (§ 1285), we find him saying that:

[PM is] neither a what, nor a quality, nor any of the other categories by which being is divided or determined.

An attempt at grasping and delineating the exact nature of PM as a metaphysical principle remains a challenge. Approaching it from the perspective of analytic philosophy, Jeffrey Brower speaks about PM as having a distinct character and suggests defining it as nonindividual atomless gunk. He adds, "it is best understood in terms of what

---

[2] See also *Phys.* I, 7 (191a 8–12); II, 7 (198a 21–22); *Meta.* VII, 3 (1029a 20–21); VIII, 4 (1044a 15–23); IX, 7 (1049a 19–22, 24).

[3] English trans. in *Selected Writings of St. Thomas Aquinas*, trans. by Robert P. Goodwin (New York: Bobbs-Merrill, 1965).

contemporary philosophers sometimes refer to as *stuff* rather than *things* (in a technical sense of both terms)." Consequently, he claims, "such matter is not merely atomless gunk, but *gunky stuff* – that is, a type of stuff whose parts are all such as to have proper parts."[4] While intriguing, this description risks hypostasing PM. For that reason, it might be useful to turn toward contemporary physics and build an analogy between PM and electromagnetic and/or quantum fields (quantum vacuum), which are believed to ground the entire physical reality as a source of potentiality. Naturally, both electromagnetic and quantum fields are physical realities (physical systems), while PM is a metaphysical principle of pure potentiality. Yet, the analogy I am proposing may help the reader get beyond all categories traditionally and intuitively associated with matter. I find it necessary in order to have an insight into what PM is. Once again, I define it as pure, unactualized possibility of there being anything at all. Even if this definition may sound abstract, it is metaphysically profound.[5]

---

[4] Jeffrey E. Brower, *Aquinas's Ontology of the Material World: Change, Hylomorphism, and Material Objects* (New York: Oxford University Press, 2014), 125.

[5] Metaphysical status of PM in both Aristotle and Aquinas became a point of division among experts in classical philosophy. Concerning Aristotle, the traditional view stating that he believed in PM as a single, everlasting, and completely indeterminate substratum of all change in nature has become an object of controversy among some contemporary Aristotelian scholars. To grasp the conversation – the analysis of which goes beyond my interest here – I refer the reader to the following articles: (1) challenging the traditional view, Hugh R. King, "Aristotle without Prima Materia," *Journal of the History of Ideas* 17 (1956): 370–89, and William Charlton, "Did Aristotle Believe in Prime Matter?," in *Aristotle, Physics: Books I and II*, trans. with introduction and notes by W. Charlton (Oxford: Clarendon Press, 1983), 129–45; (2) answering King and Charlton (successfully, in my opinion), Friedrich Solmsen, "Aristotle and Prime Matter: A Reply to Hugh R. King," *Journal of the History of Ideas* 19 (1958): 243–52, and H. M. Robinson, "Prime Matter in Aristotle," *Phronesis* 19 (1974): 168–88.

With regard to the notion of PM in the Middle Ages, already in the thirteenth and fourteenth centuries, representatives of the Franciscan school of the English Province (John Peckham, Richard of Middletown, William of Ware, John Duns Scotus, and William Ockham) claimed that it had a degree of actuality (even if it was still far from the status of physical objects available to our sensory perception), which they saw as necessary to support the thesis that God could keep it in existence as not in-formed by any SF. It seems that this position was also indirectly supported by Bonaventure. More recently, a number of commentators see Aquinas himself as being anti-realist about PM. They claim PM is for him merely "a conceptual tool" (Rebecca Konyndyk DeYoung, Colleen McCluskey, and Christina Van Dyke, *Aquinas's Ethics: Metaphysical Foundations, Moral Theory, and Theological Context* [Notre Dame, IN: University of Notre Dame Press, 2009], 19), "a theoretical terminus of form-matter analysis rather than an actual component of nature" (Norman Kretzmann, *The Metaphysics of Creation: Aquinas's Natural Theology in Summa Contra Gentiles II* [Oxford: Clarendon Press, 1998], 212),

Metaphysics of Evolutionary Transitions

Most importantly, we can say that PM, as pure potentiality, underlies each and every substance, remaining a principle of continuity in the process in which one substance (S_1) becomes another substance (S_2) (as well as in the case of accidental changes). Even if all physical aspects of S_1 change on the way to its becoming S_2, we are not dealing with a total annihilation of S_1 and coming to be out of nothing of S_2. Rather, due to PM as the principle of potentiality underlying all existing substances (that can be reidentified over time), we observe the continuity of the process of S_1 changing into S_2. Moreover, it is due to PM that both S_1 and S_2 are characterized by the persistent passive potentiality for change, which is actualized by substantial form (SF).

Substantial Form

Substantial form, on the other hand, is not merely an organizing principle, arranging the geometrical structure and shape of the constituent parts of an entity (substance).[6] Rather – described by Aristotle as "the definition" or "the statement" of the essence of an entity (ὁλόγος τοῦ τί ἦν εἶναι [*ho logos tou ti ēn einai*]) – it is an informing principle of actuality, that by which a thing (secondary matter – *materia secunda*) is what it is; an intrinsic, determining principle that actualizes PM and thus constitutes an individual being.[7] As such, similar to PM, SF is a simple

---

or "just a logical abstraction … a conceptual part of material objects" (Pasnau, *Thomas Aquinas on Human Nature* [Cambridge and New York: Cambridge University Press, 2002], 131). If this is true, adds Pasnau, then it follows that "Material beings are not composites of actuality plus some kind of elusive stuff known as matter, they are instead just composites of certain sorts of actuality. Reality is actuality all the way down, and substances are bundles of actuality, unified by organization around a substantial form" (*ibid.*). Yet, others claim that numerous fragments in Aquinas's corpus prove that he radically opposed this assertion (e.g., *ST* I, 7, 2, ad 3; *ST* I, 44, 2, ad 3; *ST* I, 66, 1, co.). See John F. Wippel, *The Metaphysical Thought of Thomas Aquinas: From Finite Being to Uncreated Being* (Washington, DC: Catholic University of America Press, 2000), 312–27; Brower, *Aquinas's Ontology*, 119–129; Christopher Brown, *Aquinas and the Ship of Theseus: Solving Puzzles about Material Objects* (London: Continuum, 2005); David P. Lang, "The Thomistic Doctrine of Prime Matter," *Laval Théologique et Philosophique* 54, no. 2 (1998): 367–85; Eleonore Stump, *Aquinas* (New York: Routledge, 2003).

[6] "'Cause' means (…) (2) The form or pattern, that is, the definition of the essence, and the classes which include this (e.g., the ratio 2:1 and number in general are causes of the octave), and the parts included in the definition" [*Meta*. V, 2 (1013a 27–28)]. See also *Phys*. II, 3 (194b 26–27).

[7] Trying to avoid the error of reducing the metaphysically robust notion of SF to geometrical shape or outward appearance, Terrence Irwin rightly notes that "if the form of the statue is essential to it, then other features besides shape must constitute the form,

Hylomorphic Notion of a Living Being

metaphysical principle (not a thing) that does not have the property of quantity or extension. For this reason, says Michael Dodds, "we cannot make an imaginative picture of a substantial form. It is not imaginable, but it is intelligible."[8] SF cannot increase or decrease. It is "educed" from the potentiality of PM and remains present in the entire substance and its parts as a fundamental principle of operation. It is expressed in essential qualities of a given substance, which classifies Aristotelian ontology as essentialist.[9]

Contrary to PM, which is a principle of continuity and a passive principle of change (as pure potentiality), SF is a principle of novelty and an active principle of change in causal processes. Hence, even if in a process of change from S_1 to S_2, PM does not change; we distinguish S_1 and S_2 as separate substances due to different substantial forms (SSFF) that inform PM in them and are educed from its potentiality. But what if S_1 changes in a way that makes it different but does not lead to its transformation into a completely new substance S_2 (e.g., a puppy growing up and becoming a mature dog)? Here, Aristotle introduces an important distinction between what was later on classified as SF and accidental form (AF). This distinction is easier to grasp in the context of Aristotle's account of accidental and substantial change:

[T]here is "alteration" when the substratum is perceptible and persists, but changes in its own properties, the properties in question being opposed to one another either as contraries or as intermediates. The body, e.g., although persisting as the same body, is now healthy and now ill; and the bronze is now spherical

---

and the reference to shape can at most give us a very rough first conception of form. If we turn from artifacts to organisms, it is even clearer that form cannot be just the same as shape." (Terence Irwin, *Aristotle's First Principles* [Oxford: Clarendon Press, 1988], 100).

[8] Michael J. Dodds, *The Philosophy of Nature* (Oakland, CA: Western Dominican Province, 2010), 25. Michael Storck notes that "not only do we not sense substantial forms, but we do not measure them with scientific instruments either. We sense the size, shape, color, and so forth, of things, and we measure their frequency, mass, temperature, electrical charge, and so on. It is only through our intellect that we are able to grasp something, often not very clearly, of the substantial forms of natural things" (Michael Hector Storck, "Parts, Wholes, and Presence by Power: A Response to Gordon P. Barnes," *The Review of Metaphysics* 62 [2008]: 55).

[9] Dismissing ontological uncertainty and the tendency to treat substantial unity as mereological structure, Aquinas distinguishes among notions of form as (1) arrangement of parts, (2) union by contact and bond, and (3) union effecting an alteration of the component parts. Only the last refers to SF, which is thus not a mere aggregation of building blocks but a source of the quiddity of an entity. See *In Meta.* V, lect. 3 (§ 779). See also Tabaczek, *Metaphysics*, 217–18.

and at another time angular, and yet remains the same bronze. But when nothing perceptible persists in its identity as a substratum, and the thing changes as a whole (when e.g., the seed as a whole is converted into blood, or water into air, or air as a whole into water), such an occurrence is no longer 'alteration'. It is a coming-to-be of one substance and a passing-away of the other – especially if the change proceeds from an imperceptible something to something perceptible (either to touch or to all the senses) (*De gen. et corr.* I, 4 [319b 10–18]).[10]

To give an example, the SF of a dog is more than just its shape or the principle uniting the dynamic activity of its parts (e.g., organs and biomolecules). As an intrinsic and constitutive principle of the essence of this particular living organism, SF radically (substantially) transformed the matter of ovum and sperm when they joined at the moment of its conception. In other words, it organized particular physical matter (ovum and sperm in the zygote) and made it exist in a particular way, proper for the particular natural kind, that is, the natural kind of a dog. The matter in question has lost its identity and (in the course of substantial change) has become a new unified being, that is, a hylomorphic unity, which is distinct from a meromorphic unity, defined as an aggregate of parts (e.g., atoms, particles, and biomolecules).

At the same time, apart from indispensable, necessary, and fixed features defined by its SF, our dog is characterized by a number of attributes that are important yet may take different "values," for example, its sex or temperament (it may be very active or phlegmatic – in analogy with human temperaments). Moreover, some of these attributes may change during its lifetime (e.g., the color of its fur, the size of its body, secretion of hormones, and its vocal cords). These characteristics are usually classified as accidental and are defined as grounded in AFs (AAFF).[11] Some of them are inseparable (or proper), that is, present as long as that particular individual exists (just as the act of burning is an inseparable or proper accident of fire). For example, our dog's temperament is such an accident. Even if it changes with time, as our dog progresses from being active to being phlegmatic and slow, it needs to have one or the other temperament at any given moment of its life. Other accidental features

[10] Aquinas discusses this distinction in *De prin. nat.* 5–7.
[11] "Accidental forms are possessed by substances via inherence (since they are properties inhering directly in substances), whereas substantial forms are possessed by substances via constituency (since they are properties inhering directly in their prime matter) ... Unlike substantial forms, which characterize substances *primarily* or *simpliciter* (in virtue of being constituents of them), accidental forms characterize them *secondarily* or *derivatively* (in virtue of being constituents of things that share the same matter as these substances)". (Brower, *Aquinas's Ontology*, 111–12, 113).

Hylomorphic Notion of a Living Being

are separable (or not proper). For example, having all teeth or being able to procreate and produce fertile offspring.[12]

Matter and form are intrinsically related for Aristotle. They cannot exist separately. In other words, we know form only as realized in prime matter, and we know prime matter only as in-formed; there is no place for Platonic dualism of separable substances here.[13] Aristotle observes a substantial unity of being at first and introduces a distinction between PM and SF to explain this unity and the fact that things can change.[14] In Book VIII of the *Metaphysics*, we read:

What then, is it that makes man one; why is he one and not many? (...) [I]f, as we say, one element is matter and another is form, and one is potentially and the other actually, the question will no longer be thought a difficulty. (...) The difficulty disappears, because the one is matter, the other form. (...) [T]he proximate

---

[12] Aquinas briefly defines inseparable (or proper) accidents in *Q de an.* 12, ad 7. Brower notes that "although the characteristics determined by accidental forms fall outside of the nature or essence of substances, and hence can be thought of as non-essential properties of substances, we must be careful not to conflate Aquinas's distinction between substantial and accidental forms with the contemporary distinction between essential and contingent properties. For even if all substantial forms are essential (in the sense of being non-contingent properties of substances), it is not true that all accidental forms are contingent properties. On the contrary, like most other medieval Aristotelians, Aquinas insists that there is a class of accidents which are possessed by substances non-contingently – the so-called *propria* or necessary accidents" (Brower, *Aquinas's Ontology*, 113).

[13] Concerning PM, Aquinas states: "Because prime matter is not a being in actuality [*ens in actu*], but merely in potentiality [*potentia tantum*], it does not exist in reality through itself [*per seipsam*]" (*ST* I, 7, 2, ad 3). In *De prin. nat.* (17) he adds: "[PM] can never exist by itself [*per se*]; because, since it does not have any form in its definition, it cannot exist in act, since existence in act is only from the form. Rather it exists only in potency [*est solum in potentia*]. Therefore whatever exists in act cannot be called prime matter." Brower notes that the notion of PM as pure potentiality "enables Aquinas to insist that not even God could create prime matter in the absence of any forms or properties, since prime matter, so understood, can have no being or actuality apart from a form or property" (Brower, *Aquinas's Ontology*, 120).

[14] We must acknowledge that apart from living beings, the question concerning substantiality of things, that is, the distinction between mere aggregates of (lower level) substances and higher substances that emerge in the process of substantial change of several lower substances, becomes a challenge. Thus, Andrew van Melsen suggests, we should speak about degrees of self-existence (individuality) and substantiality. Concerning the latter, he claims that "[T]he actual substantial forms, the actual fundamental determinations of matter do not have the idealized form which they have in our theoretical concepts. They are realized in a deficient, or rather mixed, way. For this very reason the distinction between substantial and accidental form has to be taken in a relative sense" (Andreas Gerardus Maria van Melsen, *The Philosophy of Nature*, 3rd ed. [Pittsburgh: Duquesne University Press, 1961], 147; see also *ibid.*, 130–151).

Metaphysics of Evolutionary Transitions

matter and the form are one and the same thing, the one potentially, and the other actually. (...) Therefore there is no other cause here unless there is something which caused the movement from potency into actuality.[15]

SUBSTANTIAL UNITY OF A LIVING BEING
AND VIRTUAL PRESENCE OF ITS PARTS

Yet, an intriguing and difficult question arises, with respect to substantial unity of a living being, when analyzed from the perspective of natural sciences. I have mentioned above that SF radically (substantially) transforms the matter of ovum and sperm when they join at the moment of conception of an animal. Although this explanation may seem plausible from the metaphysical point of view, it is certainly counterintuitive scientifically speaking. Trying to bring these perspectives together and answer the challenging question of what happens with basic elements and their causal activities as they go through substantial changes that lead to the emergence of complex substances, we may refer to Aquinas who – commenting on Aristotle's *De gen. et corr.* I, 10 (327b24–32) – develops a theory, which is traditionally referred to as the doctrine of the virtual (*virtute*) presence of elements in mixed substances:

The powers of the substantial forms of simple bodies are preserved in mixed bodies. The forms of the elements, therefore, are in mixed bodies; not indeed actually, but virtually (by their power). And this is what the Philosopher says in book one of On Generation: "Elements, therefore, do not remain in a mixed body actually, like a body and its whiteness. Nor are they corrupted, neither both nor either. For, what is preserved is their power."[16]

Despite its rejection by many followers of the contemporary version of atomism, the Aristotelian–Thomistic theory of virtual presence seems to offer a powerful and plausible argument against the Democritean

---

[15] *Meta.* VIII, 4 (1045a 14, 21–25, 29–30; 1045b 18–19, 21–2). We find a similar argumentation in *On the Soul*: "That is why we can wholly dismiss as unnecessary the question whether the soul and the body are one: it is as meaningless as to ask whether the wax and the shape given to it by the stamp are one, or generally the matter of a thing and that of which it is the matter. Unity has many senses (as many as 'is' has), but the most proper and fundamental sense of both is the relation of an actuality to that of which it is the actuality" (*De an.* II, 1 [412a 6–9]). See also *De part. an.*, I, 1 (640b 22–29).

[16] *De mixt. elem.* 17–18. It is important to remember that "mixture" in ancient and medieval philosophy often means a compound, that is, a unified new entity informed by a new SF, and not merely a composite or a combination of elementary particles, which, metaphysically speaking, is informed by an AF, which does not include a substantial change of the components.

Living Being and Virtual Presence of Its Parts

view of matter. Leaving it up to the physicists to specify the most basic "primary components" that can be classified as physical objects, we may assign to these entities the principles of PM and SF and claim that as such they can enter compounds and remain virtually present in them, with their powers retained yet (possibly) altered and with SSFF not entirely corrupted away but instead retrievable in the processes of corruption of these "mixed" (composite) bodies or in the reclaiming of given elements from complex substances, which nevertheless "keep" their SF (e.g., an oxygen atom leaving a dog's organism, which, nonetheless, remains the same organism).[17]

On the physical, chemical, and biochemical level of observation, a given primary component or a more complex entity such as an atom, molecule, or chemical compound may be perfectly traceable in a composite being. This fact, however, does not prevent or invalidate a philosophical (metaphysical) reflection stating that the properties and causal powers (dispositions) of that primary component, although retained, are now properties of a given compound (which is informed by a new and separate SF). Moreover, due to the fact of being "a part of" – or, better to say, "being now compounded" (e.g., a carbon atom consumed by me becomes me) – the set of properties and dispositions of a given elementary particle is usually altered, that is, we might attribute to it properties and dispositions it does not have when separated from the compound.

We may take as an example nitrogenous bases (nucleobases) that are part of the nucleotides that make up DNA. On the one hand, based on experimental science, we can conclude that their inherent activity and reactivity are entirely preserved or slightly limited in a living organism. On the other hand, the analysis of the mechanism of reading DNA proved that the order of the nucleobases carries (encodes) genetic information, the content of which contributes to the proper functioning of the entire living organism. This feature cannot be ascribed to nitrogenous bases outside a living organism (outside the structure of DNA), even though chemically speaking, these molecules have an identical structure. When tested *in vitro*, they do not contribute in any way to the maintenance of the equilibrium state of any living being.

This preliminary reinterpretation of substantial unity and virtual presence is far from being satisfactory or conclusive. Both categories

---

[17] In modern English the term "virtual" means "almost" or "nearly." For the medieval thinkers *virtualiter*, derived from *vis*, refers to the presence of a power that can produce a particular effect.

28   *Metaphysics of Evolutionary Transitions*

require further study in reference to contemporary science and philosophy of science.[18] At the same time, they need to be kept at the risk of departing from hylomorphism toward meromorphism, which assumes that SF unites parts that retain their substantial identity. This would suggest that the same "portion" of matter is actualized by more than one form, which is counterintuitive, as one thing cannot have simultaneously two separate identities.[19]

DISPOSITION OF MATTER AND LEVELS OF POTENTIALITY

My detailed presentation of the hylomorphic view of living organisms becomes an important step on the way to develop a consistent metaphysics of evolutionary transitions. One of its key aspects is the notion of the disposition of matter. In *In Meta.* V, lect. 14 (§ 963), Aquinas states, after Aristotle, that "what is capable of being acted upon in some way must have within itself a certain disposition which is the cause and principle of its passivity." He understands disposition as an order through which some qualities of a given thing direct it toward some other qualities (acquired in an accidental change) or becoming something entirely new (in a substantial change).[20]

As pure potentiality, PM can be actualized by any SF. At the same time, the type of SF actualizing PM in the case of a substantial change in which a given substance A is replaced by another substance B is not random. It depends both on the SF and on AAFF actualizing A. These principles of actuality dispose A to enter specific accidental or substantial changes, which narrows the scope of potentialities of PM that may be actualized in a given change. We might speak, respectively, about

---

[18] For more on contemporary application and interpretation of the concept of virtual presence see Christopher Decaen, "Elemental Virtual Presence in St. Thomas," *The Thomist* 64, no. 2 (2000): 271–300; Tabaczek, *Emergence*, 229–234; Mariusz Tabaczek, *Divine Action and Emergence: An Alternative to Panentheism* (Notre Dame: University of Notre Dame Press, 2021), 75–78. In the first monograph mentioned here, I also confront the classical and new Aristotelianism with emergentism, the concept of supervenience, multiple realizability of phenomena at higher levels of complexity of matter, and the theory of latent properties – as the most popular versions of nonreductionist physicalism.

[19] This view seems to find support (more or less explicit) among some of the contemporary advocates of hylomorphism. For the critical analysis of their views, see Christopher J. Austin, "Contemporary Hylomorphisms: On the Matter of Form," *Ancient Philosophy Today* 2, no. 2 (2020): 113–44; Tabaczek, *Emergence*, 216–41; Jeremy Skrzypek, "Three Concerns for Structural Hylomorphism," *Analytic Philosophy* 58, no. 4 (2017): 360–408; Brower, *Aquinas's Ontology of the Material World*, 103–184.

[20] See *ST* I–II, 49, 2, ad 1.

Disposition of Matter and Levels of Potentiality 29

"remote" and "proximate" disposition of PM. To give an example, if you put a wooden log into a fire, it does not melt but burns and turns into a pile of ash and not, let us say, into a butterfly. Although pure potentiality of PM underlying the log can be actualized by any SF ("remote disposition" of PM), the fact that it is currently actualized by the SF of wood and a number of AAFF (e.g., color, shape, and moisture) changes its disposition and sets up a limited scope of its potentialities that can be actualized within a limited range of substantial changes a wooden log may undergo ("proximate disposition" of PM).

In other words, we may say after Aquinas that – together with AAFF, which are responsible for secondary properties of a given entity (such as its size or color) and may change without it changing its identity – the SF of the entity in question disposes it, that is, becomes decisive about the array of new SSFF that may be educed from the potentiality of PM that underlies it. The action of eduction (actualization of PM) is exercised by the efficient causality of one or many agents.

Commenting on this topic in the *Metaphysics*, Aristotle states what follows:

Regarding material substance we must not forget that even if all things come from the same first cause or have the same things for their first causes, and if the same matter serves as starting-point for their generation, yet there is a matter proper [i.e., properly disposed] to each, e.g., for phlegm the sweet or the fat, and for bile the bitter, or something else; though perhaps these come from the same original matter (*Meta.* VIII, 4 [1044a 15–20]).

Aquinas, in turn, comments on this passage thus:

From the things which are said here then it is evident that there is one first matter for all generable and corruptible things, but different proper [i.e., properly disposed] matters for different things (*In Meta.* VIII, lect. 4 [§ 1730]).

And earlier, in the *Summa contra gentiles*, Aquinas has already postulated:

Thus, form and matter must always be mutually proportioned and, as it were, naturally adapted, because the proper act is produced in its proper [i.e., properly disposed] matter. That is why matter and form must always agree with one another in respect to multiplicity and unity (*SCG* II, 81, no. 7).

Consequently, we may speak about the two levels of potentiality inherent in the very fabric of the cosmos: (1) pure potentiality of PM (*materia prima*), which can be actualized by all possible types of SSFF, proper for both inanimate and animate natural kinds, and (2) potentiality of PM underlying each and every instantiation of secondary matter (*materia secunda*), which is specified (qualified) by the SF and AAFF characteristic of a particular natural kind it belongs to. To put it differently, we might classify (1) as "remote potentiality" defined in reference to the wide scope of all logically possible SSFF that may actualize PM and (2) as "proximate potentiality" defined by the narrow range of SSFF that may actualize a given "portion" of PM underlying an actually existing entity in the next substantial change it will go through. In other words, the principles actualizing entities classified as instantiations of secondary matter dispose their underlying PM in particular way, enabling thus – in the course of substantial change – an eduction of particular types of new SSFF (typical of other natural kinds) from its potentiality.

What is crucial in this account is – once again – what the Aristotelian – Thomistic metaphysics understands of the term "potentiality." It does not perceive it as the potency for a limited number of (fixed) natural kinds to unfold from the already existing secondary matter. Rather, it sees it, ultimately, as one of the most basic metaphysical principles underlying the very fabric of the universe, a potency that may be actualized by any SF. Obviously – as noted above – PM, as such, is always actualized by a given SF, which limits the range of possible future actualizations it may go through. At the same time, the flexibility of the dynamic processes is such that the fact that PM is informed at time t_1 by the substantial form SF_1, which disposes it to be actualized in the next substantial change at t_2 by the substantial form SF_2, while preventing it from being actualized (in the same substantial change at t_2) by the substantial form of SF_{2^*} does not prevent it from being actualized by SF_{2^*} after a number of substantial changes it may go through. They may dispose it such that, at one point, it may actually be "ready" to be informed by SF_{2^*}. For the potentiality of the secondary matter, although relative and limited, as ultimately grounded in the pure potentiality of PM, changes in the course of substantial and accidental transformations that a given "portion" of secondary matter enters. Refer to Figure 1.1.

Hence, the two levels of potentiality that we can define within the Aristotelian – Thomistic metaphysics seem to enable us to provide an accurate description of the dynamic and flexible character and nature of reality – the one that is in line with contemporary science. Moreover, they also allow to introduce the idea of evolutionary changes and transitions as compatible with the framework of the Aristotelian – Thomistic metaphysics and philosophical theology. But, before I offer a constructive proposal of such developments, I should first refer to one more important aspect of Aristotle's and Aquinas's thought.

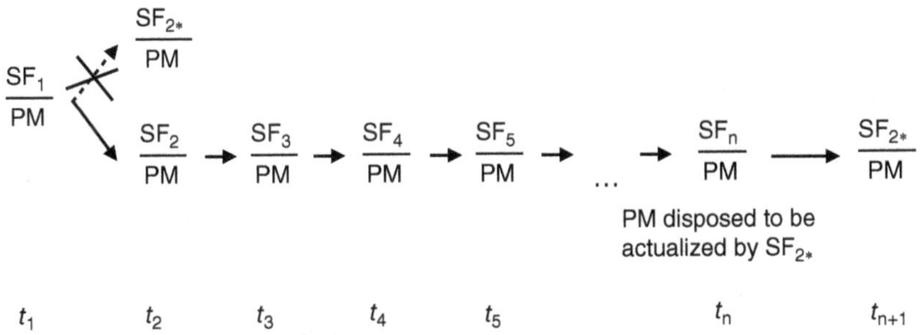

Matter as Striving for Perfection – Scala Naturae

FIGURE 1.1 Two levels of potentiality and the flexibility of the dynamic processes in nature.

MATTER AS STRIVING FOR PERFECTION – *SCALA NATURAE*

The idea of the disposition of matter is related – in both Aristotle and Aquinas – to a natural tendency of matter to be actualized (in-formed) by more perfect forms. Aristotle is the first to recognize an ascent of perfection of the beings in nature. On his *scala naturae*, we can observe a gradual crescendo from nonliving, through plant and animal, to human forms:

Nature proceeds little by little from things lifeless to animal life in such a way that it is impossible to determine the exact line of demarcation, nor on which side thereof an intermediate form should lie (*Hist. an.* VIII, 1 [588b 4–6]).

Aristotle gives an example of the ascent of nature from plants to animals:

[T]here is observed in plants a continuous scale of ascent towards the animal. So, in the sea, there are certain objects concerning which one would be at a loss to determine whether they be animal or vegetable (*Hist. an.* VIII, 1 [588b 11–13]).[21]

On another occasion, Aristotle presents us with a similar reflection concerning transitions between various forms of life:

[N]ature passes from lifeless objects to animals in such unbroken sequence, interposing between them beings which live and yet are not animals, that scarcely any difference seems to exist between two neighbouring groups owing to their close proximity (*De par. an.* IV, 5 [681a 12–15]).

Aristotle gives an example of the sponge, which here he classifies as a plant: "A sponge, then, as already said, in these respects completely resembles a plant, that throughout its life it is attached to a rock, and

---

[21] With the advance of modern science, we find it easier to define taxon-specific characteristics. However, as we shall see in Chapter 2, the very notion and precise definition of species remain a great challenge for both biology and philosophy of biology.

32   Metaphysics of Evolutionary Transitions

that when separated from this it dies" (*De par. an.* IV, 5 [681a 15–17]), whereas in *History of Animals*, he compares it to animals, due to its sensation: "Stationary animals are found in water, but no such creature is found on dry land. In the water are many creatures that live in close adhesion to an external object, as is the case with several kinds of oyster. And, by the way, the sponge appears to be endowed with a certain sensibility" (*Hist. An.* I, 1 [487b 9–10]).

Aristotle's careful empirical and speculative analysis justifies his constatation that "There is a good deal of overlapping between the various classes" (*De gen. an.* II, 1 [732b 15]). Commenting on it, O'Rourke goes as far as to say that "Without exaggerating its importance, Aristotle recognizes man's link to the primates: the ape, the monkey, and the baboon, he states, *dualize in their nature with man and the quadrupeds*" (*Hist. an.* II, 8 [502a 16–18], trans. A. L. Peck). In *De par. an.* IV, 10 (689b 31–33) Aristotle adds that: "The ape is, in form, intermediate between man and quadruped, and belongs to neither, or to both."[22]

The position of Aquinas with regards to *scala naturae* is analogous. Similar to Aristotle, he notices a spontaneous tendency of nature toward superior forms in the processes of generation and corruption. In his *Summa Contra Gentiles*, we find an important reflection on the hierarchy of degrees in substantial transformation in human embryology, which I should quote extensively:

[T]he more posterior and more perfect an act is, the more fundamentally is the inclination of matter directed toward it. Hence in regard to the last and most perfect act that matter can attain, the inclination of matter whereby it desires form must be inclined as toward the ultimate end of generation. Now, among the acts pertaining to forms, certain gradations are found. Thus, prime matter is in potency, first of all, to the form of an element. When it is existing under the form of an element it is in potency to the form of a mixed body; that is why the elements are matter for the mixed body. Considered under the form of a mixed body, it is in potency to a vegetative soul, for this sort of soul is the act of a body. In turn, the vegetative soul is in potency to a sensitive soul, and a sensitive one to an intellectual one. (...) So, elements exist for the sake of mixed bodies; these latter exist for the sake of living bodies, among which plants exist for animals, and animals for men. Therefore, man is the end of the whole order of generation (*SCG*, III, 22, no. 7).[23]

---

[22] Fran O'Rourke, "Aristotle and the Metaphysics of Evolution," *The Review of Metaphysics* 58 (2004), 39–40.

[23] This passage refers to human embryology, where Aquinas (following the science of his day) thought that a fetus was actualized successively by vegetative, sentient, and human souls. Although contemporary science proved this idea to be wrong, the more general

Matter as Striving for Perfection – Scala Naturae   33

A more general formulation of the same principle can be found in *In Meta.* XII, lect. 2 (§ 2438), where Aquinas emphasizes that in order to receive a given SF, PM must be previously under other specific SSFF. Hence, potentiality for perfection can be actualized only gradually and in accordance with some determinate order:

> [E]verything capable of being generated has a definite matter from which it comes to be, because there must be a proportion between form and matter. For even though first matter is in potentiality to all forms, it nevertheless receives them in a certain order. For first of all it is in potency to the forms of the elements, and through the intermediary of these, insofar as they are mixed in different proportions, it is in potency to different forms. Hence, not everything can come to be directly from everything else unless perhaps by being resolved into first matter.

Moreover, speaking of the importance of the proper disposition of PM for particular accidental and substantial changes of a given substance, Aquinas formulates an observation that might inspire a new development of the classical notion of hylomorphism, enabling it to provide a necessary metaphysical foundation for the contemporary version of the theory of evolution:

> From the fact that matter is known to have a certain substantial mode of existing, matter can be understood to receive accidents by which it is disposed to a higher perfection, so far as it is fittingly disposed to receive that higher perfection (*Q. de an.* 9, co.).[24]

On another occasion, we find him saying that matter, properly disposed, "turns towards the act or prepares itself to receive it" (*Super IV Sent.* 49, 3, 2, co.).[25] Once again, in his commentary on Aristotle's *On the Soul*, Aquinas comes to a similar conclusion that "everything in a lower form of existence is inclined to the maximum possible assimilation to the higher form" (*In De an.* II, lect. 7 [§ 315]).[26]

---

metaphysical principle (concerning affinity of matter to higher forms) that stands behind it may be still defended as relevant. See also Antonio Moreno, "Some Philosophical Considerations on Biological Evolution," *The Thomist* 37 (July, 1973), 440–441.

[24] See also *In De an.* II, lect. 7, (§ 315); *Q. de pot.* 5, 1, co. and ad 5; SCG III, 22, no. 7.

[25] All translations from *Super Sent.* are mine.

[26] Consequently, it should be stated that Aquinas's belief in the "tendency" of properly disposed matter to be actualized (in-formed) – in a line of consecutive accidental and substantial changes – by various new types of AAFF and SSFF (including SSFF of increasingly higher natural kinds) does not concern only his views on human embryology (as in the quoted passage from SCG III, 22, no. 7) but can be regarded as a generally binding principle in his metaphysical system.

METAPHYSICS OF EVOLUTIONARY TRANSITIONS

Our reflection on hylomorphism, substantial and accidental change, the disposition of matter, and its tendency to be in-formed by more perfect forms enables us to delineate and propose the metaphysical foundation of the mechanism of biological evolution. Here, I agree with O'Rourke who is convinced that "If Aristotle's metaphysical analysis of growth and change is correct, the principles of form and the affirmation of potency will hold *a fortiori* for the evolutionary process."[27]

Speciation

An evolutionary transition might be thus defined, in this account, as a series of minor genetic and epigenetic changes that effect minor phenotypic variations (accidental changes). These variations – remaining within the range of active and passive powers typical for a given species (natural kind) – may become permanent (i.e., transmitted from one generation to the next), which, in turn, gradually changes the "proximate disposition" of PM underlying subsequent organisms of the lineage L_I of the species S_I. This process, highly complex and extended in time, might lead to a precise instant at which the PM underlying the egg and the sperm coming from particular female and male organisms of sexually reproducing species S_I,[28] at their entering the substantial change in which they join and give an origin to a new organism, is not disposed to be actualized by the "old" type of SF that defines species S_I but by a "new" type of SF that defines species S_2, which is educed from the potentiality of PM that underlies them. The new organism (or organisms, as the process described here is commonly considered to be taking place within a population) starts a new lineage L_2, which happens to be the lineage of the new species S_2. See Figure 1.2.[29]

Anticipating our analysis presented in Chapter 2, we should emphasize that, on the proposed metaphysical/ontological model of speciation, each organism in an evolutionary lineage must belong to a distinct and clearly

---

[27] Fran O'Rourke, "Aristotle and the Metaphysics of Evolution," 27.

[28] Similar metaphysical analysis may be developed with reference to organisms reproducing asexually.

[29] The category of species used here and in all other aspects of the philosophical and theological modeling of speciation developed in this book, refers primarily to metaphysical notion of species (and of natural kinds). As such, it remains in correspondence to – while not being coextensive with – empirically based classifications used in biological attempts to formulate a definition of a species. This will become more apparent especially in light of the research presented in the remaining part of this chapter and in Chapters 2 and 5.

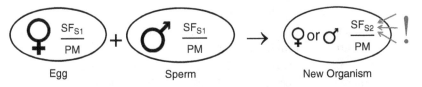

SF = substantial form
PM = primary matter
S₁, S₂ = species 1 and 2

FIGURE 1.2 Hylomorphic metaphysics of an evolutionary transition.

demarcated species. In other words, there can be no organisms that are literally "in-between" ancestral and descendant species, not belonging to either one of them. This also refers to the category of transitory or intermediate species. Albeit less numerous and less distinct in their genetic and morphological features, they form a separate natural kind. Moreover, intermediate species should be distinguished from intermediate organisms that belong to one and the same species but differ in their accidental dispositions and features – which can be captured in biological research. In other words, while intermediate species are different natural kinds, intermediate organisms belong to the same natural kind.[30]

Gametes – parental egg and sperm – are separate entities and may be treated as instrumental causes, acting under principal causation of the organisms that produced them.[31] Normally, when they join, entering thus a substantial change, which becomes an origin of the existence of a new organism, the PM that underlies them is disposed to be actualized by the original SF of the type S_1. In case of an evolutionary transition, however, accidental changes in the DNA and the epigenetic causal factors inherently affecting phenotypes of the consecutive organisms within the lineage L_1 lead to the situation in which PM, actualized by the given egg and sperm, produced by female and male organisms of species S_1, is disposed to be actualized in the substantial change these gametes enter by a new SF of the type S_2, which is educed from its potentiality. This originates the new evolutionary lineage L_2.[32]

---

[30] To put it yet another way, on the proposed model of speciation an SF "of a new type" should be distinguished from a new SF *simpliciter*. The latter actualizes an organism in a way that makes it belong to an already established natural kind, while the former actualizes and organism in a way that makes it belong to (establish) a new natural kind.
[31] See Q. de pot. 3, 11, ad 5.
[32] Even if contemporary biology is willing to acknowledge the reality of distinct species only at given points in time (due to constant genetic and phenotypic changes of

Interestingly, the described scenario finds support in Aristotle's example of the generation of a mule. Commenting on it Aquinas states: "[S]ince in the generation of a mule the sperm of a horse cannot induce the form of a horse in the matter, because it is not adapted to receive the form of a horse, it therefore induces a related form" (*In Meta.* VII, lect. 6 [§ 1432]). The "related form" here means the SF characteristic for a different species. Interpreting Aquinas's point today we may suggest that the disposition of PM underlying gametes is decisive for its potentiality to be actualized by a new SF characteristic of the same species. At rare occasions, it may happen that this condition is not met, which leads to the eduction of the "related form" that belongs to another (new) species. Reflecting on this passage from Aquinas's commentary on Aristotle's *Metaphysics*, Steven Snyder notes:

Although Aristotle had no scientific basis for asserting that semen could have formal powers and potencies not directly derived from the male, we now know that via chance mutations there can exist significant formal differences between the form of the parent and the form potential in the semen or ovum as instruments of reproduction. Mutations can arise from chance encounters with x-rays, for example, or in ways we do not yet fully understand in the process of bio-chemical union of sperm and egg. The point to emphasize is that these chance mutations in the genetic packages of the instruments of reproduction, and so differences in kind between the parents and offspring, are not alien to an Aristotelian natural philosophy.[33]

It takes many mutations and epigenetic changes (the outcomes of which are regulated by natural selection) to produce such an effect (i.e., the difference in kind between parents and their offspring), and its actual instantiation may be extremely difficult (if not impossible) to capture. But this does not exclude the possibility of its occurring, especially in a situation where some members of a species migrate to a new environment and can be modified gradually in subsequent generations, to the point where they can no longer mate with the other descendants of their ancestors. Thus, it becomes clear that, even if Aristotle's biological research was far from discovering the possibility of the transformation of species, his metaphysics, picked up and developed by Aquinas in the Middle Ages, left much room for such a possibility.[34]

---

organisms), it seems to me that the Aristotelian categories of potency/act and PM/SF provide a sufficient ground for accommodating both essentialist and processual aspects of living beings. I will say more on this in the next chapter.

[33] Steven Snyder, "Evolution and the Origin of Species: Aristotelian Reflections," https://maritain.nd.edu/jmc/ti/snyder.htm (retrieved 19 August 2022).

[34] My concept of the metaphysics of evolutionary transitions is inspired by the works of a number of Thomistic philosophers and theologians. Among them, I would like to mention in particular: (1) Antonio Moreno, "Some Philosophical Considerations"; (2)

The proposed scenario provides a clear response to a metaphysically ill-conceived argument against the possibility of evolution within the paradigm of classical metaphysics, stating that a number of accidental changes cannot lead to a substantial change that gives an origin to a new nature.[35] In answer to it, we must notice, firstly, that accidental changes indeed cannot bring a new nature in an already existing thing (this is a straw man argument on the part of an antievolutionary approach to Thomism as no follower of Aquinas that is open to evolution argues in this way). But this does not preclude the possibility of them changing the disposition of PM such that, in the course of many generations, a proper efficient cause educes from its potentiality a SF of a new type.[36] Secondly, on the proposed scheme, speciation takes place in the course of multiple substantial changes (with multiple new SSFF educed from the potentiality of PM) that accompany the processes of generation of offspring in a given evolutionary lineage. As such, it is not equivalent to any of those substantial changes in particular. Antievolutionary-oriented Thomists commit a mistake of reducing causal complexity of an evolutionary transition to its final step, in which the first organism of a new kind comes into existence (I will address this common misconception below, in a section on virtual and eminent presence of perfections). They also seem to confuse metaphysical categories assuming

---

Fran O'Rourke, "Aristotle and the Metaphysics of Evolution"; (3) William E. Carroll, "At the Mercy of Chance? Evolution and the Catholic Tradition," *Revue des questions scientifiques* 177 (2006): 179–204; and (4) Étienne Gilson, *From Aristotle to Darwin and Back Again: A Journey in Final Causality, Species, and Evolution* (Notre Dame, IN: Notre Dame Press, 1984). Concerning the question of the mono- and polygenetic character of speciation, it will be addressed in Chapter 8, on the occasion of my analysis of evolutionary anthropogenesis.

[35] This argument is repeatedly raised by Michael Chaberek. In one of his papers, he states that "accidental change will always produce only accidental differences, never bringing about a new substance or a new nature of a thing. The creation of a new substance would require substantial change: that is, the production of a new substantial form." (Michael Chaberek, "The Metaphysical Problem for Theistic Evolution: Accidental Change Does Not Generate Substantial Change," *Forum Philosophicum* 26, no. 1 [2021], 38). On another occasion, he once again emphasizes that "accidental change cannot produce substantial change" ("Classical Metaphysics, and Theistic Evolution: Why are They Incompatible?" *Studia Gilsoniana* 8, no. 1 [2019], 57).

[36] It is worth remembering that for Aquinas, substantial changes are usually preceded by a series of accidental changes. As notes Gloria Frost, "Aquinas claims that it is obvious in the case of natural substances that their powers do not produce substances immediately. Even when one substance generates another substance, it does so by gradually transforming its patient's matter" (Gloria Frost, *Aquinas on Efficient Causation and Causal Powers* [New York: Cambridge University Press, 2022], 113). See also *ibid.*, 193.

38 *Metaphysics of Evolutionary Transitions*

that speciation, which is a change in kind, is equivalent to a substantial change. This thesis is misleading, for while the latter always accompanies the former, the former does not always accompany the latter. Hence, they are not equal.

Levels of Similarity of Adjacent Species

Now, we need to acknowledge that substantial changes accompanying the conception of offspring are of a special kind. They result in coming into existence of new organisms whose SF is of the same type as that of their parental organisms. This is even more obvious in cases of asexual reproduction (e.g., by fission), yet unusual when compared with much more primitive chemical or biochemical substantial changes, which typically lead to the emergence of substances that are radically different from the reagents. Consequently, in the case of speciation, the last substantial change (conception) that crowns the entire process of an evolutionary transition is abnormal. The result is an organism whose SF belongs to a natural kind that differs from that of its parental organisms.

Understood in this way, speciation seems to violate the classical principle of similarity which says that "[E]very agent produces its like" (*SCG* II, 21, no. 9).[37] In other words, in the reproductive process the agent cause of a given type gives an origin to offspring that is similar to it. In response to this difficulty, it should be noted that according to the theory of biological evolution, the newborn first representative of the species S_2 is in most aspects and dispositions similar to the organisms of the preceding species S_1 from which it originates. Indeed, one of the major interpretations of evolutionary transitions claims that due to the specificity of speciation mechanisms and the low population size of the so-called transitional species, they have not been preserved in the fossil record. Hence, in the common understanding of evolutionary changes (based on a comparison of the forms that have been recorded in the fossil material), species differ considerably from one another. In fact, the differences between immediately adjacent phylogenetically related taxa are not so radical.

Nevertheless, the fact that the parents and their descendants do belong to different species requires some modifications in the interpretation of the classical principle in question. We need to agree that the similarity

---

[37] The principle of similarity is a particular variant of the broader principle of proportionate causation, which will be discussed below.

Metaphysics of Evolutionary Transitions 39

between parents and their offspring should not be understood as an absolute, strict, and nonexceptional qualitative identity of their SSFF. Rather, it can be defined in terms of a proportional proximity to the SF of the offspring, when compared with SSFF of its parents. It is worth noting that Aquinas himself admits departure from the strict interpretation of the principle of similarity. In *ST* I, 104, 1, co. we read:

> Sometimes, however, the effect has not this aptitude to receive the impression of its cause, in the same way as it exists in the agent: as may be seen clearly in all agents which do not produce an effect of the same species as themselves: thus the heavenly bodies cause the generation of inferior bodies which differ from them in species.[38]

The same observation made by Aquinas becomes even more apparent in his above-mentioned commentary to the seventh book of Aristotle's *Metaphysics* (lect. 6 [§ 1432–33]), where he distinguishes between substantial changes that happen by nature and substantial changes that happen by chance.[39] The latter fall outside of the normal and regular occurrences in nature, and yet they are not completely random. He suggests that the likeness defined by the principle "like produces like" can be interpreted not only as (strong) similarity in terms of belonging to the same species but also as (weak) similarity in terms of belonging to the same genus:

> [E]ach natural thing produces something similar to itself in species, unless something beyond nature [i.e., by chance] happens to result, as when a horse begets a mule. And this generation is beyond nature, because it is outside of the aim of a particular nature. For the formative power, which is in the sperm of the male, is designed by nature to produce something completely the same as that from which the sperm has been separated; but its secondary aim, when it cannot induce a perfect likeness, is to induce any kind of likeness that it can ... Hence in the generation of a mule the generator is similar in a way to the thing generated; for there is a proximate genus, which lacks a name, common to horse and to ass; and mule is also contained under that genus. Hence in reference to that genus it can be said that like generates like; for example, if we might say that that proximate genus is

---

[38] Following Aristotle, Aquinas was convinced that the energy of the sun was necessary for substantial changes to occur on earth. In reference to the example of celestial bodies causing the generation of lower bodies, one can argue that for Aquinas effects that do not resemble their causes are always ranked ontologically "lower" than their causes, while speciation, as defined above, entails the possibility of originating an organism, which is ontologically "higher," that is, one that has new and metaphysically "more perfect" dispositions in respect to its direct efficient cause. This issue will be addressed in the last section of this chapter.

[39] I will say more about chance and teleology in Chapter 3.

40 *Metaphysics of Evolutionary Transitions*

beast of burden, we could say that, even though a horse does not generate a horse but a mule, still a beast of burden generates a beast of burden.[40]

Gloria Frost rightly notes that a certain level of dissimilitude between a cause and its effect can be the outcome of the fact that many effects are caused by joined operation of a number of agents that have various active powers. She claims that according to Aquinas "In these cases, the effect will bear some similarity to each agent which produced it, and thus, it will resemble none of the individual agents perfectly."[41]

Eduction of New Substantial Forms

In my analysis so far, I have referred several times to the notion of the eduction of SSFF from the potentiality of PM. This idea (based on Latin *educere*) is found in Aquinas and seems to be his answer to one of the most challenging questions faced by classical metaphysics, that is, the one concerning the source of new SSFF. Aquinas rejects the suggestion that agents literally hand-over or pass the same numerical forms that actualize them to the substances they instantiate (act upon):

[A] hot body is not said to give off heat in this sense, that numerically the same heat which is in the heating body passes over into the heated body. Rather, by the power of the heat which is in the heating body, a numerically different heat is made actual in the heated body, a heat which was previously in it in potency. For a natural agent does not hand over its own form to another subject, but it reduces the passive subject from potency to act. (*SCG* III, 69, no. 28)[42]

Trying to clarify his position on the source of SSFF, Aquinas states that "it is not correct to say that the form is made in matter, rather should we say that it is educed from the potentiality of matter [*de materiae potentia educatur*]" (*Q. de pot.*, 3, 8, co.)[43] This is important as it

---

[40] Note that in Aquinas's example, the parental organisms belong to two different species. I believe it is legitimate to think that the interpretation of the principle "like produces like" that he suggests extends also to the cases of parental organisms that belong to one species. Nevertheless, evolutionary theory requires stretching it even more, as it assumes the reality of transitions at the level of genera and higher biological taxa.

[41] Frost, *Aquinas*, 101.

[42] In *ST* III, 77, 1, co. Aquinas offers a general formulation of the same argument, this time in reference to AAFF: "[A]ccidents do not pass from subject to subject, so that the same identical accident which was first in one subject be afterwards in another; because an accident is individuated by the subject; hence it cannot come to pass for an accident remaining identically the same to be at one time in one subject, and at another time in another."

[43] See also *Q. de pot.* 3, 4, ad 7, ad 14. In *SCG* III, 69, no. 2 Aquinas adds: "forms and accidents cannot come into being from matter, since they do not have matter as one of

reminds us that SF is not merely a combination, structure, or dynamic codependency of parts (secondary matter). Rather, matter can exist and function in different ways, and eduction of SF means actualization of one of these options. Because the principle corresponding with SF is PM, we are dealing here with a substantial change and not merely an accidental regrouping or reorganizing of atomic parts.

The language of eduction is an attempt by Aquinas to find a middle ground between treating SF as external and coming to form things "from the outside," on the one hand, and describing it as preexistent in a primitively actualized state in PM, on the other. Hence, he says that "motion is nothing else than the eduction of something from potentiality to actuality [*educere aliquid de potentia in actum*]" (*ST* I, 2, 3, co.).[44]

At the same time, we must be careful not to conceive of SSFF as somehow present or dormant in PM. This would compromise the notion of PM as pure potentiality. If we can say that form preexists in PM, it does so as entirely unactualized: "Every actuality of matter is educed from the potentiality of that matter [*educi de potentia materiae*]; for since matter is in potentiality to act, any act pre-exists in matter potentially" (*ST* I, 90, 2, ob. 2; see also ad 2). "Every form brought into being through the transmutation of matter is educed from the potentiality of matter [*forma educta de potentia materiae*]" (*SCG* II, 86, no. 6). Consequently, insofar, as the effective cause brings out the form which it realizes in the potentiality of matter, it is said to induce (*inducere*) or introduce (*introducere*) form.[45]

Speaking of the eduction of SSFF from the potentiality of PM, we must take into account efficient causes. Due to their active powers (dispositions), they are capable of actualizing PM in a particular way. They may

their parts." At the same time, in *Q. de pot.* 3, 8, ad 10 we find him saying that "form is not perfected by adding to the matter something extraneous that was not already in the matter potentially." Rather, "every form brought into being [*educitur in esse*] through the transmutation of matter is educed from the potentiality of matter, for the transmutation of matter is its reduction from potentiality to act" (*SCG* II, 86, no. 6).

[44] A similar argument can be found in *In Meta.* VII, lect. 6 (§ 1430–31): "[S]ome men were compelled to say that all forms are created; for while they held that forms come to be, they could not hold that they come from matter since matter is not a part of form; and therefore they concluded that forms come from nothing, and, consequently, that they are created. But because of this difficulty, on the other hand, some men claimed that forms actually pre-exist in matter, and this is to suppose that forms are hidden, as Anaxagoras maintained. Now the view of Aristotle, who claimed that forms are not generated but only composite things, excludes both of these other opinions. For it is not necessary to say that forms are caused by some external agent, or that they will always be present in matter actually, but only potentially, and that in the generation of the composite they are brought from potentiality to actuality."

[45] See *Quod.* 7, 4, 9, ad 4. See also *ST* I, 2, 3, co.; *ST* I, 4, 1, ad 2; *ST* I, 84, 3, co.; *ST* III, 8, 3, co.; *SCG* II, 45, no. 3.

operate individually or in groups, entering substantial changes themselves or initiating such changes in other entities. Hence, SSFF do not preexist in any way; they are not passed from one entity to the next, and they are not copied or generated (even if their origin accompanies generation of new entities). They are educed by proper efficient causes from the potency of PM, as ways of being or existence of things, making them to be what they are, at all levels of their complexity and in all quantitative and qualitative aspects of their natures. As notes Lawrence Dewan:

> The Platonists and Avicenna did not posit that forms are educed from the potency of matter, and so they were forced to say that natural agents merely *dispose matter*: the introduction of forms was from an incorporeal principle. If we say (as Thomas *does* say) with Aristotle, that substantial forms are educed from the potency of matter, then natural agents will not be merely the causes of the dispositions of matter, but even *the causes of the substantial forms*.[46]

Most importantly, this analysis tells us that the origin of SSFF should be classified as a natural occurrence, which does not require any direct supernatural causal influence.[47] The same applies to evolutionary transitions and the emergence of the first exemplars of a new species. The first SF of a given type is educed from the potency of PM. Since it is pure potentiality, all logically plausible SSFF can be educed from it by secondary efficient causes.[48] However, the proposed metaphysical foundation of evolutionary transitions and its notion of the source of new SSFF face a major challenge. Some think that it violates the principle of proportionate causation. I will address this issue in the remaining part of this chapter.

THE PRINCIPLE OF PROPORTIONATE CAUSATION AND EVOLUTION

The principle of proportionate causation (PPC) seems to be commonly accepted among classical philosophers and theologians. This becomes

---

[46] Lawrence Dewan, "The Importance of Substance," https://maritain.nd.edu/jmc/ti/dewan.htm (retrieved 19 August 2022). However, Thomas qualifies this assertion as follows: "... but just so far and no farther, viz that the forms are educed from potency into act. Consequently, the natural agents are principles of being as regards beginning to be [*essendi principia quantum ad inchoationem ad esse*], and not as regards being, absolutely [*et non quantum ad ipsum esse absolute*]" (Q. de pot. 5, 1, ad 5). I will say more on this topic in the section dedicated to the importance of *esse* in Aquinas's theology of creation in Chapter 4.

[47] One exception from this rule is human soul, which on the Thomistic scheme is created by God *ex nihilo* at the moment of conception.

[48] Once again, with the exception of the human soul.

The Principle of Proportionate Causation and Evolution   43

obvious when we take into account the variety and frequency of its formulations in Aristotle and especially in Aquinas:

[T]he begetter is of the same kind as the begotten (*Meta.* VII, 8 [1033b 30]).
[W]hatever perfection exists in an effect must be found in the effective cause
(*ST* I, 4, 2, co.). [N]o effect exceeds its cause (*ST* II-II, 32, 4, obj. 1).[49] [E]very
agent produces its like (*SCG* II, 21, no. 9). [N]othing acts beyond its species
(*Super II Sent.* 18, 2, 3).[50] [T]he order of causes necessarily corresponds to
the order of effects, since effects are commensurate with their causes (*SCG*
II, 15, no. 4). [E]very agent acts according as it is in act (*SCG* II, 6, no. 4).
No effect can be more powerful than its agent cause (*Super II Sent.* 18, 2, 3,
obj. 3).[51]

It is worth noting that Descartes forms a similar principle (often called
the Causal Adequacy Principle) when he says in the "Third Meditation"
that "there must be at least as much reality in the efficient and total cause
as in the effect of that cause."[52]

Adequacy versus *Perfection*

Before referring the PPC to the proposed metaphysics of evolutionary transitions, we need to ask about its general meaning in the wider
context of possible changes and causal relationships in nature. Here,
Stephen Boulter rightly notes that the core intuition of the PPC is that
every effect has an "adequate" (i.e., proportional or commensurate)
cause. But what constitutes adequacy? A rough yet common interpretation of the PPC is that a cause cannot give what it does not have.
However, such delineation of PPC is deficient as it rules out the emergence of new active and passive powers (dispositions) from a causal
base that does not possess them – basically in virtue of their being in
a way "new."[53]

Interpreted this way, the PPC renders implausible not only explanation provided by evolutionary biology but also a vast number, if not the

---

[49] See also *SCG* I, 67; *ST* II, 24, 6, s.c.; *Q. de pot.* 3, 16, ad 8.

[50] See also *Q. de ver.* 24, 14; *Quod.* 9, 5, 1; *SCG* III, 84; *Q. de pot.* 3, 9; *ST* I–II, 112, 1.

[51] See also *Q. de pot.* 3, 8, obj. 13; *ST* I–II, 112, 1; *Comp. theo.* 1, 93.

[52] René Descartes, *The Philosophical Writings of Descartes: Volume 2*, trans. John Cottingham, Robert Stoothoff, and Dugald Murdoch (Cambridge: Cambridge University Press,
1984), 28.

[53] See Stephen Boulter, "Evolution and the Principle of Proportionality," in *Neo-
Aristotelian Metaphysics and the Theology of Nature*, ed. William M. R. Simpson,
Robert C. Koons, and James Orr (New York: Routledge, 2021), 126.

44 *Metaphysics of Evolutionary Transitions*

majority of substantial changes observed in nature and analyzed in physics, chemistry, biology, and other sciences. These are the changes where we observe new substance(s) coming into existence, which have new properties and perfections that are not observed in the substances they originated from (the reagents that entered the reaction, which effected a given substantial change). Think about the reaction in which hydrogen and oxygen react forming water. The outcome of the process is a new substance, which has properties radically different from those of the reagents.[54]

Hence, Boulter is right when he says that what is at stake and what defines adequacy in PPC is perfection (see *ST* I, 4, 2, co. above). In other words, what PPC rules out are cases where something less perfect causes the more "perfect" or cases of an effect "exceeding" its cause or of an effect "being more powerful" than its cause (see *ST* I, 95, 1; *ST* I–II, 66, 1; *ST* I–II, 63, 2, obj. 3; *ST* II–II, 24, 6; *SCG* I, 67; *SCG* I, 41; *SCG* III, 120). Following Coffey, he traces back primary intuitions that led scholastics to formulate the PPC:

(1) The principle of causation – whatever begins to be, has a cause; whatever is contingent has a cause; nothing occurs without a cause.

(2) *Operari sequitur esse* – operational powers depend on what a given entity is.

(3) *Omnes agens agit inquantum est in actu* – all agents act insofar as they are in act. Hence, the higher an agent is on the scale of being, the more perfect its act of being, the higher its operations and effects.

(4) From a known effect, we can argue with certainty to the existence of an adequate efficient cause, which is available to our cognition (we can obtain knowledge of its nature).

(5) The principle of proportionality – an adequate efficient cause is sufficiently perfect and high on the scale of being to produce the

---

[54] Paying attention to the same problem of the popular interpretation of PPC Peter Coffey states: "The mediaeval scholastics embodied this truth in the formula: *Nemo dat quod non habet* – a formula which we must not interpret in the more restricted and literal sense of the words giving and having, lest we be met with the obvious objection that it is by no means necessary for a boy to have a black eye himself in order to give one to his neighbour!" (Peter Coffey, *Ontology or The Theory of Being: An Introduction to General Metaphysics* [Gloucester, MA: Peter Smith, 1970], 60). Brian Carl adds that "Like the claim that 'there is nothing in the intellect that is not first in the sense', the formulation that 'nothing gives what it does not have' only explicitly appears in Thomas's writings in objections," which shows that he prefers other (more precise) formulations of the PPC. See Brian T. Carl, "Thomas Aquinas on the Proportionate Causes of Living Species," *Scientia et Fides* 8, no. 2 (2020), 226.

The Principle of Proportionate Causation and Evolution 45

effect in question (otherwise the effect would be partly uncaused – which contradicts (1)).

(6) An effect cannot as such be ontologically more perfect than its adequate (created) cause, which further specifies (5).

(7) *Nihil agit ultra suam speciem; omne agens agit simile sibi* – nothing acts in a manner above its own kind; (since) everything produces its like.[55]

Delineated in this way, PPC might be considered as a real challenge for evolutionary theory, where we observe a number of fundamental transitions, including those from abiotic to biotic; from replicating molecules to populations of molecules in protocells; from independent replicators to chromosomes; from RNA to DNA; from asexual clones to sexual populations; from single-celled forms to multicell and organic forms; from individual organisms to colonies; and from primates to humans.[56] The difficulty seems to be all the more acute in reference to the metaphysical account of evolutionary transitions I delineated in this chapter.[57]

Different Notions of Perfection

The first line of response engages in an attempt at providing a metaphysically precise definition of perfection. Here, following Boulter, we need to distinguish two principal notions of what it means to be perfect.[58] The first goes back to Aristotle and ties perfection with completion, that is, the notion of ἐντελέχεια (*entelecheia*), which relates formal to final causation (anticipating my analysis of it in Chapter 3) and denotes the form as actualized in the highest state of perfection of a given entity. Within this paradigm, an entity is perfect when "in respect of excellence and goodness [it] cannot be excelled in its kind" (*Meta.* V, 16 [1021b14]). Perfection completes an entity, making it lack nothing that is proper to it, in reference to the natural kind it belongs to. Embracing this notion

---

[55] See Boulter, "Evolution," 128–31.

[56] See John Maynard Smith and Eors Szathmary, *The Origins of Life: From the Birth of Life to the Origin of Language* (Oxford: Oxford University Press, 2000), 17.

[57] Chaberek has pointed to the principles that "no being can convey more act than it possesses," that "no effect can exceed the power of its cause" and that "the perfection of the cause cannot be lesser than the perfection of the effect" as incompatible with the evolutionary emergence of novel genera of living things. See his *Aquinas and Evolution* (Lexington: The Chartwell Press, 2019), 48; "Classical Metaphysics," 56.

[58] See Boulter, "Evolution," 131–34.

46   *Metaphysics of Evolutionary Transitions*

of perfection Aquinas says: "That is perfect which lacks nothing of the mode of its perfection" (*ST* I, 4, 1, co.)

The second notion of perfection goes back to Plato and Plotinus as it is grounded in the concept of the Great Chain of Being. Boulter refers it to Anselm and his version of the Ontological Argument. On this scheme, a perfection is any property the possession of which moves one up the Chain. Yet, it is not easy to decide what all such properties have in common. Apart from rather imprecise suggestions made by scholastics, we might think about defining the common denominator of such properties in terms of rising (1) the degree of act *versus* potency; (2) the degree of immateriality; (3) immanence of action; (4) range and depth of operation and causal influence; (5) freedom from substantial change; (6) unity and simplicity of structure; or (7) natural control of other things.[59]

Most importantly, notes Boulter, even though both accounts of perfection contain the notion of completion (*entelecheia* and God's *esse*, respectively), they differ rather substantially:

According to the Aristotelian account, a perfection is a property that makes an entity better than other entities *of the same kind*, while on the Anselmian account a perfection is a property that makes an entity "better" or more "noble" than another entity, whether that entity is of the same kind or not. Anselmian perfections are thus absolute in a way Aristotelian perfections are not.[60]

Consequently, since all cases of the first (Aristotelian) notion of perfection are species and kind relative, they are inadequate in comparing and ranking entities and organisms that belong to different natural kinds. To give an example, on this notion of perfection, a fly is as perfect as an elephant, as long as both organisms lack nothing that is proper for their natural kind (i.e., they reach their kind specific state of *entelecheia*). Biologically speaking, this kind of perfection might be defined in terms of the dominance of an ecological niche and producing fertile offspring. Thus, under this notion of perfection, there can be no question of a less perfect kind of entity bringing about a more perfect kind of entity, as there is no ground for the alleged comparison.

The case of the Anselmian hierarchical notion of perfection is more nuanced. Boulter suggests, after Scotus, that we should distinguish at least two main types of hierarchy here: (1) the order of ontological dependence (based on "what depends on what") and (2) the order of

---

[59] See Bernard Wuellner, *Summary of Scholastic Principles* (Chicago: Loyola University Press, 1956), 226.
[60] Boulter, "Evolution," 133.

The Principle of Proportionate Causation and Evolution 47

eminence ("nobility" or "dignity") of entities.[61] Concerning (1) he states that the fundamental transitions in the history of life do not violate the PPC, as they do not generate effects on which they themselves depend ontologically. To the contrary, new types of being usually incorporate the old kinds of entities from which they originate as their constituent parts and thus may be said to be, to some extent, dependent on them. Even the origin of rationality from purely material causes follows the PPC, as human active intellect is only relatively independent from sense organs. With reference to (2), one might argue that the hierarchy of eminence is an anthropocentric projection or an outdated residue of Neo-Platonism, and all perfections listed in it are, in fact, Aristotelian perfections (just as life is not a perfection in a stone, sentience is not a perfection in a rose, nor rationality in an elephant). Hence, the PPC is not violated here either.[62]

However, might such a dismissive response with regards to the hierarchy of eminence be too hasty? What if Anselmian perfections are metaphysically respectable properties? What if it is metaphysically relevant to compare perfections (proper dispositions) of neighboring species on the tree of life? Would not it violate the PPC? We might think about several possible answers to this question.

Virtual and Eminent Presence of Perfections

One possible response to the observation that, in the course of evolutionary transitions, less perfect causes bring about more perfect effects is to refer to the medieval concept of dispositions and properties present in things potentially (or virtually) and not actually (or formally).[63]

---

[61] A more general account of the hierarchy of ontological dependence rules out the following relations: (1) the nonexistent being the efficient cause of any type of being; (2) a being of reason effecting a real being; (3) a potential being effecting an actual one; (4) compound entity being the efficient cause of a simple being; (5) accident efficiently causing a substance; or (6) contingent entity efficiently causing the emergence of a necessary one. In each of these relations a cause seems to depend on the effect, which violates the PPC. In other words, as notes Aquinas "effects correspond proportionally to their causes, so that we attribute actual effects to actual causes, potential effects to potential causes, and, similarly, particular effects to particular causes and universal effects to universal causes" (SCG II, 21, no. 4). See Boulter, "Evolution," 135.

[62] See, ibid., 137.

[63] Boulter mentions this idea as one of the intuitions that led scholastics to formulate the PPC (in addition to those listed above, in the section juxtaposing adequacy and perfection). He claims that they believed "The actuality of the effect need not be in its adequate created cause actually and formally, but merely potentially or virtually" (Boulter, "Evolution," 130).

48   *Metaphysics of Evolutionary Transitions*

Applying this argument in the contemporary context, Edward Feser reformulates the classical version of the PPC saying that what it means is that "whatever is in an effect must be in its *total* cause in *some* way or other, whether *formally*, *virtually*, or *eminently*."[64] In reference to this distinction, he gives an example of the $20 bill:

> Suppose I give you a twenty dollar bill. Your having it is the effect. One way in which I could cause you to have it is by virtue of having a twenty dollar bill in my wallet and handing it to you. I have the "form" of *possessing a twenty dollar bill* and I cause you to have the same form. That would be a case of what is in the effect being in the cause "formally." But it might be that I do not have a twenty dollar bill on hand ready to give you, but I do have at least twenty dollars in the bank, and I can wire the money from my account to yours so that you can withdraw it from an ATM. In that case what is in the effect was in the total cause – me plus my bank account, etc. – "virtually" rather than formally. Or it might be that I do not have even twenty dollars in my account, but I do somehow have access to a U.S. Federal Reserve Bank printing press and can get a genuine twenty dollar bill printed off for you on demand. In that case what is in the effect is in the total cause – me, the printing press, etc. – "eminently." For while in this case I don't have an actual twenty dollar bill or even twenty dollars in the bank, I would have something even more fundamental, causally speaking, namely the power to *make* twenty dollar bills.[65]

Although reasonable, this proposal needs clarification. In what way is a perfection proper for amphibians present in fish? My intuition is that the notion of virtual presence in this context differs from the one discussed above, in reference to parts present in a substantial whole through their dispositions and powers – that is, intrinsically. Here, virtual presence may be interpreted as extrinsic presence of a given perfection or its "parts" ("aspects") in what Feser calls a "*total* cause" of a given entity. Indeed, one of the major faults of the debate on metaphysical aspects of evolutionary transitions and the PPC as applied to them is a blatant oversimplification of their causal analysis. What is being taken into account is usually the last step (usually an act of fertilization or conception) of a causal process that is extremely complex, multifaceted, and extended in time. We might speak here about an evolutionary causal matrix (or causal polygeny), where relevant contributors to speciation are incredibly many. Their number might be, in fact, virtually impossible to estimate.[66]

---

[64] Edward Feser, *Scholastic Metaphysics: A Contemporary Introduction* (Heusenstamm: Editiones Scholasticae, 2014), 155.

[65] *Ibid.*

[66] The idea of causal polygeny of events was introduced in analytic philosophy of biology by John Dupré, who, in turn, takes it from genetics, which acknowledges that many

The Principle of Proportionate Causation and Evolution 49

In addition to genetic mutations, we may name a number of other accidental changes that are relevant to speciation, such as genetic recombination, gene transfer, genetic drift, and changes classified as epigenetic (i.e., permanent, nongenetic, yet heritable changes that affect DNA expression). Moreover, as already mentioned in the introduction, we currently learn more about the synergy of evolution and development (evo-devo), as well as the importance of cultural, behavioral, physiological, and ecological inheritance (biological niche construction). Among additional factors, having causal influence on speciation, we find geographic, ecological, and reproductive barriers, as well as natural selection, which – strictly speaking – is not so much a cause but rather an explanation (a descriptive principle), turning our attention toward the fact of greater reproductive success of organisms that are better adapted to the environment in which the principle of struggle for existence applies.[67] All these factors have an influence on living organisms which, by nature, seek to preserve life (maintain homeostasis) and produce offspring (reproduce). Furthermore, organisms in question are closely linked in ancestral-descendant relations within populations in a given evolutionary lineage, which extends over extremely long periods of time, counted in hundreds of thousands or millions of years.

Hence, the proportionate cause of the emergence of a new species is not a single law or force but a concurrence of many causal influences constitutive for a speciation event or rather a history of an evolutionary transition. Causal contribution of such a multiplicity of causes is stored and transmitted from generation to generation, up to the point in which a given organism is able to educe a new kind of SF from the potentiality of PM. This does not contradict the PPC. This view was expressed already by Benedict Ashley:

The proportionate cause of the emergence of new types or organisms of increasingly complex organization and independence of the environment is not any single law or force but a concurrence of many causes in an evolutionary event,

---

genes typically contribute to the production of one trait. Following Dupré, George Molnar notes not only that events are polygenic but also that causal powers, conversely, are pleiotropic and flexible, and can make a contribution to many different effects. See John Dupré, *The Disorder of Things: Metaphysical Foundations of the Disunity of Science* (Cambridge, Mass: Harvard University Press, 1993), 123–24; George Molnar, *Powers: A Study in Metaphysics*, edited by Stephen Mumford (New York: Oxford University Press, 2003), 195.

[67] I will address this issue in greater detail in Chapter 3, in a section asking whether natural selection should be regarded as teleological.

Metaphysics of Evolutionary Transitions

or better, a history. A population of interbreeding organisms interacts with the ecosystem of which it is a part so as to evolve and differentiate into new reproductively isolated species, each of which develops an integrated type adapted to a special environmental niche, clearly distinguished from other populations for many generations.[68]

Relating my argument to the notion of biological information, we may suggest that in a case of speciation, the quantity of information rises and its quality changes with respect to the first representative(s) of a new species. However, in our assessment of those differences, we must take into account not only the preceding generation, that is, the parents of the first exemplar of a new species, but also numerous causes contributing to the entire evolutionary transition. Their information input accounts for the net result and balance of the quantity of information that changes (or is being exchanged?) in this process.[69] Hence, Ashley concludes by saying:

Thus nuclear, chemical, and biological evolution, although involving very different kinds of events, have this in common: atom, molecule, and organism are products of historical events no less complex and sequentially ordered than the entities which they produce. The new species is not a "greater emerging from the less," because the amount of information it contains in integrated form is no greater than the amount of information present in the historical evolutionary process. What is spread out in history is condensed, as it were, in the emerging new species.[70]

Interestingly, this view finds a firm grounding in the thought of Aquinas who, following Avicenna, distinguishes the following four

---

[68] Benedict Ashley, "Causality and Evolution," *The Thomist* 36, (April 1972), 215. See also Norbert Luyten, "Philosophical Implications of Evolution," *New Scholasticism* 25 (July, 1951), 300–2; Leo J. Elders, "The Philosophical and Religious Background of Charles Darwin's Theory of Evolution," *Doctor Communis* 37 (1984), 56.

[69] The information input in evolutionary transitions is most likely much higher than the amount of information written and expressed in representatives of neighboring species. Much of it is possibly lost and scattered "on the way" of these highly complex and multilayered processes.

[70] Benedict Ashley, "Causality and Evolution," *The Thomist* 36, (April 1972), 215. The notion of biological information – which is notoriously difficult to define and quantify – is one of the vexing topics in philosophy of biology. See Peter Godfrey-Smith and Kim Sterelny, "Biological Information," in *The Stanford Encyclopedia of Philosophy*, ed. Edward N. Zalta, Summer 2016 (Metaphysics Research Lab, Stanford University, 2016), https://plato.stanford.edu/archives/sum2016/entries/information-biological/ (retrieved 20 July 2022); Peter Godfrey-Smith and Kim Sterelny, "Information in Biology," in *The Cambridge Companion to the Philosophy of Biology*, ed. David L. Hull and Michael Ruse (Cambridge; New York: Cambridge University Press, 2007), 103–19; Stefan Artmann, "Biological Information," in *A Companion to the Philosophy of Biology*, ed. Sahotra Sarkar and Anya Plutynski (Chichester: Wiley-Blackwell, 2010), 22–39.

The Principle of Proportionate Causation and Evolution 51

types of efficient causation: perfecting, preparing, assisting, and advising.[71] While all four categories might be attributed to natural agents, the most interesting for us are perfecting and preparing efficient causes. Aquinas's notion of the former defined as "the one which causes the ultimate perfection of a thing" (*In Meta.* V, lect. 2 [§ 766]) might be referred to the cause that brings about (directly) the final step of an evolutionary transformation. His reflection on the latter – preparing (indirect) efficient causes – can be extended to numerous causal agents contributing to the same complex evolutionary transition. He writes: "The cause disposing anything ... does not induce the final perfecting form, but rather only prepares matter for that form" (*In Meta.* V, lect. 2 [§ 767]). Hence, Aquinas is aware that natural efficient causes may be (and usually are) plugged into a network of other efficient causes and that the effect of one of them might be also attributed to others.[72] Moreover, he sometimes uses the term "order" to characterize the interconnection between many causes contributing to a joint effect (see e.g., *ST* I, 116, 2, ad 1).

Another possible answer to this query, mentioned by Feser, introduces the notion of the "eminent" presence of perfections in causes. The idea goes back to the medieval concept of a passive obediential capacity (*potentia obedientialis*) whereby the nature of a given cause can be "elevated" such that it is capable to give what by nature it does not have.[73] Naturally, just as in Feser's example, the access to a US Federal Reserve Bank printing press, which gives an eminent "power" of issuing dollar bills, is not something that lies within the capacities of a regular citizen, the "eminent" presence of perfections in contingent causes goes beyond their natural dispositions. Hence, the "elevation" of such agents is caused by the supernatural concursus of the First Cause, which enables

---

[71] See *In Meta.* V, lect. 2 (§ 766–69); *In Phys.* II, lect. 5 (§ 766–69); Frost, *Aquinas*, 192–98.

[72] Frost notes that Aquinas is concerned with positing limits to the number and scope of efficient causes potentially contributing to a given change. She says that for him "Disposing causes are those which act toward the production of that which can be immediately transformed (i.e., by a single action) into the final effect" (Frost, *Aquinas*, 196).

[73] Boulter sees it as yet another idea that motivated the formulation of the PPC in the Middle Ages. He claims the scholastics believed that "Created causes have a passive obediential capacity (*potentia obedientialis*) whereby their nature can be so elevated by the First Cause that they can produce, with His special supernatural concursus, effects of an entirely higher order than those within the ambit of their natural powers" (Boulter, "Evolution," 130). The question remains to what extent this idea, as well as the one referring to virtual presence – see note 63 above – motivated the formulation or rather explained the difficulties stemming from the PPC.

52 *Metaphysics of Evolutionary Transitions*

them to bring about effects of an entirely higher order than those within the ambit of their natural powers.

Although one could argue that divine "elevation" of contingent causes is not so much a miracle but an expression of God's agency in the universe through the instrumental causation of creatures (I will say more on this topic in Chapter 5), the argument based on *potentia obedientialis* might be less favored by the naturalistically oriented mind of a contemporary researcher and theoretician of evolutionary biology.[74] If they are not convinced by this nor by any of the preceding arguments, one could refer them to another possible response to the difficulty related to the PPC in evolutionary transitions.

Conservation of the Overall Perfection of the Universe

In reference to a growing awareness of the complexity of the notion of perfection among biologists and philosophers of biology, Boulter develops an intriguing observation that throughout the fundamental transitions in the history of life, the net "amount" of perfection of the universe remains stable. He challenges our tendency to pay attention only to increases in operation or power found in new kinds of entities. What is less immediately obvious, and for the most part neglected, is that new powers and dispositions are usually accompanied by new difficulties, problems, and defects. Hence, the balanced notion of evolution reveals that each transition in the history of life involves both increase and decrease in perfection. This allows us to postulate a principle of an overall conservation of perfection in an evolving universe.

Think about the loss of operational control – says Boulter – which we normally perceive as a decrease in perfection. Apply this rule to

---

[74] See, for example, Daniel De Haan's strong argument in favor of the naturalistic explanation of evolution from the Thomistic perspective in his "*Nihil dat quod non habet*: Thomist Naturalism Contra Supernaturalism on the Origin of Species," in *A Catholic View on Evolution: New Perspectives in Thomistic Philosophy and Theology*, ed. by Nicanor Austriaco (Washington, DC: Catholic University of America Press, 2023). In the course of his argumentation, he states: "According to Thomist naturalism, the Cosmos is endowed with all of the secondary causal potentialities required qua interacting secondary causes to eventually bring about, via adornment (*opus ornatus*), the generative eduction of all fundamental particles, atoms, molecules, galactic, stellar, and planetary systems, along with the abiogenesis and evolution of all living organisms, including the emergence of sentient conscious animals. The principled exception is the immaterial rational soul of humans that cannot be educed from any totality of hylomorphic secondary causes, because there is no material potentiality for a per se subsisting immaterial form or rational soul" (*ibid.*).

The Principle of Proportionate Causation and Evolution 53

prokaryotes entering the first eucaryotic cell, to cells of higher organisms, which depend for their activities on being part of a multicellular organism, or to individuals of sexually reproducing species that depend on populations of interbreeding organisms. He concludes that the general pattern of counterbalancing perfections continues as we mount the scale of being (*scala naturae*). In reference to John Maynard Smith and Eors Szathmary, he then offers an original reflection on this topic:

[E]ach of the transitions involves an increase in the internal complexity of the relevant entities. Yet simplicity is traditionally seen as a perfection. So whatever is gained in operational powers after a transition is offset by the increase in complexity.

Moreover, the transition from abiotic to biotic involves the emergence for the first time of *mistakes*. No doubt this is in part due to the greater internal complexity of the relevant entities. However that may be, life cannot be seen as an unqualified advance against the background of a mistake-free inanimate order, given that these mistakes are often nontrivial and introduce the very possibility of suffering for the first time.

Again, living things, animals in particular, need to be equipped to deal with their precarious form of existence in a way abiotic entities do not. In particular there is a need for forms of perception to guide movement to secure resource requirements and avoid predation. From this perspective sentience is seen to be *both* a perfection *and* a compensation for a handicap due to a need not present amongst abiotic entities and plants.

Similar remarks apply to rationality in humans. Our intellectual capacities are *both* a perfection *and* a necessary compensation for a handicap not present in the other higher animals, namely, the lack of natural weapons or defences against both predators and the elements. The lesson here is that nature provides what is *needful*; nobility is not a consideration.

Moreover, the "advance" from the sensory experiences of the sensitive soul to the abstract concepts of the intellective soul is *not* a move up from a material sensory organ to an immaterial intellect, but a *sideways* move from informationally rich to informationally impoverished but useful representations. This is because concept formation via abstraction involves *ignoring information* available in perception. But if information – truth – is a good, then this transition involves sacrificing *quantity* of information for *quality*.

Finally, voluntary action is one of the benefits associated with rationality because it involves an increase in control over behaviour; but it also introduces the possibility, not to say inevitability, of moral mistakes and suffering of a kind and intensity not known to animal, plant or inanimate entities.[75]

Boulter thus confronts us with the image of a universe that was perfect to begin with, with the emergence of life and its subsequent history

---

[75] Boulter, "Evolution," 140–41. He refers to John Maynard Smith and Eors Szathmary, *The Origins of Life*, 19.

54   *Metaphysics of Evolutionary Transitions*

revealing different but equally perfect states of the universe. If he is right, then evolutionary transitions themselves do not involve violations of the PPC, with respect to hypothetical negative perfections.

Evolution and Aquinas's Hierarchy of Causes

One last attempt at answering the challenge of the PPC applied to evolution, offered by Brian Carl, takes us back to Aquinas. He draws our attention to the complexity of causal hierarchy in Aquinas, which is often ignored by many who concentrate merely on proximate causes in their analysis of causal dependencies. For Thomas, all causal relationships in the mundane reality happen within God's providence, where God is conceived as the first and principal cause, working in nature through secondary and instrumental causes. However, between God and mundane creatures, Aquinas sees the causality of angels and celestial spheres, especially the Sun, which is the source of heat.[76] Concerning generation of animals, gametes (egg and sperm – as we know today) are instrumental causes in relation to parental organisms, which are secondary (or instrumental) causes in relation to celestial spheres (in particular, the Sun), which are secondary (or instrumental) causes in relation to angels, who are secondary (or instrumental) causes in relation to God.

Based on this observation, Carl notes that

Thomas does not in fact hold that any individual animal "has" its own nature in such a way that it is sufficient to "give" that nature to something else, for on his view an individual animal is an instrumental cause in the generation of another individual of the same species.[77]

In other words, each individual living creature does not "have" its own nature in a way that enables it to pass it on its offspring. It "has" its nature in such a manner that it can be used instrumentally by a

---

[76] It is important to remember, in this context, that the ancient and medieval idea of causation of celestial bodies is not just a relic of an outdated cosmology. It is not entirely implausible to see the energy emitted by the sun, forces of gravitation, and other universal cosmological causal principles as contributing to educing particular forms from PM in processes of substantial changes occurring in nature. At the same time, this general supposition must be distinguished from the outdated science. The ancient and medieval scientists thought that it was through heat that matter was qualitatively disposed to enter a substantial change in which its underlying PM was informed by a soul of a given type. They thought semen was a thoroughly concocted blood endowed with powers similar to blood producing flesh and organs, yet directed to do so in the conception of a new organism from the matter provided by the female (see *De gen. an.* II, 4 [740b 24]).

[77] Carl, "Thomas Aquinas," 226.

Conclusion 55

superior cause.[78] Moreover, all changes (including all cases of generation and corruption) engage the entire hierarchy of causes, since – paradoxically – higher causes (separated substances) may not be able to bring changes in mundane (physical) reality directly:

Just as the baker cannot produce the form of bread except through fire, for St. Thomas created separate substances are unable to directly cause any formal transmutation of bodily substances; they are limited to causing changes of place. If a separate substance wishes to cause any transmutation of a bodily substance, it must use a mediating body, "just as a man can heat something through fire" (*Q. de malo* 16, 9).[79]

Carl further develops this idea in reference to Aquinas who asserts that "the power of a heavenly body suffices for generating certain less perfect animals from disposed matter, for it is obvious that more [things] are required for the production of a perfect thing than for the production of an imperfect thing" (*ST* I, 91, 2, ad 2).[80] He comes to the original conclusion that:

... the only general metaphysical principle that St. Thomas invokes in order to argue for the need for the instrumental contribution of a univocal generator is not the principle of proportionate causality, but instead the principle that a remote created universal cause needs the instrumental contribution of mediating instruments to produce more powerful effects. This principle seems reconcilable with evolution as well—although to articulate this reconciliation would require much further work.[81]

This suggestion certainly remains in line with previously discussed solutions based on the notion of virtual and eminent presence of perfections and paying attention to the complexity of the evolutionary matrix of causes engaged in speciation events.

CONCLUSION

Despite an ever-present skepticism toward classical philosophy, the long-standing legacy of the Aristotelian – Thomistic tradition remains not only coherent and consistent but also vigorous, flexible, and open to the

---

[78] See *ibid.*, 235. As Thomas elsewhere puts it, endorsing what he takes to be Aristotle's view, "whatever causes generation in these lower [bodies] moves [its patient] to a species as the instrument of a heavenly body" (*ST* I, 115, 3, ad 2). See also *SCG* III, 69; *ST* I, 45, 8, ad 3.

[79] Carl, "Thomas Aquinas," 243.

[80] See also *Super II Sent.* 18, 2, 3, ad 5; *Q. de pot.* 3, 11, ad 12; *In Meta.* VII, lect. 6 (§ 1401).

[81] Carl, "Thomas Aquinas," 244–45.

new data and current ways of understanding the universe, its structures, and processes. When introduced to the evolution debate in particular, it presents itself not as an aged doctrine that is limited to humble listening and adjusting of its principles to the new scientific theories. Quite to the contrary, its fundamental principles enable us to develop a constructive proposal of the metaphysics of evolutionary transitions.

However, as promising as this perspective may seem, there are a number of queries that remain. They refer to various aspects of evolutionary theory that are widely discussed among both biologists and philosophers of biology. One of the most important issues that need to be addressed takes us back to the controversy concerning biological species. Is the classical essentialist notion of species (assumed by the proposed metaphysical notion of speciation) defensible in the context of contemporary evolutionary biology? The next chapter will provide an answer to this question.

2

Essentialist and Hylomorphic Notion of Species and Species Transformation

One of the many concerns of logical positivism in the first half of the twentieth century was the final dismissal of typological thinking in biology and philosophy of biology – a common-sense consequence of the commitment to mechanicism encouraged by the Scientific Revolution and the statistical treatment of natural selection in population genetics and the modern evolutionary synthesis. The idea that organisms have intrinsic underlying natures (essences) and belong to natural kinds – thought to arise from a naïve and uninformed view of biology – was replaced by relational and "population" thinking, which was commonly considered more fitting with evolutionary synthesis. Hence, referring to the essence of an organism as an explanatory principle was perceived for decades as indicative of dogmatic entrenchment in scholasticism and detachment from the advancements of contemporary science.

However, this radically anti-individualistic and antiessentialistic orthodoxy has been more recently challenged by a number of thinkers who claim that the relational approach in defining species requires at least supplementing with the complementary, classical view – the one that acknowledges the reality of intrinsic natures (essences) of individual organisms. Several suggestions have been made as to what should be taken to constitute an essential nature, including genetic, phenetic, and relational/historical properties, fundamental dispositions, developmental programs, and SSFF.

The aim of this chapter is to present the re-emergence of biological essentialism and its interpretation within the context of the complex and multidimensional contemporary debate concerning biological species and taxonomy. My argumentation will proceed as follows. First, I will refer briefly to the controversy concerning nominalism *versus* realism about

58 *Essentialist and Hylomorphic Notion of Species*

the species category. Next, I will introduce the division of the three levels of inquiry in the debate over species concepts and offer – as a heuristic device – a graphic classification depicting those concepts that are discussed in the text. The following section will concentrate on relational species concepts (RSCs). After listing their types, I will (1) refer to the ontological qualification of species as spatiotemporally restricted individuals with parts, (2) discuss the pluralist position in the debate on defining species, and (3) point toward the main challenges of the relational approach in the same debate. The next section will examine intrinsic species concepts (ISCs). Apart from more detailed analysis of the re-emergence and contemporary variants/aspects of the essentialist definition of biological species, it will refer shortly to the homeostatic property cluster species concept (HPCSC) and phenetic species concepts (PSC) and answer two major arguments against the compatibility of ISCs (and essentialist species concept [EssSC] in particular) with evolutionary biology. The remaining section will briefly discuss four strategies of classifying species under higher taxa. The chapter will end with a short conclusion.[1]

NOMINALISM *VERSUS* REALISM ABOUT SPECIES

Darwin's theory of evolution was undoubtedly revolutionary for the entire enterprise of biology. Moving it beyond a mere description and analysis of intrinsic natures and extrinsic relationships of countless animate entities (within their ecological niches), it boldly suggested that it is the same scientific inquiry, undertaken by biologists, that enables us to specify and describe, if not the ultimate (primary) cause, then at least proximate (secondary) causes of the origins of the profuse variety of forms of life on Earth.[2] However, a more careful scrutiny of Darwin's

---

[1] My preliminary ideas on the subject of species can be found in Mariusz Tabaczek, "An Aristotelian Account of Evolution and the Contemporary Philosophy of Biology," in *The 1st Virtual International Conference on the Dialogue between Science and Theology. Dialogo Conf 2014: Cosmology, Life & Anthropology*, ed. Cosmin Tudor Ciocan and Anton Lieskovský (Zilina: Publishing Institution of the University of Zilina, 2014), 62–64.

[2] Concerning the classical theological distinction between primary and secondary causation, toward the end of the final chapter of his seminal work, Darwin famously states: "To my mind it accords better with what we know of the laws impressed on matter by the Creator, that the production and extinction of the past and present inhabitants of the world should have been due to secondary causes, like those determining the birth and death of the individual" (Charles Darwin, *On the Origin of Species by Means of Natural Selection, or the Preservation of Favoured Races in the Struggle for Life* [London: John Murray, 1859], 488).

Nominalism versus *Realism about Species* 59

undertaking, implemented and reinterpreted within the context of the contemporary evolutionary synthesis, raises an important question concerning the scale of his revolution. On the one hand, one might think Darwin did not only aim at explaining the origin of species but, in fact, also dismissed the very concept of "species" altogether, thus, opening the way to the contemporary "population thinking" in biology.[3] In support of this thesis, one could refer to the oft cited passage from *On the Origin of Species*, where we find him saying

> I look at the term species as one arbitrarily given, for the sake of convenience, to a set of individuals closely resembling each other, (...) [I]t does not essentially differ from the term variety, which is given to less distinct and more fluctuating forms. The term variety, again, in comparison with mere individual differences, is also applied arbitrarily, for convenience's sake.[4]

On the other hand, portraying Darwin as an ardent enthusiast of radical nominalism about species begs a question. Despite his struggle to specify the unit and subject of evolutionary transformations, reflected in the quoted passage from Chapter 2 of *On the Origin of Species*, he says, in Chapter 13 of the same work, that the classification he offers – based "on the view that the natural system is founded on descent with modification," that is "that the characters which naturalists consider as showing true affinity between any two or more species, are those which have been inherited from a common parent" – "is evidently not arbitrary like the grouping of the stars in constellations."[5] On another occasion, in Chapter 6, we find him saying that "all organic beings have been formed

---

[3] The idea is that neither individual organisms with their putative intrinsic dispositions and features, nor universal categories such as the category of "species," play any explanatory role in evolutionary biology. What explains the abundance of living forms is genetic variation and the distribution of traits among organisms within populations. As Stephen Boulter notes, "In the population thinking characteristic of evolutionary biology, to determine the effects of evolutionary mechanisms one need[s] only advert to statistical laws about the interactions of the individuals in a population. One needs no knowledge of the particular properties of particular individuals. It is only properties of populations that are truly explanatory" (Stephen J. Boulter, "Can Evolutionary Biology Do Without Aristotelian Essentialism?," *Royal Institute of Philosophy Supplements* 70 [2012], 92). See also a critical evaluation of this idea in Oderberg, *Real Essentialism*, 207–208 and Denis Walsh, "Evolutionary Essentialism," *The British Journal for the Philosophy of Science* 57, no. 2 (2006), 426. I will explain below how "population thinking" inspires the "population structure" species concept.

[4] Darwin, *On the Origin of Species*, 52. This constatation by Darwin might be treated as an incentive to abandon the Linnean taxa and develop an alternative to his system. He analyses some candidates.

[5] *Ibid.*, 420, 411.

Essentialist and Hylomorphic Notion of Species

on two great laws – Unity of Type and the Conditions of Existence" – where the former law, "explained by unity of descent," should be understood in terms of "organic beings" belonging to "the same class."[6]

Hence, when one of the founding fathers of the contemporary evolutionary synthesis, Ernst Mayr, entered the conversation about the reality of the universal category of biological species, he stated categorically – in reference to the popular nominalist interpretation of Darwin's position on this matter – that "whoever, like Darwin, denies that species are non-arbitrarily defined units of nature not only evades the issue but fails to find and solve the most interesting problems of biology."[7] For "without speciation there would be no diversification of the organic world, no adaptive radiation, and very little evolutionary progress. The species, then, is the keystone of evolution."[8] What we find in this assertion is Mayr's fundamental metaphysical intuition, which states that without universal categories (taken as ontological and not merely epistemological units), we would be unable to specify the outcomes of changes occurring in the world of living creatures over time.[9]

---

[6] *Ibid.*, 206. The latter law ("Conditions of Existence") "is fully embraced by the principle of natural selection" (*ibid.*). Marc Ereshefsky thinks this only proves that Darwin was a realist about taxa (including taxa called "species") while he remained an anti-realist about the species category, based on his uncertainty whether it might be distinguished from the category of "variety." See Marc Ereshefsky, "Darwin's Solution to the Species Problem," *Synthese* 175, no. 3 (August 1, 2010): 405–25. Hence, Ereshefsky himself suggests abandoning the system of Linnean taxa and developing an alternative one, which would, nonetheless, keep the "hierarchy of categorical ranks" (Marc Ereshefsky, "Species and the Linnean Hierarchy," in *Species: New Interdisciplinary Essays*, ed. Robert A. Wilson [Cambridge, MA: A Bradford Book, 1999], 299.) Brent D. Mishler goes still further and advocates developing a "rank-free taxonomy" (Brent D. Mishler, "Getting Rid of Species?," in *Species: New Interdisciplinary Essays*, ed. Robert A. Wilson [Cambridge, MA: A Bradford Book, 1999], 307–15.). For further debate on Darwin's notion of "species" concept see Michael T. Ghiselin, *The Triumph of the Darwinian Method* (Chicago: University of Chicago Press, 1969); Ernst Mayr, *The Growth of Biological Thought: Diversity, Evolution, and Inheritance* (Cambridge, MA: Harvard University Press, 1982); John Beatty, "Speaking of Species: Darwin's Strategy," in *The Darwinian Heritage*, ed. David Kohn (Princeton: Princeton University Press, 1985), 265–82; David N. Stamos, *Darwin and the Nature of Species* (Albany, NY: SUNY Press, 2007); James Mallet, "Mayr's View of Darwin: Was Darwin Wrong about Speciation?," *Biological Journal of the Linnean Society* 95, no. 1 (2008): 3–16; David Kohn, "Darwin's Keystone: The Principle of Divergence," in *The Cambridge Companion to the "Origin of Species,"* ed. Michael Ruse and Robert J. Richards (Cambridge: Cambridge University Press, 2008), 87–108; and John S. Wilkins, *Species: A History of the Idea* (Berkeley: University of California Press, 2009).

[7] Ernst Mayer, *Animal Species and Evolution* (Cambridge, MA: Harvard University Press, 1963), 29.

[8] *Ibid.*, 621.

[9] Stamos compares and contrasts nominalism and realism about species (as classes) in David N. Stamos, *The Species Problem, Biological Species, Ontology, and the Metaphysics of Biology* (Lanham: Lexington Books, 2004), Chapters 2–3.

DEBATE OVER SPECIES CONCEPTS

However, if we decide to follow Mayr's argument in favor of the reality of the universal category of "species" and the necessity of its application in biology, we face the complexity of the debate on the proper definition of biological species. This debate has been going on for decades, and its subject remains probably the most controversial issue in contemporary biology and philosophy of biology.[10] I believe it contains at least three important levels of inquiry; the first one of which refers to the general character of the definition in question. Here, we encounter two rival schools, one (I) claiming that the definition we are looking for should be entirely relational (i.e., outlined in terms of relations among organisms in space and time), and the other (II) advocating for a definition which is, at least partially, intrinsic (i.e., outlined in terms of intrinsic features of particular organisms).

Once we make our choice between (I) and (II), we enter the second level of inquiry where one faces various attempts of members of both schools striving to provide an adequate definition of the category of "species." At this stage, the discussion proliferates in a number of definitions which I will try to shortly introduce and classify below.

Finally, the third level of inquiry undertakes the task of classifying species under higher taxa, including genera, families, and several other steps up the ladder of the Linnaean hierarchy. At this stage, one encounters at least four competing schools of biological taxonomy. I will briefly analyze their main assumptions in due time. But first, we need to address the controversy over species concepts. To help the reader navigate through the complexity of the subject matter, I offer a graphic classification that covers all major species concepts I am about to discuss. Although imperfect and limited (some species concepts go beyond the general distinction between I and II), I believe it will serve as a helpful heuristic device. Refer Figure 2.1.

---

[10] "The species problem is one of the oldest controversies in natural history" (Robert J. O'Hara, "Systematic Generalization, Historical Fate, and the Species Problem," *Systematic Biology* 42, no. 3 [1993], 231). It is "one of the thorniest issues in theoretical biology" (Philip Kitcher, *In Mendel's Mirror: Philosophical Reflections on Biology* [Oxford and New York: Oxford University Press, 2003], xii). What indicates the scale of the controversy is certainly the fact that we have around two dozen species concepts in philosophy of biology and, as claims Ereshefsky, "at least seven well-accepted ones" (Marc Ereshefsky, "Species Pluralism and Anti-Realism," *Philosophy of Science* 65, no. 1 [1998], 103). See also Richard A. Richards, "Species and Taxonomy," in *The Oxford Handbook of Philosophy of Biology*, ed. Michael Ruse (Oxford, New York: Oxford University Press, 2008), 161–88 (he defines at least 16 species concepts).

Essentialist and Hylomorphic Notion of Species

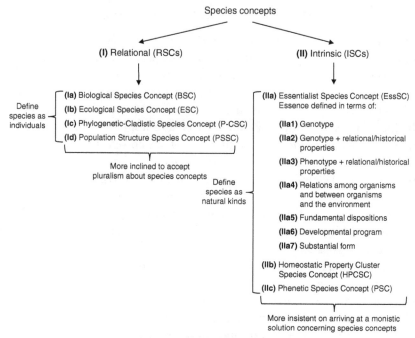

FIGURE 2.1 Classification of species concepts.

RELATIONAL SPECIES CONCEPTS

By entering the second of the proposed three levels of inquiry concerning species concepts, we shall begin with an analysis of RSCs (I). Although definitions falling into this group are much younger than historically predominant and commonly accepted intrinsic (essentialist) definitions of species as natural kinds, they quickly gained popularity in the post Darwinian milieu and are considered by many as a new orthodoxy in philosophy of biology. Hence, we shall treat them first.

The point of departure and a common presupposition of all species concepts falling within this group is the conviction that "the property in virtue of which a particular organism belongs to one species rather than another is a relational rather than an intrinsic property of the organism."[11] In other words, species should be defined in terms of spatiotemporally grounded relations among organisms rather than in terms of the intrinsic

---

[11] Samir Okasha, "Darwinian Metaphysics: Species and the Question of Essentialism," *Synthese* 131, no. 2 (2002), 201.

Relational Species Concepts

properties of particular organisms analyzed in themselves.[12] What differentiates RSCs is the nature of the relation that plays the central role in the definition.

Types of RSCs

The most popular is (Ia) biological species concept (BSC) developed by Mayr who claimed that "Species are groups of actually or potentially interbreeding natural populations which are reproductively isolated from other such groups. (...) Isolating mechanisms are biological properties of individuals which prevent the interbreeding of populations that are actually or potentially sympatric."[13] Note that this definition takes into account present causal and relational situations, rather than the historical context of common ancestors.

Another concept within this group defines species as a lineage, "which occupies an adaptive zone minimally different from that of any other lineage in its range and evolves separately from all lineages outside its range."[14] It is commonly categorized as (Ib) ecological species concept (ESC) and distinguished from the entire group of species concepts classified as (Ic) phylogenetic-cladistic (P-CSC). The latter, concentrating on the historical connections, define species as "a lineage (an ancestral-descendant sequence of populations) evolving separately from others and with its own unitary evolutionary role and tendencies."[15] Okasha says that on this view we "identify species in terms of evolutionary history ... [with] particular chunks of the genealogical nexus. ... Species come into existence when an existing lineage splits into two ... and go extinct when the lineage divides, or when all members of the species die."[16]

---

[12] "Two organisms are conspecific in virtue of their historical connection to each other, not in virtue of their similarity" (Elliott Sober, *Philosophy of Biology* [Boulder, CO: Westview Press, 1993], 150). "If species are interpreted as historical entities, then particular organisms belong in a particular species because they are part of that genealogical nexus, not because they possess any essential traits. No species has an essence in this sense" (David L. Hull, "A Matter of Individuality," *Philosophy of Science* 45, no. 3 [1978], 358).

[13] Mayr, *The Growth of Biological Thought*, 273–74.

[14] Leigh Van Valen, "Ecological Species, Multispecies, and Oaks," *Taxon* 25, no. 2/3 (1976), 70. Discussing this species concept Okasha offers a more concise definition which assumes that species "exploit the same set of environmental resources and habitats" (Okasha, "Darwinian Metaphysics," 200).

[15] George Gaylord Simpson, *Principles of Animal Taxonomy* (New York: Columbia University Press, 1961), 153.

[16] Okasha, "Darwinian Metaphysics," 200. Kim Sterelny and Paul E. Griffiths claim that "something like a consensus emerged in favor of a *cladistic* conception of systematics." See

64   *Essentialist and Hylomorphic Notion of Species*

One more relational species concept was proposed by Ereshefsky and Mohan Matthen who called it **(Id)** "population structure" species concept (PSSC). In reference to traits distribution among organisms within populations, and taking into account both the similarity and dissimilarity (polymorphism) of these characteristics, they define species genealogically as an "interpopulation structure" and claim that species are "lineages of populations."[17] As such, PSSC follows the consensus among philosophers of biology who welcomed the shift from typological toward population thinking introduced by Darwin.[18]

Species as Individuals

What remains crucial about RSCs and is thought to distinguish them ontologically from ISCs is a deep conviction of their advocates that instead of perceiving species as spatiotemporally unrestricted natural kinds that may emerge at any place and any time of the history of the universe, we should think of them as spatiotemporally restricted individuals with parts, having their beginning and end. David Hull explains:

> By "individuals" I mean spatiotemporally localized cohesive and continuous entities (historical entities). By "classes" I intend spatiotemporally unrestricted classes, the sorts of things which can function in traditionally defined laws of nature. The contrast is between Mars and planets, the weald and geological strata, between Gargantua and organisms.[19]

In other words, if we take species as units of Darwinian evolution, we must acknowledge that hereditary relations (genetic or otherwise) require generations of a given species to be causally and thus

their *Sex and Death: An Introduction to Philosophy of Biology* (Chicago and London: University of Chicago Press, 1999), 194. On another occasion, Sterelny defines species as "evolutionary linked metapopulations" or "ecological mosaics" – effects of "the relationship between evolutionary unit[s] and ecological forces" (Kim Sterelny, "Species as Ecological Mosaics," in *Species: New Interdisciplinary Essays*, ed. Robert A. Wilson [Cambridge, MA: A Bradford Book, 1999], 120).

[17] See Marc Ereshefsky and Mohan Matthen, "Taxonomy, Polymorphism, and History: An Introduction to Population Structure Theory," *Philosophy of Science* 72, no. 1 (2005): 1–21.

[18] See Ernst Mayr, "Typological Versus Population Thinking," in *Evolution and Anthropology: A Centennial Appraisal*, ed. Betty J. Meggers (Washington, DC: Anthropological Society of Washington, 1959), 409–12; Ernst Mayr, *What Evolution Is* (London: Phoenix, 2002), 83.

[19] Hull, "A Matter of Individuality," 336. See also Michael T. Ghiselin, "A Radical Solution to the Species Problem," *Systematic Zoology* 23, no. 4 (1974): 536–44.

spatiotemporally connected. This, notes Ereshefsky, has a number of important implications:

> For one, the relationship between an organism and its species is not a member/class relation but a part/whole relation. An organism belongs to a particular species only if it is appropriately causally connected to the other organisms in that species. The organisms of a species must be parts of a single evolving lineage. If belonging to a species turns on an organism's insertion in a lineage, then qualitative similarity can be misleading. Two organisms may be very similar morphologically, genetically, and behaviorally, but unless they belong to the same spatiotemporally continuous lineage they cannot belong to the same species.[20]

Pluralism of Species Concepts

One of the vexing questions concerning RSCs is their plurality and variety. What are we to make of such diversity? Whereas practicing systematists referring to RSCs are more committed to the search for a monistic solution, many philosophers signing up with (I) are willing to turn to pluralism.[21] In its pragmatic and epistemological version, species pluralism builds on the acknowledgment of the limitations of our cognitive capacities when facing the exceeding complexity of the world.[22] Those who embrace ontological pluralism about species concepts argue that it is an outcome of the fecundity of biological material and forces rather than a paucity of scientific information. At the same time, while some ontological pluralists side with Ereshefsky who argues that "the tree of life is segmented by different processes into different types of species lineages," which are captured by different species concepts that cannot be reconciled, others remain more optimistic and join Michael Ruse who speaks about a developing "consilience," which might eventually lead to a monistic solution: "There are different ways of breaking organisms into groups, and they *coincide!* The genetic species is the

---

[20] Marc Ereshefsky, "Species," in *The Stanford Encyclopedia of Philosophy*, ed. Edward N. Zalta, Fall 2017 (Metaphysics Research Lab, Stanford University, 2017), https://plato.stanford.edu/archives/fall2017/entries/species/ (retrieved 20 July 2022), section 2.2. See also Stamos, *Species Problem*, Chapter 4.

[21] Hull complains about the approach according to which "indefinitely many species concepts are needed for indefinitely many contexts." He adds that "The great danger of pluralism is 'anything goes'" (David L. Hull, "On the Plurality of Species: Questioning the Party Line," in *Species: New Interdisciplinary Essays*, ed. Robert A. Wilson [Cambridge, MA: A Bradford Book, 1999], 24).

[22] See Alexander Rosenberg, *Instrumental Biology, or The Disunity of Science* (Chicago: University of Chicago Press, 1994).

66   *Essentialist and Hylomorphic Notion of Species*

morphological species is the reproductively isolated species is the group with common ancestors."[23]

In response to Ruse's optimism, Ereshefsky notes that it does not look as if the consilience in question is really forthcoming: "Groups of organisms that have the most overall genetic similarity are not necessarily groups of interbreeding organisms. ... Some groups of interbreeding units are not monophyletic taxa. ... And some groups of organisms that form ecological units are not interbreeding units," which makes the idea of reaching a monistic position in the debate on species concepts very unlikely.[24]

Richard Mayden strives to face the same difficulty and proposes a hierarchical version of pluralism, which introduces a division of labor. He suggests treating P-CSC (Ic), which is classified by many as evolutionary species concept (EvoSC), as the main definition of species, based on its accommodating both sexual and asexual organisms, as well as those that hybridize. He sees other concepts within the category of RSCs as secondary and operational.[25] In a somewhat similar vein, Kevin de Queiroz claims that various species concepts agree on one thing, namely that species are "separately evolving metapopulation lineages."[26] He suggests that this fact defines a "conceptual," that is, "single, more general, concept of species," which allows us to treat other properties over which we tend to disagree – for example, being reproductively isolated or occupying a unique niche – as secondary, evidential (methodological), and "operational criteria" for "inferring the boundaries and numbers of species."[27] Richards suggests the division

[23] Ereshefsky, "Species," section 3.1; Michael Ruse, "Biological Species: Natural Kinds, Individuals, or What?," in *The Units of Evolution: Essays on the Nature of Species*, ed. Marc Ereshefsky (Cambridge, MA: A Bradford Book, 1992), 356.

[24] Marc Ereshefsky, *Poverty of the Linnaean Hierarchy: A Philosophical Study of Biological Taxonomy* (Cambridge New York: Cambridge University Press, 2001), 146.

[25] See Richard L. Mayden, "A Hierarchy of Species Concepts: The Denouement in the Saga of the Species Problem," in *Species: The Units of Biodiversity*, ed. M. F. Claridge, A. H. Dawah, and M. R. Wilson (London and New York: Springer, 1997), 418–22. Richards believes in the possibility of finding "a single, primary concept that colligates facts via a set of correspondence rules (not concepts) that serve to bridge the theoretical concept to the observable data" ("Species and Taxonomy," 185). He finds the EvoSC proposed by Mayden as promising as any other option among RSCs to play the role of the main species concept.

[26] Kevin de Queiroz, "Different Species Problems and Their Resolution," *BioEssays* 27, no. 12 (December 2005), 1263.

[27] Kevin de Queiroz, "Species Concepts and Species Delimitation," *Systematic Biology* 56, no. 6 (2007): 880, 882; de Queiroz, "Different Species Problems," 264. See also Kevin de Queiroz, "The General Lineage Concept of Species and the Defining Properties of the Species Category," in *Species: New Interdisciplinary Essays*, ed. Robert A. Wilson (Cambridge, MA: MIT Press, 1999), 49–90.

of conceptual labor, whereby various species concepts are useful in different theoretical and operational contexts.[28]

Ereshefsky notes that some of the pluralists who generally side with RSCs are actually willing to extend their list of viable species concepts to embrace not only those that require species to be individuals but also those based on the structural similarities among organisms sharing theoretically significant properties. Such is the view of Philip Kitcher who defines the latter in terms of spatiotemporally unrestricted sets of organisms. He distinguishes between proximate ("structural") and ultimate ("historical") types of explanation in biology and claims that while the former characterizes species in reference to structural similarities (genetic, phenotypic, and developmental), the latter sees them as lineages and thus individuals. By accepting both types of species concepts, Kitcher crosses the boundary between RSCs and ISCs.[29]

One other ontological pluralist John Dupré suggests going even further than Kitcher. According to his promiscuous realism about species, apart from concepts listed under RSCs and implemented by Kitcher's spatiotemporally unrestricted sets of organisms, we should also pay attention to nonbiological classifications, as "there are many sameness relations that serve to distinguish classes of organisms in ways that are relevant to various concerns ... [and] none of these relations are privileged."[30] He gives examples of carpenters grouping cedars on account of their aromatic timber or gastronomists grouping garlic and onions.[31] However, his view was criticized as leading to relativism and amphibolic pragmatism, which end up being antirealistic about universal categories.[32]

---

[28] See Richard A. Richards, *The Species Problem: A Philosophical Analysis* (Cambridge: Cambridge University Press, 2010).

[29] See Philip Kitcher, "Species," *Philosophy of Science* 51, no. 2 (1984): 308–33; Ereshefsky, "Species," sections 2.3. and 3.1.

[30] John Dupré, *Humans and Other Animals* (Oxford: Clarendon, 2002), 33. In Chapter 2 of the same book we find him saying: "Classification in biology has a life of its own. Biologists in areas only tangentially connected to evolutionary theory, such as ecologists, ethnobotanists, or ethologists, need to classify organisms, as do foresters, conservationists, gatekeepers, and herbalists ... for many, perhaps even most groups of organisms, evolutionary considerations are of little or no use for classificatory purposes" (*ibid.*, 82).

[31] See *ibid.*, 29, 34.

[32] See P.D. Magnus, *Scientific Enquiry and Natural Kinds: From Planets to Mallards* (London: Palgrave Macmillan, 2012), 130–33. The editors of a volume on scientific pluralism acknowledge that "promiscuous realism is hard to distinguish from radical relativism" (Stephen H. Kellert, Helen E. Longino, and C. Kenneth Waters, eds., *Scientific Pluralism* [Minneapolis, MN: University of Minnesota Press, 2006], xiii).

68 *Essentialist and Hylomorphic Notion of Species*

Difficulties of RSCs

Despite the fact that RSCs became virtual orthodoxy in philosophy of biology, each one of them faces some critical challenges. One major weakness of BSC (Ia) is that it does not allow our classification to cover all forms of living entities we distinguish. In particular, when choosing it, we exclude all asexual organisms from forming species. This is a serious drawback once we realize that the group in question is not limited to some rare examples of reptiles, amphibians, and insects, reproducing through cloning and vegetative means of self-fertilization. Indeed, asexual reproduction is rampant in plants, fungi, and bacteria, which makes it the predominant form of reproduction of living beings on Earth. Therefore, by siding with BSC, we agree that most organisms do not form species.[33] This shows the arbitrary and operational character of this species concept, which also makes it difficult to apply to organisms that have died. Another criticism of BSC draws our attention to the fact that it might be confusing cause (speciation) with effects (reproductive isolation) when saying that it is the latter that effects the former.[34] Finally, an important feature of the BSC is the assumption of smooth transitions between closely related populations.

[33] Ereshefsky acknowledges that much of the debate over species concepts (and species pluralism) focuses on multicellular organisms, while most organisms in the world are single cell microbial organisms, which do not reproduce sexually and exchange genes laterally within the same generation. He notes that microbiologists have their own species concepts, as not only BSC but also other RSCs are inadequate in the case of microorganisms. He lists four microbial species concepts: (1) recombination species concept that defines species as groups of microbes whose genomes can recombine, that is, groups that form gene pools of organisms connected by recombination; (2) ecological species concept which defines bacterial species as evolutionary lineages bound by ecotype-periodic selection; (3) phylo-phenetic species concept that aims at obtaining stable classifications of bacterial species for medical research; and (4) phylo-genetic species concept which strives to assign microbes to species according to their phylogenetic relations. See Ereshefsky, "Species," section 3.3. For further discussion he refers his readers to Maureen A. O'Malley and John Dupré, "Size Doesn't Matter: Towards a More Inclusive Philosophy of Biology," *Biology and Philosophy* 22, no. 2 (2007): 155–91; L. R. Franklin, "Bacteria, Sex, and Systematics," *Philosophy of Science* 74, no. 1 (2007): 69–95; Marc Ereshefsky, "Microbiology and the Species Problem," *Biology & Philosophy* 25, no. 4 (2010): 553–68; and Maureen O'Malley, *Philosophy of Microbiology* (Cambridge: Cambridge University Press, 2014).

[34] See Mayden, "A Hierarchy of Species Concepts," 390–91. In reference to and apart from the main argument mentioned here, BSC has been the subject of extensive criticism. See Michael Devitt, "Resurrecting Biological Essentialism," *Philosophy of Science* 75, no. 3 [2008], 356n25 for an extended list of works questioning its adequacy and usefulness in taxonomy.

Relational Species Concepts

This suggests the possibility of the existence of individuals in separate species that are able to cross the reproductive barrier. Consequently, the reproductive barrier serves only as an approximate criterion for distinguishing biological species, which once again proves the operational and pragmatic character of BSC, revealing its considerable ontological limitation.

Concerning ESC (Ib), we realize that it is difficult to apply it to large populations of organisms that often occupy various ecological niches while remaining one species (e.g., the red fox, *Vulpes vulpes*). Other organisms belonging to the same species (e.g., cichlids) can adapt to a new ecological niche within one generation, which according to ESC should qualify as a speciation event. Another difficulty is posed by microorganisms, in particular by bacterial biofilms, which bring into close cooperation many types of bacteria occupying a particular ecological niche. Such biofilms might classify as unified species according to ESC, which seems to be counterintuitive.

Even if (I) brings together several species concepts, the one among them that became predominant is P-CSC. Building upon Darwin's position cladism strives to base all classification explicitly on the phylogenesis of organisms. It defines species as "particular chunks of the genealogical nexus."[35] David Oderberg lists at least five important difficulties challenging P-CSC:[36]

1. Mere being part of a chunk of the phylogenetic tree bounded by a pair of speciation events (or splitting and extinction events) does not seem to be sufficient for conspecificity. In other words, cladism cannot define what a species is since it relies on the very concept of speciation.[37]

2. P-CSC may entail counterintuitive, if not absurd, classifications based on the traits of the most recent common ancestor while ignoring the actual behavior and forms of organisms. Oderberg gives an example of *Reptilia*, which according to P-CSC include lizards, snakes, tortoises, and turtles, as well as birds and mammals. At

---

[35] Okasha, "Darwinian Metaphysics," 200.

[36] See Oderberg, *Real Essentialism*, 214–24.

[37] Oderberg dismisses the idea of supplementing the diachronic character of P-CSC with the synchronic aspect of species grasped by BSC and ESC (see Okasha, "Darwinian Metaphysics," 201). He says a definition of species should have only one determinant. When one tries to supplement P-CSC with BSC and/or ESC, P-CSC drops out of the picture, remaining merely as an historic representation of the way the real criterion applies across space and time (see Oderberg, *Real Essentialism*, 216–17).

70 *Essentialist and Hylomorphic Notion of Species*

the same time, P-CSC would treat the two molecule-for-molecule identical organisms as members of different species.[38]

3. P-CSC suffers from a regress problem. For if classification is by descent, then what about the very first organism that did not have any ancestor? One might go down to the evolution of inanimate or even inorganic entities, still facing the same question.

4. P-CSC makes species identity an extrinsic matter, not having anything to do with the organism itself (its behavior, morphology, functioning, etc.). Oderberg claims it is not much more operative than a Platonic form in explaining what it is about a particular organism that makes it to be what it is.

5. Finally, some cladists strive to save (reintroduce) an essentialist aspect to P-CSC by claiming that historical relations among organisms define species essences. However, invoking Aristotelian typology of causes, Oderberg notes that to identify essence with descent confuses efficient and formal causes. In other words, it is true that we may say a lot about an organism's form and properties by knowing where it came from. Yet, where it came from is not equal to what it is.

The last argument might be summoned against PSSC as well. The fact that an organism is a part of a lineage of populations tells us quite a bit about its properties and form. But knowing its place in an interpopulation structure is not equal with knowing what it is. Approaching the same difficulty from another perspective, genetic variation within population depends always on the behavior of particular organisms. Hence, says Oderberg, "The biologist might be able to form hypotheses about populations without identifying which member behaves in which manner, but he still needs to know how individuals behave in order to frame any meaningful hypothesis about what population is like."[39] If this is true, population thinking needs to be implemented with individualistic thinking.

Apart from difficulties of particular RSCs, an objection has been raised to species pluralism. For it seems to be an overly liberal position, which may easily lead to virtually unlimited promiscuity about species concept (remember the view of Dupré mentioned above). This may turn against the entire undertaking of biologists and philosophers of biology who try

---

[38] One way to deal with the counterintuitive groupings under P-CSC is to accept a paraphyletic exclusion of some of the descendants of a common ancestor. However, advocates of this species concept ardently strive to perceive them as monophyletic.

[39] Oderberg, *Real Essentialism*, 208.

Intrinsic Species Concepts 71

to define species questioning the reality of species category as such.[40] Pluralists may try to provide some criteria for judging the legitimacy of a given species concept, such as empirical testability of its theoretical assumptions, its internal consistency, or intertheoretical coherence. But the question whether some commonly agreeable set of criteria might be established remains.

The version of the hierarchical solution offered by de Queiroz rises an objection on the side of the proponents of various types of RSCs who might argue that disagreements among them are not merely over evidence for the numbers and boundaries of the species. For it seems that advocates of BCS, ESC, and P-CSC believe that after all, they are identifying different types of lineages as constitutive for their classifications of species.[41]

INTRINSIC SPECIES CONCEPTS

The alternative group of species concepts builds upon the conviction that what is decisive about identities of biological taxa is intrinsic features of particular organisms. Their advocates believe species are natural kinds and claim that species concepts should, therefore, be, at least partially, intrinsic. Similar to RSCs, there are several types of ISCs. However, they are much closer to one another in their presuppositions than RSCs, which justifies the tendency among those who develop and support them toward a monistic solution to the species problem.

Essentialist Species Concept

The most popular among ISCs is (IIa) the EssSC. Commonly accepted in the ancient and medieval science and philosophy, essentialism was rejected in modernity. More recently, it was reintroduced by Kripke and Putnam in general philosophy and metaphysics, where it is considered as one of the major theories of material entities.[42] However, this new

---

[40] See Elliott Sober, "Sets, Species, and Evolution: Comments on Philip Kitcher's 'Species'," *Philosophy of Science* 51, no. 2 (1984): 334–41; Michael T. Ghiselin, "Species Concepts, Individuality, and Objectivity," *Biology and Philosophy* 2, no. 2 (April 1, 1987): 127–43; and David L. Hull, "Genealogical Actors in Ecological Roles," *Biology and Philosophy* 2, no. 2 (April 1, 1987): 168–84.

[41] See Ereshefsky, "Species," section 3.2.

[42] See Saul A. Kripke, *Naming and Necessity* (Cambridge, MA: Harvard University Press, 1980); Hilary Putnam, "The Meaning of 'Meaning'," in *Mind, Language, and Reality: Philosophical Papers, Vol. 2* (Cambridge: Cambridge University Press, 1975), 215–71.

72   *Essentialist and Hylomorphic Notion of Species*

essentialism was not welcomed among philosophers of biology who claim it is inadequate in reference to evolving organisms. Hull famously established the consensus on this matter saying that essentialism was responsible for two thousand years of stasis in systematics.[43] Rosenberg expresses the same position stating that "The proponents of contemporary species definitions are all agreed that species have no essence."[44] Sober follows him saying that "biologists do not think that species are defined in terms of phenotypic or genetic similarities."[45] Sterelny and Griffiths agree and state bluntly that "no intrinsic genotypic and phenotypic property is essential to being a member of a species."[46] Dupré accompanies them and says "it is widely recognized that Darwin's theory of evolution rendered untenable the classical essentialist concept of species."[47] Their view is followed by many other philosophers of biology, including Ghiselin, Mayr, de Queiroz, Matthen, Ruth Millikan, Ereshefsky, and Okasha.[48]

At the same time, however, the received antiessentialist consensus has been more recently challenged by a number of thinkers who claim that a reference to intrinsic dispositions/structure/constitution of organisms is necessary to formulate a viable species concept. A default version of their argument, in reference to P-CSC (which is most popular among RSCs), is suitably expressed by Crawford Elder:

If descent from certain ancestor organisms is part of what unites the members of a given species, then, the ancestor organisms in question must qualify for that crucial role by virtue of phenotypic (or perhaps genotypic) properties that they possessed – by virtue of their nonhistorical properties. Viewing biological species

---

[43] David L. Hull, "The Effect of Essentialism on Taxonomy – Two Thousand Years of Stasis (I–II)," *The British Journal for the Philosophy of Science* 15–16, no. 60–61 (1965): 314–26, 1–18.

[44] Alexander Rosenberg, *The Structure of Biological Science* (Cambridge: Cambridge University Press, 1985), 203.

[45] Sober, *Philosophy of Biology*, 148.

[46] Sterelny and Griffiths, *Sex and Death*, 186.

[47] John Dupré, "On the Impossibility of a Monistic Account of Species," in *Species: New Interdisciplinary Essays*, ed. Robert A. Wilson (Cambridge, MA: A Bradford Book, 1999), 3.

[48] See Ghiselin, "A Radical Solution"; Mayr, *The Growth of Biological Thought*; Kevin de Queiroz, "Systematics and the Darwinian Revolution," *Philosophy of Science* 55, no. 2 (1988), 238–59; Mohan Matthen, "Biological Universals and the Nature of Fear," *The Journal of Philosophy* 95, no. 3 (1998): 105–32; Ruth Garrett Millikan, *On Clear and Confused Ideas: An Essay about Substance Concepts* (Cambridge: Cambridge University Press, 2000), 19; Ereshefsky, *Poverty of the Linnaean Hierarchy*; Okasha, "Darwinian Metaphysics," 196.

Intrinsic Species Concepts 73

as "historical kinds" does not absolve us from the task of identifying nonhistorical properties that are diagnostic of membership in that species.[49]

Hence,

opponents of the idea that biological species are natural kinds are ... in much the same position as *proponents* of that idea. Each side must hold that some descent-involving property essentially characterizes any biological species. And each side must allow that there is some plurality of nonhistorical properties ... that, one way or another, essentially characterize that species as well.[50]

In other words, even if we agree to define species as spatio-temporally restricted individuals, we need to refer to their "*structural* properties." This is necessary "to avoid the consequence that all organisms belong to just a single species." Consequently, we need to acknowledge that "operationally, the 'species as individuals' view must treat species as natural kinds."[51]

Based on this line of reasoning, defenders of ISCs formulate a contemporary version of EssSC, which Christopher Austin, invoking the name of Aristotle, defines as follows: "Aristotelian essence is (a) comprised of a *natural* set of *intrinsic* properties [some claim it might be just one property] which (b) constitute *generative mechanisms* for particularised morphological development which (c) are shared among groups of organisms, delineating them as members of the same 'kind'."[52] Species can be thus defined as spatiotemporally unrestricted natural kinds.[53]

While the majority of the proponents of biological essentialism would most likely accept this definition, they seem to differ in their opinions on whether its main emphasis falls on (a) or (b) and in their answer to

---

[49] Crawford L. Elder, "Biological Species Are Natural Kinds," *The Southern Journal of Philosophy* 46, no. 3 (2008), 350.

[50] *Ibid.*

[51] *Ibid.*, 349, 353–54. Travis Dumsday offers a similar reflection in "Is There Still Hope for a Scholastic Ontology of Biological Species?," *The Thomist* 76, no. 3 (2012), 375ff. He further develops his position in Travis Dumsday, "A New Argument for Intrinsic Biological Essentialism," *Philosophical Quarterly* 62, no. 248 (2012): 486–504. Many other authors mentioned below agree with the basic line of this argument as well.

[52] Christopher J. Austin, "Aristotelian Essentialism: Essence in the Age of Evolution," *Synthese* 194, no. 7 (2017), 2540. See also Christopher J. Austin, *Essence in the Age of Evolution: A New Theory of Natural Kinds* (New York: Routledge, 2018), 12–15. A strong contemporary advocate of essentialism, Brian Ellis, defines essences in terms of universal intrinsic properties, in virtue of which entities obey universal laws of nature. However, due to the complexity of living organisms, he restricts essentialism to lower levels of organization of matter. See Ellis, *Scientific Essentialism* and Ellis, *The Philosophy of Nature*.

[53] Austin states that the categories of "natural kind" and "species" are not necessarily coextensive. See below, section on variants/aspects of EssSC, notes 66 and 67.

74   *Essentialist and Hylomorphic Notion of Species*

the question concerning particular intrinsic property/ies that defines/e essence of a given natural kind. Consequently, we find several variants of EssSC, which are listed on Figure 2.1 and shortly discussed below. Nevertheless, despite their differences, I argue that, taken together, they justify a preference for an essentialist approach to the definition of species in the contemporary setting. Moreover, as they take into account both structural and historical, as well as purely empirical and metaphysical aspects of this most basic biological taxon, these variants of EssSC provide a suitable background for a unifying definition of species that identifies essences in reference to the category of SF.[54]

Variants/Aspects of EssSC

(IIa1) Probably the most intuitive contemporary proposition of defining essences grounds them in the necessary and sufficient genetic disposition of organisms. David B. Kitts and David J. Kitts share their conviction that "The property which all the organisms of a species share and which ultimately accounts for the fact that they cannot be the parts or members of any other species is not some manifest property such as the pigmentation of a feather. It is an underlying trait."[55] They add that "Since the discovery of the structure of genetic material it has been possible to get at this underlying trait not only through the manifest properties and the reproductive behavior of organisms, but more directly by means of chemical techniques."[56]

---

[54] On the margin of my analysis, I would like to acknowledge the stark difference between biologists and philosophers of biology on the question of whether species should be treated as individuals or natural kinds. As notes Devitt, the study pursued by a group of researchers from Zagreb and based on a survey of the opinions of 193 practicing biologists from 150 biology departments in the US and the EU shows that the position supporting individualism about species is among them "utterly marginal," (only 2.94%). The majority of respondents sides with the notion of species as natural kinds. The opinion among philosophers of biology is quite opposite. The majority of them thinks species are spatiotemporally extended (scattered) individuals. See Bruno Pušić, Pavel Gregorić, and Damjan Franjević, "What Do Biologists Make of the Species Problem?," *Acta Biotheoretica* 65, no. 3 (2017): 179–209; Michael Devitt, "Individual Essentialism in Biology," *Biology & Philosophy* 33, no. 5 (2018), 4n7.

[55] David B. Kitts and David J. Kitts, "Biological Species as Natural Kinds," *Philosophy of Science* 46, no. 4 (1979), 617. They note that "No one would deny that '… to be a horse one must be born a horse' [Hull, "A Matter of Individuality," 349]. But that is not the end of it. The fact that all horses are begot by horses is something to be explained" (*ibid.*, 618). They bring this argument in support of essentialism.

[56] *Ibid.*, 622. Austin notes that "Historically, identifying the essence of a natural kind with a particular genome (or some privileged section thereof) has been a tempting thought – and not just among philosophers. The famed biophysicist Max Delbrück [Max Delbrück,

Intrinsic Species Concepts 75

Rieppel speaks about "essentialism underlying species identification by means of a DNA bar code [which] results from the claim that phylogenetic background knowledge is not needed to identify gene species that are based on nothing but bar coding gaps (discontinuities of DNA variation among contemporaneous populations)." He adds that "With bar coding, ... the typical DNA sequence becomes the underlying (intrinsic) essence of a species in the sense of Mayr's nondimensional species concept, that is, a contemporaneous time slice through a locally restricted population."[57]

(IIa2) Closely related to (IIa1) is the view that, apart from genotype, takes into account relational/historical properties of organisms. Helping to provide for the maintenance of genotype, they may be considered important for the definition of biological taxa. Crossing the boundary between (I) and (II), this variant/aspect of essentialism about species finds an explication and strong support in a series of articles by Michael Devitt. He says that "For most organisms the essential intrinsic properties are probably largely, although not entirely, genetic."[58] At the same time, however, it is "together perhaps with some historical ones" that the

---

"Aristotle-Totle-Totle," in *Of Microbes and Life*, ed. Jacques Monod and Ernest Borek (New York: Columbia University Press, 1971), 54–55], for instance, once suggested that the Nobel committee should posthumously 'consider Aristotle for the discovery of the principle implied in DNA', and even the celebrated and influential evolutionary biologist Ernst Mayr [Ernst Mayr, *This Is Biology: The Science of the Living World* (Cambridge (Mass.): Harvard University Press, 1997), 154] claimed, 'Aristotle's *eidos* [form, or essence], the seemingly metaphysical agent, is nothing else but what we now refer to as the genetic programme'. The doctrine of 'genetic essentialism' has of course been rather prominent among philosophers as well, being perhaps most notably defended in the microstructuralist theories of Kripke [*Naming and Necessity*] and Putnam ["The Meaning of 'Meaning'."]] (Austin, *Essence in the Age of Evolution*, 100).

[57] Olivier Rieppel, "New Essentialism in Biology," *Philosophy of Science* 77, no. 5 (2010), 666. He also offers a short description of the historical development of the "bar coding initiative" (see *ibid.*, 665). It should be noticed that Rieppel's argument faces an objection. While DNA barcoding is indeed widely used for identification of members of the same species, biologists are more hesitant to use it as a species definition. Austin raises another objection saying that "it seems that the inter-organismal uniformity of such sets [of organisms with shared sequence-based specificities of their genomes] is to a large extent a product of idealisation: alterations *via* mutation, absences *via* meiotic cell division, and additions *via* horizontal gene transfer, among many other commonplace genetic phenomena, strongly suggest that sequence-identity is a property shared by very few organisms, let alone by the large groups of organisms which purportedly belong to a single natural kind" (Austin, *Essence in the Age of Evolution*, 101).

[58] Devitt adds that "Sometimes those properties may not be genetic at all but in 'the architecture of chromosomes', 'developmental programs' or whatever" (Devitt, "Resurrecting Biological Essentialism," 347).

76   *Essentialist and Hylomorphic Notion of Species*

genetic properties "constitute the essence" of a given species.[59] Adopting Kitcher's terminology, Devitt distinguishes between structural and historical types of explanation in biology and finds both at least potentially important for defining species.[60]

(IIa3) Another variant/aspect of EssSC concentrates more on the phenotype and some crucial relational/historical properties that help explain its maintenance and stability across time and space. Crossing once again the boundary between (I) and (II), Elder thinks "Organisms possess the phenotypic and genotypic properties that they do simply in virtue of how matters stand during their own existences: these are nonhistorical properties. But historical properties may be crucial as well." Hence, "It would follow that the members of a biological natural kind must share not only certain phenotypic properties but also the common historical property of being descendant from the same sorts of ancestors, under the influence of the same sorts of selectional pressures."[61]

(IIa4) An alternative, somewhat unorthodox, variant/aspect of essentialism about species defines them in terms of relations among organisms and between organisms and the environment that are necessary and sufficient for the membership in particular taxon. It is classified as relational, historical, or origin essentialism. Underlying the concept of monophyly, it defines essences as relational and extrinsic, rather than intrinsic: "From

---

[59] *Ibid.*, 353. Devitt says that what constitutes a species is necessarily at least partly intrinsic and possibly partly historical. Hence, the intrinsic aspect is crucial (essential), while the historical is not. He further develops his analysis of the historical component of species concept in Michael Devitt, "Historical Biological Essentialism," *Studies in History and Philosophy of Biological and Biomedical Sciences* 71 (2018): 1–7.

[60] See Kitcher, "Species," 121; Devitt, "Resurrecting," 353. Devitt introduces a crucial distinction, saying that we need to set aside the task of distinguishing species from other taxa from the task of specifying why a given organism belongs to a particular species. He names the former (1) "the category problem" and the latter (2) "the taxon problem." He argues that although Okasha seems to be saying that RSCs answer to (1), while Sterelny and Griffiths, together with Wilson, claim they are concerned with both (1) and (2), the truth is that RSCs concentrate mainly on (1) and throw little light on (2), due to their ignorance of the intrinsic aspect of species definition. See *ibid.*, 356–58; Okasha, "Darwinian Metaphysics," 201; Sterelny and Griffiths, *Sex and Death*, 211; Robert A. Wilson, "Realism, Essence, and Kind: Resuscitating Species Essentialism," in *Species: New Interdisciplinary Essays* (Cambridge, MA: A Bradford Book, 1999), 191–92. Devitt further develops and defends his view in Devitt, "Individual Essentialism in Biology," Michael Devitt, "Defending Intrinsic Biological Essentialism," *Philosophy of Science* 88, no. 1 (2021): 67–82; and most recently in Michael Devitt, *Biological Essentialism* (Oxford: Oxford University Press, 2023). See also Rieppel, "New Essentialism," 669.

[61] Elder, "Biological Species, 347.

Intrinsic Species Concepts

the point of view of a phylogenetic taxonomy ... being descended from a particular ancestral population may seem to be the essential property of a particular taxon."[62]

(IIa5) In reference to the Aristotelian distinction between potency and act, Stan Wallace suggests that "the properties which are essential to the entities' existence cannot be genotypic or phenotypic." Rather, "an essentialist may reasonably define these essential properties as 'dispositional properties." He defines them as "tendencies or proclivities for the organism to exist in certain ways. In other words, they are dispositions of the organisms to exemplify realized, or first-order, properties and functions."[63]

Austin further develops this idea and states that "In the framework of Æ [Aristotelian essentialism], organisms are ontologically sorted into natural kinds in virtue of sharing sets of causal properties which both generate and subsequently shape their morphological development ... these 'powerful' properties are *dispositional properties*." He thus thinks that "evo-devo is a framework in which morphological variation is derived from invariant, functional causal mechanisms which serve as highly conserved 'deep homologies', underwriting a vast array of organismal diversity."[64] Speaking about the modular character of development – in reference to components operating by their own intrinsically determined principles – he suggests to call these components "phenmodulatory dispositions," which are "ontological switches" that ground the phenomenon of phenotypic plasticity (morphological variation).[65] Austin concludes by saying that "in a notable shift from the neo-Darwinian perspective, evo-devo favours a 'structuralist' approach":

An essence of a natural kind must be comprised of a nested, scalar set of a number of phenomodulatory dispositions ... [It] cannot be identified with a set of particularised morphological structures, but must instead be defined by a set of

---

[62] Dupré, *Humans and Other Animals*, 43. Similar Sterelny and Griffiths: "the essential properties that make a particular organism a platypus ... are historical or relational" (*Sex and Death*, 186). This view is also discussed by Paul E. Griffiths, "Squaring the Circle: Natural Kinds with Historical Essences," in *Species: New Interdisciplinary Essays*, ed. Robert A. Wilson (Cambridge, MA: A Bradford Book, 1999), 209–28; Ruth Garrett Millikan, "Historical Kinds and the 'Special Sciences'," *Philosophical Studies: An International Journal for Philosophy in the Analytic Tradition* 95, no. 1/2 (1999): 45–65; Okasha, "Darwinian Metaphysics"; and LaPorte, *Natural Kinds and Conceptual Change*.

[63] Stan W. Wallace, "In Defense of Biological Essentialism," *Philosophia Christi* 4, no. 1 (2002), 34–35.

[64] Austin, "Aristotelian Essentialism," 2544–45.

[65] See *ibid.*, 2546–47.

78   *Essentialist and Hylomorphic Notion of Species*

discrete morphogenetic developmental units, each individually responsible for the potential production of a unified gradient of an interrelated set of quantitative and qualitative permutations on a general architectural theme.[66]

(IIa6) Austin's suggestion is related to yet another variant/aspect of essentialism about species, which emphasizes the importance of kind-specific developmental programs (goal-directed dispositions of organisms to produce viable offspring of its own kind). Stephen Boulter suggests that biological essences "are found not in the genotype or the phenotype but in the species specific developmental programmes that map geno-types onto phenotypes." He thinks "that (i) only a portion of an organism's genome determines its species (not all of it); (ii) that developmental control genes (i.e., genes that control the expression of other genes) deter-mine the developmental pattern of an organism; and (iii) that these devel-opmental patterns are 'lineage specific', that is, shared by individuals of the same biological species understood as a smallest diagnosable clus-ter of organisms related by ancestry and descent." He concludes saying that "on this suggestion two organisms belong to the same species and have the same essence if they share the same developmental programme regardless of how else they might differ."[67]

Recognizing the tension between developmental stability and phe-notypic plasticity, in reference to evolutionary developmental biology (evo-devo), Dennis Walsh introduces the concept of an evolutionary essentialism. He refers to Mary Jane West-Eberhard and her idea of adaptive evolution based on phenotypic and genotypic accommodation,

---

[66] *Ibid.*, 2547, 2549, 2550. Note that according to Austin "natural kinds [being more inclusive] *cannot* be identified with *species*, but rather must be considered on analogy with the conceptual middle of the taxonomic tree" (*ibid.*, 2551).

[67] Boulter, "Can Evolutionary," 100. In his more recent publication, Austin seems to fol-low Boulter's position: "Thus the dispositional properties realised by the developmental modules of an organism – μ-dispositions [*morphomodulatory dispositions*] – are well suited to collectively function as its neo-Aristotelian essence as they perform the requisite causal-cum-modal role with respect to its development of a particular morphological profile: their generative competency is principally responsible not only for causally con-structing that profile but, in virtue of their "directedness" toward doing so, constraining its character. In all of these ways, μ-dispositions are evidently eminently qualified candi-dates to collectively constitute the neo-Aristotelian essences of biological natural kinds" (Austin, *Essence in the Age of Evolution*, 59). Once again, it should be noted that Austin thinks that the categories of "natural kind" and "species" are not necessarily coexten-sive: "[A]ccording to my theory, 'natural kind' is necessarily a more *inclusive* category than 'species', as the exploration of 'morphological space' afforded by the nature of μ-dispositions outstrips the narrow confines of the more particularised, well-entrenched developmental pathways, which typify the members of a species" (*ibid.*, 110, see also *ibid.*, Chapter 2, 22–37).

Intrinsic Species Concepts 79

explained as a consequence of the compartmentalization of organisms to developmental modules (local processes described as morphogenetic fields).[68] He says that "The ultimate source of variation within a population may be random genetic mutation, as the modern synthesis insists. But the *adaptiveness* of adaptive evolution seems also to require that the phenotypic variation that is visible to selection is non-random. It is regulated by the plasticity of organisms and biased by the requirements that organisms maintain viability in the face of perturbations." He thinks the latter disposition is grounded in a given species' essential features, which "should overturn the anti-individualist bias inherent in modern synthesis biology."[69]

(IIa7) Finally, one more crucial variant/aspect of EssSC, reaching toward more fundamental ontology, asks the question which – as notes Dumsday – "any essentialist philosophy of biology will be faced with," that is, "the question of what, if anything, grounds and unifies the collection of intrinsic properties generally taken to be definitive of 'organism'." Dumsday is convinced that "This issue is often left wholly unaddressed in the existing literature on the nature and origin of life, and constitutes one possible opening for the introduction of substantial form into the discussion (an introduction that would in turn help draw out the tight connection between classification and explanation that is such a prominent feature of Scholastic philosophy of nature)."[70]

Although Dumsday is not himself "aiming at the more ambitious target of a distinctively hylomorphic account" of species,[71] he does note that it is not the case that properties (be it genetic, phenetic, or dispositional) define the essence of a given type. Rather, it is the essence that grounds the properties that are associated with a given biological natural

---

[68] See Mary Jane West-Eberhard, *Developmental Plasticity and Evolution* (New York: Oxford University Press, 2003).

[69] Walsh, "Evolutionary Essentialism," 440. Similar to Austin he states that "In Aristotle's essentialist biology the nature of an organism is manifested as a goal-directed disposition to produce and maintain a living thing capable of fulfilling its vital functions in ways characteristic of its kind" (*ibid.*, 427).

[70] Dumsday, "Is There Still Hope," 394–95. The received answer to the question mentioned by Dumsday, popular among analytic metaphysicians, is usually based on the modal distinction of necessary (essential) and contingent (accidental) features, where the former are thought to define a given species in every possible world. Avoiding the complexity and challenges of hylomorphism, this view faces the need of embracing an already existing or developing a new ontology of possible worlds. See Michael Gorman, "Essentiality as Foundationality," in *Neo-Aristotelian Perspectives in Metaphysics*, ed. Daniel D. Novotný and Lukáš Novák (New York: Routledge, 2014), 122–23.

[71] *Ibid.*, 390.

80   *Essentialist and Hylomorphic Notion of Species*

kind and determines the range of behaviors of its individual members.[72] At the same time, the hylomorphic account of EssSC has already been developed within the analytic philosophical tradition by Oderberg, who says that essences are mixtures of actuality and potentiality, where the former is defined as SF and the latter as PM. Echoing Aristotle, he states SF is a metaphysical principle "*by virtue of which* the substance is what it is." As such it actualizes its complementary metaphysical principle, purely passive potentiality of wholly receptive PM, which (underlying sensible, secondary, or proximate matter) individualizes SF in a particular entity, which is further specified by its accidental properties.[73] Regarded as causes – on the assumption that causal principles, going beyond physical interactions, are understood as metaphysical principles explaining essences of natural kinds – PM and SF are closely related with efficient and final causes, as well as with the quasi (*per accidens*) causal character of chance and fortune.[74] Taken together, they ground all types of genetic, phenetic, or dispositional properties of organisms, mentioned in other variants/aspects of EssSC.[75]

This constatation is crucial. For, understood in this way, the hylomorphic aspect (dimension) of EssSC, clearly provides a necessary ontological and metaphysical ground and rationale that unifies and consolidates all other aspects proposed, discussed, and defended by the advocates of this species concept. It thus endows EssSC with plausibility and intrinsic coherence that make it a consistent and viable option in the most recent debate over species. At the same time, it proves that the reintroduction of the classical categories of SF and PM (act and potency) within the context of the contemporary evolutionary biology is not an arbitrary and forced move on the side of a stubborn minority of classically oriented Aristotelian–Thomistic thinkers, who ignore the mainstream research in

---

[72] See *ibid.*, 371.

[73] See Oderberg, *Real Essentialism*, 62–81.

[74] Note that the reference to efficient causes in causal description of an organism introduces a historical aspect to the hylomorphic variant/aspect of EssSC. Yet, as notes Oderberg, "It does not follow from the fact that a substance or species has a certain historical origin that its *essence* is to have that origin, even if it has its origin necessarily" (*ibid.*, 101). Concerning the *per accidens* causal character of chance and fortune, see below, chapter 3.

[75] In reference to the hylomorphic notion of EssSC, Oderberg argues in favor of ISCs and notes that RSCs confuse essences and properties. Properties are founded on the essence of an organism and emanate from it, determining further its nature. But essence as such is always intrinsic. Hence, while the properties of species members might be relational (e.g., the power to act in a certain way in an ecological niche or to interbreed with some other organisms), what enables a given organism to have such relational properties is its essence. See *ibid.*, 223.

Intrinsic Species Concepts

this field. To the contrary, it shows that their metaphysical and ontological commitment becomes a logical conclusion of the multifaceted research conducted by those who suggest that a good candidate for a species concept should be, at least partially, intrinsic.

In conclusion of this section, I should make an attempt at providing a hylomorphically grounded essentialist definition of species. Species can be defined as a universal category expressed in and abstracted from concrete living beings that are determined by a particular type of essence. The latter is constituted by a specific kind of SF which – as a metaphysical principle of actuality – actualizes its correlative metaphysical principle of pure potentiality, that is, PM. Causing thus an organism to be what it is, SF grounds a range of essential and accidental, intrinsic and extrinsic dispositions and properties, characteristic for a given type of living creature. A provisional list of these dispositions and properties includes particularized kind-specific morphological and physiological developmental programs, and a variety of genotypic and phenotypic traits that find their distinctive expression in historical relationships of organisms that belong to a given species.[76]

Concerning the question about the correspondence between this hylomorphically grounded essentialist (and thus metaphysical) definition of species and the notion(s) of species used in the practice of biological (and thus scientific) taxonomy, I argue that they are related, although certainly not coextensive. The correlation between them finds expression in numerous variants of EssSC that take into account structural and historical, that is, predominantly empirical aspects and features of living beings. These substantive and accidental (intrinsic and extrinsic) dispositions and properties may be treated as indicators of a particular kind of SF, which defines the metaphysical foundation of a given natural kind. Consequently, I believe that properly conducted interdisciplinary research in biology, philosophy of biology, and metaphysics enables us to arrive at the situation in which a "scientific" species, as characterized by a practicing biologist, corresponds closely to the "philosophical/metaphysical" species.[77]

---

[76] Not all active and passive dispositions proper for a given natural kind are actualized in all organisms belonging to it. Moreover, the actualization of some of these properties may move particular exemplars of a species toward its boundaries, leading thus to an evolutionary transition.

[77] Although the remaining part of the project concentrates more on the philosophical and metaphysical aspects of the EssSC, it is not ignorant about its empirically verifiable variants either. To the contrary, it aims at being continually interested in and informed by the biological practice of taxonomy.

82   *Essentialist and Hylomorphic Notion of Species*

Homeostatic Property Cluster and Phenetic Species Concepts

Apart from various types of EssSC, we can list at least two other ISCs that treat biological species as natural kinds. (**IIb**) Homeostatic property cluster species concept (HPCSC) builds on the conviction that natural kinds are groups of organisms across which some delimited phenotypic properties cluster together. None of these properties, given evolutionary forces, is essential for membership in a given species. At the same time, homeostatic causal mechanisms (e.g., interbreeding, sharing similar developmental programs, being exposed to similar selection regimes) provide for the similarity of members of a given species. Nevertheless, even if genealogical connectedness is important for HPCSC, it is similarity that plays the role of the final arbitrator of species sameness.

On the face of it, HPCSC appears to be more flexible than EssSC, as it easily allows for variations of traits within clusters that define biological species. At the same time, however, it faces the difficulty of defining borders between them. This challenge becomes all the more acute once we realize that homeostatic mechanisms may also vary over time and space (across geographic regions).[78]

(**IIc**) One more type of ISC is the phenetic species concept (PSC), which assumes that a group of organisms forms a genuine natural kind due to the same phenotypic traits cropping up in each one of them. One might assume – as does the classical formulation of the PSC – that such properties must recur across literally all organisms that belong to the same species. However, species under PSC might be defined as statistical and not discrete. On such interpretation, we might think of "dense regions" representing relatively high statistical correlations of attributes shared by a number of living beings.[79] The price of this liberalization of PSC is that it ceases to crave clear-cut boundaries between species, as it is not defined

---

[78] See Richard Boyd, "Homeostasis, Species, and Higher Taxa," in *Species: New Interdisciplinary Essays*, ed. Robert A. Wilson (Cambridge, MA: A Bradford Book, 1999), 141–85; Wilson, "Realism"; and Ereshefsky, "Species," section 2.4. Günter Wagner sees Boyd's HPCSC as "an important liberalization to the classical notion of natural kinds which was and is often expressed in fairly absolute terms" (Günter P. Wagner, "Characters, Units, and Natural Kinds," in *The Character Concept in Evolutionary Biology*, ed. Günter P. Wagner [San Diego, CA: Academic Press, 2001], 8). Elder, in "Biological Species," 355–57 offers a critical evaluation of HPCSC, showing that it needs to treat one or more properties in a given cluster as essential for a particular species.

[79] Gerry Webster and Brian Goodwin state that each species by nature occupies a place within a possibility-space, that is, a "morphological field" in which certain adaptations (and not others) are available. See their *Form and Transformation: Generative and Relational Principles in Biology* (Cambridge: Cambridge University Press, 1996).

Intrinsic Species Concepts 83

by necessary and sufficient conditions anymore. Neither does it provide unambiguous borders between natural kinds.

Probably the oldest among species concepts, PSC (oftentimes classified as morphology species concept – MSC) has a strong operational flavor to it, as it concentrates mainly on phenotypic and morphological features of organisms. It does not refer to their phylogenesis and mechanisms of speciation. As such, it seems to suffer from the difficulty of providing the general algorithm of similarity of properties. It may also be unable to distinguish between polymorphism (e.g., hierarchical and functional differences among organisms in one population) and speciation, as well as between homologies and cases of parallel and convergent evolution.[80]

At the same time, because morphology is in fact the basis of all recognition and classification – Oderberg notes that "it finds its way into ecological tests, reproductive criteria, cladistic analysis, genetic identification, mate recognition, and more" – it might be treated as an indispensable aspect of all other species concepts, even if it does not stand as a single and unique method of carving nature at its joints.[81] Undeniably morphology, meaning the study of form (*morphe*), seems to be a close ally of hylomorphic variant/aspect of EssSC, which defines essences in reference to SSFF of particular types.

Compatibility of ISCs with Evolutionary Biology

Unlike RSCs, which were developed as grounded in the contemporary evolutionary synthesis, all ISCs, and EssSC in particular, are still considered by many as incompatible with evolutionary biology. It is this conviction in particular that makes many contemporary philosophers of biology suspicious and skeptical about any attempt of reintroducing essentialist thinking in life sciences. I will now present and answer two major arguments in support of this opinion.

1. EssSC implies species fixism, which is in principle inconsistent with the view that species evolve. In other words, variation – which is crucial for natural selection and Darwinian evolution – clashes

---

[80] As an example of polymorphism, we may think of different kinds of ants or bees in a colony. Homological properties occur in two or more organisms having a common ancestor (e.g., eyes in various mammals) and is differentiated from homoplasy, which refers to a similar trait that occurs in two or more organisms and was passed down from different ancestors (e.g., octopus' and mammalian eyes), in the processes of parallel or convergent evolution.

[81] Oderberg, *Real Essentialism*, 235.

84   *Essentialist and Hylomorphic Notion of Species*

with unchangeability of species and the Aristotelian "Natural State Model."[82] On this interpretation of essentialism variation, being a result of the action of "interfering forces," takes an organism away from its "natural stage," making it thus "the result of imperfect manifestations of the idea implicit in each species."[83] Sober finds this view contrasting Darwin's, for whom "Individual differences are not *the effects* of interfering forces confounding the expression of a prototype; rather they are *the causes* of events that are absolutely central to the history of evolution."[84] Hence, adds Jody Hey, "that variation among organisms is the crucial stuff of changing life and of life's progress" is thought to be "devastating to essentialism."[85]

2. EssSC implies clear, nonbridgeable boundaries between species, but no set of properties (genotypic or phenotypic), has been identified as jointly necessary and sufficient for defining such boundaries for any biological species.[86] Moreover, a fair number of species is characterized by regularized dimorphism, especially sexual dimorphism, or polymorphism of essential properties, while others seem to show similar traits despite the fact they do not share the same evolutionary history. This further contradicts the argument in favor of there being packages of properties defining species.[87] In addition, evolution between species with clear boundaries would only be possible if nature proceeded by jumps (saltations).[88]

---

[82] Okasha, "Darwinian Metaphysics," 197. Wilson rejects genetic essentialism because "the inherent biological variability or heterogeneity of species with respect to both morphology and genetic composition is, after all, a corner stone of the idea of evolution by natural selection" (Wilson, "Realism," 190).

[83] Ernst Mayr, *Populations, Species, and Evolution, An Abridgment of Animal Species and Evolution*, Abridged edition (Cambridge, MA: Harvard University Press, 1963), 11. Griffiths says variation makes an organism belonging to intrinsically defined species to be "deviation" from an "ideal" (Paul E. Griffiths, "What Is Innateness?," *The Monist* 85, no. 1 [2001], 78–79).

[84] Sober, Elliott, "Evolution, Population Thinking and Essentialism," *Philosophy of Science* 47, no. 3 (1980), 371. He adds that "the Natural State Model presupposes that there is some phenotype which is the natural one *which is independent of a choice of environment*" (ibid., 374).

[85] Jody Hey, *Genes, Categories, and Species: The Evolutionary and Cognitive Cause of the Species Problem* (New York: Oxford University Press, 2001), 62.

[86] Sober claims that "no genotypic characteristic can be postulated as a species essence; the genetic variability found in sexual populations is prodigious" (Sober, "Evolution," 380).

[87] Referring to this argument against EssSC, Elder ("Biological Species," 346–47) mentions also "members [of species] that are abnormal or aberrant." Their existence introduces variations in a given population.

[88] See Boulter, "Can Evolutionary Biology," 92.

Intrinsic Species Concepts

In an answer to the first objection, we must note that it is based on Mayr's popular and overly Platonic phrasing of EssSC, in which he states that according to this concept "[t]here are a limited number of fixed, unchangeable 'ideas' underlying the observed variability [in nature], with the *eidos* (idea) being the only thing that is fixed and real, while the observed variability has no more reality than the shadows of an object on a cave wall."[89] However, one must not forget that, contrary to this view, on Aristotle's scheme, delineated in Chapter 1, essences or natures are not transcendental, fixed "ideas" but "goal-directed capacities immanent in the nature of the organism." In other words, they exist as realized in concrete, temporal, individual, and contingent organisms. Hence, adds Walsh, "It certainly isn't inconsistent with Aristotelian essentialism to suppose that natures could change over time in just the way we have come to think that species do. Individual organisms may well vary in their formal and material natures, in such a way that over time some variants become more common than others."[90]

In reference to the hylomorphic variant/aspect of EssSC, we may recall the notion of the two levels of potentiality inherent in the very fabric of the cosmos: (1) pure potentiality of PM, which can be actualized by all possible types of SSFF, proper for both inanimate and animate natural kinds, and (2) potentiality of PM underlying each and every instantiation of secondary (proximate and sensible) matter, which is specified (qualified) by the SF and AAFF characteristic of a particular natural kind it belongs to. The actualizing principles dispose PM underlying entities classified as instantiations of secondary matter in particular ways, enabling

---

[89] Ernst Mayr, *Evolution and the Diversity of Life: Selected Essays* (Cambridge, MA: Harvard University Press, 1976), 27.

[90] Walsh, "Evolutionary Essentialism," 431. In support of his argument, he refers to David Balme saying that "[t]here is nothing in Aristotle's theory to prevent an 'evolution of species', that is a continuous modification of the kinds being transmitted. But he had no evidence of evolution" (David M. Balme, "Aristotle's Biology Was Not Essentialist," in *Philosophical Issues in Aristotle's Biology*, ed. Allan Gotthelf and James G. Lennox [Cambridge: Cambridge University Press, 1987], 97). An expert in Aristotle's biology, James Lennox, says that "Aristotle's essentialism is not typological, nor is it in any way 'anti-evolutionary'. Whatever it is Darwin was up against, it was not Aristotelian essentialism" (James G. Lennox, *Aristotle's Philosophy of Biology: Studies in the Origins of Life Science* [Cambridge: Cambridge University Press, 2001], 162). I believe that Walsh's suggestion of natures changing over time, should be interpreted in terms of accidental changes affecting concrete organisms belonging to a given type (and thus changing the disposition of PM that underlies them), rather than in terms of gradual changes of the type of SF proper for the natural kind in question. The latter idea would be rather foreign to the Aristotelian – Thomistic metaphysics.

86   *Essentialist and Hylomorphic Notion of Species*

thus – on the way of substantial change – an eduction of particular types of new SSFF (typical of new natural kinds, i.e., new species) from its potentiality. This allows for introducing the idea of evolutionary changes and transitions within the framework of the Aristotelian philosophy of biology. I have developed this argument in Chapter 1.

Hence, concludes Dumsday, "essentialism not only allows for evolution but is plausibly required for it."[91] He notes that a similar argument was made by the scholastic scholar Richard Phillips already in 1934. In his textbook on philosophy of nature Phillips writes: "Considering, then, natural species in the strict sense, do our principles allow us to say that they could be transformed? There seems to be nothing in them to render it impossible for we should only have a striking example of substantial change."[92]

Concerning the second objection, some advocates of nonhylomorphic variants/aspects of EssSC (IIa1–6) are willing to follow the consensus grounded in RSCs and say that, ontologically speaking, "Essences are a bit indeterminate."[93] Thus, Devitt states that "the evolution of $S2$ from $S1$ will involve a gradual process of moving from organisms that determinately have [intrinsic essence] $G1$ to organisms that determinately have [intrinsic essence] $G2$ via a whole lot of organisms that do not determinately have either."[94] Walsh stipulates that "A shared nature (*genos*) does not determine any specific features of what we now call 'phenotype' (or, for that matter, genotype). Instead, it imposes a set of constraints upon the range of phenotypes that organisms sharing that nature might possess."[95] Leaning toward HPCSC, Elder states that "while there is, for a typical species, no fixed collection of properties that are individually necessary and jointly sufficient for membership in the species, it nevertheless is true that the members of the typical species are bound to present some shifting subset – some shifting majority – of the properties on a common list."[96]

---

[91] Dumsday, "Is There Still Hope," 390.

[92] Richard Percival Phillips, *Modern Thomistic Philosophy: An Explanation for Students. Volume 1: The Philosophy of Nature*, Reprint of the second reprinted edition (1962) (Heusenstamm: Editiones Scholasticae, 2013), 342. This statement is somewhat surprising as Phillips was generally skeptical about evolutionary transitions of any large significance.

[93] Devitt, "Resurrecting," 373.

[94] *Ibid.*

[95] Walsh, "Evolutionary Essentialism," 429.

[96] Elder, "biological Species," 347. The level of similarity of organisms might be defined in reference to a particular part of the underlying structure that causes in its "normal" environment, the distinctive phenotypic features of the species.

Intrinsic Species Concepts

However, according to the hylomorphic variant/aspect of EssSC (IIa7), ontological indeterminacy of species is not acceptable. If the essence of an organism is ultimately grounded in its SF, it is either present in it or not. For it is entirely unclear what a vague possession of form would amount to.[97] Consequently, notes Oderberg, we should acknowledge that:

Essence is not given by properties but by *form*, more precisely substantial form. Properties are indicators of essence, allowing fallible and provisional judgement as to the essence of an organism. ... Given the complexity of even the simplest creature, the list of necessary characteristics will be incredibly large, possibly infinite ... The same goes for sufficient properties: it may be that, for even the apparently simplest organism, listing all of the sufficient characteristics essential to it will be either technically or metaphysically impossible ... Still, the essentialist sees no cause for concern, since all the systematist should be looking for is not an exhaustive list of necessary and sufficient characteristics, but enough characteristics to enable at least a provisional judgement as to the substantial form of an organism, followed by an accumulation of characteristics to increase the well-foundedness of the judgement.[98]

If it is true that properties do not define but merely reveal the essence of an organism, which is defined as such by the SF of a given type, then all difficulties and doubts concerning classification and demarcation of species boundaries based on their empirically verifiable features are epistemological and not ontological. In other words, uncertainties in classifying forms of living beings faced by practicing biologists need not necessarily mean that essences of organisms are vague metaphysically. And vice versa, a clarity at the level of the metaphysical classification of a given species may not translate into a clear and unanimously agreeable description of its empirical properties. At the same time, as already mentioned above (toward the end of section on variants/aspects of EssSC), the contribution of numerous variants of EssSC that take into account structural and historical (i.e., empirical) aspects and features of living beings should not go unnoticed. These accidental, intrinsic, and extrinsic dispositions and properties point toward particular kinds of SSFF, which define the metaphysical foundation of distinct natural kinds.

---

[97] The tendency to treat species as ontologically indeterminate leads to a nominalist conclusion that they can be defined only in terms of a network of multilateral relationships and interactions between processes, within which it is impossible to distinguish any natural types. A species understood as a taxonomic group would simply be the result of the practical application of the species category (understood as one of the taxonomic ranks, defined in relation to selected criteria – e.g., genetic) based on a partially arbitrary decision of the researcher-systematist. Arbitrariness here is the result of fluid genetic and ecological boundaries as well as imperfect criteria for the use of species categories.

[98] Oderberg, *Real Essentialism*, 212.

88   *Essentialist and Hylomorphic Notion of Species*

As to the argument that clear boundaries between species allow only for saltations and not for steady and gradual evolutionary changes, we must not forget that these boundaries are most likely marked by sparse, if not singular mutations (changes), which bring to fulfilment complex processes of changes, extended in space and time and effected by a matrix of causes. In other words, the clarity of metaphysical boundaries between evolutionary-related species does not make them radical empirically speaking. As long as our metaphysics allows for gradual changes affecting dispositions of successive generations of offspring in a given lineage, it should welcome the possibility of an evolutionary transformation that is not saltational. Classical Aristotelian–Thomistic metaphysics certainly allows for such minute and gradual changes, disposing PM to be actualized, at some point (in a particular transition from one generation to the next), by a SF of a new type, which marks the origin of a new species. Once again, such clear metaphysical boundary between natural kinds may not easily translate or coincide with their empirical demarcation. Indeed, the latter may remain epistemologically vague. But this should not discredit our ontological assessment, at least not by default.

CLASSIFYING SPECIES UNDER HIGHER TAXA

Having discussed the controversy over the notion of species and species transformation, I shall now refer shortly to four main schools of contextualizing the species category under higher taxa. The first three contemporary schools of biological taxonomy are primarily empirical. In reference to PSC, phenetic school of taxonomy (PST) classifies species under genera, families, *etc.*, based on the overall (usually morphological) observable similarity of their members, regardless their phylogeny or evolutionary relations. Ereshefsky notes that due to the post Darwinian progress in biology, it is no longer considered a viable taxonomic school by the vast majority of taxonomists.[99]

The alternative, evolutionary school of taxonomy (EST) defines taxa in terms of common ancestry, assuming that they must be genealogical lineages. It reflects the two main evolutionary processes, that is, branching (cladogenesis), in which a single lineage splits into two, and divergence (anagenesis), in which speciation occurs in a single lineage. Refer Figure 2.2 a and b. In addition, paying attention to the extent to

---

[99] See Marc Ereshefsky, "Systematics and Taxonomy," in *A Companion to the Philosophy of Biology*, ed. Sahotra Sarkar and Anya Plutynski (Chichester: Wiley-Blackwell, 2010), 1007.

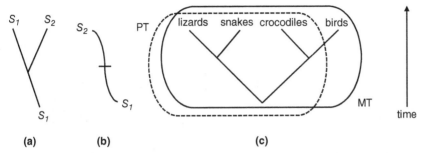

FIGURE 2.2 Depiction of evolutionary processes: (a) speciation by cladogenesis (branching); (b) speciation by anagenesis (divergence); (c) a phylogenetic tree of lizards, snakes, crocodiles, and birds – a monophyletic taxon (MT) contains all four descendants of a common ancestor, while a paraphyletic taxon (PT) excludes birds as a taxon that diverged considerably from its neighbors.

which a given taxon has diverged from its neighbors, EST distinguishes between monophyletic and paraphyletic taxa, where the former contain an ancestor and all of its descendants, while the latter contain an ancestor and some but not all of its descendants. Refer Figure 2.2c.

The third, cladistic school of taxonomy (CST) is closely related to EST yet departs from it based on its categorical conviction that classifications must be grounded on common ancestry and nothing else. Hence, unlike EST, CST accepts only monophyletic taxa (arguing that the category of "considerable difference" in definition of paraphyletic taxa is rather ambiguous) and rejects the idea of speciation by anagenesis. In response, advocates of EST argue that paraphyletic taxa are not limited to a few marginal cases. Quite the contrary, they seem to be common across the whole organic world. Nevertheless, due to its precise methods for constructing classifications, CST has become the prominent school of taxonomy.[100]

However, there is one more school I would like to mention. It has a long tradition that goes back to Porphyry (c. 234–305 A.D.). Hence, we may call it the Porphyrian school of taxonomy (PorST). What differentiates it from all three schools mentioned here is that, apart from categories of strictly empirical nature, it welcomes also those that are metaphysical. Moreover, unlike EST and CST, it sees generality and specificity as non-relative matters. Thus, the Porphyrian classification (tree) of a given entity must not be read as an account of historical origins. Rather, it is a synchronic structure designed to partition a classified species in a way that distinguishes it from everything else in the universe. As such, notes

[100] See *ibid.*, 107–10.

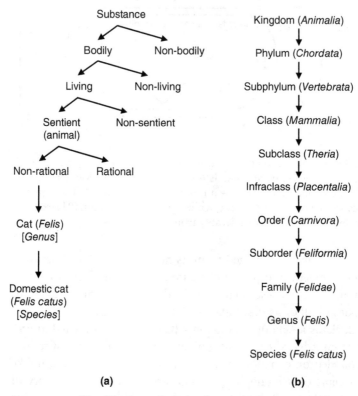

FIGURE 2.3 Classification of domestic cat (*Felis catus*) under two different schools of taxonomy: (a) Porphyrian (PorST) and (b) cladistic (CST).

Oderberg, it remains scientific in a broader, if not the broadest sense. It is a metaphysical structure informed by natural science. The higher one ascends in it, the more metaphysical categories are involved, such as substance, body, material, immaterial, simple, compound, quality, quantity, *etc.* The lower one gets, the more empirical categories are engaged, such as mammal, vertebrate, water-dweller, metal, gas, *etc.*[101]

As an example of Porphyrian classification, we may think of the one characterizing a domestic cat (*Felis catus*). Compared with the purely empirical biological taxonomy developed under CST, it converges with it only at the level of the final two categories (*genus* and *species*). However, both classifications are valid and useful in a proper context – the former in a more philosophical (metaphysical) analysis, the latter in an investigation pursued in natural sciences. Refer Figure 2.3.

[101] See Oderberg, *Real Essentialism*, 92–105.

CONCLUSION

Although the anti-individualistic and antiessentialistic orthodoxy is most likely still predominant among philosophers of biology, I hope to have shown that there is a growing group of philosophers of science and biology, who think that the received consensus defining species as spatiotemporally extended (scattered) individuals needs to be at least supplemented with the classical view that acknowledges the reality of intrinsic natures (essences) of individual organisms. Moreover, I argued that when considered in the context of its different variants or aspects, that is, referring to genetic and phenetic properties of organisms, historical relations among them, their fundamental dispositions, developmental programs, and metaphysical (hylomorphic) constitution – EssSC becomes a viable and comprehensive proposition that belongs in the age of evolution. Moving forward the conversation I offered a comprehensive hylomorphically informed essentialist definition of species, which builds upon earlier developments provided by Oderberg and Dumsday. This is important for the constructive proposal of the metaphysics of evolutionary transitions developed in Chapter 1.

However, while the strong resurgence of essentialism among analytic philosophers with a taste for metaphysics gradually finds its manifestation in contemporary philosophy of biology, which proves Ereshefsky's pronouncement of its death to be premature and most likely ill-conceived,[102] other questions concerning the interpretation of evolution within the framework of the Aristotelian–Thomistic school of philosophy remain. One of them refers to the meaning and role of natural selection, teleology, and chance in evolutionary processes. I will address it in the next chapter.

---

[102] See Ereshefsky, "species," section 2.1.

3

Natural Selection, Teleology, and Chance in Evolution

In his article on Darwin, published in 1874, Asa Gray stated: "We recognize the great service rendered by Darwin to natural science by restoring teleology to it, so that instead of having morphology against teleology, we shall have henceforth morphology married to teleology." To this Darwin replied saying: "What you say about teleology pleases me especially, and I do not think anyone else has ever noticed the point." Similar was the opinion of his son Francis, the editor of Darwin's *Autobiography*: "One of the greatest services rendered by my father to the study of Natural History is the revival of Teleology. The evolutionist studies the purpose or meaning of organs with the zeal of the older Teleologist, but with far wider and more coherent purpose."[1]

But Darwin was first and foremost a scientist, not a philosopher. In his correspondence with William Graham, the author of *The Creed of Science* (1881), Darwin acknowledged that he had no practice in abstract reasoning. We find a proof for that in the same letter to Graham in which he first denies that the existence of natural laws implies purpose but then assures him that Graham's belief that the universe is not the result of chance is his inward conviction.[2]

---

[1] Asa Gray, "Scientific Worthies," *Nature* 10 (1874); Charles Darwin, *The Autobiography of Charles Darwin, 1809–1882*, ed. Nora Barlow (London: Collins, 1958), 308, 316. Huxley's opinion, which Francis Darwin used to support his thesis, was the same: "Perhaps the most remarkable service to the philosophy of biology rendered by Mr. Darwin is the reconciliation of Teleology and Morphology, and the explanation of the facts of both, which his views offer" (Francis Darwin, *The Life and Letters of Charles Darwin, Volume II* [London: John Murray, 1887], 201).

[2] Darwin, *Autobiography*, 68. See William Graham, *The Creed of Science: Religious, Moral, and Social* (London: Kegan Paul, 1881).

Natural Selection, Teleology, and Chance in Evolution   93

This ambiguity makes it difficult to specify the exact position of Darwin in the philosophical dispute between Descartes, Bacon, and Spinoza, who rejected final causes calling them "barren virgins dedicated to God" (Bacon),[3] and Leibniz and Kant, who tried to defend the concept of final causality arguing that we must acknowledge that organisms are "natural purposes."[4] The course taken by Neo-Darwinism, however, is clear and transparent. The molecular revolution inspired a scientific atmosphere that fostered a strongly reductionist line of reasoning in theoretical biology. Having its foundation in 1869 in Von Helmholtz's praise for Darwin for bringing the study of biological form under the ambit of mechanism, it found its culmination a hundred years later in 1969, in the position of David Hull who declared: "From the point of view of contemporary biology, both vitalism and teleology are stone-cold dead."[5] Despite Quine's philosophical objections to this

---

[3] Francis Bacon, *The Dignity and Advancement of Learning* (London/New York: The Colonial Press, 1900), 99. In his *Letter to Mersenne* Descartes writes: "The number and the orderly arrangements of the nerves, veins, bones, and other parts of an animal do not show that nature is insufficient to form them, provided you suppose that in everything nature acts in accordance with the laws of mechanics" (quoted in Denis Walsh, "Teleology," in *The Oxford Handbook of Philosophy of Biology*, ed. Michael Ruse [Oxford, New York: Oxford University Press, 2008],114). Spinoza in Appendix 1 to his *Ethics* says this about teleology: "That which is really a cause it considers as an effect, and *vice versa*: it makes that which is by nature to be the last, and that which is highest and most perfect to be most imperfect" (Benedict Spinoza, "Ethics," in *The Chief Works of Benedict de Spinoza. Vol. 2*, tr. R. H. M. Elwes [New York: Dover Publications, 1951], 77).

[4] Leibniz defends the idea of final and formal cause. The internal forces of his monads can be identified with SF (according to the principle of the identity of indiscernibles). When conceived as appetites, they also have a teleological character. However, although in his system efficient and final types of causality are complementary, Leibniz does not escape entirely the problem of determinism, which in his philosophy takes the form of a pre-established harmony.

[5] David Hull, "What Philosophy of Biology Is Not," *Journal of the History of Biology* 2 (1969), 249. Having said this, we should not forget that in the first part of the twentieth century, many biologists were still convinced that teleologically oriented organization of living beings was one of the main issues of biology. This view – commonly labelled *organicism* – was represented by a group of researchers, including Joseph Henry Woodger, Joseph Needham, Conrad Hal Waddington, and Dorothy Maud Wrinch. They formed the "Theoretical Biology Club," that promoted anti-reductionist and holistic approach to the phenomenon of life. Their work inspired Ludwig von Bertalanffy. Moreover, further interest in the nonreductionist explanation of biological organization came from (1) some physicists associated with the development of quantum theory (see, e.g., Erwin Schrödinger, *What Is Life? The Physical Aspect of the Living Cell* [Cambridge: Cambridge University Press, 1944]), (2) the cybernetic movement (e.g., the work of the American physiologist Walter B. Cannon, who developed the concept of "homeostasis," and others who proposed mathematical models of biological systems and developed the

94   *Natural Selection, Teleology, and Chance in Evolution*

reductionist dogma,[6] teleology retained its bad reputation in the second half the twentieth century, among many philosophers and scientists, who suggested to replace it with chance. Driven to the extreme, this position led Richard Dawkins formulate his famous metaphysical manifesto in which he declares: "The universe we observe has precisely the properties we should expect if there is, at bottom, no design, no purpose, no evil and no good, nothing but blind pitiless indifference."[7]

However, this antiteleological crusade characteristic for logical positivism is mostly over.[8] A number of contemporary philosophers of biology acknowledge that Darwin was a "teleologist" and did not raise chance and randomness to the point of being *causa prima* of evolutionary changes. On the course toward presenting and evaluating their ideas concerning natural selection, teleology, and chance, I will first go back to the classical notion of teleology as developed by Aristotle. The next two sections of this chapter will be dedicated to Aristotle's and Aquinas's understanding of the interplay of teleology and chance in nature. In the next step, I will refer to an observation made by Aristotle in *Physics* and commented on by Aquinas in *In Phys.*, which might be interpreted as a preliminary formulation of the principle of natural selection. Moving to the contemporary conversation on natural selection, teleology, and chance, I will first present a recent argument portraying Darwin as reinventing teleology. The next section will present the debate on teleology among the founding fathers of the twentieth-century evolutionary synthesis. The remaining subsections will be dedicated to the current status of teleology in philosophy of biology, and the question of whether natural selection should be understood as teleological. The final section will refer once again to the idea of the interplay between teleology and

---

theory of *autopoiesis*), and (3) the research inspired by Ilya Prigogine's notion of self-organization in conditions that are far-from-equilibrium (see Alvaro Moreno and Matteo Mossio, *Biological Autonomy: A Philosophical and Theoretical Enquiry* [Dordrecht: Springer, 2015], xxv–xxvi).

[6] Willard van Orman Quine, "Two Dogmas of Empiricism," in *From a Logical Point of View* (Cambridge, MA: Harvard University Press, 1953), 20–46.

[7] Richard Dawkins, *River Out of Eden: A Darwinian View of Life* (New York: Basic books/Harper Collins, 1995), 132–3.

[8] Moreno and Mossio speak about the "second theoretical biology," which picked up the ideas developed by the "Theoretical Biology Club" from the early-twentieth century and further developed them in the second half of the same century, in response to logical positivism and a purely mechanical approach to the phenomenon of life. Among pioneering authors of this movement, they list Robert Rosen, Jean Piaget, Humberto Maturana, and Francisco J. Varela, Howard H. Pattee, and Tibor Gánti (see Moreno and Mossio, *Biological Autonomy*, xxvi).

Classical Notion of Teleology 95

chance; this time in reference to the contemporary philosophical account of evolution delineated in this and the previous chapters. It will be followed by a short conclusion.

CLASSICAL NOTION OF TELEOLOGY

Searching for an adequate and effective theory of scientific explanation, Aristotle came to the conclusion that the complete account of the fact that things are what they are, keep their identity while going through accidental changes, and change into something else on entering into processes leading to substantial changes requires – apart from hylomorphism and the categories of material and formal causes – an introduction of the two additional types of causality. He was convinced that we need to know the source of change and/or rest of a given entity (its efficient cause) and the end of this activity or a lack of it (its final cause). Leaving the category of efficient cause to be discussed in Chapter 5, I will now concentrate on goal-directedness (finality).

Definition

Aristotle defines final cause as "that for the sake of which" a thing is done, or a good that can be attained and that is proper for a being.[9] It takes its other name, "teleology," from the Greek τέλος (*telos*), which translates as "end" or "goal." Although he invokes necessity as an explanation of the availability of suitable matter, Aristotle acknowledges the need for an explanation in terms of purpose as a function of nature, to explain why given matter acquires the particular shape and structure it does.[10]

---

[9] "Again (4) in the sense of end or 'that for the sake of which' a thing is done, e.g. health is the cause of walking about. ('Why is he walking about?' we say. 'To be healthy,' and, having said that, we think we have assigned the cause.) The same is true also of all the intermediate steps which are brought about through the action of something else as means towards the end, for example, reduction of flesh, purging, drugs, or surgical instruments are means towards health. All these things are 'for the sake of the end, though they differ from one another in that some are activities, others instruments" (*Phys.* II, 3 [194b 29–195a 2]). A similar definition can be found in *Meta.* V, lect. 2 (1013a 29–1013b 2). See also *Phys.* II, 7 (198a 18–20); *Meta.* I, 2 (983a 30–32).

[10] See, for instance, *De part. an.* III, 2 (663b 12–14); IV, 5 (679a 25–30); *De gen. an.* II, 4 (739b 27–31); III, 4 (755a 17–30). Bostock lists a number of scholars claiming that "Aristotle would concede (at least for the sake of argument) that a complete materialist explanation might perhaps be available, and yet still insist that a teleological account was also needed" (David Bostock, *Space, Time, Matter, and Form: Essays on Aristotle's*

96 Natural Selection, Teleology, and Chance in Evolution

This observation inspires Aristotle to suggest a general proposition stating that "generation is a process from something to something, from a principle [ἀρχή, *archē*] to a principle – from the primary efficient cause, which is something already endowed with a certain nature, to some definite form or similar end [τέλος]" (*De part. an.* II, 1 [646a 31–34]).[11]

Aquinas notes that teleology may refer to both immanent (intrinsic) and transeunt (extrinsic) agency of a given thing.[12] He speaks about a natural inclination, that is, a natural impetus that each substance has for engaging in determinate actions that produce determinate goals: "In natural beings there is a desire for or an inclination toward some end or goal, to which the will of a rational nature corresponds; and for this reason a natural inclination is itself called an appetite" (*In Meta.* V, lect. 6 [§ 829]). He thinks natural agents strive to follow this inclination to the greatest extent possible in realization of their own intrinsic good or perfecting other beings: "natural things have a natural inclination not only towards their own proper good, to acquire it if not possessed, and, if possessed, to rest therein; but also to spread abroad their own good amongst others, so far as possible" (*ST* I, 19, 2, co.). He also claims that natural inclinations are grounded in SSFF of agents: "things of nature have forms, which are the source of action, and inclinations resulting from the forms, which we call natural appetites, and actions result from these inclinations" (*Q. de malo*, 6, 1). At the same time, he acknowledges, after Aristotle, that "the end is the cause of causes, because it is the cause of the causality in all causes" (*De prin. nat.* 29).[13]

It is important to note that both Aristotle and Aquinas extend teleology (goal directedness) – which is usually associated with conscious human decisions – to other living and nonliving entities. Indeed, as notes

---

"Physics" [Oxford: Clarendon Press, 2006], 58). He suggests this "seems to be roughly the position that we ourselves are in nowadays" (*ibid.*, 60).

[11] Aristotle's profound conviction that "nature does nothing in vain" makes him think that there has to be a purpose for everything in nature. At the same time, he is careful to note that the final cause is not acting sensu stricto: "The active power is a 'cause' in the sense of that from which the process originates: but the end, for the sake of which it takes place, is not 'active'. (That is why health is not 'active,' except metaphorically.) For when the agent is there, the patient becomes something: but when 'states' [ἕξεων, *hexeōn*, dispositions] are there, the patient no longer becomes but already is – and 'forms' [εἴδη, *eidē*] (i.e. 'ends') [καὶ τὰ τέλη, *kai ta telē*] are a kind of 'state' [ἕξεις, *hexeis*]" (*De gen. et corr.* I, 7 [342b 14–18]).

[12] See, for example, *Q. de ver.* 14, 3.

[13] "Plainly, however, that cause is the first which we call that for the sake of which. For this is the account of the thing, and the account forms the starting-point, alike in the works of art and in works of nature" (*De part. an.* I, 1 [639b 14–16]).

Bostock, in *Meteo.* IV, 12 (389b 25–390a 21), "Aristotle does explicitly say that the elements, and the inorganic compounds that are formed from them, are 'for the sake of something', equating this with the view that they have a 'function' (ἔργον [*ergon*]) which in turn is a power (δύναμις [*dynamis*]) to act or be acted upon."[14] Moreover, Aristotle and Aquinas help us understand that when predicated about inanimate and animate but unconscious nature, teleology must not be understood as a mysterious – quasi-efficient – cause, directing things according to a pre-established harmony. Quite the contrary, it should be seen as a natural tendency of things to realize what is proper to their nature (e.g., a tree blossoming and bearing fruit) – a tendency that does not have to be known or intended by a conscious agent.[15] That is why Aristotle delineates in *Phys.* II, 8 (199b 26–27) that "it is absurd to suppose that purpose is not present because we do not observe the agent deliberating."[16] Obviously, an inorganic compound does not have a soul. But it does have a SF, which might fulfill the same task of holding elements and transforming them into a composite entity. Hence, by analogy, just as the soul of a living organism can be identified with its goal and actions that realize it, so the form of an inorganic compound has a similar task to perform.

Normative Aspect of Teleology

Moreover, in this context, it becomes apparent that teleology has a normative import. It can be clearly seen in case of animals, whose natures transmitted in the processes of generation function as causes, by way of being goals toward which animals develop, and which are their proper

---

[14] Bostock, *Space*, 71.

[15] In response to the objection that the end – existing upon the completion of the agent's action – cannot be its cause, Aquinas says that "Although the end be last in the order of execution, yet it is first in the order of the agent's intention. And it is this way that it is a cause" (*ST* I–II, 1, 1, ad 1). Concerning natural causes that do not have cognition, Aquinas thinks their "intention" is expressed in their natural inclinations: "to intend ... is nothing else than to have a natural inclination to something" (*De prin. nat.* 19).

[16] Aquinas has something similar to say in *De prin. nat.* 19: "we should notice that, although every agent, both natural and voluntary, intends an end, still it does not follow that every agent knows the end or deliberates about the end. To know the end is necessary in those whose actions are not determined, but which may act for opposed ends as, for example, voluntary agents. Therefore it is necessary that these know the end by which they determine their actions. But in natural agents the actions are determined, hence it is not necessary to choose those things which are for the end." See also Bostock, *Space*, 48–78; Allan Gotthelf, "Aristotle's Conception of Final Causality," *The Review of Metaphysics* 30 (1976): 226–54; W. K. C. Guthrie, *A History of Greek Philosophy*, vol. 6, *Aristotle: An Encounter* (New York and Cambridge: Cambridge University Press, 1981), 114–18.

98   *Natural Selection, Teleology, and Chance in Evolution*

good. Commenting on this normative aspect of teleology, Bostock states that we can speak about a "law of goodness" in Aristotle, which assumes that "there is something that counts as good, namely what is good for the animal or plant concerned." Consequently, "whatever parts a living thing needs, in order to live a life that is good for it, will for that very reason tend to be present in it (and therefore will grow as it grows). The law is limited in its application, of course, by the fact that the 'laws of matter' will only permit some kinds of parts to develop, and not others. ... It is for him [Aristotle] a law that is basic and irreducible."[17]

However, normativity of teleology is apparent not only at the level of living organisms but also in the case of inanimate entities (objects). In other words, teleology – as notes Mark Bedau – is, generally speaking, "value-centered," and this fact cannot be neutralized by either (1) relating it, in a Humean way, to minds and their designs (the mental approach) or (2) explaining it in terms of goal-directedness of natural systems (the systems approach) or (3) rationalizing it in reference to causal histories of teleological phenomena (the etiological approach). Bedau successfully shows that all three ways of striving to eliminate teleology's reference to value end up reorienting the conversation back to the value approach.[18]

Naturally, the evaluative element of teleology thus understood – that is, understood as the proper good of a given entity – need not consist in any moral good. Neither does it have to confer an important or the best good. Quite the opposite, it is enough for it to refer to some good: "moral or non-moral or even immoral, important or insignificant, and intrinsic or merely instrumental."[19] The good in question is always related to what kind of thing a given entity is (its formal principle). Thus, even if properly classified and named in philosophical investigation performed by conscious beings, it is, nonetheless, real and intrinsic to the entity in question, independently of the operation of any human mind.[20]

---

[17] Bostock, *Space*, 77–78. For more information on teleology in Aristotle's biology see Allan Gotthelf, *Teleology, First Principles, and Scientific Method in Aristotle's Biology* (Oxford: Oxford University Press, 2012).

[18] See Mark Bedau, "Where's the Good in Teleology?," *Philosophy and Phenomenological Research* 52 (1992): 783–87. See also Bedau's response to the criticism of the value analysis of teleology as viciously circular and spurious in reference to the cases of supposedly value-free teleology in *ibid.*, 793–94.

[19] *Ibid.*, 791.

[20] See also Lenny Moss and Daniel J. Nicholson, "On Nature and Normativity: Normativity, Teleology, and Mechanism in Biological Explanation," *Studies in History and Philosophy of Science* Part C: *Studies in History and Philosophy of Biological and Biomedical Sciences* 43, no. 1 (2012): 88–91.

ARISTOTLE ON TELEOLOGY AND CHANCE

As a source of regularity and order in observed reality, teleology is often opposed to chance. However, the classical approach helps us realize that the relationship between these two fundamental categories is more nuanced. With regards to chance, Aristotle considers it to be, first of all, the ontological aspect of reality and not merely an epistemological unexpectedness of certain occurrences due to the limitations of human understanding. He sees it as a kind of event that (metaphysically) demands the agency/intentionality of nature or human will, since it appears to "happen for an end," but no such agency is involved in its occurrence. To better understand this position, we should follow Aristotle's distinctions introduced in the chapters of *Physics* dedicated to chance.[21]

Aristotle distinguishes chance events from occurrences that happen necessarily and those happening in the same way for the most part. Chance events also have a unique character in his second classification, in which he distinguishes between events that come to be for a purpose (due to a deliberate intention or as a result of nature) and those that do not happen for a purpose. He says that "even among the things which are outside the necessary and the normal, there are some in connexion with which the phrase 'for the sake of something' is applicable. (...) Things of this kind, then, when they come to pass incidentally are said to be 'by chance'" (*Phys.* II, 5 [196b 20–24]). Refer Figure 3.1a.

---

[21] Aristotle criticizes philosophers of the past for either not finding a place for chance on their list of causes, or not paying enough attention to it. He refers specifically to Empedocles who attributed to chance certain events, such as movement of air in the process of the separation of elements, or the origin of the parts of animals, but did not analyze the nature of chance in more detail. He is also critical about Democritus who attributed the origin of the universe to spontaneity, claiming at the same time that chance is not responsible for the generation of plants, animals, or mind. Finally, he rejects the view of those who claim that chance is full of mystery and a divine thing (see *Phys.* II, 4 [196a 19–196b 7]). It is possible that these difficulties with the classification of chance in the writings of pre-Socratics are due to the fact that in their description of causality in nature they referred predominantly to material and efficient causes and did not consider formal and final causation. Aristotle notices it in *De gen. an.* V, 1 (778b 7–10) and *De part. an.* I, 1 (640b 4–11).

Dudley claims that the view of chance presented by Democritus and atomists resembles that of Hume and corresponds with the opinion of many contemporary scientists, who claim that everything in the universe obeys the necessary laws of physics, while the order in the universe itself came into being by chance. See John Dudley, *Aristotle's Concept of Chance: Accidents, Cause, Necessity, and Determinism* (New York: Sunny Press, 2012), 152–53.

(a)

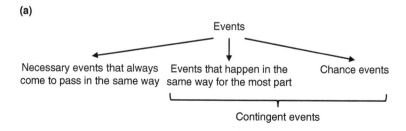

(b)

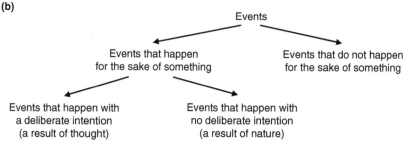

FIGURE 3.1 Two divisions of events in Aristotle (see *Phys.* II, 5 [196b, 10–20]).

Another distinction introduced by Aristotle separates chance (ταύτόματον – *tautomaton*) and luck or fortune (τύχη – *tyche*). We can refer once again to the second distinction of events presented above (refer Figure 3.1b) and characterize the scope of both categories in a way depicted on Figure 3.2.

To explain the nature of chance, Aristotle refers to yet another distinction between *per se* (καθ' αὑτὸ αἴτιον, *kath' hauto aition*) and incidental (κατὰ συμβεβηκὸς, *kata symbebēkos*), or *per accidens* causes. He sees *per se* causes as fundamental and essential efficient causes that come from nature (φύσις, *physis*) or intellect (νοῦς, *nous*). As such, they are naturally related to the formal and final causality of a given agent. In other words, an efficient cause is acting *per se* when its activity is performed by an agent, in accord with the agent's SF, to produce its proper effect.[22] The character of the second *per accidens* (accidental) type of causes, on the other hand, can be explained in reference to Aristotle's metaphysics of substance. Just as an accident (accidental formal feature) of an entity has

---

[22] See *Phys.* II, 7, (198a 23–26).

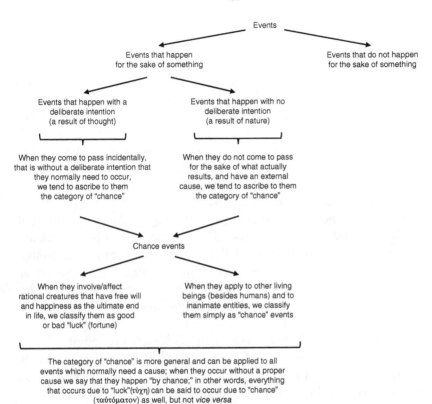

FIGURE 3.2 The distinction between chance and luck (fortune).[23]

no existence of its own but is rooted in its substantial formal features, an accidental cause must be related to a *per se* cause.[24]

To give an example taken from Aristotle, the essential efficient cause of a statue is the sculptor. If he happens to be fair-skinned and musical as well, it seems just to say that a musician or a fair-skinned man made a

---

[23] Dudley offers a detailed analysis of the distinction between "chance" and "luck" in Aristotle's *Physics*. He presents it in the second and third chapter of his book, with several substantial textual conclusions concerning the structure and dating of *Phys.* II, 4–6. See Dudley, *Aristotle's Concept of Chance*, 58–100. See also *ibid.*, 42–54. Note that in the most popular translation of *Physics* by R. P. Hardie and R. K. Gaye in McKeon's edition of the works of Aristotle, ταὐτόματον is translated as "spontaneity" and τύχη as "chance." In Dudley, both terms are translated respectively as "chance" and "luck." His version is more accurate. It is also followed by Richard Hope in his translation of Aristotle's *Physics*.

[24] See *Phys.* II, 3 (195a 26–34); II, 5 (196b 24–29).

102 Natural Selection, Teleology, and Chance in Evolution

statue. But his musical skills and the fact that he is fair-skinned are only incidental (coincidental, *per accidens*) causes related to the *per se* cause of his being a sculptor.[25]

Keeping this distinction in mind, Aristotle defines chance as an unusual incidental (*per accidens*) cause, which is inherently unpredictable, although it still falls in the category of events that "happen for the sake of something" (since it refers and is related to such occurrences). Thus, chance events are in a way posterior, since their occurrence and analysis require always a reference to *per se* causes of a given causal situation. Consequently, trying to specify its ultimate nature, Aristotle states that "chance is an incidental cause. But strictly it is not the cause – without qualification – of anything."[26] And yet, because it is distinguished as a unique type of occurrence which is not primary and which yet is inherently related to nature (φύσις, *physis*) and intellect (νοῦς, *nous*), chance needs to be defined in reference to *per se* formal and final causality rather than blind material necessity. This tells us that delineating it in a stark opposition to these causes is an unjustified simplification.[27]

To give an example, when riding on my bicycle through the downtown, I met my friend walking to the store. While my intention was to get out of the city to take a break, my friend's intention was to get to the store and do some shopping. Our intentions (final causes), our actions (efficient causes), and the essence of each one of us (hylomorphic union of PM and SF) were *per se* causes of our activities but not of our accidental encounter. In other words, tracing back *per se* causes of our activities does not eliminate the chance character of our encounter, making it to be inevitable (predetermined). The accidental nature of our meeting was something real, in addition to *per se* causes of our actions, and it could not have transpired without these causes. Hence, one might say that, in a way, it was ontologically parasitic upon them. Moreover, as notes Snyder, this shows that there must be some correlation and proportionality of active and passive powers of entities that

---

[25] See *Phys.* II, 3 (195a 34–195b 6). Aristotle also uses a similar example of a house builder in *Phys.* II, 3 (196b 25–29). See also *Phys.* II, 3 (195b 24); II, 5 (196b 27–29).

[26] *Phys.* II, 5 (197 a 12–14).

[27] "No incidental cause can be prior to a cause *per se*. Spontaneity and chance, therefore, are posterior to intelligence and nature. Hence, however true it may be that the heavens are due to spontaneity, it will still be true that intelligence and nature will be prior causes of this all and of many things in it besides" (*Phys.* II, 6 [198a 8–13]).

Aristotle on Teleology and Chance

enter chance occurrences, even if they are not specifically and directly ordered to one another. "For, chance events are not so completely random that any two natures can interact in any chance way to produce any outcome whatsoever."[28]

Consequently, we may say that the need of reference to *per se* causes in the case of chance occurrences protects Aristotelian metaphysics not only from blind material necessity – defined as "tychism" (from the Greek τύχη, *tychē*),[29] that is, attributing everything to chance – but also from absolute determinism, which sees chance simply as lack of human knowledge of causes.[30] This fact has a significant influence on Aristotle's philosophy of nature and his understanding of necessary occurrences in the physical world. Necessity as such is never absolute for him, but always suppositional. Things happen in accordance with causal patterns but on the supposition that nothing interferes with given causal occurrences. In other words, what we observe in nature is a nomological necessity governing relations between metaphysically contingent entities and the processes they enter.[31]

---

[28] Snyder, "Evolution." Snyder adds that "The requisite proportionality of active and receptive powers in the interacting natures arises not from the specific formalities of the natures but from more general and generic characteristics and formalities they have." He gives an example referring to evolution: "Thus cosmic rays mutate a gene not qua gene but qua the gene's more generic molecular properties. It is not the teleology of a gene to be mutated but to be stable. But because of the kind of chemical bonds, etc., that a gene has, it can be mutated when acted on by ultraviolet radiation, for example, On account of the *specific* formalities and character of natures, they are stable and tend to reproduce an offspring of the same kind. But because of the *generic* formalities, characteristics, and potencies things have, they are open to chance, and to a substantial difference-in-kind between parent and offspring" (*ibid.*).

[29] As already explained above in Figure 3.2 and in note 23, Aristotle's category of ταὐτόματον (*tautomaton*) would be more appropriate here, as it is more general. Nonetheless, it is the category of τύχη (*tyche*) that has been used to specify the position of material necessity or radical contingency (indeterminism) of occurrences in nature.

[30] "For Aristotle it is not legitimate to view the present condition of the world as the outcome of the interaction of chains of necessary causes, as many contemporary scientists and philosophers would hold. For Aristotle the human intellect can only trace back one chain of causes at a time, and will always have to stop the process when it reaches a free choice or a [sc. unusual] accidental cause, both of which introduce contingency into chains of causes, since the effect of free choices and [sc. unusual] accidents on the course of events is inherently unpredictable" (John Dudley, *Aristotle's Concept of Chance*, 323).

[31] For Aristotle on hypothetical necessity, see *De part. an.*, I, 1 (639b 23–6); IV, 2, (677a 15–19); *De gen. an.*, IV, 8 (776b 31–3). Aquinas embraces Aristotle's distinction between absolute and conditional (suppositional) necessity. See *De prin. nat.* 33.

104   *Natural Selection, Teleology, and Chance in Evolution*

AQUINAS ON TELEOLOGY AND CHANCE

Aquinas's teaching on final causation follows – for the most part – the position of Aristotle.[32] He is also in agreement with him on the philosophical notion of chance. In his lengthy commentary on the part of the *Second Book Physics* dedicated to this topic, Aquinas states that as a *per accidens* cause, chance must be related to *per se* causality of nature and intellect. Along the way, he raises an interesting question, asking whether everything that happens due to a *per accidens* cause should be regarded as a chance event, to which he answers that such events must occur rarely, for "what is always or frequently joined to the effect falls under the intention itself."[33]

There is one more important development proposed by Aquinas, which has a substantial influence on the proper understanding of his own and Aristotle's approach to the problem of chance. It is often thought that since Aristotle in his reflection on chance and fortune uses an example of two lines of causality crossing at a certain point of time and space, it would be enough to trace back each to find a proper (*per se*) cause of a chance event. Chance would then have merely an epistemological character. Toward the end of the *Prima Pars* of his *Summa theologiae*, Aquinas is clear that such a reasoning is intrinsically wrong:

> Consequently what results from this clashing of causes is not to be reduced to a further preexisting cause, from which it follows of necessity. For instance, that some terrestrial body take fire in the higher regions of the air and fall to the earth, is caused by some heavenly power; again, that there be on the surface of the earth some combustible matter, is reducible to some heavenly principle. But that the burning body should alight on this matter and set fire to it, is not caused.[34]

In other words, although a chance event can be described as an intersection of two or more *per se* efficient causes acting for an end, according to their formal dispositions and their manifestations, none is of itself a cause of the chance event. Nor is such a coincidence of the lines of causation itself a proper (*per se*) cause of the chance occurrence. The whole situation still begs the question of what made this intersection of *per se* causes happen. We can either say such an event does not have

---

[32] See *In Meta.* V, lect. 2 (§ 775); V, lect. 3 (§ 781–82); *In Phys.* V, lect. 11 (§ 246); *De prin. nat.* 19, 34–36.

[33] *In phys.* II, lect. 8 (§214). Moreover, we should also remember that, "among the per accidens causes, some are nearer [to the *per se* cause] and others are more remote. Those which are more remote seem less to be causes" (*ibid.*, lect. 9 [§ 221]).

[34] See *ST* I, 115, 6, co.

a cause and call it chance (an unintelligible noncause), or we can say it has an accidental cause and call it chance.[35] In both cases, chance has an ontological character.

NATURAL SELECTION IN ARISTOTLE AND AQUINAS

Before I address the contemporary debate concerning natural selection, teleology, and chance, I must remain for a little longer with Aristotle and Aquinas. For it turns out that in one of his works, Aristotle offers a view that might be interpreted as a preliminary notion of natural selection. If true, this observation would be quite remarkable, taking into account the distance in time between his biological research and reflection and that of Darwin.

Indeed, it is in Aristotle's *Physics*, where we find the Philosopher's peculiar reference to some thinkers who, rejecting teleology, suggest that everything in nature happens out of necessity. It may seem, they say, that things in nature come to be for an end; yet, in spite of appearance, they are actually organized "spontaneously in a fitting way," which helps them survive, unlike those things or organisms that grew otherwise, which "perished and continue to perish" (*Phys.* II, 8 [198b 29–32]).

This passage from Aristotle, which already looks like a primitive description of natural selection, was commented on by Aquinas, whose own description is even closer to the one formulated by Darwin and modern evolutionary theory. Referring to the same group of thinkers who rejected teleology and argued for the necessity of natural events, Aquinas says that

they say that from the beginning of the formation of the world the four elements [earth, water, air, fire] were joined in the constitution of natural things, and thus the many and varied dispositions of natural things were produced. And in all these things only that which happened to be suitable for some utility, as if it were made for that utility, was preserved. For such things had a disposition which made them suitable for being preserved, not because of some agent intending an end, but because of that which is *per se* vain, that is, by chance. On the other hand, whatever did not have such a disposition was destroyed, and is destroyed daily. Thus Empedocles said that in the beginning things which were part ox and part man were generated (*In Phys.* II, lect. 12 [§ 253]).

---

[35] Commenting on Aristotle's reflection on chance in *The Physics*, Massie emphasizes the role of time, which seems to be the only factor holding together two lines of *per se* causation in the chance event: "The coincidence of simultaneity has no rule and no other unity than the instant of its occurrence" (Pascal Massie, "The Irony of Chance: On Aristotle's *Physics* B, 4–6," *International Philosophical Quarterly* 43 [2003], 25). And yet, we must remember that time cannot be regarded as a causal factor.

106   *Natural Selection, Teleology, and Chance in Evolution*

Both descriptions are striking. Clearly, to assume *prima faciae* that Aristotle and Aquinas either developed or accepted a theory of evolution or natural selection would be anachronistic. As notes David Depew, Empedocles's position, commented by Aristotle and Aquinas, is not *sensu stricto* an evolutionary one:

> Those enamored of this similarity must discount the fact that Empedocles' theory is about the survival of suddenly congealed and henceforward stable species. In Darwinism the evolution of species comes about over many generations from the differential reproductive success of subspecific populations that at first just happen to possess variations that are environmentally helpful.[36]

At the same time, it seems legitimate to argue that both Aristotle and Aquinas, carefully observing changes and processes in nature, developed a metaphysics that might be thought as an introductory philosophical foundation for evolutionism (see Chapter 1) and, indeed, seems to remotely allude to the principle of natural selection.

Assuming that their analysis does introduce a preliminary description of natural selection, we ought to acknowledge that neither Aristotle nor Aquinas say plainly whether they find the very idea plausible. In fact, they seem to reject it. Why? Interestingly, the thinkers quoted by Thomas as first describing such a process did so while intending to prove that, in natural processes, the necessity of chance is the rule; a rule that would nowadays be described as a "blind" or "absolute" chance. This stood in stark contrast to the philosophical principle that nature always acts for an end. For Aristotle and Aquinas, this end, or final cause, is natural and intrinsic to things and organisms. Simply put, they found the rejection of teleology to be unacceptable.[37]

However, in spite of Aristotle's and Thomas' initial rejection of the primal description of natural selection, might we still find room to justify it within their philosophy? It seems that they both thought that teleology does not exclude chance and vice versa. For just as teleology is suppositional and does not introduce a radical determinism, chance and fortune are neither absolute nor blind. Consequently, one might expect that in the universe in which both teleology and chance are at play, the pursuit of living creatures toward excellence, that is, *entelechy* (a complete and full realization of their natures) will take place with varying degrees of

---

[36] David J. Depew, "Aristotelian Teleology and Philosophy of Biology in the Darwinian Era," in *The Cambridge Companion to Aristotle's Biology*, ed. Sophia M. Connell, New edition (Cambridge: Cambridge University Press, 2021), 265.

[37] See *ibid.*, 265–68.

Contemporary Debate on Teleology

success. In fact, in his commentary on Aristotle's *Physics*, Aquinas presents us with another observation that brings him closer to accepting the notion of natural selection within the context of Aristotelian metaphysics, which he embraced:

> The very fact (...) that there happens to be error in art is a sign that art acts for the sake of something. The same thing also happens in natural things in which monsters are, as it were, the errors of nature acting for the sake of something insofar as the correct operation of nature is deficient. And this very fact that error occurs in natural things is a sign that nature acts for the sake of some thing. The same thing is true of those substances which Empedocles said were produced at the beginning of the world, such as the 'ox-progeny', that is, half ox and half man. For if such things were not able to arrive at some end and final state of nature so that they would be preserved in existence, this was not because nature did not intend this [a final state], but because they were not capable of being preserved (*In Phys.* II, lect. 14 [§ 263]).

If Aristotle's and Aquinas's ideas presented here can be treated as a remote anticipation of the principle of natural selection – which I think they are – then we might feel justified to think that Darwin's theory, far from being a nineteenth-century *deus ex machina*, instead has philosophical precedence as early as in ancient Greece and Medieval Paris. Far from being antithetical to ancient philosophy, Darwin seems to further develop it.

CONTEMPORARY DEBATE ON TELEOLOGY

John Dudley rightly says that our contemporary debate on the mechanism of biological evolution resembles the ancient struggle between Empedocles, who would understand evolution as an entirely random process of coming to be of new organisms, without any *per se* or final causes, and Aristotle, who, when observing and describing changes in nature, would always refer to final and formal causation. Of course, neither Empedocles nor Aristotle assumed a theory of evolution in its modern version, but – as we have seen – the philosophical system of the latter remains by all means relevant to its main premises.[38]

Darwin as Teleologist

The first point in contemporary debate readdresses the question of Darwin's attitude to teleology. On the one side, we find those who agree

---

[38] See Dudley, *Aristotle's Concept of Chance*, 337.

108   *Natural Selection, Teleology, and Chance in Evolution*

with Michael Ghiselin's critical evaluation of the point made by Asa Gray, Francis Darwin, and Thomas Huxley, which opened this chapter:

... a myth has grown up, partly the work of [Asa] Gray, partly the work of Darwin's son and biographer, Francis Darwin, that Darwin somehow "brought teleology back into biology." In any nontrivial sense of that word, he did the exact opposite, getting rid of teleology and replacing it with a new way of thinking about adaptation ...[39]

One might argue that Darwin's agreement with Gray's comment was motivated by him trying to smooth over differences and controversies in the Darwinian fold. However, as notes James Lennox, to see in above-mentioned comments, a piece of political maneuvering on Darwin's part simply will not work. Hence, on the other side of the conversation, we find those who emphasize that there must be something going on if Huxley – a stark enemy of the teleological argument from design – praises Darwin for reconciling teleology and morphology.[40]

Lennox argues that Darwin, who by his own admission admired the argument from design in William Paley's work – while at Cambridge – and seemed ready to accept creation by design as the most plausible explanation for adaptation – when the Beagle sailed – did not change his view to the point of rejecting teleology altogether.[41] Quite contrary, in his *Species Notebooks*, he consistently used the term "final cause," in contexts where the central question related to various phenomena was "What is S for?"[42] The general direction of his views on teleology can be seen in his notes on John Macculloch's *Proofs and Illustrations of the Attributes of God*,[43] where Darwin systematically tests natural selection against Macculloch's Creator in accounting for various natural phenomena. It is true that, based on his knowledge of Francis Bacon through William Whewell, he most likely did consider whether – once one gives

---

[39] Michael Ghiselin, "Introduction" in Charles Darwin, *The Various Contrivances by Which Orchids Are Fertilized by Insects*, 2nd Revised edition (Chicago: University of Chicago Press, 1984), xiii. See also M. Solinas, *From Aristotle's Teleology to Darwin's Genealogy: The Stamp of Inutility*, trans. James Douglas (London: Palgrave Macmillan UK, 2015).

[40] James G. Lennox, "Darwin *was* a Teleologist," *Biology and Philosophy* 8 (1993), 410.

[41] Paley argued that living things have the structure and behaviors that they do because they were designed for certain purposes by a benevolent Creator. See William Paley, *Natural Theology: Or, Evidences of the Existence and Attributes of the Deity, Collected from the Appearances of Nature* (London: R. Faulder, 1802).

[42] See Paul H. Barrett, ed., *The Collected Papers of Charles Darwin: Two Volumes in One* (Chicago, IL: The University of Chicago Press, 1987), 167–455.

[43] *Ibid.*, 631–641.

Contemporary Debate on Teleology

up the idea of special designs of an intelligent and benevolent creator, as the cause of adaptations – one should also give up the language of "final cause" altogether. But his answer to this question must have been "No," as he continued to use the term both in *On the Origin of Species* and later.[44] Moreover, he consistently argued that "natural selection acts *for the good* of each being, and that its products *are present for* various functions, purposes and ends."[45] Consequently, states Lennox:

Darwin essentially re-invented teleology. Encouraged by many close followers to drop the term 'natural selection', Darwin steadfastly refused. He saw, better than his followers, that it could not easily be dropped. In the context of viewing variation as the provision of a random set of alternatives, a mechanism for selecting among them is crucial. The concept of selection permits the extension of the *teleology* of domestic breeding into the natural domain, without the need of conscious design. ... In a historical context where one's teleological choices were either the goals of goal-directed vital forces or divinely designed adaptation, no one was prepared for Darwin's accomplishment: a selection-based teleology. Far from leaving the doctrine of Final Causes just where it was, Darwin had given it a fundamentally new theoretical base. Unlike Gray [who thought Darwin left the doctrines of Final Causes, utility, and special design, just where they were before], Huxley seems to have, at least implicitly, understood this. ... [For] while he thought Darwin's theory had dealt "the death blow" to special creation, he also insisted that "there is a wider teleology which is not touched by the doctrine of Evolution, but is actually based upon the fundamental proposition of Evolution" (in F. Darwin 1887, 316). If by "the fundamental proposition of Evolution" Huxley intended the principle of natural selection, this remark seems to describe Darwin's practice correctly.[46]

Similar argument, yet in different context, that is, in reference to medical examples and evolutionary medicine, was developed by Harry Smit. He

---

[44] See Charles Darwin and Ernst Mayr, *On the Origin of Species: A Facsimile of the First Edition* (Cambridge, Mass.: Harvard University Press, 2001), 216, 435, 448.

[45] *Ibid.*, 149, 152, 224, 237, 451. See Lennox, "Darwin," 410–11. He also examines Darwin's teleological reasoning on two examples: (1) *Primula* and (2) *Orchids* (see *ibid.*, 412–16).

[46] Lennox, "Darwin," 417, 416. He refers to Charles Darwin, *The Life and Letters of Charles Darwin* (London: John Murray, 1887). Lennox emphasizes that Gray and Huxley were right that Darwin reconciled morphology and teleology, that is, a disagreement over whether priority in biological explanation should be given to references to the basic anatomic plan of the class to which a given organism belongs (the approach of Linnaeus) or to those based on its functional needs (the approach of Cuvier). Darwin indeed finds the middle ground when he says: "It is generally acknowledged that all organic beings have been formed on two great laws – Unity of Type, and the Conditions of Existence. ... On my theory, unity of type is explained by unity of descent. The expression of conditions of existence, so often insisted on by the illustrious Cuvier, is fully embraced by the principle of natural selection" (Darwin and Mayr, *On the Origin of Species*, 206).

110   *Natural Selection, Teleology, and Chance in Evolution*

suggests that it is far more preferable to study goal-directed phenomena as intrinsic parts of nature rather than as phenomena explicable by analogy with human intentional behavior and/or with the help of an argument from design. His conclusion is parallel to the one offered by Lennox:

> Darwin did not replace teleology by evolutionary explanations but showed that we can understand teleology without referring to a Designer. He eliminated the concept of design and rehabilitated Aristotelian teleological explanations. The implication is that adaptations should not be investigated as if designed, but with the help of both teleological and evolutionary explanations.[47]

Hence, we may conclude that Darwin was a teleologist. Moreover, it becomes clear that his notion of teleology was, in fact, a rediscovery of the classical notion of this concept, which I have outlined in previous sections. Indeed, in 1882, Darwin wrote his famous letter, in response to a gift by his friend, William Ogle of Ogle's recent translation of Aristotle's *Parts of Animals*, in which he remarks that his "two gods," Linnaeus and Cuvier, were "mere school-boys to old Aristotle."[48] Allan Gotthelf proves that this remark was not merely an extravagantly worded gesture of politeness. What Darwin realized based on his reading of *Parts of Animals* (even if he has read only a part of it before sending his letter) was that Aristotle, centuries before Linnaeus of Cuvier, had a systematic and plausible scheme of animal classification, and that he sought to identify functions of animal parts, which would explain their presence in complex organisms:

> [T]here is an *isomorphism* between Darwin's biological vision and Aristotle's ... [T]here is much in Darwin's biological theorizing that reflects what one gets if one imagines Aristotle having to accept into his system (i) full evidence of the evolution of species and (ii) a more powerful biochemistry than was projectible in his time.[49]

---

[47] Harry Smit, "Darwin's Rehabilitation of Teleology Versus Williams' Replacement of Teleology by Natural Selection," *Biological Theory* 5, no. 4 (2010), 357. See also Depew, "Aristotelian Teleology," 268–75; David J. Depew, "Consequence Etiology and Biological Teleology in Aristotle and Darwin," *Studies in History and Philosophy of Biological and Biomedical Sciences* 39, no. 4 (December 2008): 379–90.

[48] Charles Darwin, "C. Darwin to W. Ogle," (letter from Feb. 22, 1882) in *The Life and Letters of Charles Darwin. vol. 3*, edited by Francis Darwin (London: John Murray, 1887), 252. In his response to Darwin Ogle wrote: "I am glad ... to have added a third person to your gods and completed the Trinity" (quotation after Allan Gotthelf, "Darwin on Aristotle," *Journal of the History of Biology* 32, no. 1 [1999], 24).

[49] Gotthelf, "Darwin on Aristotle," 21–22. Gotthelf responds in his article to Simon Byl and his article "Le jugement de Darwin sur Aristote," *L'Antiquité Classique* 42 (1973), 519–521.

Contemporary Debate on Teleology

Moreover, Gotthelf thinks this is particularly true with respect to biological teleology, where Darwin's insight seems to go beyond that of Ogle, taking him back to Aristotle's notion of natural intrinsic finality of living systems:

Darwin has understood something about Aristotelian teleology that Ogle did not ... Ogle's Aristotle combines elements of the two approaches [mechanism and teleology], since he recognizes the limitations material necessity places in teleology, but he is still fundamentally a teleologist, who views "Nature" as an "intelligent ... foreseeing agent." But, contrary to Ogle's sentiment, Aristotle's natures are *not* literally intelligent, not literally planners, and arguably the philosopher's genius lies in plotting a *third* course between these two pictures, and defending it as scientifically legitimate. This third course involves the postulation not of an "intelligent Nature" but of inherent *natures* – that is, of natural capacities (in Greek, *dunameis*) *directed at form*, capacities for the production of a living organism of a particular type that are irreducible to the capacities of the elements that constitute such an organism.[50]

Contextualizing and grounding functionality in his theory Darwin seems to "locate" it in natural selection explanations, which he saw as inherently teleological, in the sense that a value consequence (Darwin most often uses the term "advantage") of a trait explains its increase, or presence, in a population. This brings our attention to one of the founding fathers of the modern evolutionary synthesis – Francisco Ayala – and his notion of teleology.

Teleology and the Twentieth-Century Evolutionary Synthesis

Despite the evidence for teleological aspects of Darwin's theory, the success of molecular and cell biology, biochemistry, and genetics inspired not only the reductionist program of logical positivism but also some reductionist interpretations of evolutionary theory. It all created the image of Darwin as promoting mechanism and materialism. However, that this reductionist and antiteleological view of biological evolution is highly problematic and inconsistent, has become evident for many. Yet, the way back to the acknowledgment of the role of finality and goal-directedness in evolutionary transitions was not straightforward.

---

[50] Gotthelf, "Darwin on Aristotle," 22. Gotthelf admits "Aristotle's teleology is a *stronger* teleology than Darwin's, since Aristotle postulates a primitive or basic *directiveness on an end*, an irreducible (yet non-conscious) directiveness built into each ontogenic process which cannot be explained by reference to anything simpler (such as a series of selections leading to parent organisms which then reproduce themselves); but against the background of a pure Democritean mechanistic world-view, it is the *similarity* between Aristotle and Darwin, not the *difference*, that one notices" (*ibid.*, 23).

112   *Natural Selection, Teleology, and Chance in Evolution*

The first signs of the recovery of teleology in biology came with the work of three important evolutionary biologists: Theodosius Dobzhansky, Ernst Mayr, and Francisco Ayala. The first one among them simply notes that "mutation alone, uncontrolled by natural selection, would result in the breakdown and eventual extinction of life, not in the adaptive or progressive evolution."[51] Similar is the position of Francisco Ayala, who strives in addition to explain in more detail the nature of natural selection. Defined as differential reproduction, dependent on differential survival, mating success, fecundity, and survival of offspring, natural selection is determined by the environment. At the same time, having been trained in classical philosophy, Ayala notes and emphasizes that natural selection is not only a purely negative mechanistic end-directed process that promotes the useful and gets rid of harmful mutants increasing thus reproductive efficiency. Quite to the contrary:

[It] is able to generate novelty by increasing the probability of otherwise extremely improbable genetic combinations. Natural selection is creative in a way. It does not "create" the genetic entities upon which it operates, but it produces adaptive genetic combinations which would not have existed otherwise. (...) Natural selection is teleological in the sense that it produces and maintains end-directed organs and processes, when the function or end-state served by the organ or process contributes to the reproductive fitness of the organisms.[52]

Hence, continues Ayala, while "The overall process of evolution cannot be said to be teleological in the sense of proceeding towards certain specified goals," still, in reference to functional characteristics of various parts of organisms, we must acknowledge that:

A teleological explanation implies that the system under consideration is directively organized. For that reason, teleological explanations are appropriate in biology. (...) Moreover, and most importantly, teleological explanations imply that the end result is the explanatory reason for the existence of the object or process which serves or leads to it. A teleological account of the gills of fish implies that gills came to existence precisely because they serve for respiration.[53]

Consequently, Ayala maintains that "teleological explanations in biology are not only acceptable but indeed indispensable," which finds

---

[51] Theodosius Dobzhansky, *Genetics of the Evolutionary Process* (New York: Columbia University Press, 1970), 65.

[52] Francisco J. Ayala, "Teleological Explanations in Evolutionary Biology," in *Nature's Purposes. Analyses of Function and Design in Biology*, ed. Colin Allen, Marc Bekoff, and George Lauder (Cambridge, MA/London: A Bradford Book/The MIT Press, 1998), 35, 41.

[53] *Ibid.*, 44.

Contemporary Debate on Teleology 113

further support in the opinion of Michael Ruse who testifies saying that "Purpose in evolution is obviously alive and well and mixing in the best circles!"[54]

This attempt to legitimize teleology was criticized by Mayr, for whom teleology is equivalent to goal-directedness implying a sort of "backwards causation," that is, causal activity of a future goal on the present situation, which he thinks is not acceptable in Neo-Darwinism. He finds teleological notions in biology to be vitalistic, incompatible with modern mechanistic explanation and "mentalistic."[55] For these reasons, he suggests replacing teleology with "teleonomy" and "teleomatics." He defines the former term as a process or behavior "that owes its goal directedness to the operation of a program." The latter one refers in his view to "processes that reach an end-state caused by natural laws."[56] However, it turns out that the explanatory power of the proposed cybernetic replacements for teleology is doubtful. For who, one may ask, is the author of a "program" operating toward goal-directedness? As notes Terrence Deacon "The major problem with the term *teleonomy* is its implicit agnosticism with respect to the nature of the mechanism that exhibits this property."[57] The question of the ground and source of natural and

---

[54] Michael Ruse, *Darwin and Design: Does Evolution Have a Purpose?* (Cambridge (Mass.): Harvard University Press, 2003), 286. Ayala further distinguishes between "internal" (natural end-directedness) and "external" (product of purposeful activity) teleology. He also talks about "determinate" (end-state reached in spite of environmental fluctuations, for example, physiological or developmental homeostasis), and "indeterminate" (end-state as a result of a selection of one from among several alternatives) teleology. See Ayala, "Teleological Explanations in Evolutionary Biology," 43; Francisco J. Ayala, "Teleological Explanations," in *Philosophy of Biology*, ed. Michael Ruse (New York, MacMillan Publishing Company, 1989), 190.

[55] See Ernst Mayr, "The Multiple Meanings of Teleological," in *Toward a New Philosophy of Biology: Observations of an Evolutionist* (Cambridge, Mass.: Harvard University Press, 1989), 38–66.

[56] Ernst Mayr, "Teleological and Teleonomic: A New Analysis," in *Evolution and the Diversity of Life. Selected Essays* (Cambridge, MA/London: The Belknap Press of Harvard University Press, 1976), 387–90, 403. Mayr compares his idea of operational program in nature with a computer program: "The purposive action of an individual, insofar as it is based on the properties of its genetic code, therefore is no more nor less purposive than the actions of a computer that has been programmed to respond appropriately to various inputs. It is, if I may say so, a purely mechanistic purposiveness" (Ernst Mayr, *Toward a New Philosophy of Biology. Observations of an Evolutionist* [Cambridge, MA/London: Harvard University Press, 1988], 31).

[57] Terrence W. Deacon, *Incomplete Nature: How Mind Emerged from Matter* (New York: W. W. Norton, 2012), 121. Mayr seems to forget about the fact that the computer program has its conscious designer. His analogy begs a question of the source of the properties of the genetic code.

114   *Natural Selection, Teleology, and Chance in Evolution*

intrinsic goal-directedness is simply replaced by the one concerning the ground and source of a "program."

Moreover, Mayr's objection about the alleged causal activity of future goals with reference to the present is an outcome of his misunderstanding and misrepresenting of the classical view of causation. He seems to share it with Pittendrigh, who coined the term "teleonomy." In his letter to Mayr, Pittendrigh says: "Teleology in its Aristotelian form has, of course, the end as immediate, 'efficient', cause. And this is precisely what the biologist (...) cannot accept."[58] What we find here is a clear example of the post-Humean reduction of the complex fourfold Aristotelian notion of causality to the efficient cause alone. If an end-state operated simply as an efficient cause, we would have no reason to speak about final causality at all. Unfortunately, it seems that even Ayala succumbs to this type of reductionism at one point, when, in his response to Mayr's critique, he follows Ernst Nagel saying that "Teleological explanations can be reformulated, without loss of explicit content, to take the form of nonteleological ones."[59]

Current Status of Teleology

The most recent philosophy of biology offers a more nuanced albeit critical approach to the notion of teleology and its importance in evolutionary theory. On the one hand we find "teleonaturalists" who claim that references to teleology in biological explanation are burdened with the error of anthropomorphism. According to them, the category of finality (purposefulness) is appropriate for psychology, social sciences (e.g., sociology), and economics, where it grounds the language of motivational and functional explanations. In case of biology, following Mayr, we can speak at most about quasi-purposeful character of teleonomy, defined as

---

[58] Colin S. Pittendrigh, "Adaptation, Natural Selection and Behavior," in *Behavior and Evolution*, ed. Anne Roe and George Gaylord Simpson (New Haven, CT: Yale University Press, 1958), 390–419 (quotation after Mayr, *Teleological*, 392n1). His idea was also picked up by George Christopher Williams. See his *Adaptation and Natural Selection: A Critique of Some Current Evolutionary Thought* (Princeton: Princeton University Press, 1966).

[59] Ayala, *Teleological*, 43. Nagel states that "teleological explanations are fully compatible with causal accounts. (...) Indeed, a teleological explanation can always be transformed into a causal one." By "causal explanation" he means an explanation in terms of efficient causes. See Ernst Nagel, "Types of Causal Explanation in Science," in *Cause and Effect*, ed. D. Lerner (New York: Free Press, 1965), 24–5. See also the criticism of Ayala in Walsh, "Teleology," 123.

Contemporary Debate on Teleology

a process of actualization of a specific (genetic) program. Otherwise, the explanation in life sciences should be mechanistic.

On the other hand, there are those who think that, due to the specificity of entities, phenomena, and processes studied in biology, Hempel-Oppenheim models of explanation are replaced in it not only by genetic-historical and structural (based on the analysis of parts within a whole) but also functional and teleological types of explanation.[60] They claim that our study of living systems should take into account goal-directedness. Natural and normative, yet free from anthropomorphism, it manifests in keeping homeostasis and producing offspring.

These two approaches are noticeable in the debate on functional explanation. According to Robert Cummins, functional explanations boil down to definitions of the role of a given disposition (power) or organ in the functioning of a living system taken as an integral whole. Grounded in the structural model of explanation, it is referred to as the "causal" concept of function, free from any teleological overtones. Cummins's ideas about functional analysis have been incorporated in more recent discussion on mechanisms in the biological sciences. For instance, Carl Craver draws on Cummins in his argument for moving teleological descriptions down to the molecular level.[61] According to the alternative "etiological" concept of function developed by Larry Wright, the presence of a given feature or organ should be explained in relation to the evolutionary process of its formation – an approach he describes as neo-teleological, that is, defined in terms of naturalized teleology.[62]

---

[60] Hume's radical causal skepticism led to the rejection and replacement of causal explanation with deductive-nomological and inductive-statistical (probabilistic) models of explanation in science, developed by Hempel-Oppenheim. The former, deductive-nomological model, indicates a general law or set of laws (explanans) that can be applied, in a given set of conditions, to the phenomenon that is being explained (explanandum). The latter, inductive-statistical (probabilistic) model, admits laws of a statistical (probabilistic) nature. See Carl G. Hempel and Paul Oppenheim, "Studies in the Logic of Explanation," *Philosophy of Science* 15, no. 2 (1948): 135–75.

[61] See Robert Cummins, "Functional Analysis," *Journal of Philosophy* 72, no. November (1975): 741–64; Carl F. Craver, "Functions and Mechanisms: A Perspectivalist View," in *Functions: Selection and Mechanisms*, ed. Philippe Huneman (Dordrecht: Springer, 2013), 133–58.

[62] See Larry Wright, "Functions," *Philosophical Review* 82, no. 2 (1973): 139–68; Larry Wright, *Teleological Explanations: An Etiological Analysis of Goals and Functions* (Berkeley: University of California Press, 1976).

For more on the debate concerning teleology and function in contemporary philosophy of biology see Colin Allen and Jacob Neal, "Teleological Notions in Biology," in *Stanford Encyclopedia of Philosophy*, ed. Edward N. Zalta (Stanford University, 2020), https://plato.stanford.edu/archives/spr2020/entries/teleology-biology/ (retrieved 20 July

Among those in favor of teleological explanations, apart from scholars pursuing important historical studies, including those presented above, in section on Darwin as teleologist,[63] we find others who strive to defend and redefine teleology in the context of contemporary evolutionary biology. In his chapter on teleology in *The Oxford Handbook of Philosophy of Biology*, Denis Walsh offers an answer to the three standard objections concerning teleological explanations:

1) To the argument of the backward causation of nonfactual future states of affairs, he answers that it is *goal-directedness*, as an intrinsic property of a system, and not unactualized goals, that explains the presence of traits in an organism.

2) To the argument that all teleological explanations require intentionality, he answers that, for Aristotle, teleology is present in both nonrational and rational nature. Intentionality is not necessary to apply a teleological explanation.

3) To the argument that all teleological explanations appear to have normative import, he answers that "Teleology does not require a category of value-bearing goal states; it only requires goal-directedness."[64]

Walsh recognizes the immanent, naturalistic, and functional character of Aristotle's teleology (in opposition to its anthropocentric, transcendent, and creationist version found in Plato). He finds an irreducible example of this immanence in the adaptiveness and phenotypic

---

2022); Colin Allen, Marc Bekoff, and George Lauder, eds., *Nature's Purposes: Analyses of Function and Design in Biology* (Cambridge, Mass: A Bradford Book, 1998); Walsh, "Teleology"; Mark Perlman, "The Modern Philosophical Resurrection of Teleology," in *Philosophy of Biology: An Anthology*, ed. Alex Rosenberg and Robert Arp (Oxford: Blackwell, 2010), 149–63; Marjorie Grene and David J. Depew, *The Philosophy of Biology: An Episodic History* (Cambridge and New York: Cambridge University Press, 2004), 313–21; Alex Rosenberg and Daniel W. McShea, *Philosophy of Biology: A Contemporary Introduction* (New York, NY: Routledge, 2008), 87–93; Sober, *Philosophy of Biology*, 83–88; Peter Godfrey-Smith, "A Modern History Theory of Functions," in *Philosophy of Biology: An Anthology*, ed. Alex Rosenberg and Robert Arp (Oxford: Blackwell, 2010), 175–88.

[63] See also Allan Gotthelf's detailed study of teleology in Aristotle: *Teleology, First Principles, and Scientific Method in Aristotle's Biology*; Allan Gotthelf and James G. Lennox, eds., *Philosophical Issues in Aristotle's Biology* (Cambridge: Cambridge University Press, 1987), and James G. Lennox, *Aristotle's Philosophy of Biology*.

[64] Wash, "Teleology," 116–21. I have said above that normativity is an integral part of teleological explanations. Walsh reacts against the argument that it must necessarily refer to some consciously accepted norms, defending thus teleological notions in biology against the charge of anthropocentrism.

Contemporary Debate on Teleology

plasticity of organisms, which is manifested in their self-organizing goal-directedness and capacity to make compensatory changes to form or physiology during their lifetime (e.g., acclimatization or immune response). On the level of evolutionary changes, lineages undergo selection to thus become ever more suited to the conditions of their environment. Walsh shows that the Darwinian process of iterated mutations and selection does not provide a satisfactory explanation for adaptive evolution. A careful observer notices that the explanatory role of phenotypic plasticity brings back a genuine Aristotelian teleology. It gives a reason why organisms of one species resemble one another, despite genetic variations and environmental influences. It also illuminates Aristotle's idea of hypothetical necessity, by showing that alterations to development are hypothetically necessary for the continued existence of an organism in its environment.[65]

In his approach to teleology, Walsh is by no means an isolated thinker. Mark Perlman in his article entitled "The Modern Philosophical Resurrection of Teleology," presents a very clear and systematic description of the actual views on teleology in evolutionary biology and philosophy of biology. He distinguishes between nonnaturalistic, quasi-naturalistic, and naturalistic explanations of finality in nature. He categorizes both Aristotle's teleological explanation and teleological explanations proposed by the science of emergent properties as quasi-naturalistic. In opposition to these quasi-naturalistic theories, he classifies naturalistic theories as those that strive to reduce teleology to a present, past, or future functional analysis. Perlman ascribes to Aristotle's teleology a quasi-naturalistic character due to some commentators (e.g., Aquinas, *ST*, I, 6, 1, ad 2) who would say that acting for an end means achieving the "good." For someone who does not acknowledge the existence of natural values, this statement may seem nonnatural. However, in light of my former comments on the type of normativity required for teleology, it becomes clear that Aristotelian teleology can be treated as a fully natural phenomenon.[66]

---

[65] See *Ibid.*, 128–32. For more on Aristotle's final cause in relation to other types of causality in philosophical analysis of living systems see Gotthelf, "Aristotle's Concept of Final Causality."

[66] See Mark Perlman, "The Modern Philosophical Resurrection of Teleology," 152–53. Another attempt at developing a contemporary interpretation of teleology may be found in William Wallace who distinguishes three different meanings of the word "end": (1) terminus, that is, a moment when an action stops (e.g., a terminus of a natural fall of an object, or a chemical reaction reaching equilibrium); (2) higher level of perfection of a nonliving or living entity, reached in a natural process (e.g., a certain configuration of a

118   *Natural Selection, Teleology, and Chance in Evolution*

The rediscovery of this naturalistic character of Aristotle's notion of goal-directedness inspires a number of contemporary biologists and philosophers of biology to provide accounts of teleology that go along with the theory of evolution by natural selection and map some of Darwin's observations on this topic. Apart from Francisco Ayala (whose thought I have discussed above), we may think about George Ch. Williams, William Wimsatt, Ruth G. Millikan, Karen Neander, Robert N. Brandon, and Harry Binswanger.[67]

Natural Selection as Teleological?

Our analysis so far shows that those who argue in favor of teleology in the context of the contemporary evolutionary synthesis usually invoke natural selection explicitly when explaining functional claims, either in an etiological sense, based on the history of selection, or in a dispositional sense, based on the fitness of organisms possessing the traits. Hence, we might say that, following Ayala, they see natural selection as teleological. But this interpretation does not come without a challenge.

Most importantly, the concept of natural selection itself has been criticized as tautology. It is claimed that it falls into tautology when we formulate it as follows: those that survive are the fittest, and the fittest are those that survive. The problem arises from a casual inspection of the phrase "survival of the fittest" and then asking what defines the fittest. If the answer is those that reproduce the most, then it seems we are explaining a phenomenon, differential reproduction, in terms of itself, which is

---

chemical compound, which makes it fitting for becoming a building block of an organic substance, or a higher survival rate of an organism, reached through the process of chance mutation and natural selection); (3) intention or aim (proper for cognitive agents: animals and humans). See William A. Wallace, *The Modeling of Nature: Philosophy of Science and Philosophy of Nature in Synthesis* (Washington, DC: Catholic University of America Press, 1996), 15–18.

[67] See respectively Williams, *Adaptation and Natural Selection*; William C. Wimsatt, "Teleology and the Logical Structure of Function Statements," *Studies in History and Philosophy of Science* Part A 3, no. 1 (1972): 1–80; Robert N. Brandon, "Biological Teleology: Questions and Explanations," *Studies in History and Philosophy of Science* Part A 12, no. 2 (June 1, 1981): 91–105; Ruth Garrett Millikan, *Language, Thought, and Other Biological Categories: New Foundations for Realism* (Cambridge, Mass: MIT Press, 1984); Karen Neander, "Functions as Selected Effects: The Conceptual Analyst's Defense," *Philosophy of Science* 58, no. 2 (1991): 168–84; Robert N. Brandon, *Adaptation and Environment* (Princeton, N.J Chichester: Princeton University Press, 1995); Harry Binswanger, *The Biological Basis of Teleological Concepts* (Los Angeles, CA: TOF Publications, Inc., 1990).

Contemporary Debate on Teleology

no explanation at all. The principle of natural selection needs a criterion of fitness, other than survival.[68]

One possible answer to this problem was offered by Michael Ruse. He mentions three points that invalidate the objection. (1) Natural selection depends upon the fact that more offspring are produced than can survive. This is an observation that predates Darwin. (2) There are traits that differ between those members of the population that survive and those that do not. These trait differences can, in fact, be shown to be related to survivability. (3) Successful traits can be shown by experiment to yield like results in like situations. Ruse thinks these three criteria show that the apparent tautology is actually an observational fact of some merit to the Darwinian model.[69]

Another answer to the problem suggests defining fitness as "expected fitness" rather than actual fitness. This is oftentimes described as "propensity approach." As notes Tam Hunt:

The propensity interpretation of fitness allows statements such as: "We expect population A to grow by x percent as a result of a y percent increase in seed stock." The "x percent growth" prediction is the "expected fitness" of population A. This re-framing allows a definition of (testable) natural selection as follows: *Natural selection is a theory that predicts differential survival and reproduction of organisms with the highest expected fitness.*[70]

The propensity interpretation may indeed save natural selection from tautology because "expected fitness" does not reduce to "survival." The former is defined as a theoretical expectation, while the latter is defined

---

[68] This argument has been raised by many. See, for example, Samuel Butler, *Evolution: Old and New*. London: Boque, 1882; T. H. Morgan saying "For it may be little more than a truism to state that the individuals that are best adapted to survive have a better chance of surviving than those not so well adapted to survive" (quoted in Tom Bechtel, "Darwin's Mistake" *Harper's* 252:1509 [1976], 72); C. H. Waddington, *Evolution after Darwin* (Chicago: University of Chicago Press, 1960); Norman Macbeth, *Darwin Retried: An Appeal to Reason* (Boston: Gambit, 1971); Alexander Rosenberg and Frederic Bouchard, "Fitness," in *The Stanford Encyclopedia of Philosophy*, (Spring 2020 Edition), https://plato.stanford.edu/cgi-bin/encyclopedia/archinfo.cgi?entry=fitness&archive=spr2020 (retrieved 20 July 2022).

[69] See Michael Ruse, *Taking Darwin Seriously: A Naturalistic Approach to Philosophy* (Amherst, N.Y.: Prometheus Books, 1998), 24.

[70] Tam Hunt, "Reconsidering the Logical Structure of the Theory of Natural Selection," *Communicative & Integrative Biology* 7, no. 6 (2014): e972848. The propensity argument was developed by Robert N. Brandon and Grant Ramsey in "What's Wrong with the Emergentist Statistical Interpretation of Natural Selection and Random Drift," in *The Cambridge Companion to the Philosophy of Biology*, ed. David L. Hull and Michael Ruse (Cambridge University Press, 2007), 66–84.

120   *Natural Selection, Teleology, and Chance in Evolution*

based on empirical observation. However, this move comes at the price of "expected fitness" becoming simply the biologist's tool for making predictions about expected evolution in actual organisms or populations, rather than some property that inheres in organisms or populations. This may speak in favor of the argument that in biology, we do not observe laws of nature such as those captured in physics or in chemistry.[71]

Moreover, classically oriented metaphysics asks even deeper question about the status of the laws of nature and science as such. Here, we may refer to William Stoeger who, as both a physicist and theologian, emphasized on numerous occasions that the laws of nature are epistemological descriptions rather than ontological prescriptions:

---

[71] Frost notes that "Many believe that the notion of a law of nature is a post-medieval concept invented by Descartes. Research has shown, however, that there were medieval figures such as Robert Grosseteste and Roger Bacon who discussed general laws that govern natural causation and prioritized these laws of nature over the immanent features of material substances (e.g. active forms) in causal explanations of natural events" (Frost, *Aquinas*, 31).

Some claim that it is impossible to formulate any general laws in biology. Although it does introduce many generalizations, they do not seem to meet the criteria of scientific laws, due to multiple exceptions (based on the evolutionary variability of biological structures) and the limitation of their scope in space and time (the historical aspect of biological sciences). See Pierre-Alain Braillard and Christophe Malaterre, eds., *Explanation in Biology: An Enquiry into the Diversity of Explanatory Patterns in the Life Sciences* (Dordrecht: Springer, 2015), 9–14; Michel Morange, "Is There an Explanation for ... the Diversity of Explanations in Biological Studies?," in *Explanation in Biology: An Enquiry into the Diversity of Explanatory Patterns in the Life Sciences*, ed. Pierre-Alain Braillard and Christophe Malaterre (Dordrecht: Springer, 2015), 31–46.

Even those generalizations in biology that have acquired the status of scientific laws become problematic for the Hempel-Oppenheim models. For example, the central dogma of molecular biology saying that biological information always flows in one direction from DNA, through RNA to protein, does not seem to meet the conditions of a universal law of science. This becomes clear once we consider: (1) the possibility of copying information from RNA to RNA (RNA replication); (2) the possibility of DNA synthesis from the RNA template (so-called reverse transcription); (3) the possibility of protein synthesis directly from the DNA template, excluding mRNA; and (4) the phenomenon of prions, that is proteins with specific structure that replicate in the host cell by introducing configurational (conformational) changes in other proteins with the same amino acid sequence. However, the situation changes if the central dogma is defined as the principle saying that once the information has been conveyed and translated into a protein, it cannot be transferred (rewritten) to another protein or nucleic acid (Francis Crick formulated it along these lines already in 1957). This formulation may allow for special transfers described in points 1–3. At the same time, the transfer of biological information from protein to protein in the case of prions is indeed an exception that does not allow us to classify the central dogma as a law of science in the strict sense of the Hempel-Oppenheim models.

Contemporary Debate on Teleology 121

Although the laws of nature reveal and describe fundamental patterns of behavior and regularities in the world, we cannot consider them the source of those regularities, much less attribute them the physical necessity these regularities seem to manifest. Nor can we ascribe to them an existence independent of the reality whose behavior they describe. Instead I claim that they are imperfect abstract descriptions of physical phenomena, not prescriptions dictating or enforcing behavior. Thus, a Platonic interpretation of these laws is unjustified.[72]

Indeed, according to Aristotle's moderate realism, the universe is what it is because of the natures of things that are present in it. Scientific laws and laws of nature that we name describe the reality, tracing regularities related to the phenomena of stability and changeability of things. Hence, the law (principle) of natural selection reveals and describes the regularity of a greater reproduction success of organisms that are better fitted in their environment. Yet, it does not causally make them to be such or to reach reproduction success. Consequently, teleology – indispensable for evolutionary transitions – is not so much "located" or grounded in natural selection but rather in organisms that strive to survive and produce fertile offspring. This observation becomes a substantial contribution of the classical metaphysics to our contemporary understanding and interpretation of evolutionary theory.[73] As such, it more recently finds support in the position of Moreno and Mossio, who emphasize that

---

[72] William R. Stoeger, "Contemporary Physics and the Ontological Status of the Laws of Nature," in *Quantum Mechanics: Scientific Perspectives on Divine Action*, ed. Robert J. Russell et al. (Berkeley, CA: Vatican Observatory & Center for Theology and the Natural Sciences, 2001), 208.

[73] See also Antonio Moreno, "Finality and Intelligibility in Biological Evolution," *The Thomist* 54, no. 1 (1990): 1–31. Already in 1917 I. W. Howerth notes that the phrase "survival of the fittest" – introduced by Herbert Spencer, favored by Alfred Russell Wallace (as avoiding apparent danger of personification of nature in the use of the phrase "natural selection"), and eventually (albeit reluctantly) accepted by Darwin in the fifth and sixth editions of *On the Origin of Species* – is not, as all pioneers of the evolutionary theory mentioned here assumed, identical in meaning and interchangeable with Darwin's originally defined rule. He suggests that "natural selection is a process while the survival of the fittest is a result; the one is a principle of limited application, the other a universal law. Natural selection would obviously be powerless without something to select and something to reject and, although the selection is unconscious, it implies also a mode of selection. Natural selection, then, involves, first, a plurality of objects to select from, and these are presented in the organic world through the immense fertility of living things" (I. W. Howerth, "Natural Selection and the Survival of the Fittest," *The Scientific Monthly* 5, no. 3 [1917], 254). Moreover, Howerth points out that selection may be both artificial and natural, yet "the law of the survival of the fittest applies to artificial selection as well as to natural selection. It is universal. The fittest always survive." As such, this law "is as rigid as the law of gravitation" (*ibid.*, 256). Naturally, Stoeger's

122   *Natural Selection, Teleology, and Chance in Evolution*

[E]volutionary mechanisms operate because they are embodied in the complex organization of organisms. Thus, if we look for the roots of the impressive capacity of life to proliferate, to create an enormous variety of forms, to adapt to completely different environments, and particularly, to increase its complexity, we shall focus on individual living entities, namely on organisms, because evolution as an explanatory mechanism actually presupposes the existence of organisms.[74]

Interestingly, this observation seems to find confirmation in the contemporary research on the explanatory and causal interconnectedness between evolution and development (evo-devo, i.e., evolutionary developmental biology), which studies how the dynamics of development determine phenotypic variation that arises from genetic variation, and how this, in turn, affects phenotypic evolution. As already mentioned in the Introduction, the discovery that differences in genetic make-up may lead to differences in development while the differences in development may lead to genetic changes shows how considerably different organisms "use" the same genes in various ways to produce different phenotypes. This definitely shows that natural selection is not as important as the gene-centered emphasis of the contemporary

observation still applies. The law in question is descriptive, rather than prescriptive, as it depends on the existence and operation of intrinsically goal-directed (directed towards survival) (teleological) organisms.

This understanding of teleology might be referred to Immanuel Kant's *Critique of Teleological Judgement*, in which he reverts to the original Aristotelian notion of goal-directedness as related to creature itself, and not to God's intentions to bring about humankind. Kant says that that an organism is "both cause and effect of itself" (Immanuel Kant, *Critique of the Power of Judgment*, ed. Paul Guyer, trans. Eric Matthews and Paul Guyer [Cambridge: Cambridge University Press, 2002], §64, 371).

[74] Moreno and Mossio, *Biological Autonomy*, xxi–xxii. Earlier on, in 1979, Francisco J. Varela argued that "evolutionary thought, through its emphasis on diversity, reproduction, and the species in order to explain the dynamics of change, has obscured the necessity of looking at the autonomous nature of living units for the understanding of biological phenomenology" (Francisco J. Varela, *Principles of Biological Autonomy* [New York: North Holland, 1979], 5). Chiu states that "From the EES [Extended Evolutionary Synthesis] perspective, evolutionary theory should be a theory of phenotypic evolution ... The EES is a research program centered on organisms as the core causes of the evolution of their phenotypes" (Chiu, *Extended*, 45, 46). Even more acute is the opinion expressed by Robert Rosen who states, "We cannot answer the question (...) 'Why is a machine alive' with the answer 'Because its ancestors were alive'. Pedigrees, lineages, genealogies, and the like, are quite irrelevant to the basic question. Ever more insistently over the past century, and never more so than today, we hear the argument that biology *is* evolution; that living systems instantiate evolutionary processes rather than life; and ironically, that these processes are devoid of entailment, immune to natural law, and hence outside of science completely. To me it is easy to conceive life, and hence biology, without evolution" (Robert Rosen, *Life Itself: A Comprehensive Inquiry into the Nature, Origin, and Fabrication of Life* [New York: Columbia University Press, 1991], 254–55).

Evolution and the Interplay of Teleology and Chance 123

evolutionary synthesis thought. Similar conclusions can be drawn from the field of epigenetics, which shows that the direction and speed of evolutionary changes depend not only on selection (gene frequency) but also on various circumstances and environmental factors that may induce changes in hormonal system of an organism, having a causal impact on which genes are available and how they are expressed (e.g., activating previously hidden genetic variations).[75]

We may thus refer to Scott Gilbert, John Opitz, and Rudolf Raff, who stated, already in 1996: "Thus, the evidence for evolution is better than ever. The role of natural selection in evolution, however, is seen to play less an important role. It is merely a filter for unsuccessful morphologies generated by development. Population genetics is destined to change if it is not to become as irrelevant to evolution as Newtonian mechanics is to contemporary physics."[76] An even earlier constatation made by Mivart is surprisingly relevant here as well:

[I]t seems that the origin of a new species must be due, first, to the inherent nature of the parent organism, responding in definite ways to the action of the environment; secondly, to the surrounding influences which stimulate such action; and thirdly, to the destructive forces which eliminate variations exceeding the bounds of physiological propriety. These two latter agencies are, however, but the occasions and the limitations of variations which must be due above all to the inner nature of the organism itself.[77]

EVOLUTION AND THE INTERPLAY OF TELEOLOGY AND CHANCE

The question of teleology and the character of natural selection is usually accompanied by the further question concerning the role and nature of chance in evolutionary processes. Going back to Darwin, we find him first, in one of his letters, torn between the extreme positions of attributing everything to a "blind" chance or to a direct supernatural divine action of the Creator (design as understood by William Paley): "I cannot look at the Universe as the result of blind chance, yet I can see no evidence of beneficent design, or indeed of design of any kind in the details."[78] A deeper

---

[75] See Jablonka and Lamb, *Evolution in Four Dimensions*, Chapter 7.

[76] S. F. Gilbert, J. M. Opitz, and R. A. Raff, "Resynthesizing Evolutionary and Developmental Biology," *Developmental Biology* 173, no. 2 (1996), 368.

[77] St. George Jackson Mivart, "Darwin's Brilliant Fallacy," *The Forum* 7 (1889), 102.

[78] Charles Darwin, "Letter no. 7273," in *Correspondence Project*, www.darwinproject .ac.uk/letter/DCP-LETT-7273.xml (retrieved 20 July 2021).

124   *Natural Selection, Teleology, and Chance in Evolution*

insight into his views on chance shows that he did not see it as the first cause of all changes in nature, including evolutionary transitions. In his *On the Origin of Species,* we find him saying:

Mere chance, as we may call it, might cause one variety to differ in some character from its parents, and the offspring of this variety again to differ from its parent in the very same character and in a greater degree; but this alone would never account for so habitual and large an amount of difference as that between varieties of the same species and species of the same genus.[79]

I have hitherto sometimes spoken as if the variations – so common and multiform in organic beings under domestication, and in a lesser degree in those in a state of nature – had been due to chance. This, of course, is a wholly incorrect expression, but it serves to acknowledge plainly our ignorance of the cause of each particular variation.[80]

The second quotation does not mean, in my opinion, that Darwin thought chance was merely epistemological. Rather, taken together with other quoted passages, it shows that he was aware of the fact that ontologically real chance events that produce minor variations remain in a synergy with the regularity and teleological character of life cycles and transmission of features between generations. This allows for the accumulation of accidental changes that may lead, in extended periods of time, to speciation. To put the same argument in Aristotelian terms, we may say that although mutations are truly unpredictable and occur by chance, they have a *per accidens* character in reference to the *per se* cause of living beings that strive to survive and produce offspring. The acceptance of this plural notion of causality helps us understand that the absence of a direct efficient cause of mutations does not exclude other kinds of causality from being active. Aristotle's philosophy of nature reminds us that we need to take formal and final causality into account in our attempt to explain the nature of evolutionary changes.

Consequently, it seems to me that Darwin would be utterly surprised with the famous utterance of Jacques Monod saying that:

It necessarily follows that chance alone is at the source of every innovation, and of all creation in the biosphere. Pure chance, absolutely free but blind, at the very root of the stupendous edifice of evolution: this central concept of modern biology is no longer one among many other possible or even conceivable hypotheses. It is today the sole conceivable hypothesis, the only one that squares with

---

[79] Charles Darwin, *On the Origin of Species,* 111.
[80] *Ibid.,* 131.

Conclusion   125

observed and tested fact. And nothing warrants the supposition – or the hope – that on this score our position is ever likely to be revised.[81]

In the light of what I have said about teleology and natural selection, it becomes clear that evolution cannot be attributed to blind chance, which would actually mean giving up the possibility to explain reality. It is possible that Darwin shared and, at least indirectly, expressed a similar intuition.[82]

CONCLUSION

The world is full of teleological dimensions. When we search for them, we can easily see that virtually any of the main aspects of our world can be taken as a particular case of teleology. Although this holds especially for living beings, the physicochemical world also exhibits many directional features that acquire a special meaning when seen as necessary conditions for the existence of living beings. Directionality indicates the existence of tendencies toward goals, which is the hallmark of natural teleology. ... It is not difficult to find examples of directionality and cooperativity. If we begin with the most elementary components of the world, we find out that subatomic particles and the four basic interactions behave according to well-known specific patterns and collaborate to build up successive levels of organization – atoms, molecules, macromolecules, and the bigger inorganic and organic beings. The entire construction of our world is the result of the deployment of tendencies that collaborate to make up unitary systems.[83]

This quotation from Mariano Artigas shows that the history of the philosophical notion of teleology has gone a full circle. Discovered and defined

---

[81] Jacques Monod, *Chance and Necessity: An Essay on the Natural Philosophy of Modern Biology*, trans. Austryn Wainhouse (New York: Vintage Books, 1970), 112.

[82] Anticipating the second part of this volume which will be dedicated to theology, I find fitting the opinion of the International Theological Commission shared in the document *Communion and Stewardship*: "In the Catholic perspective, neo-Darwinians who adduce random genetic variation and natural selection as evidence that the process of evolution is absolutely unguided are straying beyond what can be demonstrated by science. Divine causality can be active in a process that is *both* contingent and guided. Any evolutionary mechanism that is contingent can only be contingent because God made it so. An unguided evolutionary process – one that falls outside the bounds of divine providence – simply cannot exist because "the causality of God, Who is the first agent, extends to all being, not only as to constituent principles of species, but also as to the individualizing principles. ... It necessarily follows that all things, inasmuch as they participate in existence, must likewise be subject to divine providence" (*Summa theologiae* I, 22, 2)" (International Theological Commission, *Communion and Stewardship: Human Persons Created in the Image of God* [Vatican City: Libreria Editrice Vaticana, 2004], no. 28).

[83] Mariano Artigas, *The Mind of the Universe: Understanding Science and Religion* (Philadelphia: Templeton Foundation Press, 2000), 129.

126   *Natural Selection, Teleology, and Chance in Evolution*

in ancient philosophy, further developed and commented on throughout the Middle Ages, closely tightened to the argument from design (at least in some circles) around the time of the scientific revolution, rejected and denied in modernity and the first part of the twentieth century, it has a moderate revival in the most recent philosophy of biology, including its reflection in the theory of evolution. Understood along the line of reasoning developed by Aristotle as a natural intrinsic principle of each entity, and referred to randomness and chance, it becomes an indispensable aspect of the framework that grounds the metaphysical analysis of evolutionary transitions presented in the previous chapters. Hence, we may conclude the present chapter with one more observation, this time coming from Walsh who states:

> The "Aristotelian purge" was seen as a pivotal achievement of early modern science. As a consequence of the scientific revolution, the natural sciences learned to live without teleology. Current evolutionary biology, I contend, demonstrates that quite the opposite lesson needs now to be learned. The understanding of how evolution can be *adaptive* requires us to incorporate teleology – issuing from the goal-directed, adaptive plasticity of organisms – as a legitimate scientific form of explanation. The natural sciences must, once again, learn to live with teleology.[84]

This remark closes the first part of the book, addressing philosophical (ontological and metaphysical) aspects of evolutionary theory. The remaining second part will begin with the investigation of some crucial aspects of the classical theology of creation (Chapter 4). Their analysis will serve as a point of departure for a theological interpretation of evolution developed in the remaining Chapters 5–8.

[84] Walsh, "Teleology," 133.

4

Aquinas's Account of Creation

Aquinas's teaching on creation provides a good example of his intellectual skills, revealing the considerable clarity and consistency of his philosophical theology and proving the effectiveness of his method. The secret of this method is very simple: Aquinas never leaves philosophy behind him. Rather, he constantly holds to it as an indispensable conceptual tool for any theological reflection. Therefore, it is not a coincidence that Thomas does not begin his treatise on creation with an analysis of the account of the cosmogony in Genesis. To interpret it properly, one must be equipped with the right philosophical terminology. That is why Aquinas first explains the nature of *creatio ex nihilo* from the perspective of metaphysics. He points to the necessary distinction between creation and change, which helps him differentiate the three main stages of the work of the six days as depicted in his commentary on the *Hexameron* in the *Summa theologiae*. The same philosophical approach to the doctrine of creation makes Augustine's notion of *rationes seminales* appealing to Aquinas. All these provide the necessary ground to propose a Thomistic theological interpretation of the theory of evolution, which I will develop in the remaining chapters of this book (5–8).

The analysis of Aquinas' notion of creation presented in this chapter will begin with a reference to Augustine's interpretation of Genesis in which he introduces the concept of *rationes seminales*, and an attempt at specifying the meaning of this term in his work. Next, I will critically evaluate the interpretation of Augustine's notion of creation as evolutionary. The central part of this chapter opens with Aquinas's philosophical theology of creation. I will, first, emphasize the importance of *esse* for his understanding of this doctrine. In the next step, I will provide a

128   *Aquinas's Account of Creation*

brief and precise formulation of Aquinas's metaphysical understanding of what creation is and discuss the importance of both *esse* and *essentia* in formulating a comprehensive notion of how creation implies "dependence on God." Moving toward Aquinas's commentary on Genesis in his *Summa theologiae*, I will begin with a short presentation of his distinction of the three stages of the work of the six days. The next two sections will discuss in detail Aquinas's use of Augustine's *rationes seminales* in his analysis of the *Hexameron* and suggest an Aristotelian redefinition of this conceptual tool that will open a way for developing a Thomistic version of theistic evolution. The chapter will end with a short conclusion.

AUGUSTINE'S NOTION OF CREATION

The point of departure for our analysis is the thought of Augustine commenting on the creation accounts in Genesis 1 and 2 in his *De Genesi ad litteram libri duodecim*.[1] Concerning the very act of creation, Augustine clearly states that "God made everything together without any moments of time intervening."[2] Hence, he does not think we should understand literally the six days of the Genesis account: "We should not think of those days as solar days."[3] For how could there be solar days before the sun itself came to be (in the Genesis account it was created on the

---

[1] Ernan McMullin notes: "Twice Augustine attempted a commentary along allegorical lines on the disputed text of Genesis, but he was unsatisfied with the results. Finally in 415 A.D., after fourteen years of labor, he completed the *De Genesi ad litteram*, a detailed study of all the alleged points of conflict according to the 'proper historical meaning', with frequent prescriptions as to how such conflict ought to be handled" ("Introduction: Evolution and Creation," in *Evolution and Creation*, ed. Ernan McMullin [Notre Dame, IN: University of Notre Dame Press, 1986], 1). Among these prescriptions, adds McMullin, one was to bring an attention of future generations, most notably of Galileo. He found inspirational and relevant Augustine's advice that, when conflict arises between a literal reading of the Bible and a truth about nature which has been demonstrated by reliable argument, the Christian should strive to reinterpret the biblical text in a metaphorical way (see *De Gen. ad litt.* 1.21). My account of Augustine's concept of *rationes seminales* follows the one offered by McMullin. See Augustine, *The Literal Meaning of Genesis*, trans. John Hammond Taylor (New York: Newman Press, 1982).

[2] *De Gen. ad litt.* 5.11.

[3] *De Gen. ad litt.* 5.5. Following J. H. Taylor's introduction to the English translation of *De Gen. ad litt.*, McMullin notes: "It ought be noted that Augustine's usage of the term 'literal' was much broader than ours. The 'literal meaning' alluded to in the title of his book, the meaning he searches for so painstakingly, was the meaning intended by the original author. 'Literal' for him was opposed to 'allegorical', not to 'metaphorical'. Thus he could claim that 'day' in the Genesis account clearly had to be taken metaphorically, that this was the author's plain intention. Hence the 'literal' meaning here (in his sense) was the metaphorical one" (McMullin, "Introduction," 50n29).

Augustine's Notion of Creation

fourth day)? At the same time, unlike the contemporary advocates of old earth creationism, he does not extend the ordinary 24-hour days of the creation account in Genesis 1 into much longer periods of time (thousands, millions, or billions of years).[4] Quite to the contrary, he thinks that God's creative act was instantaneous, and that the six days in the biblical description might be interpreted allegorically as referring to the six stages of the angelic knowledge about creation.[5]

[4] Among old-earth creationists we find: (1) gap creationists (ruin-restoration creationists), who think that, although the six-*yom* creation period in Genesis did involve six twenty-four-hours-long days, literally interpreted, there was an extended temporal gap between the two distinct stages of creation (as described respectively in Gen 1:1–2 and 1:3–31); (2) progressive creationists, who, accepting microevolution, think that God created so-called "natural species" (species defined at the level of family or order in the modern classification) through direct divine intervention, yet gradually, over a period of hundreds of millions of years; (3) day-age creationists, who hold that the six days referred to in the Genesis account of creation were not ordinary twenty-four-hour days, but rather were much longer periods (thousands or millions of years); and (4) cosmic time creationists, who, in reference to contemporary physics, consider the period of the six days in the Genesis account under the conditions of quark confinement, when the universe was approximately a trillion times smaller and hotter than it is today, and suggest it is equal to fifteen billion years of earth time today (due to space expansion after quark confinement). Proponents of theistic evolution are oftentimes classified as day-age creationists (3), which is rather inadequate in the case of Augustine and those who follow him in his assertion that creation of the universe was instantaneous. For more information on (1), see Tom McIver, "Formless and Void: Gap Theory Creationism," *Creation/Evolution Journal* 8, no. 3 (1988): 1–24; for more on (2), see Alan Hayward, *Creation and Evolution: Rethinking the Evidence from Science and the Bible* (Ada, Ml: Bethany House, 1985), and Hugh Ross, *A Matter of Days: Resolving a Creation Controversy* (Colorado Springs, CO: NavPress, 2004); for more on (3), see Ronald L. Numbers, *The Creationists: From Scientific Creationism to Intelligent Design*, *Expanded Edition* (Cambridge, MA: Harvard University Press, 2006), chapters 2–4; for more on (4), see Gerald Schroeder, *Genesis and the Big Bang Theory: The Discovery Of Harmony between Modern Science And the Bible* (New York: Bantam, 1990).

[5] As notes Aquinas: "For Augustine understands by the word 'day', the knowledge in the mind of the angels, and hence, according to him, the first day denotes their knowledge of the first of the Divine works, the second day their knowledge of the second work, and similarly with the rest. Thus, then, each work is said to have been wrought in some one of these days, inasmuch as God wrought nothing in the universe without impressing the knowledge thereof on the angelic mind, which can know many things at the same time, especially in the Word, in Whom all angelic knowledge is perfected and terminated. So the distinction of days denotes the natural order of the things known, and not a succession in the knowledge acquired, or in the things produced. Moreover, angelic knowledge is appropriately called 'day', since light, the cause of day, is to be found in spiritual things, as Augustine observes [*De Gen. ad litt.* 4.28]. In the opinion of the others, however, the days signify a succession both in time, and in the things produced" (*ST* I, 74, 2, co.).

McMullin values Augustine's cautiousness and openness for further clarifications of the proper interpretation of the "day" metaphor: "Whoever, then, does not accept the meaning that my limited powers have been able to discover ... let him search and find a solution with God's help" (*De Gen. ad litt.* 4.28).

130   *Aquinas's Account of Creation*

Naturally, Augustine did not think that all things, including Sun, Earth, seas, plants, animals, and so on, came to be fully formed in that first moment. Comparing and contrasting the two creation accounts opening the book of Genesis, he suggests that what were present in the first instant of the existence of the universe were only the "seed-principles" (*rationes seminales*; *logoi spermatikoi* [λόγοι σπερματικοί]) of all natural kinds and that over the history of the universe, God "unfolds the generations which He laid up in creation when He first founded it."[6] In other words, "[God] created all [creatures] together ... whose visible forms He produces through the ages, working even until now."[7]

What inspired Augustine's thesis were not only the metaphysical principles of stoicism and neo-Platonism but also some biblical passages. First, in the Vulgate and, presumably, in the *Vetus Latina* version of the Bible available to Augustine, in the short passage from Sirach 18:1a, we read "Qui vivit in aeternum creavit omnia simul," which translates as "He that liveth for ever created all things together."[8] Secondly, in the same version of the Bible, the passage from Genesis 2:4–5a reads as follows: "Istae sunt generationes caeli et terrae, quando creata sunt, in die quo fecit Dominus Deus caelum et terram, et omne virgultum agri antequam oriretur in terra, omnemque herbam regionis priusquam germinaret." This translates into English as: "These are the generations of the heaven and the earth, when they were created, in the day that the Lord God made the heaven and the earth: and every plant of the field before it sprung up in the earth, and

---

[6] *De Gen. ad litt.* 5.20. Augustine calls *rationes seminales* also *causales rationes, rationes primordiales, primordia causarum,* or *quasi semina futurorum* (see 253n67 in Taylor's translation of *De Gen. ad litt.*).

[7] *De Gen. ad litt.* 5.23. Later on, in book 7, he adds: "The things [that God] had potentially created ... [came] forth in the course of time on different days according to their different kinds ... [and] the rest of the earth [was] filled with its various kinds of creatures, [which] produc[ed] their appropriate forms in due time" (*De Gen. ad litt.* 7.22). When speaking of ontologically defined natural kinds in the context of Augustine's and Aquinas's commentaries on Genesis, we should distinguish them from the notion of biblical created kinds, as there is clearly no one-to-one correspondence between them. I believe that both Augustine's and Aquinas's argumentation (grounded in their non-literal reading of Genesis 1) departs from the latter and aims at being applied also in the context of the former. An additional classification of these and other key categories referred to in the model of creation and evolution proposed in this volume is offered in Chapter 5.

[8] This is the reading of the Douay-Rheims which represents Augustine's understanding of simultaneity in the statement. In The New American Bible, Revised Edition (NABRE), the same passage reads: "He who lives forever created the whole universe." The Greek version in the Septuagint is closer to the older translations, with the Greek *panta* more in its usual sense of "all" or "whole," rather than in the sense of the Latin *simul*: "Ho Zōn eis tōn aiōna ektisev ta panta koinē ['Ο ζῶν εἰς τὸν αἰῶνα ἔκτισεν τὰ πάντα κοινῇ]."

The Meaning of Rationes Seminales

every herb of the ground before it grew."[9] It is commonly accepted that both passages mentioned here inspired Augustine's use of the concept of *rationes seminales* in the context of his commentary on Genesis.

Going back to his work, even if he thought that the first account of creation in Genesis was summarized by the second one, Augustine emphasized the difference between the two descriptions and claimed that the latter referred to the later stage of divine action in the already created universe, bringing about from the primitive matter new kinds of entities (new species), that pre-existed in it as *rationes seminales*. Hence, we may say that for Augustine, all species had been created at once, while their unfolding was (is?) extended in time.[10]

This reading of Genesis, notes McMullin, was not entirely a novel one. The Alexandrine fathers already thought that the universe began from a single divine act and that six days in Genesis 1 should be taken allegorically. Gregory of Nyssa went even further saying that what came to be in the act of creation were the potencies of all that would come later:

The sources, causes, and potencies of all things were collectively sent forth in an instant, and in this first impulse of the Divine Will, the essences of all things assembled together: heaven, aether, star, fire, air, sea, earth, animal, plant – all beheld by the eye of God. ... There followed a certain necessary series according to a certain order ... as nature the maker [*technikē physis* (τεχνικὴ φύσις)] required ... appearing not by chance ... but because the necessary arrangement of nature required succession in the things coming into being.[11]

THE MEANING OF *RATIONES SEMINALES*

But what exactly are *rationes seminales*? They do not seem to be empirically verifiable seeds in the common understanding of the term. They are hidden from our sight. Augustine compares them to the principle

---

[9] Douay-Rheims. In NABRE the same passage reads: "This is the story of the heavens and the earth at their creation. When the LORD God made the earth and the heavens – there was no field shrub on earth and no grass of the field had sprouted." A purely formal-equivalence translation from Hebrew would follow the old translation: "These [are] the generations the heavens and the earth when they are created in the day that Yahweh God made the earth and the heavens, before any plant of the field was in the earth and before any herb of the field had grown" (see biblehub.com/interlinear/genesis/2.htm).

[10] Although he may not state it clearly, we can assume Augustine understood divine action in unfolding of the *rationes seminales* as the activity of God working through contingent (secondary) causes.

[11] Gregory of Nyssa, *Apologia in hexaemeron* (PG, 44:72); quoted by Ernest C. Messenger in *Evolution and Theology: The Problem of Man's Origin* (New York: Macmillan, 1932), 24 (trans. slightly modified).

132   *Aquinas's Account of Creation*

whereby we grow old, which lies in each one of us already when we are young.[12] Even if such a principle cannot be seen by our eyes, "by another kind of knowledge we conclude that there is in nature some hidden force by which latent forms are brought into view."[13] In other words, says Augustine: "There is, indeed, in seeds some likeness to what I am describing, because of the future developments stored up in them. Indeed, it is the seed-principle which is the more basic of the two, since it comes before the familiar seeds we know."[14] Hence, each seminal reason (seed-like principle) is best described as potentiality – a very specific potentiality of a particular and fixed type of entity or natural kind (species). Augustine introduces an analogy of the tree that originates from the seed that itself originates from another tree, noting that they both originate from the Earth:

> In the seed, then, there was invisibly present all that would develop in time into a tree. And in this same way we must picture the world, when God made all things together, as having had all things which were made in it and with it when day was made. This includes not only heaven with sun, moon and stars ... but also the beings which water and earth produced in potency and in their causes before they came forth in the course of time.[15]

And here comes a major difficulty in interpretation. On the one hand, Augustine seems to claim that when the proper conditions are met, gradual and spontaneous unfolding of *rationes seminales* occurs naturally: "All things were created by God in the beginning in a kind of blending of the elements, but they cannot develop and appear until the circumstances are favorable."[16] On the other hand, however, he sometimes tends to interpret Genesis more literally as implying that each new kind originates in its adult form. This, naturally, makes it hard to imagine how an adult form may originate from a seed without going through a normal process of development and growth. Hence, it becomes apparent that such an origin might require a more direct and instantaneous divine intervention.

---

[12] "The principle which makes this development possible is hidden to the eyes but not to the mind; but whether such a development must necessarily come about is completely unknown to us. We know that the principle which makes it possible is in the very nature of body; but there is no clear evidence in that body that there is a principle by which it must necessarily take place" (*De Gen. ad litt.* 6.16).

[13] *De Gen. ad litt.* 6.16.

[14] *De Gen. ad litt.* 6.6.

[15] *De Gen. ad litt.* 5.21.

[16] Augustine, *De Trinitate* 3.9, quoted in Eugène Portalié, *A Guide to the Thought of St. Augustine* (Chicago: Regnery, 1960), 138.

The Meaning of Rationes Seminales 133

Consequently, on the occasion of his analysis of the origin of Adam, Augustine forms a more general assertion that the seed principles might have a double potentiality: (1) the potentiality that manifests in the slow growth (unfolding) in the favorable conditions of the environment and/or (2) the potentiality that provides a suitable ground for the instantaneous and direct (general or special) divine production of the first adult form of a new kind.

If (1) is true with regard to the origin of natural kinds of living organisms, then no special divine intervention seems to be necessary. And yet, says Augustine:

God has established in the temporal order fixed laws governing the production of kinds of beings and qualities of beings and bringing them forth from a hidden state into full view, but His will is supreme over all. By His power He has given numbers to His creation, but He has not bound His power by these numbers.[17]

The "numbers" here might be compared with the contemporary notion of the laws of nature.[18] Even if the seed principles unfold according to these "numbers," this does not exclude the possibility of divine intervention that is able to bring about an outcome that would not "naturally" occur. Hence, "whichever way God made Adam [and he might have made him through a direct divine intervention], He did what was in accordance with his almighty power and wisdom."[19]

If (2) is true with regard to the origin of natural kinds of living organisms, then no *rationes seminales* seem to be needed, since the Creator is able to transform anything into anything at his divine will. And yet, says Augustine,

---

[17] *De Gen. ad litt.* 6.13.

[18] McMullin says this was Augustine's influential interpretation of Wis 11:20: "Thou hast ordered all things in measure and number and weight" (see *De Gen. ad litt.* 4.3–5; McMullin, "Introduction," 51n47). Avoiding overly simplistic and anachronistic reading of the modern concept of the laws of nature into the patristic era, we must not ignore its early foundations. Going further back than the opinion of Frost, mentioned above in chapter 3, note 71, Christopher Kaiser shows that it was already "Ambrose of Milan [who] wrote a Latin paraphrase of Basil's *Hexaemeron* which used the phrase *lex naturae* ("law of nature") at this point [in reference to Genesis 1:11] (*Hexaemeron* V.6.16), and this concept became commonplace in Western discourse long before its more specialized use in modern science" (Christopher B. Kaiser, "Early Christian Belief in Creation and the Beliefs Sustaining the Modern Scientific Endeavor," in *The Blackwell Companion to Science and Christianity*, ed. J. B. Stump and Alan G. Padgett [Malden, MA: Wiley-Blackwell, 2012], 7.)

[19] *De Gen. ad litt.* 6.13. Augustine seems to assume that God indeed brought Adam into existence as an adult man.

134   *Aquinas's Account of Creation*

If we should suppose that God now makes a creature without having implanted its kind in His original creation, we should flatly contradict Sacred Scripture which says that on the sixth day God finished all his work.[20]

In other words, even if God directly intervenes to make man (and, arguably, other natural kinds of living organisms), he does not do this *ex nihilo*, as in the first creation, but takes the earth (the elements or matter on a lower level of its complexity) and draws on its potencies, even if what he does goes beyond its natural active and passive dispositions.

Augustine discusses both possible interpretations of the potentiality of *rationes seminales* and asks which option (1 or 2) is ultimately true. Unfortunately, he does not seem to provide us with a clear-cut and satisfying answer to this question. He thinks we should acknowledge that natural kinds came (come) into being in both ways: "We must conclude, then, that these reasons [*rationes seminales*] were created to exercise their causality in either one way or the other: by providing for the ordinary development of new creatures in appropriate periods of time, or by providing for the rare occurrence of a miraculous production of a creature, in accordance with what God wills as proper for the occasion."[21] None of them is preferred, and God is free to actualize particular *rationes seminales* the way he wants. In other words, while it becomes apparent that Augustine believed both Adam and Eve came to be without an observable process of development and growth (i.e., through direct divine intervention), he does not seem to clarify how many and which other species might have been produced/created in the same way.[22]

---

[20] *De Gen. ad litt.* 5.20.

[21] *De Gen. ad litt.* 6.14.

[22] Concerning the origin of Adam, Augustine claims that he was "formed from the slime of the earth in accordance with the causal reason [seminal notion] in which he had been originally created." The actualization of this particular seed-like principle required the direct intervention of God (*De Gen. ad litt.* 6.15). Similarly, with respect to the origin of Eve, Augustin clearly states that God created her in "causal reasons" (*rationes seminales*), and their actualization (determination) was not so much spontaneous (and thus necessary) but "hidden in God's plans" (i.e., requiring God's direct intervention). See *De Gen. ad lit.* 9.17–18.

    Note that with respect to the origin of human souls Augustine – before he came to the conclusion that they are directly created by God – supported the idea of traducianism, claiming that souls are passed on from parents on their children in a spiritual aspect of their procreative union. This was a spiritual version of traducianism which Augustine proposed in opposition to material traducianism of Tertullian, who spoke about souls passing from parents to children in a form of material seed-principles (*rationes seminales*). Augustine also considered generationism, assuming that parental souls give birth to their child's soul, just as a flame (considered as fleeting and in a sense immaterial) gives rise to a flame.

AUGUSTINE'S CREATION THEOLOGY AS EVOLUTIONARY

Despite the difficulty in explaining the nature of the potentiality of *rationes seminales*, Augustine's interpretation of the creation account in Genesis became an attractive point of reference in the advent of the debate concerning Darwin's theory of evolution. It was in this context that an attempt was made to describe Augustine's theory as "evolutionary." Such was the opinion of a number of theologians and philosophers, especially at the early stage of the controversy over Darwin's *On the Origin of Species*, when the attitude of the Church and of Christians to this new theory was, to say the least, reserved and skeptical. Having the authority of Augustine in support of the preliminary version of theistic evolution was regarded by them as a major argument in favor of the credibility of their theory.

To give some examples, in 1871, in his *On the Genesis of Species*, St. George Jackson Mivart, a British biologist, member of the Royal Society and convert to Catholicism, although critical about strictly naturalistic (agnostic or atheistic) interpretations of Darwin's ideas, claimed that theistic evolution was "thoroughly acceptable to the most orthodox theologians." In doing so, he referred to the works of Augustine, Aquinas, and Francisco Suárez. He thought that (educated) Christianity has never gone in search of "miraculous powers and perpetual 'catastrophes'" and instead has searched for "institutions of laws" not "interference with the laws of nature."[23] Similar to Mivart, John Zahm, C.S.C., in 1896, in his *Evolution and Dogma*, claimed that the "most venerable philosophical and theological authorities" of the Catholic Church (including Augustine and Aquinas) supported theistic evolution.[24] In 1921, Henry de Dorlodot,

---

[23] St. George Jackson Mivart, *On the Genesis of Species* (New York: D. Appleton, 1871), 317, 19–20. See also *ibid.*, 302–5. More information about Mivart and the criticism of his position may be found in Artigas, Glick, and Martínez, *Negotiating Darwin*, 236–69 (ch. 7: "Happiness in Hell: St. George J. Mivart"); and O'Leary, *Roman Catholicism and Modern Science*, 78–93, 103–8.

[24] John Augustine Zahm, *Evolution and Dogma* (Chicago: McBride, 1896), 312. Zahm's book was well received and became a bestseller in the United States. It also received some good reviews in Europe, but not in Rome. Some officials of the Roman Curia accused Zahm of presenting Augustine and Aquinas as evolutionists. His book was denounced to the Congregation of the Index on November 5 of 1897 with the recommendation of issuing a public condemnation of the book. The Congregation did not accept this suggestion but issued a decree of personal condemnation to Zahm, channeled through the Superior General of his congregation. After that Zahm quietly withdrew from his role as an apologist of the Church in matters of theology and science dialogue. See Artigas,

136   *Aquinas's Account of Creation*

the director of the Catholic University of Louvain's geological institute, in his *Le Darwinisme au point de vue de l'orthodoxie catholique*
(translated in 1922 by E. C. Messenger as *Darwinism and Catholic
Thought*), argued that Catholics were at liberty to accept Darwin's
idea of the transformation of species. Similar to Mivart and Zahm, he
was confident that he remained within the bounds of orthodoxy and
invoked the works of Augustine in particular for support. He referred
extensively to *De Genesi ad litteram*.[25]

But one has to be careful not to make too strong a claim. For
Augustine certainly did not hold that one species can arise from the
other. Within the context of his neo-Platonist theory of forms as eternal
and unchangeable ideas in the mind of God, participated by created
beings, such hypothesis would not be acceptable.[26] In his understanding
of nature, species unfold at the proper time out of their own seed principles, which were already present at the first moment of the existence of
the universe. Hence, although he accepted gradualism (without contradicting the possibility of direct divine interventions in the actualization
of *rationes seminales*), he should not be regarded as a precursor of the
modern evolutionary theory.

Indeed, it was precisely Augustine's strong conviction that God
made everything simultaneously at the moment of creation *ex nihilo*
(without any moments of time intervening) that made his theory unacceptable for Darwin, who wanted to argue in favor of the historical
origin of new species, which were not present before.[27] Moreover, the

---

Glick, and Martínez, *Negotiating Darwin*, 124–202 (ch. 4: "Americanism and Evolutionism: John A. Zahm"), and O'Leary, *Roman Catholicism*, 97–100.

[25] See: Henry de Dorlodot, *Le Darwinisme au point de vue de l'orthodoxie catholique*
(Brussels: Lovanium, 1921); de Dorlodot, *Darwinism and Catholic Thought* (New
York: Benziger, 1922). Dorlodot's tribute to Darwin was warmly received in England
but invoked some criticism in Belgium (see O'Leary, *Roman Catholicism*, 126–28). Messenger also discusses Dorlodot's ideas in his *Evolution and Theology*. It is worth men-
tioning that Dorlodot was instructed not to apply his evolutionary ideas to humans. This
warning resulted in his not publishing his nearly completed volume on human evolution.
This reflects a more general attitude of the Roman curia, which mostly accepted evolutionary theorists' appeals to Augustine, while remaining skeptical about the idea of the
evolution of the human species.

[26] See *De Gen. ad litt.* 4.5.

[27] In his study on Aristotle and Darwin Gilson shows that Darwin did not regard himself
originally as a herald of evolutionary theory. In fact, in *On the Origin of Species* the word
"evolution" appears only once, in the last of the six editions of the book published during Darwin's lifetime. Darwin was skeptical about Augustine claiming that after creation
nothing has been added to the world, and that everything originally contained in nature
in the form of seminal notions (*rationes seminales*) gradually "e-volves," "un-folds," or

Aquinas's Philosophical Theology of Creation 137

uncertainty regarding the possibility, if not a necessity, of a direct and instantaneous divine intervention in the actualization of *rationes seminales*, made Augustine's position even less tolerable for the proponents of Darwinian evolution.[28]

Augustine's world appears to be a kind of a pre-established harmony in which everything has been decided and "written" down in the potentiality of the first primitive matter. He did not understand the potentiality he spoke about as a general metaphysical principle underlying the very fabric of the universe. Rather, he saw it as a potentiality for unfolding and coming into existence of concrete and fixed types of entities (natural kinds). It becomes apparent that his view of potency differs significantly from the one developed by Aristotle and Aquinas. Hence, even if he says that "it is obvious that in accordance with those kinds of creatures which He first made, God makes many new things which He did not make then," Augustine adds that "we cannot believe that He establishes a new kind, since He finished all His works on the sixth day."[29] Consequently, the question arises of whether the unfolding new natural kinds are truly new or just appear to us to be new, while in fact they are not.

AQUINAS'S PHILOSOPHICAL THEOLOGY OF CREATION

Augustine's concept of *rationes seminales* and his interpretation of the opening chapters of the book of Genesis found acceptance and support among various thinkers, including Bonaventure, Albert the Great, Roger Bacon, and Nicolas Malebranche. Yet, the most prominent and

---

"en-velops" in time. He would also reject Herbert Spencer's definition of evolution with its philosophical overtones. His was the idea of "transmutation of species" or "change of species by descent," which he would propose and defend as a biological hypothesis. See Gilson, *From Aristotle to Darwin and Back Again*, 59–61.

[28] Darwin explicitly criticized the concept of God independently creating each species: "To my mind it accords better with what we know of the laws impressed on matter by the Creator, that the production and extinction of the past and present inhabitants of the world should have been due to secondary causes, like those determining the birth and death of the individual. When I view all beings not as special creations, but as the lineal descendants of some few beings which lived long before the first bed of the Cambrian system was deposited, they seem to me to become ennobled" (Darwin, *On the Origin of Species*, 428). In the same, concluding chapter of his book, Darwin quotes from the letter received from his friend the Reverend Charles Kingsley, who had written that he had "gradually learnt to see that it is just as noble a conception of the Deity to believe that He created a few original forms capable of self-development into other and needful forms, as to believe that He required a fresh act of creation to supply the voids caused by the actions of His laws" (422).

[29] *De Gen. ad litt.* 5.20.

138 *Aquinas's Account of Creation*

influential follower of his ideas was most likely Thomas Aquinas. As is well known, he contrasted Augustine's position with the opinion of Ambrose and other fathers of the Church, who read the Bible more literally and considered the act of creation not as instantaneous, but rather extended in time (six days or six longer periods of time). Aquinas is known for his balanced evaluation of both opinions. Early on, in his *Commentary on the Sentences of Peter Lombard*, we find him saying:

Thus with respect to the beginning of the world something pertains to the substance of faith, namely that the world began to be by creation, and all the saints agree in this. But how and in what order this was done pertains to faith only incidentally insofar as it is treated in Scripture, the truth of which the saints save in the different explanations they offer (*Super II Sent.*, 12, 1, 2, co.).

Similar is Aquinas's opinion offered in his *Quaestiones disputatae de potentia Dei*:

This incorporeal agent by whom all things, both corporeal and incorporeal are created, is God, as we have proved above (*Q. de pot.*, 3, 5; 6; 8), from whom things derive not only their form but also their matter. And as to the question at issue it makes no difference whether they were all made by him immediately, or in a certain order as certain philosophers have maintained (*Q. de pot.* 5, 1, co.).

Later on, in *Q. de pot.*, commenting on the positions of Augustine and Ambrose, Aquinas adds:

The first explanation of these things, namely that held by Augustine is the more subtle, and is a better defense of Scripture against the ridicule of unbelievers: but the second, which is maintained by the other saints, is easier to grasp, and more in keeping with the surface meaning of the text. Seeing however that neither is in contradiction with the truth of faith, and that the context admits of either interpretation, in order that neither may be unduly favored we now proceed to deal with the arguments on either side (*Q. de pot.*, 4, 2, co.).

However, although he is supportive of both interpretations of Genesis, Aquinas seems to be following Augustine's opinion more than the one offered by Ambrose. Before I will discuss the way in which he implements Augustin's notion of *rationes seminales* in his treatise on the work of the six days, I will first analyze his philosophical theology of creation developed in *Summa theologiae* and his other works. This will prove important for the Thomistic response to the theory of evolution developed in the remaining part of this project.[30]

---

[30] See also the account offered by Gaven Kerr in *Aquinas and the Metaphysics of Creation* (New York: Oxford University Press, 2019), and Kretzmann in *The Metaphysics of*

Aquinas's Philosophical Theology of Creation

The Importance of Esse

After he became familiar with and adopted Aristotle's hylomorphism, Thomas Aquinas made an original metaphysical discovery that proved crucial for the entire framework of his philosophy and theology. He realized that PM and SF, defining the essence (*essentia*) or nature of any contingent entity, are not identical with its act of existence (*esse*). Thus, he introduced one more ontological distinction characteristic of each contingent being – the one between essence and existence. He also regarded *esse* as the most perfect among all principles:

Being properly signifies: something-existing-in-act (*ST* I, 5, 1, ad 1). [It] means that-which-has-existence-in-act (*In Meta.* XII, lect. 1 (§ 2419]). [Hence,] being ... is the actuality of all acts, and therefore the perfection of all perfections (*Q. de pot.* 7, 2, ad 9). [It is] innermost in each thing and most fundamentally inherent in all things since it is formal in respect of everything found in a thing (*ST* I, 8, 1, co.). [Taken simply,] as including all perfection of being, [*esse*] surpasses life and all that follows it (*ST* I–II, 2, 5, ad 2).

Moreover, shifting his reflection toward a theological analysis of the perfection of *esse* Aquinas attributes its primary source to the Creator who is the only being in whom *esse* is identical with his essence (*essentia*). He thus claims all creatures have their own *esse* by participation in God's *esse*:

[B]eing itself belongs to the first agent according to His proper nature, for God's being is His substance (*SCG* II, 52, no. 8). In Him essence does not differ from existence (*ST* I, 3, 4, co.). Since therefore God is subsisting being itself, nothing of the perfection of being can be wanting to Him (*ST* I, 4, 2, co.) [*Esse*] belongs to all other things from the first agent by a certain participation (*ST* I, 44, 1, co.). God alone is actual being through His own essence, while other beings are actual beings through participation, since in God alone is actual being identical with His essence (*SCG* III, 66, no. 7).[31]

Creation. The latter states that "the very wording of the first chapter of Genesis, and his idea of the level of sophistication in the audience for whom it was originally intended, let him [Aquinas] to join Augustine in taking a remarkably enlightened view of the way to read the story of the six days – a view that would, I think, have equipped Augustine and Aquinas to appreciate judiciously, rather than denounce, scientific accounts of evolution" (*ibid.,* 190). See also *ibid.,* 190–93.

[31] See also *ST* I, 4, 3, ad 4; 104, 1, co.; *Super I Sent.* 37, 1, 1, co.; *Q. de ver.* 5, 8, ad 9; *SCG* III, 65, no. 3; *Super De causis,* 24. On the meaning of *ipsum esse subsistens* see Rudi A. te Velde, *Participation and Substantiality in Thomas Aquinas* (Cologne: Brill, 1995), 119–25. On the way Aquinas introduces the concept of *esse* in his writings see Wippel, *The Metaphysical Thought of Thomas Aquinas,* 238–53.

140   *Aquinas's Account of Creation*

His strong emphasis on the importance of *esse* and its ultimate origin in the divine being of God leads Aquinas to define *creatio ex nihilo* not as any kind of motion or change but bringing into existence (into being) something that has not existed before:

> [W]hat is created, is not made by movement, or by change (*ST* I, 45, 3, co.). Creation is not change (*ST* I, 45, 2, ad 2). [B]eing is the most common first effect and more intimate than all other effects: wherefore it is an effect which it belongs to God alone to produce by his own power (*Q. de pot.* 3, 7, co.). [I]t must be that all things which are diversified by the diverse participation of being, so as to be more or less perfect, are caused by one First Being, Who possesses being most perfectly (*ST* I, 44, 1, co.). [T]he proper effect of God creating is what is presupposed to all other effects, and that is absolute being (*ST* I, 45, 5, co.).

Consequently, thinking of the continual dependency of creatures on God in their being, Aquinas thus defines the notion of divine *conservatio* of things:[32]

> [C]reation in the creature is only a certain relation to the Creator as to the principle of its being (*ST* I, 45, 3, co.) [T]he being of every creature depends on God, so that not for a moment could it subsist, but would fall into nothingness were it not kept in being by the operation of the Divine power (*ST* I, 104, 1, co.).[33]

An important clarification needs to be added at this point, which will prove crucial for our model of divine and natural causality in evolution proposed in Chapter 5. Even though Aquinas clearly states that *esse* has its ultimate source and can only be "produced" by God, he admits that creatures can be causes of coming into existence of other created entities. As such, they may be called causes but not of existence (*esse*) as such, (i.e., *causa essendi*) but of coming into existence, (i.e., *causa fiendi*).[34] In

---

[32] It is important to remember that the act of the Creator sustaining being of his creatures in time can – and for Aquinas must – be still eternal (timeless). In other words, one does not have to reject Aquinas's concept of divine eternity as timeless to defend the idea of divine *conservatio*.

[33] On the unity of *creatio ex nihilo* and divine *conservatio* of creatures see Rudi A. te Velde, *Aquinas on God: The "Divine Science" of the Summa Theologiae* (Aldershot, Hants, U.K.: Ashgate, 2006), 125.

[34] See *Super I Sent.* 7, 1, 1, ad 3; *Q. de ver.* 5, 8, ad 8; *Q. de pot.* 5, 1; *ST* I, 104, 1. It is worth noticing that in his *Super Sent.* Thomas might be considering the plausibility of the emanationist view of creation in which intermediate spiritual creatures are instruments of the creation of lower creatures as such. Since he gave up this idea in his later works, the same claim that created entities can be instrumental causes of coming into existence (becoming) but not of existence as such (being) should be understood as an emphasis on the fact that creatures cannot, *sensu stricto*, create anything. Only the cause of existence (*esse*) as such can be called the creator and this is God. Creatures are merely instruments

Aquinas's Philosophical Theology of Creation 141

other words, they may be called secondary causes of coming into existence (acting under the primary causation of God) but only instrumental causes of existence as such. For even if all actions of efficient causality involve a bestowal of existence (being), whether substantially or accidentally, no creature can be a source of existence for another creature. It "gives" something that is beyond its own capacities to offer or rather provides some suitable circumstances in which God bestows *esse* on a new contingent entity. Hence, contingent entities must be classified as instrumental causes of being as such (*esse*), dependent on the principal agency of God, the only source of being:

[N]o lower agents give being except in so far as they act by divine power. Indeed, a thing does not give being except in so far as it is an actual being. But God preserves things in being by His providence... Therefore, it is as a result of divine power that a thing gives being (*SCG* III, 66, no. 1–2).[35]

Aquinas's Philosophical Definition of Creation

Remembering the importance of *esse* in Aquinas's philosophy and theology, we can now try to formulate a unified and coherent summary of his teaching on creation. I want to suggest that *creatio* has for him

of coming into existence of other creatures. Note that this view is not occasionalist as the action of creatures is not only apparent, while everything is, in fact, caused by God. For Aquinas causation of secondary and instrumental causes is real and autonomous within the immanent order of causation, while it always depends on the primary and principal causation of God.

The phrase "as such" – introduced here and used repeatedly in the remaining parts of the book (especially in Chapter 5) in reference to the metaphysical categories of existence and essence (including PM and SF) – is thought as a way of describing them in a more static aspect of what they are. It is contrasted with the complementary dynamic side of the same metaphysical categories, expressed in terms such as "coming into existence (into being)," "informing (actualizing) PM," "educing (eduction of) SF from the potentiality of PM."

35 See also *SCG* III, 67, no. 1; *SCG* II, 21; *Q. de pot.* 3, 7, co.; ad 3; ad 16; *Q. de pot.* 5, 1, co.; *ST* I, 45, 5, co.; 104, 1, co. Wippel notes that "[F]or Thomas, whenever a new substance is efficiently caused by a natural or created agent, that agent's causation applies both to the act of being itself (*esse*) of the new substance and to a particular determination of esse as realized in that substance. Causation of the particular determination (this or that kind of form) is owing to the created efficient cause insofar as it operates by its own inherent power as a principal cause. Causation of the act of being itself (*esse*) is assigned to it as an instrumental cause acting with the power of God and to God himself as the principal cause of the same. From this it follows that one should not maintain that Thomas denies that created causes can efficiently cause the act of existing or the act of being, at least in the process of bringing new substances into being" (Wippel, *The Metaphysical Thought of Thomas Aquinas*, 213).

two principal and intrinsically related aspects: (I) creation understood as active divine agency on the part of God and (II) creation understood as the passive reception of divine agency on the part of creatures. Concerning (I) Aquinas distinguishes between (Ia) the primordial creative act, defined as bringing all beings into existence out of nothing (*ex nihilo*), without any preexisting matter, and (Ib) sustaining and preserving (upholding) all contingent entities both in the fact that they are (their existence – *esse*) and in what they are (their essence – *essentia*). As a consequence of (Ia) and (Ib), all contingent entities depend entirely on God – again, both in the fact that they are (their existence) and in what they are (their essence). This dependency explains the passive aspect of creation (II).

Concerning (Ia) Aquinas – taking a more Neoplatonist attitude to emphasize the fact that nothingness cannot be a subject of divine act of creation – states that "we must consider not only the emanation of a particular being from a particular agent, but also the emanation of all being from the universal cause, which is God; and this emanation we designate by the name of creation" (*ST* I, 45, 1, co.). Note that the matter that comes into existence in the act of creation is not unspecified (unqualified). Rather, according to Aquinas, "we must assert that primary matter was not created altogether formless, nor under any one common form, but under distinct forms" (*ST* I, 66, 1, co.).[36] In his analysis of the account of the Genesis, he lists all four elements – earth, water, air, and fire – while acknowledging "That air and fire are not mentioned by name is due to the fact that the corporeal nature of these would not be so evident as that of earth and water, to the ignorant people to whom Moses spoke" (*ST* I, 66, 1, *resp.* to second argument *sc*).

Concerning (Ib), we must emphasize that Aquinas defines God's act of sustaining and preserving (upholding) all contingent entities in their existence and essence as conservation of things (*conservatio rerum*).[37] Even if he emphasizes that "The preservation of things by God is a continuation of that action whereby He gives existence" (*ST* I, 104, 1, ad 4), he never uses the term "continual creation" (*creatio continua*), which

---

[36] From the metaphysical point of view SF cannot be unspecified (unqualified). Quite contrary, its very character consists in being a SF of a particular type.

[37] See, for example, *Super II Sent.* 15, 3, 1, ad 5. where Aquinas speaks of *conservatio rerum in esse*, and *ST* I, 103, 4, co. where he discusses *conservatio rerum in bono*. It is worth noting that while Aquinas does agree that "a thing simultaneously is being created and is created" (*SCG* II, 19, no. 6), he says so in the context of his strong emphasis on the fact that creation is instantaneous and there is no succession in it.

Aquinas's Philosophical Theology of Creation 143

gained much popularity in a more recent philosophy of religion and theology of creation. I think that closer to his understanding of (Ib) would be yet another modern term, that is, *conservatio a nihilo* – preserving contingent entities from falling into nothingness.[38]

Concerning (II) Aquinas, emphasizing the crucial role of the dependence of contingent entities on God for their existence, seems to be asserting that this, in fact, has a definitive importance for our understanding of what creation is. In *Q. de pot.* 3, 3, co. we find him saying that "creation is really nothing but a relation of the creature to the Creator together with a beginning of existence."[39] Note that on the account of this aspect of the definition, the primordial act of *creatio ex nihilo* seems to be, in a way, subordinated to a principal idea of the relation of dependence of the created entities on God in their *esse*. Hence, one might say that whereas the idea of *prima creatio* (Ia) touches merely on the origin of the existence of matter, the essence of what it means to be created is defined by (II) the relation of dependence of material entities (as well as immaterial ones – that is the angels) on God in their *esse*, which naturally implies the divine act of their conservation (Ib).[40]

---

[38] For the introduction to the debate on whether conservation is a continuation of *creatio ex nihilo* or needs to be distinguished from the first act of calling the universe into existence see David Vander Laan, "Creation and Conservation," in *The Stanford Encyclopedia of Philosophy*, ed. Edward N. Zalta, Winter 2017 (Metaphysics Research Lab, Stanford University, 2017), https://plato.stanford.edu/archives/win2017/entries/creation-conservation/ (retrieved 20 July 2022).

[39] Answering to the sixth objection in the same third article of *Q. de pot.* 3 Aquinas explains: "Creation denotes this relation [of dependence on God in existence] together with inception of existence: hence it does not follow that a thing, whenever it may be, is being created, although its relation to God ever remains. Yet even as the air as long as it is light is illuminated by the sun, so may we say with Augustine (*Gen. ad lit.* viii, 12) that the creature, as long as it is in being, is made by God. But this is only a distinction of words, inasmuch as creation may be understood with newness of existence or without." Hence, divine *conservatio* must be understood as a constant dependence of creatures on God in existence, and not in terms of the occasionalist notion of their continual (re)creation *ex nihilo*, at each instance of time, with all the differences – a process which only in the mind of an observer generates a false illusion of the actual continuity of this entity in space and time.

[40] I hope my account of Aquinas's notion of creation shows that it needs to be considered both in its metaphysical and theological (historical) aspects. My impression is that some Thomists tend to emphasize the former (dependence of creatures on God in *esse*), while paying less attention to the latter (the beginning of the universe in time). See, for example, the otherwise accurate account of the classical notion of creation reinterpreted in the age of science, offered by Carroll. Although he mentions creation in both philosophical and theological senses, he nonetheless concludes that "The root sense of creation does not concern temporal origination; rather it affirms metaphysical

144 *Aquinas's Account of Creation*

Creation as Dependence on God in Esse *and* Essentia

Note that, speaking of the status of being created in terms of (II), Aquinas concentrates almost exclusively on the dependence of creatures on God in their *esse*, with little attention paid to their dependence on God in their *essentia*. On the one hand, this does not surprise us once we realize the importance of *esse* in his metaphysics, where he sees it as the highest and most fundamental principle. On the other hand, acknowledging together with Aquinas that the existence of each creature is not identical with its essence, it seems to me that a somewhat more plausible and consistent definition of creation in terms of (II) should emphasize the dependence of created entities on God in both their existence and their essence, that is, in the fact *that* they are, as well as in *what* they are. Among the few places in his writings where Aquinas actually does present an argument of this kind, we find *ST* I, 45, 3, sc., *ST* I, 65, 3, co., and *Q. de pot.* 3, 2, ad 2. In all three passages creation is defined as the act "whereby a thing is made according to its whole substance (*per quam fit [res] secundum totam substantiam suam*)."[41]

In fact, on several occasions, Aquinas emphasizes that all four Aristotelian types of causation, and even the *per accidens* (i.e., quasi-causal) character of chance – all of them being crucial for explaining the way things are, remain stable, and change into one another – have their ultimate origin and source in God. This fact can be explained as follows:

1. **Material cause.** Although it would be erroneous to assert that God (total actuality) is the ultimate PM (total potentiality) of each being, PM does come from God and retains a likeness to him:

---

dependence" (Carroll, "Creation, Evolution, and Thomas Aquinas, section "Thomas Aquinas' Understanding of Creation"). See also Carroll, "Creation in the Age of Modern Science" and Carroll, "At the Mercy of Chance?".

Robert John Russell sees temporal contingency as an important secondary contribution to the meaning of *creatio ex nihilo*. He defines finitude in terms of a Lakatosian research program in a series of auxiliary hypotheses and claims that it serves as "a bridge between the core theory, ontological origination, and the data for theology, here seen in terms of the origin of the universe at t=0" (Robert J. Russell, "Finite Creation Without a Beginning: The Doctrine of Creation in Relation to Big Bang and Quantum Cosmologies," in *Quantum Cosmology and the Laws of Nature*, edited by Robert John Russell, Nancey Murphy, and C. J. Isham [Vatican City State: Vatican Observatory; Berkeley, Calif.: Center for Theology and the Natural Sciences, 1999], 306).

[41] See also *Super II Sent.*, 1, 1, 2, sc.

Aquinas's Philosophical Theology of Creation 145

"also primary matter is created by the universal cause of being" (*ST* I, 44, 2, co.). God's action finds its expression in creating and providing PM as a source and principle of potentiality and of all changes in nature.

2. **Formal cause.** Because formal cause reduces PM from potentiality to act, we may appropriately consider God as the ultimate source of formal causation. Hence, states Thomas, "Form is something divine and very good and desirable." The reason we can say it is divine is because "every form is a certain participation in the likeness of the divine being, which is pure act. For each thing, insofar as it is in act, has form" (*In Phys.* I, lect. 15 [§ 135]). In other words, through their SSFF, creatures possess, in part, the actuality that is infinite in the Creator. Consequently, God can be said to act in the world as the Creator of all forms and the source of all actuality. Creatures' dependence on God in the formal aspect of their essence provides for their intelligibility.[42]

3. **Efficient cause.** Aquinas sees God as the first source of all efficient causation. He states, "all agents act in virtue of God himself: and therefore He is the cause of action in every creature" (*ST* I, 105, 5, co.).[43] Moreover, he thinks that the likeness between the agent, *that is*, the efficient cause, and its effects observed in nature, makes it unreasonable to pass over the natural generators of SSFF and to claim that God obviates the causality of natural agents. It is this way of thinking that makes him suggest distinctions between primary and secondary and between principal and instrumental causation of God and his creatures – distinctions which I will discuss in more detail in Chapter 6.

---

[42] At this point Aquinas goes beyond the metaphysics of Aristotle and his theory of intrinsic formal causation, introducing the Platonic idea of external exemplar forms (causes), which he sees not as subsisting entities, but as ideas in the mind of God: "[I]n the divine mind there are exemplar forms of all creatures, which are called ideas, as there are forms of artifacts in the mind of an artisan" (*Quod.* 8, 2).

[43] In *SCG* III, 67, no. 2 and no. 3 Aquinas states: "Now, every power in any agent is from God, as from a first principle of all perfection. Therefore, since every operation results from a power, the cause of every operation must be God ... [J]ust as God has not only given being to things when they first began to exist, and also causes being in them as long as they exist, conserving things in being ... so also has He not merely granted operative powers to them when they were originally created, but He always causes these powers in things. Hence, if this divine influence were to cease, every operation would cease. Therefore, every operation of a thing is traced back to Him as to its cause."

146   *Aquinas's Account of Creation*

4. **Final cause.** Similar to other modes of causation, all forms and cases of natural teleology (which Aquinas calls after Aristotle a "cause of causes") find their ultimate source in God. He notes that "the end of all things is some extrinsic good," which is "outside the universe" (*ST* I, 103, 2, co.). It is desired by all creatures as they are looking for the fulfillment of their nature. In other words, ἐντελέχεια (*entelecheia*), an ultimate actualization of form in the final state of an entity, bears some likeness to God and his goodness. It brings Aquinas to the conclusion that "everything is (...) called good from the divine goodness, as from the first exemplary effective and final principle of all goodness" (*ST* I, 6, 4, co.). Consequently, we may assert that "All things desire God as their end, when they desire some good thing, whether this desire be intellectual or sensible, or natural, that is, without knowledge; because nothing is good and desirable except forasmuch as it participates in the likeness to God" (*ST* I, 44, 4, ad 3). On another occasion, we find Aquinas saying that:

> God moves all things to their own actions to which they are inclined by their own proper forms. And thus it is that He disposes all things sweetly, because to all things He gives forms and powers inclining them to that which He Himself moves them; so that they tend toward it not by force, but as if it were by their own free accord. (*De vir.* 2, 1, co.)[44]

5. **Chance.** I have already mentioned in Chapter 3 that Thomas agrees with Aristotle that chance and fortune are not causes *per se*. At the same time, as *per accidens* types of causality, they must be related to proper material, formal, efficient, and final causes, relevant to entities and dynamical systems in which they occur (see *In Phys.* II, lect. 7–10 [§ 198–238], especially § 218). As such, chance events are classified as contingent events, which Aquinas sees as remaining under God's providence: "God, Who is the governor of the universe, intends some of His effects to be established by way of necessity, and others contingently" (*SCG* III, 94, no. 11). "Things are said to be fortuitous as regards some particular cause from the order of which they escape. But as to

---

[44] See also *SCG* III, 67, no. 6: "[E]very agent is ordered through his operation to an ultimate end, for either the operation itself is the end, or the thing that is made, that is, the product of the operation. Now, to order things to their end is the prerogative of God Himself."

Aquinas on the Three Stages of the Work of the Six Days 147

the order of Divine providence, 'nothing in the world happens by chance', as Augustine declares" (*ST* I, 103, 7, ad 2).[45]

All four causes (material, formal, efficient, and final), as well as the quasi-causality of chance occurrences, are crucial for the eduction of a given SF from the potentiality of PM in each substantial change. They may be thus classified as causes of the essence of a new entity that comes into being. In analogy to the perfection of *esse*, we must say that God as Creator of PM and all forms, source of efficient causality and natural teleology, as well as the transcendent cause of the occurences attributed to chance and fortune, is the first and ultimate cause of the essence (*essentia*) of each contingent entity. At the same time, created agents can be regarded both as secondary causes of essences of other contingent beings, *that is*, secondary causes of the eduction of a given SF from the potentiality of PM (also through properly disposing it to go through a suitable substantial change), as well as instrumental causes of the essence (*essentia*) as such of a given being (dependent on the principal causality of God).

Consequently, for Aquinas, to be created means to be dependent on God in *esse* and in *essentia* (in existence and in essence). This rule applies both to entities that came into being *ex nihilo* at the beginning of creation and existed or still exist in time, as well as to those that come into being throughout the history of the universe from already existing matter, due to causality of other creatures. The latter can be classified as secondary causes of the essence (*essentia*) of a given entity (through the eduction of a proper SF from the potentiality of PM) and instrumental causes of the essence as such, as well as secondary causes of coming into existence (*esse*) of the entity in question and instrumental causes of its existence as such.[46]

AQUINAS ON THE THREE STAGES OF THE WORK OF THE SIX DAYS

Keeping in mind the principles of Aquinas's philosophical theology of creation, we can now move to his *Treatise on the Work of the Six Days* (*ST* I, 65–74). Here, we should emphasize, one more time, that Thomas

---

[45] On divine action through chance, in the context of the theory of evolution, see Kretzmann, *The Metaphysics of Creation*, 203–16.

[46] The origin of each new human being is an exception here. Aquinas believes God creates an immortal soul *ex nihilo* when a new human person begins to exist.

148 *Aquinas's Account of Creation*

understands creation *ex nihilo* as the coming into being out of nothing (i.e., not from a preceding being of any kind) of the most primitive
types of contingent entities: the elements. He thus sees it as an act that
was instantaneous, rather than extended in time. We infer this based on
Aquinas's differentiation between the work of creation (*opus creationis*)
and those of distinction (*opus distinctionis*) and adornment (*opus ornatus*), in his analysis of the work of the six days in the first part of the
Summa theologiae.[47]

The outcome of the work of creation (*opus creationis*) was the coming into existence of the most primitive matter (*materia secunda*), which
was, in fact, inseparable from the first three stages of distinction (*opus
distinctionis*), the second of which was the distinction "of the elements
according to their forms."[48] The outcome of the work of distinction
(*opus distinctionis*) was the separation of land from the sea, accompanied by the preliminary stage of the work of adornment (*opus ornatus*),
the production of plants.[49] The outcome of the work of adornment (*opus
ornatus*) was the production of celestial bodies and animals and the creation of man.[50] Refer Figure 4.1.

Following Aquinas's distinction, we should acknowledge that the subsequent production (*productio*) of more complex contingent beings was, in a
way, mediated through the most basic forms of material stuff – the origin
of which was the outcome of the work/act of creation (*opus creationis*). In
other words, more complex entities, in some respect, came "from" them.[51]

---

[47] See Aquinas's introduction to *ST* I, 65. Kretzmann notes that this distinction, present
also in *In II Sent.* 13, 1, 1; 14, 1, 5; 15, 1, 1; 15, 2, 2 and 17, 2, 2, is not fully present in
SCG II, 39–45, where *opus distinctionis* covers also *opus ornatus*: "[F]urnishing [*opus
ornatus*] is never even mentioned in SCG II or, for that matter, anywhere else in SCG.
So, if 'distinguishing' in II.39–45 designates Aquinas's explanation of the origin of all
species ... then in SCG 'distinguishing' covers also what is carefully separated off as
the work of furnishing not only in ST, written after SCG, but also in Aquinas's earlier
Commentary on the *Sentences*" (Kretzmann, *The Metaphysics of Creation*, 186).

[48] Following the account of Genesis, Aquinas defines the remaining two distinctions as the
distinction of the heaven from the earth, which is joint to the very act of creation – "In the
beginning God created heaven and earth." (Genesis 1,1) – and the distinction of place "since
the earth is said to be under the waters that rendered it invisible, whilst the air, the subject of
darkness, is described as being above the waters" (*ST* I, 66, 1, ad 3, reply to sc 2 of obj. 3).

[49] We must remember that in antiquity many thought plants were not living organisms
because they do not move and allocate themselves. Hence, the production of plants in
the account of Genesis preceded the actual *opus ornatus*.

[50] Aquinas's distinction between *creatio* and *productio* seems to correspond with the distinction between Hebrew "to create" (*bara* [בָּרָא]) and "to make" (*asah* [עָשָׂה]).

[51] I will say more on the terminological distinction between *creatio* and *productio* in
Chapters 5 and 6.

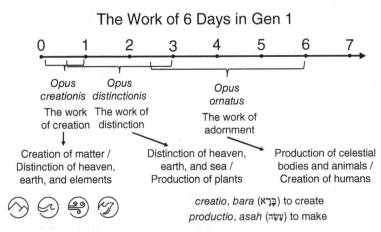

FIGURE 4.1 Graphic depiction of the sequence of the work of the six days in the account of Genesis 1.
Four elements – source: (author) Dawid Socha

AQUINAS'S USE OF AUGUSTINE'S NOTION OF *RATIONES SEMINALES*

Aquinas realizes that even a literal interpretation of Genesis suggests that (1) it was Earth that brought forth plants, the green herbs and fruit trees; (2) it was water that brought forth an abundance of swimming creatures and birds (although Genesis does not say explicitly where they came from); (3) it was Earth that brought forth all kinds of living creatures, such as cattle, creeping things, and wild animals of all kinds. Hence, following Augustine's concept of *rationes seminales*,[52] Aquinas states that plants and trees might have been produced "in their origin or causes," that is, the earth "received ... the power to produce

---

[52] Although Aquinas uses the term *rationes seminales* explicitly on numerous occasions in his commentary on the *Sentences*, in other parts of *ST*, in *Q. de ver.*, *Q. de pot.*, and *Q. de malo*, and in some biblical commentaries, he paradoxically does not use it in his analysis of the works of the six days (*ST* I, 65–74). At the same time, however, he does refer in these questions directly to the authority of Augustine and his concept of all types of creatures existing in *statu potentiae* in the earth (the primitive elements) and unfolding at the proper time, contrasting his view with the one held by "other holy writers." Having said this, we must not forget that Aquinas explicitly rejects the "latent forms" theory. For him the prior existence of forms in matter is *potentialiter* but not *simpliciter*. In other words, when a given thing has a form potentially, in no sense it is present in it in actuality. His position on this issue is much clearer than the one of Augustine. See, for example, *ST* I, 45, 8, co. On this topic, see also Kretzmann, *The Metaphysics of Creation*, 198–202.

150 *Aquinas's Account of Creation*

them." They were subsequently brought into existence in "the work of propagation."[53] Similar with fishes and birds, which Augustine saw as produced by "the nature of waters on that [fifth] day potentially,"[54] and animals, whose "production was potential" as well.[55]

This clear reference to Augustine's concept of *rationes seminales* faces the challenge of their double potentiality, that is, (1) their potentiality to naturally and spontaneously unfold in favorable circumstances and (2) their potentiality understood as providing a suitable ground for the instantaneous and direct (special) divine intervention in the production of new forms of living creatures. Unlike Augustine, who, as we have seen, remained uncertain as to whether the production of each animate species involved(s) a direct divine intervention, Aquinas introduces an important distinction, which strives to further clarify Augustine's position.

Commenting on the second book of *Sentences* of Peter Lombard Aquinas claims that the origin of plants requires merely causal principles proper for the work of distinction (*opus distinctionis*) and adds that the role of fathering in this process belongs to the powers of celestial

---

[53] *ST* I, 69, 2, co.: "In these first days God created all things in their origin or causes, and from this work He subsequently rested. Yet afterwards, by governing His creatures, in the work of propagation, 'He worketh until now'. Now the production of plants from out the earth is a work of propagation, and therefore they were not produced in act on the third day, but in their causes only."

[54] *ST* I, 71, 1, co.

[55] *ST* I, 72,1, co. See also *Q. de pot.* 4, 2, ad 28: "Before the plants were produced causally, nothing was produced, but they were produced together with the heaven and the earth. In like manner the fishes, birds and animals were produced in those six days causally and not actually." Aquinas alludes to the concept of *rationes seminales* on several other occasions: (1) "God is said to have stopped creating new creatures on the seventh day because nothing was made afterwards that did not come first in some likeness according to genus or species, at least in a seminal principle ... Therefore, I say that the future renewal of the world indeed came first in the works of the six days in a remote likeness" (*Super IV Sent.*, 48, 2, 1, ad 3); (2) "For we see that all things which, in the process of time, being created by the work of Divine Providence, were produced by the operation of God, were created in the first fashioning of things according to seedlike forms [*seminales rationes*], as Augustine says [*De Gen. ad litt.* 7.3], such as trees, animals, and the rest" (*ST* I, 62, 3, co.); (3) "In the first production of things matter existed under the substantial form of the elements. ... In the first instituting of the world animals and plants did not exist actually. ... On the day on which God created the heaven and the earth, He created also every plant of the field, not, indeed, actually, but 'before it sprung up in the earth', that is, potentially [*potentialiter*]. ... God created all things together so far as regards their substance in some measure formless. But He did not create all things together, so far as regards that formation of things which lies in distinction and adornment" (*ST* I, 74, 2, co. and ad 1–2).

Aquinas's Use of Augustine's Notion of Rationes Seminales 151

bodies, while the role of the mother is fulfilled by the primordial matter (i.e., elements).[56] Similar is his opinion presented in *De potentia*, where we find him saying:

> Now the production of plants from the earth into actual existence belongs to the work of propagation, since the powers of the heavenly body as father, and of the earth as mother suffice for their production. Hence the plants were not actually produced on the third day but only in their causes: and after the six days they were brought into actual existence in their respective species and natures by the work of government (*Q. de pot.* 4, 2, ad 28).[57]

However, the case of animals might look different. Concerning their origin Aquinas emphasizes that:

> Those things that are naturally generated from seed cannot be generated naturally in any other way. ... In the natural generation of all animals that are generated from seed, the active principle lies in the formative power of the seed. ... The material principle, however, in the generation of either kind of animals, is either some element, or something compounded of the elements. But at the first beginning of the world the active principle was the Word of God, which produced animals from material elements, either in act, as some holy writers say, or virtually [*virtute*], as Augustine teaches (*ST* I, 71, 1, ad 1).[58]

This theological opinion of Aquinas leaves space for an interpretation assuming that no direct divine intervention is needed in the actualization of animal species. They might have been produced virtually (as *rationes seminales*), and similar to the plant species, they may spontaneously unfold in the proper conditions of the environment. However, we must not forget that, concerning the origin of Adam, Thomas clearly states that a direct divine intervention was necessary:

> The first formation of the human body could not be by the instrumentality of any created power, but was immediately from God. ... Therefore as no pre-existing body has been formed whereby another body of the same species could be generated, the first human body was of necessity made immediately by God (*ST* I, 91, 2, co.).[59]

---

[56] See *Super II Sent.*, 14, 1, 5, ad 6.

[57] It should be remembered that the second part of the corpus and all responses to arguments in this article were probably written by Vincentius Castronovo and not by Aquinas himself, who most likely left the article in question unfinished.

[58] See also *Super II Sent.* 14, 1, 5, ad 6.

[59] We should also remember that because heavenly bodies were thought of as indestructible, they could not have come into existence from any preexisting destructible matter. Hence, in accordance with Augustine's view, they could not have unfolded from *rationes seminales*. It seems they must have been created through a direct divine intervention as well. However, McMullin notes that even if Aquinas

152 Aquinas's Account of Creation

This assertion concerns Adam's body. When it comes to his soul, Aquinas emphasizes that "the rational soul can be made only by creation." At the same time, he adds this "is not true of other forms," which means they may be generated by contingent causes.[60] Indeed, on another occasion, Aquinas claims that "the form of the thing generated depends naturally on the generator in so far as it is educed from the potentiality of matter" (*Q. de pot.* 5, 1, co.).[61] This might suggest, once again, that the occurrence of new animate (including animal) species may proceed from the natural processes of actualization (unfolding) of *rationes seminales*. However, one may argue that what Aquinas has in mind here is the generation of new exemplars of an already existing species and not the coming to be of the first exemplar of a new species. For, indeed, on yet another occasion, Thomas seems to be saying that the origin of the first member of each new animal species requires, in fact, a direct divine intervention:

[Some things come into being neither through motion nor through generation] because of the necessity that generation always generates what is similar in species. For this reason the first members of the species were immediately created by God, such as the first man, the first lion, and so forth (*Super II Sent.*, 1, 1, 4, co.).[62]

Consequently, we must acknowledge that, although he tried to, Aquinas did not succeed in clarifying Augustine's position on the exact nature of the potentiality of *rationes seminales*. Similar to Augustine, he remained unclear in specifying which types of natural kinds may

---

asserts Augustine was "not at variance" with other writers in regard to the heavenly bodies ("For he says that they were made actually and not merely virtually, since the firmament has not the power of producing luminaries, as the earth has of producing plants" [*ST* I, 70, 1, co.]), the reference to the text he cites from Augustine (*De Gen. ad litt.* 5.5) makes his reading dubious. For although Augustine does say there that "on the fourth day, the lights and stars were created," he makes this claim in a paragraph about "those beings which were formed from formlessness (unformed matter) and are clearly said to be created." He appears to be using the term "created" here in the sense of "drawing forth from a prior matter," the sense that Aquinas wants to exclude (See McMullin, "Introduction," 52n65).

60 See *ST* I, 90, 2, co.

61 On Aquinas's defense of the unity of man, see *ST* I, 76, 4.

62 However, this might not be true about at least some species of insects, of which Aquinas says here that they originated from putrefaction: "Man, for instance, can only be generated from man. It is, however, otherwise with those things which are not generated by an agent that is similar to them in species. For these, rather, the power of celestial bodies along with appropriate matter is sufficient, as, for example, those things which are generated by putrefaction" (*ibid.*). I will say more on this topic in Chapter 5.

Aquinas's Use of Augustine's Notion of Rationes Seminales   153

originate through natural unfolding (actualization) of seed principles and which require a direct divine intervention.[63] Moreover, assuming his theology in this matter follows faithfully the original thought of Augustine, it might be considered as being unable to fit within the context of the modern and contemporary versions of the evolutionary theory.

However, we must not forget that Aquinas's reference to Augustine's concept of *rationes seminales* was accompanied by his general acceptance of Aristotle's moderate realism about universals, including species, grounded in his hylomorphic metaphysics of substance (I have alluded to it in Chapter 2, in my analysis of the compatibility of ISCs with evolutionary biology). Aristotle is known for criticizing Plato's concept of species conceived as immutable forms, separated from matter and existing in the realm of eternal ideas. For him, species are real and immutable, in the sense that each one of them is defined by an SF of a particular kind, which causes each organism belonging to a given species to be what it is and to exhibit a set of fixed and permanent traits. At the same time, however, every species exists only as realized in concrete, temporal, individual, and contingent organisms. Thus, while the essential intrinsic traits of a species are immutable, their existential exemplifications and realizations in nature are not. Aristotelian metaphysics allows us to argue that all representatives of a species share a "common nature" (defined by an SF of a particular kind), which finds its expression in the variety of interactions and inter-relations between unique individuals that differ in terms of many accidental features. This understanding of species provides an opportunity for redefining Augustine's concept of *rationes seminales* in terms of the hylomorphic theory of matter, its disposition, and the two levels of potentiality grounded in it.[64]

---

[63] On several occasions Aquinas distinguishes between imperfect and perfect animals, where the latter are defined as having "a supreme diversity in their organs." (*SCG* II, 72; see also *ST* I, 76, 5, ad 3; *ST* I, 76, 8; *Q. de an.* 10 and 15). He might have been of the opinion that plants and imperfect animals may arise by spontaneous generation, while the emergence of perfect animals required direct divine intervention. Naturally, the category of "perfect animals," as defined by Aquinas, is far from being precise by the standards of contemporary philosophy and natural science.

[64] It could be argued that Aristotelian species are perpetual. Not as Platonic transcendental forms or as types of SSFF perpetually exemplified in real organisms. For we know that species go into extinction. However, even if they do, they may still exist potentially (in the potentiality of PM – the weakest form of "existence") and as ideas in the mind of God. Nevertheless, the question remains whether evolutionary theory allows for the (natural)

EVOLUTIONARY REDEFINITION OF THE
CONCEPT OF *RATIONES SEMINALES*

The constructive proposal of the Thomistic metaphysics of evolutionary transitions presented in Chapter 1 enables us to reframe both Augustine's notion of *rationes seminales* and Aquinas's interpretation of its main objectives, within the context of the core principles of Aristotelian metaphysics in its encounter with contemporary science. I suggest seed principles should not be defined as organisms virtually present in their dormant forms, hidden forces, or potencies (fixed and limited in number), that are inherent to the most primitive matter created with the origin of the universe. We might redefine them, instead, in terms of the two levels of potentiality specified in Chapter 1: (1) pure potentiality of PM, which can be actualized by all possible types of SSFF, proper for both inanimate and animate natural kinds; and (2) potentiality of PM underlying all instantiations of secondary matter (*materia secunda*), which is specified (qualified) by the SF and AAFF characteristic of a particular natural kind it belongs to.

The principles actualizing entities classified as instantiations of secondary matter dispose their underlying PM in a particular way. This opens the way to substantial changes that lead to the eduction of particular types of new SSFF (characteristic of other natural kinds) from its potentiality. This allows, in turn, for introducing the idea of evolutionary changes and transitions within the framework of the Aristotelian – Thomistic metaphysics and philosophical theology.

The advantage of the proposed model is that, on the one hand, it does not constrain the idea of *rationes seminales* to their interpretation in terms of the potentiality of mere unfolding of what has always been actually present in some latent form in the fabric of the cosmos. In other words, it allows for the genuine novelty of evolutionary processes, leading to the origin of new natural kinds, which were not present before at any level of actuality. On the other hand, the originating new types of natural kinds do not come into existence out of nothing (*ex nihilo*). Rather, they are "written" in the above-mentioned, clearly distinguished and specified two levels of potentiality inherent to the reality of the universe and the entities it contains. This, in turn, enables the proposed

---

re-exemplification of an extinct species. Also, on the side of metaphysics, one could object that a given type of SF (that grounds a particular natural kind) is a form of act and not of potency, hence the idea of its "potential" way of existence in PM is doubtful.

Conclusion   155

model to accommodate the idea of the gradual transformation of species along the line of the research presented in Chapter 1.

CONCLUSION

The analysis of the classical notion of creation presented in this chapter brings several important conclusions. First, we saw Aquinas precisely distinguishing the work (primordial act) of creation (*opus creationis*) from nothing (*ex nihilo*) from the consequent transformations of already existing matter (*opus distinctionis* and *opus ornatus*). Although primitive, it possessed *rationes seminales*, that is, intrinsic potentiality grounding possible future transformations, which take place within processes of accidental and substantial changes, including propagation. Second, Aquinas's philosophical theology of creation offers a precise description of the way in which creatures depend on God in their *esse* and *essentia*. Third, although neither Augustine nor Aquinas presented us with clear and precise information concerning species (*rationes seminales*), the emergence of which requires direct divine intervention, it seems that both are inclined to think that coming to be of the first representatives of all higher animals and humans does require such intervention. This conclusion naturally depends on the level of scientific knowledge in antiquity and in the Middle Ages. At the same time, their view remains open to the proposed redefinition of the concept of *rationes seminales* along the lines of Aristotelian metaphysics of evolutionary transitions (developed in Chapters 1–3). I claim it may be further developed in reference to the classical distinctions between primary and principal causation of God and secondary and instrumental causation of creatures.

I believe that all these provide necessary material and conceptual tools that enable us to develop a Thomistic version of theistic evolution. A constructive proposal of such interpretation will be offered in the following chapters.

5

Aquinas and Evolution

The first part of the book, dedicated to philosophical aspects of evolutionary theory, proved that the classical Aristotelian–Thomistic metaphysics is not hostile to the notion of evolutionary transitions. Quite to the contrary, it provides a necessary background and speculative categories that help us capture and describe the dynamism of natural processes effecting the origin of new species. The question concerning the openness of the Thomistic theology to evolution is much more complex and nuanced. On the one hand, the analysis of Aquinas's philosophical theology of creation offered in Chapter 4 seems to open his system to the idea of God working in the universe in and through evolutionary processes. I am thinking here in particular about the precise distinction of creation *ex nihilo* from transformation of an already existing matter and the theological interpretation of the concept of *rationes seminales*, where we might speak of God as the primary cause actualizing potentiality of matter in the course of the history of the universe, with the effect of multiple new natural kinds coming into existence.

On the other hand, however, it would be anachronistic and intellectually dubious to claim that evolutionism fits easily with Thomistic theology. Although he is not entirely clear on all aspects of his theistic reflection on protology, Aquinas seems to be inclined to argue that (1) only God can create; (2) the origin of the first exemplars of all higher forms of life, including human beings, required his direct divine intervention; (3) the number of species in the universe is pretty much fixed (the counterexamples of new species emerging from putrefaction and crossbreeding are rare exceptions rather than proofs for an ongoing natural process of production of new species); (4) *opus ornatus* is accomplished and current processes of generation and corruption do not give origin to new species – rather, they effect emergence of new exemplars of already existing natural kinds.

Consequently, an attempt at developing a consistent and relevant Thomistic version of theistic evolutionism requires some adjustments to Aquinas's theological system. As we shall see these are rather minor, yet necessary changes that need to be introduced. Most importantly, they do not contradict nor radically transform the most fundamental doctrinal aspects of the system in question. Quite to the contrary, they go with it smoothly, proving once again its flexibility and openness to ever-changing scientific knowledge about the universe we live in. All these enable us to discover and learn through a particular example that one aspect of the truth does not contradict the other.

My goals in this chapter are the following. In the opening section, I will present and discuss various textual arguments in Aquinas's corpus, relevant to the topic of emergence of new species. I believe this will show both the complexity of the debate on whether there is a "space" for evolution in his theology, as well as the openness for reinterpretation and further development of his ideas on this matter in reference to contemporary metaphysical analysis of speciation, developed in the first part of this book. In the following section, I will delineate a constructive proposal of the Thomistic account of theistic evolution, grounding it in Aquinas's theology, yet pointing toward necessary changes that need to be introduced for it to be relevant with respect to evolutionary theory. The last section will comment on an objection against the proposed version of theistic evolutionism coming from Michael Chaberek. The chapter will end with a short conclusion.

AQUINAS ON THE EMERGENCE OF NEW SPECIES

As is well known, Aquinas reflects upon the origin of the universe, and all it contains on numerous occasions. Some of these accounts inspire him to ask further questions concerning the perfection of the universe and whether there is a possibility for the emergence of new species in it. On other occasions, he comments on rare cases of the actual origin of new species (as he saw it, based on the science of his time), through putrefaction and crossbreeding. I gathered the most important and relevant textual evidence in Table 5.1. I numbered all passages for the sake of convenience of the analysis that follows the table.

TABLE 5.1 *Selection of the passages from the works of Aquinas showing the complexity of the debate on the possibility of the emergence of new species through biological evolution in reference to his theology of creation – both philosophical and based on revelation and tradition* (some of these passages appear in other parts of this volume)

On the possibility of the emergence of new species in general		
	(1) *Q. de pot.* 4, 2, ad 22	"In its beginning the universe was perfect with regard to its species (*quantum ad species*)."
	(2) *Q. de pot.* 3, 16, ad 17	"[T]he universe which has been produced by God is the best with respect to those things that are, but not with respect to those things that God can do."
	(3) *Super I Sent.* 44, 1, 2, co.	"[T]he universe can be made better, either through the addition of many parts, that is to say, so that many other species would be created, and that many degrees of goodness that can exist would be complete, since the distance between the highest creature and God is still infinite; and thus God could have made [in this way] the universe better and can still do it."
	(4) *ST* I, 25, 6, ad 3	"The universe … cannot be better, on account of the most beautiful order given to things by God; in which the good of the universe consists … Yet God could make other things, or add something to the present creation; and then there would be another and a better universe."
	(5) *ST* I, 118, 3, ad 2	"To the perfection of the universe there can be added something daily with regard to the number of individuals, not, however, with regard to the number of species."
	(6) *ST* I, 69, 2, co.	"[T]he first constitution of species belongs to the work of the six days, but the reproduction among them of like from like, to the government of the universe."
	(7) *ST* I, 73, 1, ad 3	"Nothing entirely new was afterwards made by God, but all things subsequently made had in a sense been made before in the work of the six days. (…) Species, also, that are new, if any such appear, existed beforehand in various active powers; so that animals, and perhaps even new species of animals, are produced by putrefaction by the power which the stars and elements received at the beginning. Again, animals of new kinds arise occasionally from the connection of individuals belonging to different species, as the mule is the offspring of an ass and a mare; but even these existed previously in their causes, in the works of the six days. Some also existed beforehand by way of similitude, as the souls now created."

(8) *ST* I, 45, 5, co.	"[I]t is impossible for any creature to create, either by its own power or instrumentally – that is, ministerially."
(9) *ST* I, 65, 3, co.	"[N]o secondary cause can produce anything, unless there is presupposed in the thing produced something that is caused by a higher cause. But creation is the production of a thing in its entire substance, nothing being presupposed either uncreated or created. Hence it remains that nothing can create except God alone, Who is the first cause. Therefore, in order to show that all bodies were created immediately by God, Moses said: 'In the beginning God created heaven and earth'."
(10) *ST* I, 65, 4, co.	"[I]n the first production of corporeal creatures no transmutation from potentiality to act can have taken place, and accordingly, the corporeal forms that bodies had when first produced came immediately from God, whose bidding alone matter obeys, as its own proper cause."
(11) *Q. de pot.* 4, 2, ad 28	"Now the production of plants from the earth into actual existence belongs to the work of propagation, since the powers of the heavenly body as father, and of the earth as mother suffice for their production."
(12) *Super II sent.* 1, 1, 4, co.	"[Some things come into being neither through motion nor through generation] because of the necessity that generation always generates what is similar in species. For this reason the first members of the species were immediately created by God, such as the first man, the first lion, and so forth."
(13) *ST* I, 91, 2, co.	"The first formation of the human body could not be by the instrumentality of any created power, but was immediately from God. ... Therefore as no pre-existing body has been formed whereby another body of the same species could be generated, the first human body was of necessity made immediately by God."
(14) *SCG* III, 66, no. 4, 6	"[B]eing is the proper product of the primary agent, that is, of God; and all things that give being do so because they act by God's power. ... [S]econdary agents, which are like particularizers and determinants of the primary agent's action, produce as their proper effects other perfections which determine being."

(*continued*)

TABLE 5.1 (*continued*)

(15) *Super II Sent.* 12, 1, 2, co.	"[W]ith respect to the beginning of the world something pertains to the substance of faith, namely that the world began to be by creation, and all the saints agree in this. But how and in what order this was done pertains to faith only incidentally insofar as it is treated in scripture, the truth of which the saints save in the different explanations they offer."
(16) *Q. de pot.* 5, 1, co.	"[T]his incorporeal agent by whom all things, both corporeal and incorporeal are created, is God, as we have proved above (*Q. de pot.*, 3, 5; 6; 8), from whom things derive not only their form but also their matter. And as to the question at issue it makes no difference whether they were all made by him immediately, or in a certain order as certain philosophers have maintained."
(17) *Q. de pot.* 3, 10, ad 2	"The universe in its beginning was perfect (...) as regards nature's causes from which afterwards other things could be propagated, but not as regards all their effects."
(18) *Q. de pot.* 4, 1, co.	"[W]hen he [God] made things out of nothing he did not at once bring them from nothingness to their ultimate natural perfection, but conferred on them at first an imperfect being, and afterwards perfected them, so that the world was brought gradually from nothingness to its ultimate perfection."
(19) *Q. de pot.* 5, 5, ad 13	"God in bringing all creatures into being out of nothing, himself instituted the first perfection of the universe, consisting in the principal parts thereof, and the various species of things: and that in order to give it its final perfection, consisting in the completion of the ranks of the blessed, he ordained the various movements and operations of creatures, some of which are natural, for instance, the movement of the heavens and the activities of the elements, whereby matter is prepared to receive rational souls, while others are voluntary such as the ministrations of the angels who are sent to minister for them who shall receive the inheritance of salvation."
(20) *Super II Sent.* 1, 1, 4, co.	"Man, for instance, can only be generated from man. It is, however, otherwise with those things which are not generated by an agent that is similar to them in species. For these, rather, the power of celestial bodies along with appropriate matter is sufficient, as, for example, those things which are generated by putrefaction."

Emergence of New Species in General

The first question we need to ask is more general. What does Aquinas think about the possibility of the emergence of new species throughout the history of the universe? An answer to this question in *Q. de pot.*, which is one of the mature works by Aquinas, seems to fall into a contradiction. On the one hand, Aquinas clearly states (1) that "In its beginning the universe was perfect with regard to its species (*quantum ad species*)" (*Q. de pot.* 4, 2, ad 22). Yet, in the same work, we find him saying (2) that the perfection of the created universe is, in fact, relative. Perfect with regards to things created, the universe might still become more perfect in reference to things God could possibly bring about. Hence, Aquinas would reject Leibniz's suggestion that we live in the best possible world. But does the possibility of greater perfection of which he speaks include the possibility of the emergence of new species?[1] While we do not find a clear answer to this question in *Q. de pot.*, we do encounter Aquinas's surprising opinion on this issue in his commentary to the first book of the *Sentences of Peter Lombard* (3), which Thomas writes at the very beginning of his theological career. This text requires more attention on our part.

The context of Aquinas's claim that the universe can be made more perfect through addition of many new species is, once again, the general question concerning its perfection. In answer to this query, Thomas lists three possible ways in which the universe may grow in perfection. With regard to the parts of the universe, it can be made better by the addition of new parts, that is, new species.[2] According to Aquinas' teaching in this particular work, it is still possible:

If [we look at the problem] with regard to the parts in themselves, then it can be understood that the universe can be made better, either through the addition of many parts, that is to say, so that many other species would be created, and that many degrees of goodness that can exist would be complete, since the distance between the highest creature and God is still infinite; and thus God could have made [in this way] the universe better and can still do it.[3]

---

[1] On this topic see Kretzmann, *The Metaphysics of Creation*, 216–23.

[2] Olivia Blanchette explains in reference to Albert the Great that in thirteenth-century discussions about the universe, the somewhat technical term "part" was understood as species: "Pars universi non sunt individua, sed species" (Albert the Great, *Quaestiones super de Animalibus*, 13, ad 1; for the English translation see *Questions concerning Aristotle's On animals*, trans. Irven M Resnick and Kenneth F Kitchell [Washington, DC: Catholic University of America Press, 2008]). See Olivia Blanchette, *The Perfection of the Universe According to Aquinas* (University Park, PA: Pennsylvania State University Press, 1992), 100n13.

[3] "Si quantum ad partes ipsas, tunc potest intelligi universum fieri melius, vel per additionem plurium partium, ut scilicet crearentur multae aliae species, et implerentur multi

162 Aquinas and Evolution

Following the principle of the continuity, Thomas adds that the universe enriched with new species would not be exactly the same nor radically different from the present one. It will be related to it as a whole to part. The addition of goodness will occur by mode of discrete quantity.[4]

While the first way of perfection of the universe assumes the possibility of the addition of new parts different in form, the second one consists of the possibility of the mutation of all parts of the universe to a better proportion and harmony, a finer tuning, so to speak:

> Or, it [the universe] can be understood to be made better quasi-intensively, as it were through the mutation of all its parts for the better, because if some parts were made better while other were not made better, the goodness of order would not be as great; as it is seen with the lyre, if all strings are made better, its harmony becomes sweeter, but if only some of them are made better, there is dissonance.[5]

This higher proportion and harmony of the universe might be an outcome of an action or interaction among already existing parts of it. In this case, an essential goodness of the universe remains unchanged. But God is able to make it still more perfect in what may be characterized as an instantiation of an accidental perfection, increasing and enhancing the original order in nature.

Finally, from the standpoint of the order of all things to the final end, as they draw closer to it, creatures can attain greater similitude to the divine goodness and thus contribute to the greater perfection of the universe as a whole:

> [S]o far as the goodness of the parts of the universe and their order to one another would increase, the order to the end might improve as well, because they would come closer to the end, and they would attain more similitude to the divine goodness, which is the end of all things.[6]

gradus bonitatis qui possunt esse, cum etiam inter summam creaturam et Deum infinita distantia sit; et sic Deus melius universum facere potuisset et posset" (*Super I Sent.* 44, 1, 2, co.).

[4] "[T]hat universe would be related to the present one as whole to part, and so it would be neither completely the same nor completely different, and this addition of goodness would be by way of discrete quantity" (*ibid.*).

"[I]llud universum se haberet ad hoc sicut totum ad partem; et sic nec penitus esset idem, nec penitus diversum; et haec additio bonitatis esset per modum quantitatis discretae."

[5] "Vel potest intelligi fieri melius quasi intensive, quasi mutatis omnibus partibus ejus in melius, quia si aliquae partes meliorarentur aliis non melioratis, non esset tanta bonitas ordinis; sicut patet in cithara, cujus si omnes chordae meliorantur, fit dulcior harmonia; sed quibusdam tantum melioratis, fit dissonantia" (*ibid.*).

[6] "[E]t sic secundum quod cresceret bonitas partium universi et ordo earum ad invicem, posset meliorari ordo in finem, ex eo quod propinquius ad finem se haberent, quanto similitudinem divinae bonitati magis consequerentur, quae est omnium finis" (*ibid.*).

Aquinas on the Emergence of New Species 163

This analysis is striking. Nowhere else in Aquinas' works can we find a direct suggestion concerning the possibility of the addition of new species. His opinion expressed in (4) follows the one shared in (3) only indirectly, as it is not clear whether "other things" (*alias res*) and "something" (*alias*) can be interpreted as new species. Nevertheless, we need to emphasize once again that the argumentation encountered in (3) is by no means a definitive proof for the presence of the seeds of the modern concept of evolution in Aquinas. The *Commentary on the Sentences* is one of the earliest works written by Thomas,[7] and the idea of the creation of new species will never return in his mature theological writings. Moreover, even if new species can emerge, they would be actualizations of *rationes seminales*. There is no place for transformism in Aquinas, just as there was none in Augustine, whose interpretation of Genesis he embraces. Finally, the next two passages from the *Summa theologiae* quoted in the Table (5–6) go into the opposite direction. Thomas claims in them that it is only with regards to the number of individuals and not of species that the perfection of the universe can grow. He also adds that the first constitution of the species belongs to the work of the six days. Yet, we do not learn from him when exactly the work of adornment (*opus ornatus*) was accomplished. All that he seems to be telling us is that at present, we may observe only reproduction within already existing species.

However, one more passage related to the same topic (6) becomes yet another "game changer." Here Aquinas, following moderate Aristotelian realism, faces the scientific fact of new species emerging from putrefaction and crossbreeding. Although this fact does not fit easily in his theological view assuming that no new species come into existence after the work of the six days was accomplished, Aquinas does not deny it. Rather, he tries to interpret it in reference to Augustine's notion of *rationes seminales*, which he adopts for his own theology. What is crucial for our analysis, however, is the very possibility of the emergence of new species even today. Still, we cannot forget that for Aquinas such occurrences are exceptions rather than regularities.

---

[7] Aquinas wrote his *Commentary on the Sentences* during his first teaching years in Paris between 1252/53–1254/55, although its composition was not fully complete even when Thomas began his activities as a master in 1256. The authorization permitting public teaching of the Aristotelian corpus, approved at this time at the University of Paris, was a great inspiration for Aquinas as a beginning scholar. Torrell notes that "The young bachelor did not hide his aims, and his choices show up immediately. There are more than 2000 quotations from Aristotle in the commentary on Lombard's four books" (Jean-Pierre Torrell, *Saint Thomas Aquinas. Vol. 1: The Person and His Work* [Washington, DC: The Catholic University of America Press, 2005], 41, 332).

164   *Aquinas and Evolution*

Emergence of New Species through Transformism

The second question we can ask is more specific. Is Aquinas's theology open to the notion of the emergence of new species through the transformation of already existing ones? The first two passages (8–9) in the second part of the table remind us, first of all, that no creature can create. This becomes obvious on account of my description of Aquinas's philosophical theology of creation in Chapter 4. For creation is *ex nihilo* and involves the continual bestowal of *esse,* which requires an infinite power. However, one might say – and I will develop an argument in favor of this supposition in the next chapter – that species transformism is not a part of the work of creation (*opus creationis*) but rather an aspect of the work of adornment (*opus ornatus*). First exemplars of new species come into existence from already existent matter (their SSFF are educed from it). This might potentially open a "space" for evolutionary thinking. Yet, Aquinas's reflection on the possible ways of actualization of *rationes seminales,* discussed in Chapter 4 and summarized in the Table (10–13), is neither clear nor entirely consistent – possibly due to the fact that the questions he asked in his time were different from those we ask nowadays.

According to (10), even if the emergence of all "corporeal creatures" (all species) is classified as "production," they nonetheless "came immediately from God" (hence, there is no space for transformism).[8] Yet, "the production of plants" as described in (11) might be possibly

---

[8] Note that when Thomas emphasizes that "the corporeal forms that bodies had when first produced came immediately from God" (*ST* I, 65, 4, co.), he speaks about immediate origin of forms from God in opposition to Plato and Avicenna who thought corporeal forms were derived from spiritual substances. At the same time, we need to remember that Aquinas does speak about causal influence of spiritual (separated) substances (angels) in creation: "Corporeal forms, therefore, are caused, not as emanations from some immaterial form, but by matter being brought from potentiality into act by some composite agent. But since the composite agent, which is a body, is moved by a created spiritual substance, as Augustine says (*De Trin.* III, 4,5), it follows further that even corporeal forms are derived from spiritual substances, not emanating from them, but as the term of their movement" (*ST* I, 65, 4, co.). Moreover, as I have already mentioned towards the end of Chapter 1, in reference to Aristotle's cosmology, Aquinas also speaks about the influence of the celestial bodies (sun and stars) on the events taking place on earth: "The heavenly bodies inform earthly ones by movement, not by emanation" (*ST* I, 65, 4, ad 3). See also *SCG* III, 67, no. 5; *SCG* III, 69, no. 24; *ST* I, 118, 1, ad 3; *Q. de pot.* 3, 8, ad 15. Both of these claims are intriguing and defendable philosophically and theologically. However, we must remember that separated substances and celestial bodies are not mediators of divine action, but participants entering a complex nexus of secondary and instrumental causes engaged in substantial transformations taking place in the universe.

Aquinas on the Emergence of New Species

interpreted in terms of transformism, as they come "from the earth." But in (12), Aquinas seems to take again the same position as expressed in (10). This time, however, he speaks in terms of "immediate creation" and not production and in reference to higher animals ("the first man, the first lion, and so forth" – he does not specify whether the rule he comments on refers to all species). Finally, in (13), Thomas refers specifically to the first human body. This time he goes back to the categories of "forming" and "making," yet he emphasizes that this act was an outcome of an immediate divine intervention, which seems to exclude (natural) transformism.

To make things even more perplexing and vague, we might refer what I have said on (8–9) to (14), where Aquinas says that contingent entities can, in fact, "give being" to other creatures acting "by God's power." Having mentioned this argument in Chapter 4, I will further develop it in Chapters 6 and 7, showing that it does not contradict Aquinas's own claim that only God can create. Here, it suffices to note that Aquinas does not specify whether created entities could give being to new creatures that belong to a different natural kind. Hence, the question about the opening of his theology to species transformism remains, once again, unanswered.

The next two passages (15–16) take us back to Aquinas's general view on what belongs to the core of the creation dogma (see the section on Aquinas's philosophical theology of creation in Chapter 4), opening anew a space for speculation concerning "how and in what order" various species came into existence. Using the freedom he gives us, we might suggest reading the remaining passages (17–20) in evolutionary terms. The new "effects" (17) that come into existence "gradually" (18) and through "the movements and operations of creatures" (19) might be understood to be actualized through the transformation of already existing "appropriate" matter (20). Naturally, this would be an interpretation, as Aquinas could not have thought evolution in his time. I will now try to delineate the main principles of this interpretation.[9]

---

[9] Steven Baldner and William Carroll offer a commentary to (19) in their translation of Aquinas's work: "Aquinas, following the ancients, thought that worms, for instance, could be generated from the rotting of garbage. The garbage had to have the appropriate matter (the right active and passive qualities) and the action of a celestial body (the sun) was required. The biology here is incorrect, of course, but the philosophical point is what is important. Aquinas is saying that animal and plant generation need not, in principle, always take place from parent members of the species. That such, in principle, could happen is needed for a doctrine of evolution. Aquinas, of course, did not hold a doctrine of evolution, but the point that he is making here is important if his philosophy

166   *Aquinas and Evolution*

THOMISTIC VERSION OF THEISTIC EVOLUTIONISM

The fundamental and most intuitive definition of the position of theistic evolutionism (or theistic evolution) – which has its origins already in eighteenth-century reflection of some scientists, including Linnaeus – states that the belief in creation is compatible with the modern scientific understanding of cosmological, geological, chemical, biochemical, and biological evolution. Among many contemporary proponents of this view, we find the former director of the US National Human Genome Research Institute and later convert to Christianity, Francis Collins who simply states that evolution is real, but it was set in motion by God.[10] Claude E. Stipe expressed the same intuition back in 1985 saying that "Evolution occurred as biologists describe it, but under the direction of God."[11]

Since it is embraced by many Christians, coming from different denominations and philosophical and theological traditions, theistic evolutionism covers a wide range of beliefs about the extent of God's direct and indirect interventions in the processes of emergence of new species. Hence, it is not easy to form a consistent list of theses embraced by the proponents of this theological position. Francis Collins, in his attempt, mentions the following:

1. The universe came into being out of nothingness approximately 14 billion years ago.
2. Despite massive improbabilities, the properties of the universe appear to have been precisely tuned for life.
3. While the precise mechanism of the origin of life on Earth remains unknown, once life arose, the processes of evolution and natural selection permitted the development of biological diversity and complexity over very long periods of time.

---

is to be held to be compatible with a doctrine of evolution" (Thomas Aquinas, *Aquinas on Creation: Writings on the "Sentences" of Peter Lombard, Book 2, Distinction 1, Question 1,* trans. Steven E. Baldner and William E. Carroll [Toronto: Pontifical Institute of Mediaeval Studies, 1997], 85, footnote 51.

[10] See Francis S. Collins, *The Language of God: A Scientist Presents Evidence for Belief* (New York: Free Press, 2006). In 2009, Pope Benedict XVI appointed Collins to the Pontifical Academy of Sciences.

[11] Claude E. Stipe, "Scientific Creationism and Evangelical Christianity," *American Anthropologist* 87, no. 1 (1985), 149. According to Eugenie Scott "In one form or another, TE [Theistic Evolutionism] is the view of creation taught at the majority of mainline Protestant seminaries, and it is the official position of the Catholic church" (Eugenie Carol Scott, *Evolution Vs. Creationism: An Introduction* [Berkeley, CA: University of California Press, 2005], 64.

Thomistic Version of Theistic Evolutionism 167

4. Once evolution got under way, no special supernatural intervention was required.
5. Humans are part of this process, sharing a common ancestor with the great apes.
6. But humans are also unique in ways that defy evolutionary explanation and point to our spiritual nature. This includes the existence of the Moral Law (the knowledge of right and wrong) and the search for God that characterizes all human cultures throughout history.[12]

Although Collins's list might be considered to be representative for the vast majority of theistic evolutionists, his claim shared in point 4 becomes contentious for those who claim that some direct divine action is necessary for speciation events. We find early examples of those who shared this view in Russell Wallace and Zeferino González, who thought that the final steps of evolutionary formation of the first human body required God's intervention (I will say more on this topic in Chapter 8). Among contemporary evangelical Christians, we see many who view God as more actively involved in evolution of all species. Another question refers to the understanding of the distinction between the primary (and principal) causation of God and the secondary (instrumental) causation of creatures, where some interpretations might lean toward deism, while others show the tendency to predicate about divine and creaturely agency univocally (more on this in Chapter 7).

Approaching this topic from the Aristotelian–Thomistic perspective, I would like to propose the main postulates of the Thomistic version of theistic evolution (TVTE). I organized them into a list, similar to the one proposed by Collins:

1. TVTE pays attention to natural science and accepts the biological notion of evolution. It carefully follows the research and critical debate concerning the mechanisms of speciation. It also actively engages in the analysis of philosophical aspects and interpretations of the past and current versions of evolutionary theory.
2. TVTE is grounded in Aristotle's and Aquinas's hylomorphism and ontology of living beings, emphasizing their unity, in reference to the principles of their stability and changeability (see Chapter 1).
3. TVTE is also grounded in the metaphysical model of evolutionary transitions as delineated in Chapters 1–3, with the special emphasis

---

[12] Collins, *The Language of God*, 200.

168 *Aquinas and Evolution*

on the categories of the disposition of matter, levels of potentiality, and the notion of matter understood as directed toward perfection. Another crucial aspect of the same model is its assumption and defense of the essentialist notion of species (see Chapter 2), and the interpretation of the interplay of teleology and chance offered in the classical metaphysics (see Chapter 3). This foundation safeguards TVTE from the pitfalls of materialist reductionism and causal monism.

4. Theologically speaking, TVTE emphasizes, after Aquinas, that the initial act of creation is restricted to the *creatio ex nihilo* of the most basic physical matter of the elements and keeping the ever transforming and changing universe in existence (*conservatio rerum*). Hence, it clearly distinguishes between creation and the processes of emergence of new things from already existing secondary matter of the universe.

5. TVTE interprets the continual and ongoing processes of micro- and macro-evolution as belonging to the work of adornment (*opus ornatus*), whose subsequent stages are not limited to the closed and past time interval but extend through the entire history of the universe.

6. TVTE acknowledges that the perfection of the universe can grow daily not only with regard to the number of individuals but also with regard to the number of species.

7. TVTE holds that the origin of species occurs through "production" (*productio*) from pre-existing matter with ancestry, in a process of universal common descent, in which God's agency concurs with the secondary and instrumental causation of creatures. This proposal is grounded in the reinterpreted version of Augustine's concept of *rationes seminales*, which Aquinas introduces in his theology of creation.

8. TVTE does not require a direct divine intervention in the origin of a new plant or animal species. The exception is the human species, where the first human soul was created *ex nihilo* at the final step of the speciation process, and all subsequent human souls are created *ex nihilo* at the moment of conception of each new human being. The first human soul actualized PM properly disposed within evolutionary processes. TVTE remains open-minded in the debate on mono- *versus* polygenism (see Chapter 8).

It is worth noting that even if points (5–8) might be considered as going beyond the way Aquinas understood and explained creation, their

A Response to an Objection

169

introduction seems to be necessary, taking into account contemporary science, the current status of evolutionary biology in particular, and the most recent scientific and philosophical analysis of causation and causal relationships in nature. At the same time, they certainly do not contradict any of the core principles of the Aristotelian–Thomistic philosophy and theology as described in Chapters 1–4. Quite the contrary, the possibility of harmonizing them with the main objectives of the classical thought proves the flexibility of the latter and its relevance within the context of contemporary science.[13]

A RESPONSE TO AN OBJECTION

While the vast majority of contemporary Thomists would most likely agree that the version of theistic evolution proposed here is consistent with their master's teaching,[14] Michael Chaberek – a supporter of

---

[13] My position is inspired by Kretzmann who states: "Aquinas, of course, had no inkling of any scientific evidence that might prompt an attempt to provide a non-literal interpretation of the biblical account. But the very wording of the first chapter of Genesis, and his idea of the level of sophistication in the audience for whom it was originally intended, led him to join Augustine in taking a remarkably enlightened view of the way to read the story of the six days – a view that would, I think, have equipped Augustine and Aquinas to appreciate judiciously, rather than denounce, scientific accounts of evolution" (Kretzmann, *The Metaphysics of Creation*, 190).

[14] Apart from the already mentioned works by Carroll, Elders, Gilson, Luyten, McMullin, Moreno, and O'Rourke, see Mortimer J. Adler, "Problems for Thomists: I. – The Problem of Species (Parts One–Five)," *The Thomist* 1, nos. 1–3 (1939): 80–122; 237–70; 381–443; *The Thomist* 2, nos. 1–2 (1940): 88–155; 237–300; Nicanor Pier Giorgio Austriaco *et al.*, *Thomistic Evolution: A Catholic Approach to Understanding Evolution in the Light of Faith* (Tacoma, WA: Cluny Media, 2016); F. F. Centore, "Darwin on Evolution: A Re-Estimation," *The Thomist* 33, no. 3 (1969): 456–96; F. F. Centore, "Evolution after Darwin," *The Thomist* 33, no. 4 (1969): 718–36; John N. Deely, "The Philosophical Dimensions of the Origin of Species. Part I–II," *The Thomist* 33, nos. 1–2 (1969): 75–149; 251–335; Charles DeKoninck, "Darwin's Dilemma," *The Thomist* 24, no. 2 (1961): 367–82; Joseph Donceel, "Causality and Evolution," *New Scholasticism* 39 (1965), 301–302; Michael J. Dodds, *Unlocking Divine Action: Contemporary Science and Thomas Aquinas* (Washington, DC: Catholic University of America Press, 2012); Ryan Fáinche, "Aquinas and Darwin," in *Darwin and Catholicism: The Past and Present Dynamics of a Cultural Encounter*, ed. Louis Caruana (London; New York: T&T Clark, 2009), 43–59; James R. Hofmann, "Some Thomistic Encounters with Evolution," *Theology and Science* 18, no. 2 (2020): 325–46; George P. Klubertanz, "Causality and Evolution," *Modern Schoolman* 19 (1941): 11–14; Jacques Maritain, "On the Philosophy of Nature (I): Toward a Thomist Idea of Evolution," in *Untrammeled Approaches* (Notre Dame, IN: University of Notre Dame Press, 1997), 85–131; Raymond J. Nogar, "From the Fact of Evolution to the Philosophy of Evolutionism," *The Thomist* 24 (1961): 463–501; Raymond J. Nogar, *The Wisdom of Evolution* (New York: Doubleday, 1963);

170   *Aquinas and Evolution*

the theory of intelligent design (ID) – finds it at odds with some fundamental elements of Aquinas's system of thought (refer to my comments on some of his arguments in Chapter 1) and claims that the only evolutionary model that can be accepted is a version of progressive creation, that is, a diversification of species from ancestral, divinely produced, "natural species."

Categorical Distinctions

The main argument by Chaberek can be found in his *Aquinas and Evolution* where he thus defines species:

Natural species – natural kinds of living organisms, such as dogs, cats, cows, and horses. From a theological perspective, natural species could be identified with "kinds" mentioned in Genesis 1. From a metaphysical perspective, a natural species includes organisms that share the same nature. In this context "nature" is defined by Aquinas as "the essence of a thing as it is ordered to the proper operation." From the same, metaphysical perspective, natural species can be seen as living beings (composites of form and matter) that share the same substantial form. From the biological perspective these are organisms that belong to one taxonomic group of family or genus.[15]

Chaberek's position is similar to the position proposed by the Jesuit Erich Wasmann already in 1906, in response to a critical evaluation of the first attempts at reconciling Catholic theology and evolutionism, developed by theologians such as Augustin Zahm C.S.C. or Marie-Dalmace Leroy O.P.[16] James Hofmann, in his article on the legacy of

---

Edward T. Oakes, "Dominican Darwinism: Evolution in Thomist Philosophy After Darwin," *The Thomist* 77, no. 3 (2013): 333–65 Gerard M. Verschuuren, *Aquinas and Modern Science: A New Synthesis of Faith and Reason* (Kettering, OH: Angelico Press, 2016).

[15] Chaberek, *Aquinas and Evolution*, 21. See also Michael Chaberek, *Knowledge and Evolution: How Theology, Philosophy, and Science Converge in the Question of Origins* (Eugene, OR: Resource Publications, 2021). Educated in the Thomistic tradition (as a Dominican), Chaberek has openly declared – at the conference in Waidhofen an der Thaya in 2019 – that he is not a Thomist.

[16] See the English translation of Wasmann's work: *Modern Biology and the Theory of Evolution* (London: Kegan Paul, Trench, Trübner & Company, 1910). It is known that in the second edition of *On the Origin of Species* (page 481, Peckham ed. 1959, page 748) Darwin referred with an approval to the letter of Charles Kingsley, who – accepting the idea of what we might call "natural species" – claimed: "I have gradually learnt to see that that it is just as noble a conception of deity to believe that he created primal forms capable of self development (...) as to believe that he required a fresh act of intervention to supply the lacunas which He himself had made" (Letter [2534] from Charles Kingsley, 18 November 1859, www.darwinproject.ac.uk/letter/DCP-LETT-2534.xml [retrieved 20 July 2021]).

the concept of "natural species" in the Catholic debate on evolution, mentions and analyzes other thinkers using this term in their argumentation. Among them we find: Hermann Muckermann, Joseph Gredt, Richard P. Phillips, Mortimer Adler, and Anthony C. Cotter. He traces the origin of this notion of species, which was motivated by the attempt at bringing together evolutionary biology and the literal interpretation of Genesis. He argues that the use of the concept of "natural species" in contemporary debate is retrograde as it did not stand up to the criticism of biological science. It was abandoned around the 1960s, after "population genetics and molecular data such as protein sequencing opened up powerful new sources of evidence for ... universal common descent."[17]

The main difficulty of Chaberek's position is its vagueness and idiosyncratic character. He inappropriately and unproductively conflates a number of fundamental categories that include: SF, metaphysical species, biological species (and other categories of biological taxonomy), ontologically defined natural kinds, and the biblical notion of created kinds. One of the main objectives of the project developed in this volume is to keep them separate, while engaging each one of them in a constructive proposal of a plausible and intrinsically coherent model of theistic evolution. Hence, it might be helpful, at this point, to list their definitions and comment on possible relationships among them (remembering that we approach this topic from a particular – that is, Aristotelian–Thomistic – perspective). See Table 5.2.

The information provided in Table 5.2 makes it clear that – apart from the direct relation between (1) and (2) – all the other relations between fundamental categories referred to in the proposed version of theistic evolutionism require the introduction of some important qualifications and presuppositions. Nevertheless, despite the fact that there seems to be no single and simple way to come up with a unified definition of a species, the proposed classification shows that it is possible to find a meaningful correspondence between (2), (3), and (4), which makes my interdisciplinary project intelligible and coherent (this conclusion corresponds with the one formulated toward the end of the section dedicated to variants/aspects of EssSC in Chapter 2). Moreover, the correlation between seemingly most important categories (2) and (3) appears to be beneficial for both of them. On the one hand, a reference

---

[17] See James R. Hofmann, "Erich Wasmann, S.J.: Natural Species and Catholic Polyphyletic Evolution during the Modernist Crisis," *Journal of Jesuit Studies* 7 (2020), 262.

172   *Aquinas and Evolution*

TABLE 5.2 *Categories used in the proposed model of theistic evolutionism*

Category	Definition	Relation to Other Categories
(1) Substantial form	A metaphysical principle of actuality that makes a given entity to be what it is A principle in-forming PM in an individual entity (inanimate or animate)	• Fundamental for understanding (2) • Related to (4) – on the interpretation of (4) that defines essences in reference to hylomorphism
(2) Metaphysical species	A universal category that classifies a number of entities as belonging to one and the same ontological class, based on a particular type of SF that actualizes them Members of metaphysical species are individualized by signified matter (*materia signata*), and distinguished on the base of their accidental features (grounded in AAFF)	• Fundamentally grounded in (1) • Related to (3) on the interpretation that sees SSFF – defining (2) – as accessible through an analysis of empirically traceable structural and dispositional properties of entities (animate entities in particular) • Related to (4) – on the interpretation of (4) that defines essences in reference to hylomorphism
(3) Biological species	A universal category that classifies a number of living organisms as belonging to one group on the base of empirically observable phenomena such as: interbreeding, occupying an ecological niche, evolutionary history, population structure, intrinsic features (genotype, phenotype, dispositional properties, developmental program, homeostatic cluster of properties), etc. Grouping in biological species is usually pragmatic and operational	• Related to (1) and (2) – on the interpretation that sees the empirically observable phenomena listed in its definition as indicators of a particular kind of SF, which provides a metaphysical foundation of a given biological species • Related to (4) – on the interpretation of (4) that defines essences in reference to some intrinsic properties or structures, which are empirically traceable

A Response to an Objection

TABLE 5.2 *(continued)*

Category	Definition	Relation to Other Categories
(4) Natural kind	A universal category that classifies a number of entities as belonging to one group on the base of a common essence and in reference to necessary and sufficient intrinsic properties or structure(s), uniquely possessed by all and only members of a kind (essentialist definition of natural kind) Grouping in natural kinds reflects the structure of the natural world rather than the interests and cognitive skills of human beings[18]	• Related to (1) and (2) – on the interpretation that grounds essentialism in hylomorphism • Related to (3) – on the interpretation of (3) that aspires to go beyond purely pragmatic and operational approach, in order to reflect the objective structure of the world
(5) Biblical kind	The original forms of life as they were created by God, i.e., original (Genesis) kinds or Baramins (combining Hebrew *bará*, "created" and *min* "kind") Category based on a literal (pre-philosophical and pre-scientific) reading of Genesis 1	• Potentially open to (1), (2), (3), and (4) – on the perspective of a critical methodological approach to (5) defined as "faith seeking understanding"

to empirically traceable structural and dispositional properties of organisms on the side of (2) makes its grounding category of SF accessible beyond a purely speculative analysis. On the other hand, an openness to interpret the variety of empirically observable phenomena, listed in the definition of (3), as indicators of a particular kind of SF (understood as a principle that makes things to be what they are), provides for its unifying metaphysical grounding. Consequently, when using the category

---

[18] Proponents of the Homeostatic Property Cluster Species Concept (HPCSC) – mentioned in Chapter 2 (Section 4.3) – define natural kinds less rigorously in terms of a shared subset of properties that tend to cluster together due to some underlying common causes. Even more liberal is the approach of promiscuous realism about species (mentioned in Section 3.3 of Chapter 2). My approach follows the more restrictive essentialist approach to natural kinds.

174   *Aquinas and Evolution*

of species on the model of theistic evolution proposed in this volume, I mean (2) in correspondence (yet not coextensively) with (3). In other words, I suggest to perceive biological species are contingent empirically based classifications that do not always rise to the more precise level of reality assigned to the category of metaphysical species. Finally, one should note that on the proposed model, the last category (5) does not play a significant role (as a natural consequence of the fact that Aquinas's reading of Genesis 1 was not literal). Nevertheless, it remains an important point of reference that triggers an interest and development of the remaining categories (1–2–3–4).

The interrelatedness of clearly differentiated categories defined here is missing in the proposal developed by Chaberek. His effort to provide a unified definition of species confuses and conflates all five categories listed in Table 5.2. I claim that this makes his unified category of "natural species" unattractive for all members of the conversation (i.e., biologists, philosophers, and theologians). Concerning biology, the category of "natural species" compromises and uses biological taxonomy in an instrumental way. From the point of view of philosophy, Chaberek makes a fundamental category mistake. According to principles of Aristotelian metaphysics – which he declares to value and follow – organisms cannot share the same SF. Chaberek hypostasizes and attributes SF with the characteristics of a universal. In this way, his views converge with the stance taken by Plato, which Chaberek wants to avoid at all costs.[19] Finally, theologically speaking, the category of "natural species" tends toward biblical fundamentalism, which is foreign to the Thomistic and more generally Catholic theology.[20]

---

[19] As emphasized in my model, organisms belonging to one species are actualized by individual SSFF of a particular type, but do not participate in one universal SF that defines their species. Chaberek's erroneous interpretation of moderate realism about species/natural kinds is also apparent in Logan P. Gage "Can a Thomist Be a Darwinist?," in *God and Evolution*, ed. Jay W. Richards (Seattle: Discovery Institute Press, 2010), 187–202. In *In Meta.* VII, lect. 6 (§ 1335) we find Aquinas directly rejecting this position: "'And every form' which is in the matter, namely, 'in this flesh and these bones', is some singular thing, such as Callias or Socrates. And this form which causes a likeness in species in the process of generation, also differs numerically from the form of the thing generated because of difference in matter; for material diversity is the principle of diversity among individuals in the same species; for the matter containing the form of the man who begets and that of the man who is begotten are different. But both forms are the same in species; for the form itself is 'indivisible', that is, it does not differ in the one who generates and in the one who is generated. Hence it follows that it is not necessary to posit a form apart from singular things, which causes the form in the things generated, as the Platonists claimed."

[20] A more extended account of my polemic with Chaberek can be found in the following three articles published in *Nova et Vetera*: Mariusz Tabaczek, "Afterword to the Polish Edition of *Thomistic Evolution: A Catholic Approach to Understanding Evolution in the*

A Response to an Objection 175

Methodological and Ontological Naturalism

Apart from the substantive argument questioning possible openness of Aquinas's system of philosophy and theology to the theory of evolution, and his own support for the category of "natural species" and the concept of progressive creationism, Chaberek – as notes James Hofmann – engages in an ideological crusade, presenting us with a position that seems to revive the spirit of nineteenth-century antimodernism. He accuses Thomists who accept macroevolution of succumbing to the influence of naturalism and reductionism (in his approach, methodological naturalism necessarily entails ontological naturalism and reductionism). He argues that many modern Thomists, while advocating theistic evolution with regard to the human body, inevitably accept "principles of naturalism," that is, principles that include "unjustified acceptance of scientific theories as criteria by which we must judge theological doctrines."

> Once they [Thomists] gave into the naturalistic paradigm, their goal changed: from defending Christianity they moved to tinkering with Christian doctrine in order to make it 'compatible' with naturalism. This is how theistic evolution came about.[21]

Chaberek argues that adopting a new synthesis of intelligent design and progressive creationism requires "courage to challenge the neo-pagan worldview."[22] He thinks Thomism and evolutionism are incompatible:

> Aquinas believed literally in Genesis, in the separate creation of species, and the formation of the first human body directly by God. ... This cannot be changed by tinkering with some of his secondary doctrines. The incompatibility enters the very foundations of his philosophy and theology, because these two worldviews are built upon two different paradigms – the Christian paradigm based on the Bible and faith, and the evolutionary paradigm based on naturalism and materialism.[23]

He thus suggests Thomists should be open to Intelligent Design (ID) theory. In his understanding:

> *Light of Faith* by Nicanor Pier Giorgio Austriaco, O.P., James Brent, O.P., Thomas Davenport, O.P., and John Baptist Ku, O.P." *Nova et Vetera* 21, no. 2 (2023): forthcoming; Michael Chaberek, "Where Do Substantial Forms Come From? – A Polemic with the Theistic Evolution of Mariusz Tabaczek," *Nova et Vetera* 21, no. 2 (2023): forthcoming; Mariusz Tabaczek, "Evolution and Creation – A Response to Michael Chaberek's Polemic with Theistic Evolution," *Nova et Vetera* 21, no. 2 (2023): forthcoming.

[21] Chaberek, *Aquinas and Evolution*, 255.

[22] *Ibid.*, 234.

[23] *Ibid.*, 236–37.

176 *Aquinas and Evolution*

The theory of intelligent design holds that certain features of the universe and of living things are best explained by an intelligent cause, not undirected processes (such as natural selection) or the laws of nature alone.[24]

The fact that the nature of intelligence in ID is rather unclear is not a problem for him, for

[T]his theory says that intelligence must have caused the design of the organic structures, or maybe even whole species, but it does not say how it was done. The question of how exceeds the competence of ID as much as it exceeds the competence of science. (...) Explaining the origin of species belongs to theology, not to science.[25]

Leaving aside Chaberek's argument in favor of ID – its analysis and response to it go beyond the scope of this project – I would like to emphasize, once again, the difficulty of his position in which he identifies methodological and ontological versions of naturalism. As notes Hofmann, the need for a clear distinction between these positions has been emphasized in the dialogue between religion and science for decades.[26] Another difficulty is Chaberek's rigid reading of Aquinas that allows little room for any development of his doctrine if this would conflict with literal reading of Thomas's own position. In his approach, a stiff orthodoxy in the interpretation of Aquinas takes over an open-minded search for truth within his system of philosophy and theology, with space left for necessary actualizations, reinterpretations, or carefully proposed and well-argued changes.[27]

CONCLUSION

I believe to have shown, in the course of the present and preceding chapters, that contemporary Thomistic philosophy and theology remain open to the theory of evolution. The proposed Thomistic version of theistic

---

[24] *Ibid.*, 263.

[25] *Ibid.*, 211, 82.

[26] See, for example, Gregory W. Dawes and Tiddy Smith, "The Naturalism of the Sciences," *Studies in History and Philosophy of Science Part A* 67 (2018): 22–31.

[27] See Hofmann, "Some Thomistic Encounters," 12–18. My exposition and criticism of Chaberek's views concerning Thomism and ID follows the one proposed by Hofmann. More recently, Hofmann has published another article in which he expresses his critical account of the position developed by Chaberek: James R. Hofmann, "The Evolving Taxonomy of Progressive Creation," *Scientia et Fides* 11, no. 1 (2023): 199–214. In the upcoming issue of the same journal, he will publish another research paper in which he compares Chaberek's and mine view of theistic evolution: James Hofmann, "Thomistic Hylomorphism and Theistic Evolution," *Scientia et Fides* 11, no. 2 (2023): forthcoming.

Conclusion 177

evolutionism proves to be grounded in crucial metaphysical and theological presuppositions and categories of the Aristotelian–Thomistic system. Thus, faithful to classical thought, it moves it forward and advances in a way that enables it to serve as an intriguing point of reference in the age of science.

Yet, although my analysis so far forms a comprehensive and coherent view, still more can be said on the theological presuppositions and consequences of the proposed version of theistic evolution. In the next two chapters, I will address two crucial topics, already mentioned, yet requiring further clarification and specification. The first is my claim that evolutionary transitions do not belong to the work of creation (*opus creationis*) but to the work of adornment (*opus ornatus*) and divine governance (*gubernatio*) of the created universe. I will address it in greater detail in the following chapter, offering a necessary contextualization of my constructive proposal developed here.

6

Evolution and Creation

My argument concerning the theological status of evolutionary transitions, which I am about to present in this chapter, is straightforward. A number of contemporary advocates of theistic evolution – striving to prove that the scientific notion of evolution does not contradict the theological belief in divine creation – develop and support an image of God who creates within and through evolutionary processes. They define their position as "evolutionary creation" (or "evolutionist creationism") and conceive God as sharing his divine power to create with his creatures, to whom they assign a unique status of being co-creators with God.

I argue that the notion of "evolutionary creation" (as well as the theologically interpreted concept of "creative evolution") is a blind alley, as it comes at risk of falling into (or developing from) one of two (or both) significant theological errors. First, it may be grounded in both philosophically and theologically unjustified extension of the doctrine concerning divine governance of the universe – which introduces a vital notion of the cooperation (concurrence) of the transcendent (primary and principal) causation of God and immanent (secondary and instrumental) causation of his creatures – to the unique and untransferable act of creation, which can be attributed only to God and thus cannot be shared by any created entity.

Second, "evolutionary creation" may have its foundation in a philosophically and theologically doubtful reinterpretation of the notion of creation – defined in Chapter 4 as bringing the universe into existence *ex nihilo* and keeping it in existence – which extends it to the origin of the first exemplars of new species. Taking into account that those first exemplifications of new species come into existence as outcomes of accidental

The Meaning of Theistic Evolutionism 179

and substantial changes caused by contingent beings in already existing matter, "evolutionary creation," paradoxically, diminishes the uniqueness and significance of the act of divine creation. This becomes apparent in the idea of attributing to the contingent creatures a power to co-create with God, as well as in the conviction that God's creation through evolutionary processes becomes yet another aspect of divine kenosis.

Critical of the concept of "evolutionary creation," I will show that evolutionary transformations can certainly be thought as particular exemplifications of the concurrence of divine and natural causes, where the latter are regarded as secondary and instrumental agents "moved" by the primary and principal transcendent causation of God. At the same time, because they occur within already existing matter, they should not be conceived as an aspect of divine creation but rather as an important part of divine providential governance and guidance of the created universe toward its end, along the path which abounds in astonishing beauty of new types of inanimate and animate creatures.

My argumentation will proceed in the following steps. First, I will shortly introduce the main thesis of theistic evolutionism, and the way in which it provides a space and context to think about evolution in terms of it being an important aspect of divine creation. Next, I will give an account of some important proponents of theistic evolutionism who – more or less directly – speak of God as creating through evolution. I will refer both to the general context of Christian theology and to the tradition of the Aristotelian–Thomistic school of philosophy and theology. The following section will discuss the terminological shift from "theistic evolutionism" to "evolutionary creationism." Moving toward my critical response to the latter position, I will investigate the three vital distinctions: (1) between creation and transformation of already created matter, (2) between divine creation and divine government of the created universe, and (3) between creation of SSFF of the first exemplars of new species and their eduction from the potentiality of matter. Based on these distinctions, I will present my argument against the position of "evolutionary creationism." A short conclusion will close the chapter.

THE MEANING OF THEISTIC EVOLUTIONISM

I have mentioned in Chapter 5 that the fundamental and most intuitive definition of the position of theistic evolutionism states that the belief in creation is compatible with the modern scientific understanding of cosmological, geological, chemical, biochemical, and biological evolution.

180   *Evolution and Creation*

Although it sounds modest, a closer analysis of the philosophical and theological consequences of this claim and its developments raises some important questions concerning (1) our understanding of creation and (2) our understanding of evolution in relation to the faith in creation.

Concerning (1), theistic evolutionists commonly emphasize that the divine act of creation is not limited to the original bringing of the universe into existence out of nothing (*ex nihilo*) but is extended in time. In support of this assertion, they willingly refer to the category of continuous creation (*creatio continua*), perceived as a modern expression of the classical doctrine of divine conservation (*conservatio*).[1] Reinterpreting it in the context of the theory of evolution, they portray *creatio continua* as accommodating the idea of God's bringing into existence new types of inanimate and animate entities in the course of the history of the cosmos. Consequently, in reference to (2), many theistic evolutionists characterize evolutionary processes and transformations as creative, that is, they tend to classify them as being a part (an important aspect) of the divine act of creation. In addition, based on this understanding of evolution and creation, they also claim that through evolutionary processes, God allows contingent agents to participate in his creative activity.

GOD AS CREATING THROUGH EVOLUTION

The theological position described here finds more or less direct exemplifications in writings of many Christian authors coming from different traditions and denominations. In one of the statements given by the Pontifical Academy of Sciences, we read that "One could see in … evolutionary processes a confirmation of the theological concept of *creatio continua* (*creatio* and *conservatio*) which states that creation is a permanent process of participation of being."[2] Distinguishing within *creatio continua* two

---

[1] Fabien Revol traces the origin of the term *creatio continua* back to one of the metaphysical meditations of Francisco Suarez written in 1597, in which he (wrongly) attributes it to Aquinas saying "That is why S. Thomas claims that conservation is, as it were, a continual creation" (*Et ideo saepe dicit divus Thomas, conservationem esse quasi continuatam creationem*) (Francisco Suarez, *Opera Omnia*, Vol. 25, ed. Carolo Berton [Paris: Louis Vivès, 1861], D. 21, 2, 4, 791). Revol thinks Suarez and other scholastic thinkers who introduce the term *creatio continua* are clearly referring to *ST* I, 22, 103, and 104. However, Aquinas himself never uses the term in question. See Fabien Revol, "The Concept of Continuous Creation Part I: History and Contemporary Use," *Zygon* 55, no. 1 (2020): 229–50.

[2] Pontifical Academy of Sciences, "Statement by the Pontifical Academy of Sciences on Current Scientific Knowledge on Cosmic Evolution and Biological Evolution," in *Scientific Insights into Evolution of the Universe and Life*, edited by W. Arber, N. Cabibbo, M. Sánchez Sorondo (Vatican City: Pontificia Academia Scientiarum, 2009), 586.

God as Creating through Evolution

acts: conservation and creation, this statement seems to suggest that apart from keeping created matter in existence, God continually creates (also through evolution). Similar was the opinion of John Paul II who, addressing participants of the symposium on Christian faith and evolution, said that

[E]volution does indeed presuppose creation; creation is placed in the light of evolution as an event that extends along time – as a *"creatio continua"* [a continuing creation] – in which God is made visible to the believer's eyes as the Creator of heaven and earth.[3]

The idea of creation understood as extended in time and unfolding through evolutionary processes may also be found in the thought of Joseph Ratzinger. In one of his works, he states "The cosmos is not a kind of closed building, a stationary container in which history may by chance take place. It is itself movement, from its one beginning to its one end. In a sense, creation is history."[4] Earlier on, in his unpublished Münster lecture on creation, delivered in 1964, he speaks about "creation understood evolutionarily" (the term "evolutionarily" stands as an adverb in the German phrase "Schöpfung evolutionistisch verstehen"). He boldly argues that

To understand creation evolutionarily means to understand being from within in terms of time … Creation is thus not a one-time remote beginning, in such a way that the whole block of being is present there. Neither is it a beginning divided into several stages. Rather, creation is a statement that concerns being as such. It concerns being as temporal and becoming. Temporal, becoming being is as such and as a whole encompassed by the one creative act of God, which we can only grasp over the course of time and in temporal extension.[5]

---

[3] John Paul II, *Address to the Symposium "Christian Faith and the Theory of Evolution,"* Rome, 1985, April 26, trans. Paolo Zanna, http://inters.org/John-Paul-II-Faith-Evolution-1985, "[L]'evoluzione infatti presuppone la creazione; la creazione si pone nella luce dell'evoluzione come un avvenimento che si estende nel tempo – come una 'creatio continua' – in cui Dio diventa visibile agli occhi del credente come Creatore del Cielo e della terra." (www.vatican.va/content/john-paul-ii/it/speeches/1985/april/documents/hf_jp-ii_spe_19850426_studiosi-evoluzione.html [retrieved 15 May 2021]).

[4] Joseph Cardinal Ratzinger, *The Spirit of the Liturgy* (San Francisco, CA: Ignatius Press, 2000), 28.

[5] This passage is quoted in German and translated into Spanish by Santiago Sanz Sánchez in "Joseph Ratzinger y la doctrina de la creación: los apuntes de Münster de 1964 (II). Algunos temas fundamentals," *Revista española de Teología* 74 (2014), 238n122. I want to thank Matthew Ramage for turning my attention to this text and for translating it into English. Javier Novo distinguishes two clearly demarcated periods in Ratzinger's attitude towards the theory of evolution, separated by a transitional period of almost two decades. The Münster lecture belongs to the first, more optimistic period, in which he was trying to specify "in what form the evolutionary worldview, too, may be understood as

Evolution and Creation

Ratzinger's longtime friend Christoph Schönborn agrees with him and claims creation is being-in-movement and becoming, which inspires reflection of those who characterize evolutionary processes as an aspect of the divine act of creation. Building on Ratzinger's position he argues that

The Creator endows the creatures not only with existence, but also with effective activity ... his creatures become fellow creators ... What Darwin called "secondary causes" can thus perfectly well be reconciled with belief in creation. The natural causes are an expression of the activity of creation.[6]

The notion of *creatio continua* is also present in the thought of Pope Francis. First, in his address to the Pontifical Academy of Sciences, in 2014, we heard him saying that "creation continued for centuries and centuries, millennia and millennia, until it became what we know today, precisely because God is not a demiurge or a magician, but the creator who gives being to all things."[7] Second, in reference to the ecological crisis, in the second chapter of his Encyclical Letter *Laudato Si'*, entitled "The Gospel of Creation," Francis states: "God is intimately present to each being, without impinging on the autonomy of his creature, and this gives rise to the rightful autonomy of earthly affairs. His divine presence, which ensures the subsistence and growth of each being, 'continues the work of creation'."[8]

---

an expression of creation" (Joseph Ratzinger, "Belief in Creation and the Theory of Evolution," In *Dogma and Preaching* [San Francisco: Ignatius Press, 2011], 138, originally published in 1969 as *Schöpfungsglaube und Evolutionstheorie*). Novo traces "a change in Ratzinger's attitude towards the theory of evolution at the beginning of the 1980s, when he becomes aware that evolution was being portrayed as an impersonal and irrational process governed by chance, and used as an argument against theism." He finds some of the Ratzinger's critical remarks rather unfortunate. See Javier Novo, "The Theory of Evolution in the Writings of Joseph Ratzinger" *Scientia et Fides* 8, no. 2 (2020): 323–349.

[6] Christoph Schönborn, *Chance or Purpose? Creation, Evolution and a Rational Faith* (San Francisco, CA: Ignatius Press, 2007), 65. In support of his argument Schönborn (*ibid.*, 83) refers to Leo Scheffczyk who wrote: "Thus evolution becomes in a sense comprehensible as creation that does not exclude or eliminate creative co-operation, but brings it wholly into play: for in this way of conceiving it, the act of becoming something new presupposes the presence and activity of creaturely reality, with all its proper forces, its dynamics, and its causality. This, then, is a communal act in which God and the creatures both participate" (Leo Scheffczyk, "Gottes fortdauernde Schöpfung," in "Leo Scheffczyk, *Schwerpunkte des Glaubens: Gesammelte Schriften zur Theologie* [Einsiedeln: Johannes-Verlag; Auslfg. Benziger, 1977], 200.

[7] Catholic News Agency, "Francis inaugurates bust of Benedict, emphasizes unity of faith, science," www.catholicnewsagency.com/news/francis-inaugurates-bust-of-benedict-emphasizes-stewardship-43494 (retrieved 9 January 2021).

[8] Pope Francis, *Laudato Si': On Care for Our Common Home* (Huntington, IN: Our Sunday Visitor, 2015), §80.

God as Creating through Evolution   183

Among Protestant thinkers, Denis Alexander encourages us to "Think of creation like one great book. Running through the text is an evolutionary narrative thread, which describes how God brought biological diversity into being and continues to sustain it all moment by moment." He also characterizes God as creating through the evolutionary processes.[9] Within the panentheistic camp, Philip Clayton, speaking of *creatio continua*, distinguishes it from the first creation *ex nihilo* and says "it connotes that God uses indirect means to bring about creative purposes within the world."[10] Arthur Peacocke similarly speaks of God continuously creating through the processes of the natural order, working from inside the universe. He thinks "creation goes on all the time and is not just a one-off event."[11] On another occasion, he confidently emphasizes that

God is continuously creating, continuously giving existence to, what is new; God is *semper Creator*, and the world is a *creatio continua*. The traditional notion of God *sustaining* the world in its general order and structure now has to be enriched by a dynamic and creative dimension ... God is creating at every moment of the world's existence in and through the perpetually-endowed creativity of the very stuff of the world. God indeed makes "things make themselves," as Charles Kingsley put it.[12]

Following this train of thought, various advocates of theistic evolutionism go as far as to say that God gives a co-creative role to nature, allowing the creatures to participate in his own creative activity: "God is creating at every moment of the world's existence through perpetually giving creativity to the very stuff of the world" – says Peacocke.[13]

---

[9] Alexander, *Creation or Evolution*, 213. See also *ibid.*, entire Chapter 8.

[10] Philip Clayton, *God and Contemporary Science* (Grand Rapids, Michigan: Wm. B. Eerdmans Publishing, 1997), 23–24. The category of "indirect means" might be treated as an indirect allusion to secondary and instrumental causation of creatures in the classical Aristotelian – Thomistic framework.

[11] Arthur Robert Peacocke, *Theology for a Scientific Age: Being and Becoming – Natural, Divine, and Human* (Minneapolis: Fortress Press, 1993), 170; see also Arthur Peacocke, "Articulating God's Presence in and to the World Unveiled by the Sciences," in *In Whom We Live and Move and Have Our Being: Panentheistic Reflections on God's Presence in a Scientific World*, ed. Philip Clayton and Arthur Robert Peacocke (Grand Rapids, Michigan/Cambridge, UK: William. B. Eerdmans Publishing, 2004), 147–51.

[12] Arthur Robert Peacocke, "Biological Evolution – A Positive Theological Appraisal," in *Evolutionary and Molecular Biology: Scientific Perspectives on Divine Action*, ed. Robert J. Russell, William R. Stoeger, and Francisco José Ayala (Berkeley, CA: Vatican Observatory & CTNS, 1998), 359. On numerous occasions Peacocke emphasizes the interplay of chance and order in nature. He says, "it is chance operating within a lawlike framework that is the basis of the inherent creativity of the natural order, its ability to generate new forms, patterns, and organizations of matter and energy" (*ibid.*, 363).

[13] Peacocke, "Articulating," 144.

184   *Evolution and Creation*

Similar is the conclusion of Clayton who claims that "God invites creatures to participate in God's own creative activity within the world – a state of affairs that Lodahl calls *creatio ex creatione* (or, following Paul van Buren, *creatio ex amore*), which makes us *created co-creators* with God (Philip Hefner)."[14] In the same vein, Paul Davies speaks of God who "is able to bestow a reach creativity on the cosmos ... to give a vital, cocreative role to nature itself,"[15] while Robert Russell deliberates about "*Creator who, together with nature, brings about what science describes in a neo-Darwinian framework as the biological evolution of life on earth* (creatio continua)."[16]

It is worth paying attention to the fact that the notion of God creating through evolution finds an ally or becomes an important aspect of the kenotic strain of contemporary theology, which states that "God empowers and fulfills finite beings by negating Godself."[17] In other words, "By creating the world out of love, God *kenotically refrains from the exercise of detailed predetermination* in order to give room for creaturely self-development."[18] Adopting this view of kenosis in evolutionary creationism, John Haught, in his *God after Darwin*, states that

The divine infinity may be thought of – in our imperfect human concepts – as "contracting" itself, foregoing any urge to direct the creation forcefully or to absorb it into the divine. An unrestrained display of infinite presence or "omnipotence"

[14] Philip Clayton, "Kenotic Trinitarian Panentheism," *Dialog* 44, no. 3 (2005), 252. Clayton refers to Philip J. Hefner, *The Human Factor: Evolution, Culture, and Religion* (Minneapolis: Fortress Press, 1993).

[15] Paul Davies, "Teleology without Teleology: Purpose through Emergent Complexity," in *In Whom We Live and Move and Have Our Being: Panentheistic Reflections on God's Presence in a Scientific World*, ed. Philip Clayton and Arthur Robert Peacocke (Grand Rapids, Michigan/Cambridge, U.K.: William. B. Eerdmans Publishing, 2004), 104.

[16] Robert John Russell, "Special Providence and Genetic Mutation: A New Defense of Theistic Evolution," in *Evolutionary and Molecular Biology: Scientific Perspectives on Divine Action*, ed. Robert J. Russell, William R. Stoeger, and Francisco José Ayala (Berkeley, CA: Vatican Observatory & CTNS, 1998), 194.

[17] Daniel J. Peterson, "The Kenosis of the Father: Affirming God's Action at the Higher Levels of Nature," *Theology and Science* 11, no. 4 (2013), 453.

[18] Niels Henrik Gregersen, "Deep Incarnation and Kenosis: In, With, Under, and As: A Response to Ted Peters," *Dialog* 52, no. 3 (2013), 257. Gregersen adds that this position is followed, among others, by Jurgen Moltmann, John Polkinghorne, and Arthur Peacocke. John Polkinghorne joins them when he says that "divine power is deliberately self-limited to allow causal space for creatures" (J. C. Polkinghorne, "Kenotic Creation and Divine Action," in *The Work of Love: Creation as Kenosis*, ed. J. C. Polkinghorne [Grand Rapids, MI and Cambridge, UK: Eerdmans, 2001], 102).

THOMISTIC NOTION OF GOD CREATING THROUGH EVOLUTION

would leave no room for anything other than God, and so it would rule out any genuine evolutionary *self-transcendence* on the part of the cosmos. It is a humble "retreat" on God's part that allows the cosmos to stand forth on its own and then to evolve as a relatively autonomous reality distinct from its creative ground. In this sense, creation and its evolutionary unfolding would be less the consequence of an eternal divine "plan" than of God's humble and loving "letting be."[19]

THOMISTIC NOTION OF GOD CREATING THROUGH EVOLUTION

Within Thomistic circles, in the co-authored popular volume on the Thomistic approach to evolution, we find an essay by Nicanor Austriaco, in which he seems to follow some crucial aspects of the described view of God as creating through evolution. Referring to another theological category of divine governance of the created universe (God's *gubernatio*), Austriaco notes, after Aquinas, that "God shares his perfection with his creatures by inviting them to participate in his causality, which in the world manifests itself in his governance of his creation."[20] Having said this, Austriaco takes yet another step, which goes beyond what was originally said by Aquinas and claims that "in doing so, he [God] was able to give his creation – the material universe and the individual creatures within it – a share in his causality to create."[21] Being a Thomist, Austriaco immediately amends his conclusion saying that the causality in question "is not the causality that allows one to create from nothing, because this causality is the sole prerogative of God who alone is creator." Nonetheless, classifying it as secondary causation he does assert it "allows one to create novelty and diversity from pre-existing matter."[22] Most importantly, bringing his argument to its logical conclusion, he refers to the theory of evolution and states that

---

[19] John F. Haught, *God After Darwin: A Theology of Evolution* (Boulder, CO: Westview Press, 2000), 112.

[20] Nicanor Pier Giorgio Austriaco, "The Fittingness of Evolutionary Creation," in Nicanor Pier Giorgio Austriaco et al., *Thomistic Evolution: A Catholic Approach to Understanding Evolution in the Light of Faith* (Tacoma, WA: Cluny Media, 2016), 185. Commenting once again on *ST* I, 103, 6, co. where Thomas notes that "God so governs things that he makes some of them to be causes of others in government" Austriaco adds that "according to St. Thomas it is a greater perfection, and therefore, more fitting, for God to share his causality with his creatures, making them authentic causes that can cause by their own natures, than for God to remain the sole cause acting within creation" (Austriaco, "The Fittingness," 186).

[21] *Ibid.*, 187.

[22] *Ibid.*

Evolution and Creation

[O]nce God has chosen to create through his creatures, it was fitting that he used evolution to create rather than another means, because evolution is the most efficient way for Divine Providence to use non-personal instrumental causes to generate novel and adaptive life forms on a dynamic and ever changing planet.[23]

Note that this statement, asserting that God does create through his creatures, speaks about evolution both in terms of creation (God uses evolution to create) and generation (God uses evolution to bring about novel and adaptive life forms). This remains in line with Austriaco's conviction that the divine act of creation extends to (includes) bringing about (originating) novelty from the already existing matter.[24]

It seems that other Thomists who find the theory of evolution compatible with the classical philosophy and theology are rather hesitant to state that God creates through evolution and to attribute to creatures the power to co-create with God. Much more modest in their conclusions, they simply strive to prove that evolutionary theory does not oppose the principles of classical philosophy and the Christian dogma of creation. However, Austriaco does have predecessors. In the summary of an article written in 1965, in which he presents a survey of a number of neo-scholastic thinkers writing on causality and evolution, Joseph Donceel speaks about God who indeed "makes them [contingent beings] transcend their own possibilities, thus in a certain sense *creating* new realities through and with them."[25] Similarly, in conclusion of his article written in 1972, Benedict Ashley states that "if 'creation' and 'creativity' are used (as common usage has it today) not in view of the material but the final cause, that is, the novelty and uniqueness of what is produced, then even in Thomistic metaphysics God can and does share his creativity with his creatures." He claims this view is possible provided that we use "the terms 'creation' and 'creativity' in the broad sense in which

---

[23] *Ibid.*, 188.

[24] I believe Austriaco's position is similar to the one offered by Mivart who distinguishes between "absolute" and "derivative" creation, where the former is the "absolute origination of anything by God without pre-existing means or material, and is a *supernatural* act," and the latter is "the divine action by and through natural laws ... [which brings changes in the] pre-existing matter [that] has been created with the potentiality to evolve from it, under suitable conditions, all the various forms it subsequently assumes" (Mivart, *On the Genesis of Species*, 290–91, 301).

[25] Donceel, "Causality and Evolution," 315. The article analyzes positions of Karl Rahner, Edmond Brisbois, Norbert Luyten, Jacques Maritain, Joseph Finance, Pierre Teilhard de Chardin, and Piet Schoonenberg. They all emphasize the role of secondary causes in evolutionary transformations. Yet, they do not speak of them in terms of their alleged ability to co-create with God.

creatio ex nihilo is the mode of activity proper to God, while creatures participate in this only in their own mode as secondary causes acting to perfect the *existing* universe."[26]

"THEISTIC EVOLUTIONISM" *VERSUS* "EVOLUTIONARY CREATIONISM"

Such understanding of creation and evolution finds continuation in a terminological shift suggested by Denis Lamoureux who claims that the word arrangement in the term "theistic evolution" is rather unfortunate as it places "the process of evolution as the primary term, and makes the Creator (creation) secondary as merely a qualifying adjective." He thus prefers to speak about "evolutionary creation" or "evolutionary creationism" – making "creation" the primary term and "evolutionary" a qualifying one. He states, "Evolutionary creation claims that the Father, Son, and Holy Spirit created the universe and life through an ordained, sustained, and design-reflecting evolutionary process."[27]

The roots of "evolutionary creation" might be traced back to yet another term "creative evolution" that was first introduced by Henri Bergson as the title of his book published in 1906 (*L'évolution créatrice*).[28] Obviously, what Bergson had in mind when he proposed it was the popular (folk) meaning of the term "creation," which he used to develop a philosophy capable of accounting both for the continuity of all living beings, as well as their discontinuity (divergence and differentiation). He saw the latter as grounded in creative processes of evolution. Hence, he equated life with creation and creativity, understood as processes capable of bringing novelty out of already existing matter.[29] And yet, the meaning of Bergson's "creative evolution" has changed with Teilhard de Chardin who saw it as an adequate expression of his deep philosophical and theological conviction that God as Creator uses evolution to bring about (unfold) his divine plan.[30] Enthusiastic about this shift in meaning

---

[26] Ashley, "Causality and Evolution," 230, note 52.

[27] Denis O. Lamoureux, "Evolutionary Creation: Moving Beyond the Evolution Versus Creation Debate," *Christian Higher Education* 9, no. 1 (2009), 28–30.

[28] Henri Bergson, *Creative Evolution*, trans. by Arthur Mitchell (New York: Henry Holt and Company, 1911).

[29] See Leonard Lawlor and Valentine Moulard Leonard, "Henri Bergson," in *The Stanford Encyclopedia of Philosophy*, ed. Edward N. Zalta, Summer 2016 (Metaphysics Research Lab, Stanford University, 2016), https://plato.stanford.edu/archives/sum2016/entries/bergson/ (retrieved 17 April 2020), section 5.

[30] See Pierre Teilhard de Chardin, *The Phenomenon of Man* (New York: Harper, 1959), 105, 263, 268.

of the term in question, a French Dominican Marie Joseph Nicolas commented on it in 1973 asserting that when we speak about creative aspects of evolutionary transitions, "It is not a creative evolution [in Bergsonian terms – that we have in mind] but a creation [understood as God's act] expressing itself completely only through evolution."[31]

It turns out that the term "evolutionary creation" was accepted by many thinkers, including a number of theistic evolutionists like Austriaco – who puts it in the title of his essay, in which he also speaks about "the fittingness of evolutionary creation"[32] – or Denis Alexander, who gives the title "Evolutionary Creationism" to one of the core chapters of his popular book discussing creation and evolution.[33] Hence, although it was proposed as an alternative to "theistic evolutionism," "evolutionary creationism" was, in fact, gradually embraced by its chief advocates. Is it then possible to distinguish these positions? Scott suggests it is and states that "The differences between EC [evolutionary creation] and theistic evolution lie not in science but in theology, with EC being held by more conservative (Evangelical) Christians, who view God as being more actively involved in evolution than do most theistic evolutionists."[34]

However, the proposed demarcation line is rather conventional since, on the one hand, we find scholars such as Jim Stump who – being the vice president of the BioLogos Foundation, founded in 2007 by the evangelical Christian Francis Collins (mentioned above), who put evolutionary creation as one of its core commitments – describes divine interventions in the natural order of the universe as indirect, in the manner resembling the classical notion of God working through secondary and instrumental causes. On the other hand, we find Catholic thinkers such as Avery Robert Dulles who perceive divine action in evolution in terms of more direct interventions:

If God is so active in the supernatural order, producing effects that are publicly observable, it is difficult to rule out on principle all interventions in the process of evolution. Why should God be capable of creating the world from nothing but incapable of acting within the world he has made? The tendency today is to say

---

[31] Marie Joseph Nicolas, *Evolution et christianisme. De Teilhard de Chardin à saint Thomas d'Aquin* (Paris: Fayard, 1973), quotation after Fiorenzo Facchini, "Man, Origin and Nature," in *Interdisciplinary Encyclopedia of Religion and Science*, 2002, http://inters.org/origin-nature-of-man (retrieved 17 April 2020).

[32] Austriaco, "The Fittingness," 182–83.

[33] Denis Alexander, *Creation or Evolution*, Chapter 8.

[34] Eugenie Scott, "The Creation/Evolution Continuum," *National Center for Science Education*, 2016, https://ncse.ngo/creationevolution-continuum (retrieved 17 April 2020).

Distinctiveness of Creation

that creation was not complete at the origins of the universe but continues as the universe develops in complexity.[35]

Nevertheless, putting aside these terminological queries, what comes out from my analysis so far is a more or less consistent image of God whose creative act is extended in time, who thus creates also through evolutionary processes and transformations, giving to his creatures a power to co-create with him (i.e., sharing with them his divine power to create). It is precisely this view that will be an object of my criticism in the remaining part of this chapter.

DISTINCTIVENESS OF CREATION

Anyone familiar with the classical philosophical theology of Aquinas realizes that the image of God co-creating with contingent beings contradicts his, already-mentioned, clear-cut assertion that "It is impossible for any creature to create, either by its own power or instrumentally – that is, ministerially" (*ST* I, 45, 5, co.).[36] Having defined in Chapter 4 Aquinas's understanding of creation of the universe, we can now distinguish it clearly from all the transformations that created entities may and do enter in the course of its history.

Creation *versus* Transformation

As I have already pointed out in the section dedicated to Aquinas's philosophical definition of creation in Chapter 4, and referred to in Chapter 5,

---

[35] Avery Robert Dulles, "God and Evolution," in *First Things*, 176 (2007): 19–24.

[36] "Now the proper effect of God creating is what is presupposed to all other effects, and that is absolute being. Hence nothing else can act dispositively and instrumentally to this effect, since creation is not from anything presupposed, which can be disposed by the action of the instrumental agent" (*ibid.*). See also *ST* I, 65, 3, co. In *SCG* II, 20–21, Aquinas presents a series of arguments in support of his thesis that no (created) body is capable of creative action, which in turn belongs to God alone. In *SCG* II, 21, no. 2 he states categorically that "creation is exclusively proper to God, who is the first agent." In *SCG* II, 21, no. 7 he further explains: "If, therefore, there exists a creature which participates in the work of creation as an instrument of the first creator, it must do so by an action due and proper to its own nature. Now, the effect answering to an instrument's proper action is prior, in the order of productive process, to the effect corresponding to the principal agent ... Hence, by the proper operation of the creating instrument, something will have to be produced that is prior, in the order of production, to being – which is the effect corresponding to the action of the first agent. But this is impossible, because, the more universal a thing is, the greater its priority in the order of production ... That any creature should exercise creative action, either as principal agent, or instrumentally, is, therefore, impossible."

190   *Evolution and Creation*

Aquinas – following Augustine – perceives the production (*productio*) of more complex contingent beings as mediated through the more basic forms of material stuff, the origin of which was the outcome of the work/ act of creation (*opus creationis*). Consequently, with reference to the primordial act of *creatio ex nihilo* (Ia), he sees plants and animals as indeed originating from it but not as fully actualized but rather "in potency," that is "in their origin or causes," subsequently brought into final actualization in "the work of propagation."[37]

Having said this, I acknowledge that when it comes to the above-mentioned distinction between *creatio*, on the one hand, and *productio* and *formatio* on the other, Aquinas is not entirely precise and consistent in his use of these terms. For it is true that sometimes, we find him (1) speaking of *productio* in reference to both the primordial act of *creatio ex nihilo* and to the creation of man, while on some other occasions, he (2) explains *opus ornatus* as an important aspect of divine *creatio* of the universe.

To give an example of (1), in *ST* I, 45, 4, ad 3, Aquinas defines creation as "the production of the whole being" (*creatio est productio totius esse*). In the introduction to question 90 of the same *Prima pars* of his *Summa theologiae*, he informs his readers that he is about to discuss "the production of man himself" (*de productione ipsius hominis*), in reference to both his body and soul (*de productione hominis quantum ad animam ... quantum ad corpus viri*). He also uses the same category of production in reference to the origin of the first woman (*quantum ad productionem mulieris*). Moreover, speaking of the origin of human soul, Aquinas juxtaposes "making" (*utrum anima humana sit aliquid factum*) with "creating" (*supposito quod sit facta, utrum sit creata*). At the same time, speaking of (2), we find him describing, in *Q. de pot.* 5, 9, ad 8, the effects of *opus ornatus* in categories of divine *creatio*. We read about "the work of creation whereby the earth was adorned with animals and plants" (*opus creationis per ornatum animalium et plantarum*). However, these references and examples should not be treated as a final argument against the distinction between *creatio* and *productio* and *formatio* that I strive to trace in Aquinas's philosophical and theological account of creation. I think this distinction is real, even if Aquinas is not always consistent in using it.

---

[37] In reference to Chapter 4, (Ia) stands for the primordial creative act (*creatio ex nihilo*), (Ib) for sustaining and preserving (upholding) all contingent entities both in the fact that they are (their existence – *esse*) and in what they are (their essence – *essentia*), (II) for the passive aspect of creation (dependence on God in *esse* and *essentia*).

Consequently, the picture of the universe that emerges from my analysis is the one in which the most primitive, that is, least actualized, complex, and structured matter, brought by God into existence *ex nihilo* in the primordial act of creation (Ia) and kept in existence in divine act of its conservation (Ib), entered (immediately after it had been created) and continues to go through the incessant processes of multidimensional accidental and substantial transformations, which give origin to new entities (elements, mixtures, chemical and biochemical compounds, living systems, etc.), which either belong to already existing natural kinds (types) or establish, that is, give origin to new kinds (types) of inanimate or animate creatures.

It is important to remember that whenever new entities come into existence within an already existing universe, they are created in terms of (Ib) and (II), that is, in terms of the conservative activity of God who prevents them from falling into nothingness (*conservatio a nihilo*), which activity is passively received by them in their total dependence on God in their *esse* and *essentia*. At the same time, however, we must acknowledge that they are not created in terms of (Ia), that is, they do not come into existence out of nothing (except for the human soul in the origin of each human being, a topic I will address in more detail below). Quite to the contrary, they come into existence from an already existing "portion" of matter. Hence, while we may still be willing to assert that they are created *ex nihilo*, we need to add that this characteristic (feature) should not be predicated of them literally – that is, they are created *ex nihilo* in a derivative meaning of the term. Without clearly stating that our predication is analogical (metaphorical), we risk devaluing or diluting the meaning of the term "creation" in its strict sense.

Creation *versus* Governance

If this conclusion is correct, it enables us to better grasp the ambiguity of the term *creatio continua*, which is commonly understood as God's bringing new entities and their properties into the already existing universe. Because these new entities and properties were not present before, many theistic philosophers and theologians tend to relate and perceive their origin as the continuation of the initial act of *creatio ex nihilo*, which also brought into existence something that had not existed before.[38]

---

[38] It is important to further distinguish the theological meaning of the term "creation," which refers to divine action and is the subject matter of our reflection, from its popular

Evolution and Creation

But I think these are false companions. I claim that, bringing Aquinas's philosophical and theological account of creation to its logical conclusions, we should acknowledge that the very act of primordial *creatio ex nihilo* (Ia) was instantaneous and is finished once and for all. Naturally, as I have said before, it does find continuation in divine conservation (Ib) of all things which, as such, depend on God for their existence and essence (II). But the processes of transformation of the already existent matter through which God – acting as primary and principal cause, working through secondary and instrumental causation of creatures – effects (brings about) many new, including unprecedented, entities, and properties, belong to God's providential governance of the universe and not to the act of its creation. If we want to describe these processes as creative, we need to qualify our assertion acknowledging that this term is used in this context in an analogical (derivative) sense.

This refers, I think, to numerous situations where Aquinas says, for example, that the "incorporeal agent by whom all things, both corporeal and incorporeal are created, is God" (*Q. de pot.* 5, 1, co.). He certainly does not suggest that all material beings throughout the history of the universe came/come into existence *ex nihilo*, as all angels did at the first moment of its existence and all subsisting human souls (as incorporeal things) do as it continues in existence. I suggest that if we still speak of all material things coming into existence from the pre-existing matter as created, we do so based on their indirect and remote relation to original (first) substances which, after they came to be *ex nihilo*, entered the continuous chain of processes of generation and corruption that "produced," down the line, some material entity(ies) that directly preceded them in existence. Their direct material predecessors entered a particular substantial change (or changes) that effected the origin in space and time of the entities in question.[39]

---

and colloquial usage, simply noting and describing novelty of properties, entities and processes occurring in nature. Among natural scientists and philosophers, we find those who use the term in question informally and loosely, asserting, for example, that "Evolution ... created progressively more complex and adaptively more secure organizations," or that "Natural selection is creative and, much more than a sieve, creates new wonders." See respectively Theodosius Dobzhansky, *The Biology of Ultimate Concern*, Later Printing edition (New York: The New American Library, 1967) 129; Antonio Moreno, "Finality and Intelligibility," 19.

[39] This is what I mean by saying that all material entities are created (*ex nihilo*) in an analogical or derivative meaning of the term.

Distinctiveness of Creation

To put this point in a different way, we may refer to Aquinas's account of God's providence over everything in which he states:

Two things belong to providence – namely, the type of the order of things foreordained towards an end; and the execution of this order, which is called government. As regards the first of these, God has immediate providence over everything, because He has in His intellect the types of everything, even the smallest; and whatsoever causes He assigns to certain effects, He gives them the power to produce those effects. Whence it must be that He has beforehand the type of those effects in His mind. As to the second, there are certain intermediaries of God's providence; for He governs things inferior by superior, not on account of any defect in His power, but by reason of the abundance of His goodness; so that the dignity of causality is imparted even to creatures (*ST* I, 22, 3, co.).[40]

What I infer from this reflection – in reference to Aquinas's notion of creation – is that, having brought the universe into existence *ex nihilo* (Ia), and keeping in existence all the entities that constitute it (Ib) – and thus depend on God both in their *esse* and in their *essentia* (II) – God orders everything toward an end. In so doing, he bestows causal efficacy on created entities, which both participate in (due to their passive potencies) and initiate (due to their active potencies) various accidental and substantial changes of created (already existing) matter. These changes constitute an incessant flow of generation and corruption of beings on various levels of complexity of matter.

Within the processes of generation and corruption described here, new beings that belong to already existent natural kinds or give origin to new natural kinds come into existence as actualizations of the potentiality of matter. Such is Aquinas's interpretation of the later stages of the work of six days described in Genesis (*opus distinctionis* and *opus ornatus*). All species of plants and animals (or rather all first exemplars of these species) came into existence in the course of the history of the universe as unfolding *rationes seminales*, that is, they came into existence through actualization of particular potentialities of the pre-existing matter, which I believe belongs to the work of divine government.

In Chapter 4, I spent a considerable amount of time trying to answer the question of whether processes of unfolding/actualization of *rationes seminales* were considered by Augustine and Aquinas as (1) occurring spontaneously, in favorable conditions or (2) requiring a direct divine intervention (special divine action). They thought that if the latter were true, new things, especially first exemplars of new types of animal species,

---

[40] See also *ST* I, 103.

194 *Evolution and Creation*

would come into existence instantaneously in an adult (fully actualized) state, that is, outside of the regular processes of development and growth. I have shown that while Augustine assumed that all natural kinds came (come) into existence simultaneously in both ways, Aquinas seems to consider *rationes seminales* of plants to unfold spontaneously and those of animals with the assistance of direct divine interventions.

However, even if such interventions were required, they should be conceived as occurring within the processes of God's governance of the created universe and not as belonging to the divine act of its creation. For as such they would introduce changes in pre-existing matter, while Aquinas strongly emphasizes that "What is created, is not made by movement, or by change. For what is made by movement or by change is made from something pre-existing" (*ST* I, 45, 3, co.). This refers both to *creatio ex nihilo* (Ia) and *conservatio a nihilo* (Ib and II), as neither of them is movement or change.[41]

Creation *versus* Eduction

However, one might object and say that while movement and change of matter leading to the origin of the first exemplar of a new animate species do not belong to the divine act of creation *per se*, the SF of each first exemplar of a new biological kind that actualizes matter in its origin and its act of existence (*esse*) must be (have been) created by God *ex nihilo*. And if this is the case, then this particular aspect of divine governance, which is bringing into existence the first exemplar of each new animate species, actually does belong to God's creative activity.

Trying to answer this challenge with Aquinas, we must first pay attention to his thoughts on the origin of SSFF of new exemplars of already existing natural kinds (including animate species). Because SF is decisive for the identity and functioning of a given individual entity (organism), it becomes clear for Aquinas that new SSFF are actualizations of the potentiality of matter. As I have said in Chapter 1 (in section on eduction of new substantial forms), he speaks about "educing" – Latin *educere*, which in this context means "bringing out," "bringing forth," or "drawing out" – of SSFF from the potentiality of matter in the course of

---

[41] Note that direct divine interventions do not have to be considered as miraculous. If they are necessary for new animate species to come into existence, we may assume it is a part of the natural order of things wanted by God. He simply might have decided, "when" creating the universe, that they will be actualized in this particular way.

Distinctiveness of Creation
195

substantial changes. Thinking about the efficient cause of such processes and changes Aquinas distinguishes two levels (orders) of causation. In *Q. de pot.* 5, 1, co. he speaks about (1) the causality of "an incorporeal principle on which the form directly depends" (i.e., God – see also *Q. de pot.* 3, 5; 3, 6; 3, 8) and (2) the causality of "a corporeal agent whose action consists in moving something." Hence, although God is the first and ultimate cause of SSFF of entities coming into existence in the course of the history of the universe, as such they are not educed from the potentiality of matter directly by God but rather indirectly, through secondary causes.

Lower corporeal agents are not the cause of the forms in things made, except to the extent of their causality in ... transmuting matter [*in quantum disponunt materiam*] and educing the form from the potentiality of matter [*educunt formam de potentia materiae*]. Hence the form of the thing generated depends naturally on the generator in so far as it is educed from the potentiality of matter, but not as to its absolute existence [in this aspect they depend on God] (*Q. de pot.* 5, 1, co.).

Applying this general model to philosophy of biology and changes within developmental lineages of living organisms, we realize (as mentioned in Chapter 1) that when they reproduce, they do not pass onto their offspring their own SF (if they did that, they themselves would cease to exist) nor do they copy or reproduce it, but – acting teleologically as efficient causes – they educe SSFF, proper to the natural kind they belong to, from the potentiality of matter. This happens through substantial changes effecting the origin of new organisms of the same species. In the case of sexual reproduction, the change in question involves a combination of gametes, that is, fertilization, as a result of which they cease to exist, and a new organism begins to exist. Taking into account that gametes are separate entities, I have suggested (in Chapter 1) that they are, in fact, secondary (instrumental) causes acting "on behalf of" the parental organisms.

Given Aquinas's conviction that new kinds of living beings (first exemplars of new species) arise as a result of changes in already existing matter (remember his reference to Augustine's *rationes seminales*), it should be emphasized that the SSFF of their representatives are also educed from the potentiality of matter. The causal factors here are God and the secondary causes, whose action introduces movement and change. Moreover, applying the distinction of the two levels (orders) of agency to the metaphysical interpretation of generation, we should make a distinction between being the cause of an eduction of a given type of SF

196   *Evolution and Creation*

from the potentiality of PM within the order of secondary causes and being the (first) cause of a given species *per se* (i.e., a species taken as universal category). Aquinas notes that in begetting offspring of the same species, its parental organisms – acting as efficient causes making "this matter" to receive "this form" (proper for the natural kind they belong to) – are not, at the same time, causes of SSFF of this particular natural kind taken as such (*per se*). Otherwise, they would have been causes of themselves. In other words, while the coming into existence of the new organism depends on active efficient (physical) causes, its SF – which determines its belonging to a particular type of contingent beings – as well as its *esse*, depend on an immaterial and ultimate cause, which is God.[42]

Analogically, in the case of speciation, parental organisms of a given generation within the lineage L_1 of species S_1, while efficiently causing their offspring, bring to the final completion a complex nexus of accidental and substantial changes extended over time and space, which effects actualization of a given "portion" of *materia signata* by an SF that turns out to be the SF of a new species S_2, originating a new lineage L_2.[43] At the same time, we must not consider them as causes of this new species as such (i.e., species taken as universal category). Its first and ultimate cause with this regard is God.

Similar to the essence (SF) of the first exemplar of a new species, its act of existence is not directly created by God *ex nihilo*. Unlike in creation out of nothing, where "God, simultaneously giving esse, produces that which receives esse: and thus it is not necessary that he work on something already existing" (*Q. de pot.* 3, 1, ad 17); in the origin of beings

---

[42] "Now it is clear that of two things in the same species one cannot directly cause the other's form as such, since it would then be the cause of its own form, which is essentially the same as the form of the other; but it can be the cause of this form for as much as it is in matter – in other words, it may be the cause that 'this matter' receives 'this form'. And this is to be the cause of 'becoming', as when man begets man, and fire causes fire. Thus whenever a natural effect is such that it has an aptitude to receive from its active cause an impression specifically the same as in that active cause, then the 'becoming' of the effect, but not its 'being', depends on the agent" (*ST* I, 104, 1, co.). See also *SCG* II, 21, no. 8; III, 65, no. 4; *ST* I, 13, 5, ad 1.

[43] Aquinas defines *materia signata* as characterized by quantitative definitiveness, that is, concrete and measurable dimensions (actual size) and other individualizing parameters (*individuantia*). He says "the principle of individuation is not matter taken in just any way whatever, but only designated matter" (*De ente*, 23). As such, it assigns particular essence to (identifies it with) a particular individual entity, while its SF assigns it to (identifies it with) a particular species: "essence [is] terminated in a species by [a given entity's] form, and confined to individuality by matter" (*ST* I, 7, 3, co.).

Distinctiveness of Creation

within an already existing universe, God does work on something that already exists. He does it through secondary and instrumental causation of other contingent beings. This is true not only with regard to the essence of things coming into existence (especially, their SSFF educed from the potentiality of matter) but also their existence (*esse*). That is why, as already mentioned in Chapter 4 (section on the importance of *esse*) and in Chapter 5 (section on emergence of new species in general), Aquinas is not afraid to say that contingent things give being. He states they "do so because they act by God's power" (*SCG* III, 66, no.4). I claim this rule applies both to cases of regular generation of offspring of already existing species and the special cases of generation that bring to conclusion complex processes of speciation. The *esse* of new exemplars – being a participation "by likeness" in the first and pure act, subsistent existence, that is, God[44] – is nonetheless "given" or "passed on" by instrumental efficient agents, rather than directly bestowed as created by God *ex nihilo*.

This fact becomes more apparent, once we realize that *esse* must not be thought as an agent, separated from the essence of a given entity, coming "from the outside" and actualizing it. Quite the contrary, on Aquinas's scheme *esse* remains in a close relation to SF. In *Q. de ver.* 27, 1 Aquinas answers the objection suggesting that our *esse* comes directly from God: "God causes natural existence in us without the intervention of any other cause, because He created us immediately" (*Q. de ver.* 27, 1, arg. 2). He states that "God causes natural existence in us by creation without the intervention of any agent cause, but nevertheless with the intervention of a formal cause; for a natural form is the principle of natural existence" (*Q. de ver.* 27, 1, ad 2). Commenting on the same topic, Lawrence Dewan says that

When matter acquires form, matter acquires being. Thus, it is a doctrine expressed by St. Thomas that "*form gives being to matter*" [*De ente*, ch. 4]. Matter, just in itself, *can* participate in being. It is potentially a being [see *In Phys.* I, lect. 15 (§ 131)]. Thus, it has kinship with *being*, but not as strongly as *form* has. Form is the factor through which the matter comes to participate in being. Form is thus very close in nature (or ontological character) to what we call "esse." Indeed, form and being are *indissociable*; being follows upon or necessarily accompanies form, just because of the kind of thing form is.[45]

---

[44] See John F. Wippel, "Metaphysics," in *The Cambridge Companion to Aquinas*, ed. Norman Kretzmann and Eleonore Stump (Cambridge: Cambridge University Press, 1993), 93–99, esp.97.

[45] Lawrence Dewan, *Form and Being: Studies in Thomistic Metaphysics* (Washington, DC: Catholic University of America Press, 2006), 198.

CREATION AND EVOLUTION

Bearing in mind all three distinctions introduced in previous sections – that is, (1) the distinction between creation and transformation, understood in terms of the complex nexus of changes that created entities enter in the course of the history of the universe, (2) the distinction between divine creation and divine governance of the created universe toward an end, and (3) the distinction between creation of SSFF of the first exemplars of new species and their eduction from the potentiality of matter – I shall now address the main subject of my concern in this chapter, that is, the question of whether it is proper to say that God creates through evolution.

I believe it becomes clear that, from the Aristotelian–Thomistic point of view, the concept of "evolutionary creation" is rather problematic, if not altogether ill-conceived. The idea that God's creative act is extended in time and that he creates through evolutionary processes and transformations does not seem to agree with Aquinas's definition of creation in terms of (I) and (II). Even more problematic is the suggestion that God gives to his creatures a power to co-create with him, that is, shares with them his divine power to create. This suggestion stands in opposition to Aquinas who states that "It is impossible for any creature to create, either by its own power or instrumentally – that is, ministerially." For if "to create" means "to produce being absolutely, not as this or that being ... it is manifest that creation is the proper act of God alone" (*ST* I, 45, 5, co.). In the same treatise on creation in his *Summa theologiae*, answering the question comparing creation to the works of art – performed by creatures – Aquinas adds that "in the works of nature creation does not enter, but is presupposed to the work of nature" (*ST* I, 45, 8, co.).[46]

Consequently, I argue that if evolutionary processes and transformations do occur throughout the history of the created universe (and we have vast scientific evidence in support of the claim that they do), they should not be considered as an aspect of divine creation. This claim, paradoxically, diminishes the ultimate distinctiveness of creation from all phenomena and occurrences we may observe, verify, and think of. Rather, we should treat evolutionary processes as an integral part of divine governance of the created universe, leading it to its eschatological fulfilment. In other words, in the course of the complex matrix of the processes effecting particular cases of speciation, God does act as the first and primary cause

---

[46] See also *ST* I, 45, 8, ad 1, ad 4.

of novelty, working through secondary and instrumental causation of contingent creatures. But what he thus shares with them (if such language is appropriate at all) is not so much his power to create but rather his power to providentially guide and lead the contingent reality to its final end, along the path which abounds in astonishing beauty of new types of inanimate and animate creatures.

Consequently, associated with the proposed view is a strong conviction that the observable novelty of entities, their properties, and processes that they enter does not require a creative activity of God, as understood in (Ia) to occur. As such, it emerges in already existing matter, in the course of actualization of its potentiality – a potentiality with which God himself endowed it. Hence, I suggest we should leave behind the somewhat confusing concept of "continual creation" (*creatio continua*) and stick to the traditional Aquinas's distinction of intrinsically interrelated: (Ia) divine creation out of nothing (*creatio ex nihilo*) and (Ib) divine conservation (*conservatio*) of created beings. As such, they enter the incessant processes of generation and corruption, which, in turn, effect the coming into existence of new entities that belong to already existing natural kinds or give origin to new natural kinds of contingent beings. These entities naturally and necessarily depend on God for their existence and essence, which Aquinas grasps and expresses in the passive aspect of his definition of creation (II).

This conclusion enables us to avoid the both philosophically and theologically doubtful claim that extends creation beyond bringing the universe into existence *ex nihilo* and keeping it in existence. That such a claim, paradoxically, diminishes the uniqueness and exceptionality of creation becomes clear from the fact that its proponents are willing to attribute to contingent creatures a power to co-create with God, which they consider to be yet another aspect of divine self-limitation. This certainly contradicts a legitimate and valid intuition of Aquinas, who emphasizes that creation can be effected by God alone, as no creature can participate (even "ministerially," that is, instrumentally) in this act of primordial effusion of God's goodness and love, that is beyond time and space, hence, beyond any movement and change. This refers not only to *creatio ex nihilo* but also to divine *conservatio* of created things which is "a continuation of that action whereby He [God] gives existence, which action is without either motion or time" (*ST* I, 104, 1, ad 4).

If my position presented here is not mistaken, it introduces an important amendment to the view concerning evolution and creation expressed by many important and influential Christian scholars, including some followers of the Aristotelian – Thomistic school of thought, such as Austriaco,

Evolution and Creation

Donceel, and Ashley. With respect to Ashley's position in particular, I believe my analysis has shown that the broad sense of "creation" and "creativity" he recommends is actually not helpful and may distort the proper understanding of the terms in question.[47]

CONCLUSION

The idea of God creating through evolutionary processes and sharing his divine power to create with his creatures remains very popular within the circles of contemporary advocates of theistic evolutionism. I believe that what stands behind it is an originally much more modest and nuanced argument, which strives to prove that the science of evolution does not contradict the faith in divine creation. It might have been the case that, trying to defend this important position, both scientifically informed philosophers and theologians and philosophically and theologically informed scientists, began gradually to merge the two perspectives and to speak about "evolutionary creation" and "creative evolution," where divine creation is conceived as "expressing itself completely only through evolution."

I believe I have shown that the classical tradition of the Aristotelian–Thomistic philosophy and theology offers a still actual, thorough, and consistent terminological (categorical) background that enables us to avoid the pitfalls of this view. A clear distinction between creation – on the one hand – and transformations of already created (existing) matter, through the eduction of new SSFF from its potentiality, conceived as part of the divine governance of the universe – on the other – helps us develop a philosophically and theologically sound reflection concerning evolution and creation.

The next topic that requires a more careful examination is the concurrence of divine and created causes in evolutionary transitions, in reference to the classical distinctions between primary and principal agency of God and secondary and instrumental causality of creatures. The following chapter will be dedicated to it.

---

[47] It needs to be mentioned that the position I present and defend here, brings an important correction and clarification of my own ideas as well. See Tabaczek, "Does God Create Through Evolution?," 462–466, 480–481.

7

Concurrence of Divine and Created Causes in Evolutionary Transitions

Many theologians who support the position of theistic evolution willingly accept Aquinas's distinction between primary and secondary causes, to describe theologically "the mechanics" of evolutionary transformism. Their description of the character of secondary causes in relation to God's agency, however, oftentimes lacks precision. It is not entirely clear how they understand secondary causation of creatures and how they relate it to God's action in evolutionary changes. Moreover, their tendency to marry divine concurrence, defined in terms of the distinction between primary and secondary causes, with the particular version of the free-will defense argument – which entails God's free decision to limit his divine power to allow for creaturely self-determination (including human free will) – seems to be self-contradictory.

The situation within the Thomistic camp is similar, to some extent, when it comes to specifying the exact nature of secondary and instrumental causes at work in evolution. Important questions arise whether it is right to ascribe all causation in evolution to creatures – acting as secondary and instrumental causes – and whether there is any space for a more direct divine action in evolutionary transitions. This chapter offers an original model of explaining the complexity of the causal nexus in the origin of new species, analyzed in reference to both the immanent and transcendent orders of causation. Formulated within the framework of Aristotelian–Thomistic philosophy and theology, it should prove helpful for all those who refer to the secondary causation of creatures in theological reflection on evolution.

The plan of the research presented in this chapter is as follows. The first section will shortly introduce the topic of divine action and delineate

202 *Concurrence of Divine and Created Causes*

its crucial characteristics. The following two sections will describe references and understanding of secondary and instrumental causation in theistic evolution outside and within Thomistic theological circles. The following two sections will present my constructive model of the concurrence of divine and natural causes in evolutionary transformations. The last section will address the difficult question concerning the unity of the nexus of causes engaged in an evolutionary change. The chapter will close with a short conclusion.

DIVINE ACTION

The claim that God acts purposefully to call the world into being and to guide its history is one of the most fundamental themes in the theistic religious traditions. The conversation on divine action in the context of the transition from sacred texts in the Bible to theological claims about God's agency in the universe and in reference to natural science and scientific and philosophical notions of causation has a long tradition. We can think about a number of distinctions and descriptions of divine agency that were proposed in this discussion.[1]

---

[1] The most important among more recent works on divine action include: Álvaro Balsas, *Divine Action and the Laws of Nature: An Approach Based on the Concept of Causality Consonant with Contemporary Science* (Braga: Axioma, 2018); Michael J. Dodds, "Science, Causality, and God: Divine Action and Thomas Aquinas," *Angelicum* 91, no. 1 (2014): 13–36; Dodds, *Unlocking Divine Action*; Denis Edwards, *How God Acts: Creation, Redemption, And Special Divine Action* (Minneapolis: Fortress Press, 2010); Karl W. Giberson, ed., *Abraham's Dice: Chance and Providence in the Monotheistic Traditions* (New York: Oxford University Press, 2016); John Henry and Mariusz Tabaczek, "Causation," in *Science and Religion: A Historical Introduction*, ed. Gary B. Ferngren (Baltimore: Johns Hopkins University Press, 2017); Simon Maria Kopf, *Reframing Providence: New Perspectives from Aquinas on the Divine Action Debate* (New York: Oxford University Press, 2023); Ian T. Ramsey, *Models for Divine Activity* (Wipf and Stock, 2011); Robert J. Russell et al., eds., *Scientific Perspectives on Divine Action (vols. 1–5): Quantum Cosmology and the Laws of Nature (1993); Evolutionary and Molecular Biology (1998); Neuroscience and the Person (1999); Chaos and Complexity (2000); Quantum Mechanics (2001); Twenty Years of Challenge and Progress (2008)*, (Berkeley, CA: Vatican Observatory & CTNS, 1993–2008). Nicholas Saunders, *Divine Action and Modern Science* (Cambridge and New York: Cambridge University Press, 2002); Ignacio Silva, *Providence and Science in a World of Contingency: Thomas Aquinas' Metaphysics of Divine Action* (New York: Routledge, 2022); Ignacio Silva, "A Cause Among Causes? God Acting in the Natural World," *European Journal for Philosophy of Religion* 7, no. 4 (2015): 99–114; Ignacio Silva, "Revisiting Aquinas on Providence and Rising to the Challenge of Divine Action in Nature," *Journal of Religion* 94, no. 3 (2014): 277–91; Southgate, ed., *God, Humanity and the Cosmos*, Chapter 10. Owen C. Thomas, ed., *God's Activity in the World: The Contemporary Problem* (Chico, CA: Scholars Press, 1983).

Divine action in the world can be understood first [I] as (1) direct (immediate) or (2) indirect (mediated). The former mode consists in God's affecting causal factors and natural occurrences at the level of their operation, which presupposes univocal predication of divine action and the causality of creatures (however, one may argue that the Thomistic idea of God's direct action of bestowing *esse* on each contingent entity is conceived in nonunivocal terms). The latter mode is defined as sustaining and bringing changes in nature by God as the primary and principal (transcendent) cause, working (immanently) through secondary and instrumental causation of creatures. As a side note, occasionalism may be treated as an extreme version of (1).

Secondly [II], divine action in the world may be conceived as (3) instantaneous or (4) extended in time. On another (third [III]) approach to its objective character and nature, divine action can be defined as (5) ordinary (general) or (6) special (particular, or miraculous). The former refers to God's regular action in the world, while the latter describes his particular actions to achieve some specific purposes in its history independently of the course of nature. God may achieve those purposes through: (a) producing effects that are beyond the power of nature (directly yet not univocally), (b) restraining secondary causes from producing their normal effects or producing those same effects directly (but not univocally) by his causal power alone, or (c) the mediation of secondary causes acting as instruments in working miracles.

On yet another, fourth [IV] level of the debate concerning divine action, another distinction is made based on whether the world on which God acts is (7) deterministic or (8) indeterministic. The possibility of (7) assumes theo-physical compatibilism (which is opposite to theo-physical incompatibilism, stating that God could not act in the world that is deterministic). Finally [V], in reference to human beings, we may conceive God's action on them as (9) entities having true freedom of the will or (10) merely an elusive impression of it. The possibility of (9) assumes anthropo-theological compatibilism (which is opposite to anthropo-theological incompatibilism, stating that God could not act on a truly free human being).

The five distinctions mentioned here result in a plurality of positions concerning divine action in the world. Some of the possible combinations are: 1/3/5/7; 1/3/5/8; 2/4/5/7/9 (in the Cartesian-type of a universe in which human freedom occurs in otherwise completely deterministic world); 2/4/5/7/10; 1/3/6a/8/9; etc. In search for more specific examples, Augustine's notion of God's intervention in bringing about the occurrence of the first exemplar of a given species in the mature stage of its development should be classified as 1/3. With regard to the third distinction mentioned here, it seems that it might be considered as an instantiation of either 5, 6a, or 6b. God might have designed the world such that an instantiation of a new animal (or a new plant?) species requires his direct (immediate) and instantaneous intervention, which, nonetheless, belongs to its natural way of operation. Equally reasonable is an alternative scenario in which such an intervention is special and goes beyond God's regular causal activity in the world. Naturally, neither 1/3/5 nor 1/3/6a//6b is acceptable for Darwinian evolutionists because of 1/3. Concerning the fourth distinction, Augustine's notion of *rationes seminales* – regardless of whether their unfolding is spontaneous or requires direct and instantaneous divine intervention – will most likely opt for (7). The last distinction is irrelevant in this context, but we may assume that Augustine's weak theological determinism places him somewhere in between (9) and (10), most likely closer to (9), although this might be considered debatable.

I believe the above-mentioned distinctions [I–V] and the example of classification of Augustine's view of a particular case of divine agency in the origin of the first exemplar of a new species show the complexity of the debate on divine action. What interests us in this chapter is the notion of the concurrence of divine and created causes in evolutionary transitions. To specify its character, we need to discuss first the meaning of the classical distinctions between primary and principal agency of God and secondary and instrumental causality of creatures.

SECONDARY CAUSATION IN THEISTIC EVOLUTION OUTSIDE OF THOMISTIC CIRCLES

Building on my description of theistic evolution in Chapter 5, I agree with Ted Peters and Marty Hewlett who say that it is in fact a collection of views ranging from those that reluctantly consent to the truth of evolutionary theory on the grounds of its scientific credibility, to those that embrace with great enthusiasm both developmental and evolutionary worldviews. Hence, the variety of theologians who may be classified as proponents of theistic evolution goes from more conservative or even fundamentalist thinkers such as Benjamin B. Warfield to radically progressive adherents of transformism such as Pierre Teilhard de Chardin for whom the concept of evolutionary advance become a foundation for his comprehensive epistemology, metaphysics, and spirituality. Between these two extreme positions, Peters and

Secondary Causation outside of Thomistic Circles

Hewlett list a number of thinkers whose ideas gradually descend or ascend (depending on the opinion of their reader) from one end of the spectrum to the other. They mention: a cell biologist Kenneth Miller, a biochemist and theologian Arthur Peacocke, systematic theologians Denis Edwards and John Haught, physicist and theologian Robert John Russell, and systematic theologian Philip Hefner.[2]

The analysis of convergences and divergences among these theologians concerning deep time, natural selection and teleology, common descent, divine action, and theodicy shows that the majority of them value the concept of secondary causation.[3] They seem to find attractive the idea of God as the primary cause working through the secondary causation of his creatures, as it enables them to assert the autonomy of both nature and God, working on separate yet connected planes of reality. A closer analysis of their use of the distinction between primary and secondary causation, however, reveals a lack of precision in defining it. Warfield uses it primarily to explain the simultaneously divine and human origin of the Holy Scripture and only secondarily as a base for his theological incorporation of evolutionary theory.[4] Others seem to compromise the concept of primary/secondary causation by joining it to the particular version of the free-will defense argument, which entails God's free decision to limit his divine power to permit creaturely self-determination, including human free will.[5]

---

[2] See Peters and Hewlett, *Evolution from Creation to New Creation*, Chapter 6, 115–57.

[3] The idea of primary/secondary causation is not so important for de Chardin who sees divine action as uniformitarian, yet not in a deistic sense (God initially selects the laws that are operative through cosmic and evolutionary history and withdraws from any further individual interventions) but rather as an ongoing pantheistic divine guidance of evolution, internal to nature as it is internal to divine life. See de Chardin, *The Phenomenon of Man*. Philip Hefner seems to side with de Chardin on this issue. See Hefner, *The Human Factor*. The position of Kenneth Miller on divine action is close to deism (even if he strives to avoid it). He does not point toward anything God could do within the natural world, which seems to make him responsible only for its existence. See Kenneth R. Miller, *Finding Darwin's God: A Scientist's Search for Common Ground Between God and Evolution* (New York: Cliff Street Books, 1999).

[4] See Benjamin Breckinridge Warfield, *Evolution, Scripture, and Science: Selected Writings*, ed. Mark A. Noll and David N. Livingstone (Grand Rapids: Baker Books, 2000), 56–57.

[5] The free-will defense is a logical argument developed by Alvin Plantinga in response to the challenge formulated by John Leslie Mackie, who claimed that the key attributes of the God of Christian theism (his omniscience, omnipotence, and omnibenevolence) are logically incompatible with the existence of evil (see Alvin Plantinga, *God, Freedom, and Evil* [Grand Rapids, MI: Eerdmans, 1977], Chapter 4; John Leslie Mackie, "Evil and Omnipotence," *Mind* 64 [1955], 200–212). Plantinga's original argument emphasized the moral value of human free will as a justified reason for God's permitting the existence

206 *Concurrence of Divine and Created Causes*

This tendency may be clearly seen in the position of Peacocke. While he does speak about God making "things make themselves" and the interplay of order and chance as secondary causes working in nature, Peacocke writes extensively about God's self-limitation in his omnipotence and omniscience as a condition for the coming into existence of free self-conscious human beings and finds a new level of God's presence in creation expressed in his sharing the world's sufferings.[6] The idea of self-limitation of God – a fellow sufferer who thus, affected by the world, shares in the very life of his creatures – is even more transparent in the versions of theistic evolution offered by Denis Edwards and John Haught. They both perceive God as engaged in self-restraint and self-removal, *that is*, creating through letting-be.[7]

Peters and Hewlett note that free-will defenders seem to contradict their own choice of applying the distinction between primary and secondary causation in their versions of theistic evolution. In fact, they "tacitly and perhaps unintentionally reject secondary causation, presuming rather that divine power and creaturely freedom belong on the same plane. ... The fallacy presupposes a fixed pie of power. According to the fixed pie image, if God gets a big slice then creation gets a proportionately smaller slice. If God would be all-powerful, then creation would be totally powerless."[8] This criticism rightly shows that many contemporary theologians, who strive to reconcile faith with the scientific view of the universe, tend to speak about divine action in the world in univocal terms, locating it on the same ontological level as the causation of contingent creatures.

Robert John Russell tries to avoid this difficulty. In doing so, however, he seems to be getting close to the other extreme of the spectrum. Acknowledging the importance of secondary causation of creatures, he speaks about the direct divine action on the quantum level as the origin of evolutionary changes. He claims that this type of divine action is objective

---

of evil. The same argument from the defense of human free will (accompanied by the more general concept of creaturely self-determination), was later used to argue in favor of divine self-limitation in creation of the universe.

[6] See Peacocke, *Theology for a Scientific Age*, 99–134.

[7] See Denis Edwards, *The God of Evolution: A Trinitarian Theology* (New York: Paulist Press, 1999); and, *God After Darwin*. Any logically coherent theory that includes the claim that God limits his own power uses the term "God" in a sense quite different from that of Aquinas, for whom God is, of necessity, omnipotent. This will become more apparent in the latter sections of this chapter. The use of the term "God" in Peacocke, Edwards, and Haught, seems to be nearer to the one proposed by Hegel or Whitehead than to Aquinas's. See Mariusz Tabaczek, "Hegel and Whitehead: In Search for Sources of Contemporary Versions of Panentheism in the Science–Theology Dialogue," *Theology and Science* 11 (2013): 143–61.

[8] Peters and Hewlett, *Evolution*, 130–31, 143.

Secondary Causation within Thomistic Circles

and noninterventionist (NIODA = noninterventionist objective divine action), since – according to the Copenhagen interpretation of quantum mechanics – we cannot expect natural causes to operate in these events, as they are ontologically indeterminate. Nevertheless, Russell's version of theistic evolution may still be in danger of univocally predicating causation of God and creatures, since he suggests that God withdraws his causal activity with the advent of consciousness and human free will. This might suggest he needs to "make a space" for specifically human action.[9]

SECONDARY CAUSATION IN THEISTIC EVOLUTION WITHIN THOMISTIC CIRCLES

Within the Thomistic theological camp, the situation looks different. Proponents of theistic evolution among Thomists carefully avoid the mistake of the univocal predication of God's and creatures' causal activity. At the same time, they do side with Aquinas's assertion that "God's immediate provision over everything does not exclude the action of secondary causes; which are the executors of His order" (*ST* I, 22, 3, ad 2).[10] Since God as the Creator has gifted every creature with its proper causality, according to its nature, his influence cannot interfere with this causality but must rather be its source. On the other hand, they emphasize that, while we can say that a particular natural effect comes to be through the combined agencies of God and the natural agent, we must remember

that the same effect is not attributed to a natural cause and to divine power in such a way that it is partly done by God, and partly by the natural agent; rather, it is wholly done by both, according to a different way, just as the same effect is wholly attributed to the instrument and also wholly to the principal agent (*SCG* III, 70, no. 8).[11]

Thus, Thomistic advocates of theistic evolution acknowledge that, metaphysically speaking, the divine action of a transcendent God does not

---

[9] See Robert J. Russell, *Cosmology from Alpha to Omega: The Creative Mutual Interaction of Theology and Science* (Minneapolis: Fortress Press, 2008), Chapters 5–6, 151–225.

[10] See also *ST* I, 19, 6, ad 3; 19, 8, co.; 23, 5, co.; 105, 5, ad 2; I–II, 10, 4, ad 2; Étienne Gilson, *The Christian Philosophy of St. Thomas Aquinas* (New York: Random House, 1956), 176, 182–84; te Velde, *Participation and Substantiality in Thomas Aquinas*, 170–75. It is worth noting that the medieval distinction between primary and secondary causation has its roots in the neo-Platonic tradition.

[11] "[J]ust as it is not unfitting for one action to be produced by an agent and its power, so it is not inappropriate for the same effect to be produced by a lower agent and God: by both immediately, though in different ways" (*SCG* III, 70, no. 5).

208   *Concurrence of Divine and Created Causes*

belong to the same order of causation as that of his creatures. Even if "all created things, so far as they are beings, are like God as the first and universal principle of all being" (*ST* I, 4, 3, co.) immanently present in their operations, the causation of the Creator infinitely transcends causation of all contingent creatures. The influence of the first cause is therefore not only more intense, so that we can assert with Aquinas that "God is more especially the cause of every action than are the secondary agent causes" (*SCG* III, 67, no. 5).[12] We must also realize that God's agency belongs, in its essence, to an entirely different ontological and metaphysical order of causation.[13] Consequently, Thomistic evolutionists do not see any need of introducing divine self-limitation or the self-restriction of God's attributes of omnipotence and omniscience, to explain the indeterministic character of some occurences in nature, and the phenomenon of human free will.

Moreover, Thomistic theology offers one more important distinction concerning causal efficiency that might be helpful in explaining the position of theistic evolution. The passage from Aquinas's *Summa contra gentiles* quoted above, in which he attributes causal effects observed in nature to the agency of both God and creatures, introduces a further distinction in the realm of secondary causes. Some of them act according to their natural dispositions, while others produce effects beyond their capacities. Aquinas classifies the latter as instrumental causes and emphasizes their dependence on principal causes for their operation (e.g., an ax in the hand of a lumberjack). In other words, instrumental causes can be classified as a special kind of secondary causes, since every cause that acts under the influence of another is a secondary cause. At the same time, a cause that produces an effect exceeding its natural capacity should be regarded as an "instrumental secondary cause (*causa secunda instrumentalis*)" (*ST* I, 45, 5, co.).[14]

---

[12] "Therefore, to be the cause of the effect belongs first to the primary cause and second to the secondary cause. That which is first in all things is greater because the more perfect are naturally prior. Therefore, the primary cause is more a cause of the effect than the secondary cause" (*Super De causis*, 1). See also *ST* I, 21, 4, co.; 36, 3, ad 4; *Q. de ver.* 5, 9, ad 10; *Q. de pot.* 3, 7, co.

[13] The International Theological Commission has adopted this doctrine stating that "divine causality and created causality radically differ in kind and not only in degree. Thus, even the outcome of a truly contingent natural process can nonetheless fall within God's providential plan for creation" (The International Theological Commission, *Communion and Stewardship*, no. 69).

[14] Explaining the relation between the principal and instrumental agents Aquinas says "An instrument performs its instrumental activity inasmuch as it is moved by the principal

Secondary Causation within Thomistic Circles

Aquinas's further explication of how exactly God acts in the world through secondary and instrumental causes can be found in his *Q. de pot.* 3, 7. Summarizing the crucial part of the response (the corpus of the article), Ignacio Silva suggests distinguishing four aspects of efficient divine action in the world, in reference to Aquinas's list of four ways of being the cause of action of something else:[15]

1. To be a cause of something else means, first of all, to give it power to act, since every action, as a manifestation of a certain power, is ascribed to the giver of that power as effect to cause. "In this way" – says Aquinas – "God causes all the actions of nature, because he gave natural things the forces whereby they are able to act" (*Q. de pot.* 3, 7 co.).

2. To be a cause of something else means, secondly, to uphold (preserve) a natural power in its existence. Thus, "a remedy that preserves the sight is said to make a man see" (*ibid.*). In this sense, we may say that "God not only gives existence to things and their causal powers when they first begin to exist, but also causes existence in them as long as they exist, by preserving or sustaining them in existence. If the divine causality were to cease, all operation would come to an end."[16]

3. To be a cause of something else means, thirdly, to apply the power (a thing) to act. "A thing is said to cause another's action by moving it to act" – says Aquinas – "as a man causes the knife's cutting by the very fact that he applies the sharpness of the knife to cutting by moving it to cut" (*Q. de pot.* 3, 7 co.). Hence, God can be thought to cause the action of every natural thing by moving and applying its power to act.

4. To be a cause of something else means, finally, to act as a principal agent working through the thing in question as an instrument.

---

agent and through this motion shares in some way in the power of the principal agent, but not so that that power has its complete existence in the instrument, because motion is an incomplete act" (*Q. de ver.* 26, 1, ad 8). In other words, while it is proper to say that "the instrument acts not according to its own form, but according to the power of that by which it is moved" (*ST* III, 64, 5), one must not forget that "An instrument is related to an action more like that by which it is done than like that which does it; for the principal agent acts by means of the instrument" (*Q. de ver.* 27, 4, ad 8).

[15] Silva presents similar accounts of the same typology in: Ignacio Silva, "Thomas Aquinas Holds Fast: Objections to Aquinas within Today's Debate on Divine Action," *Heythrop Journal* 48 (2011), 5–7; Silva, "Revisiting Aquinas," 280–85; Ignacio Silva, "Divine Action and Thomism: Why Thomas Aquinas's Thought Is Attractive Today," *Acta Philosophica* 25, no. 1 (2016), 71–74, and Silva, *Providence and Science*, 98–102.

[16] Silva, "Thomas Aquinas Holds Fast," 6.

"In this way" – adds Aquinas – "again we must say that God causes every action of natural things" (*Q. de pot.* 3, 7 co.).[17] What Thomas has in mind here is the fact of which I have spoken before, that is, that each efficient action includes causing ("giving") being (*esse*) in one way or the other. Since it is an effect (a perfection) that belongs to God alone to produce by his own power, created efficient agents must be considered as instrumental causes of (esse).[18]

Having listed all four aspects of efficient divine action in the universe, Silva suggests classifying the first two of them as "founding" and the other two as "dynamic."[19]

The distinction between secondary and instrumental causes may be applied to the theological explanation of cases of the origin of new species, in which parental organisms of species S_1 give an origin to the first organism belonging to the new species S_2, acting thus – in some respect – both in accordance with and beyond their own causal dispositions, that is, as both secondary and instrumental causes "in the hands" of God. However, Thomistic proponents of theistic evolution oftentimes do not seem to engage in more detailed analysis of divine action in the coming to be of new species. Their argumentation seems to be limited to a very careful presentation of Aquinas's understanding of creation and his distinction between primary causation of God and secondary (and instrumental) causation of his creatures, followed by a general application of these principles to evolutionary transformism. N. Luyten, for instance, commenting on causality in evolution, states:

[17] In other words, "God is the cause of every action, inasmuch as every agent is an instrument of the divine power operating" (*Q. de pot.* 3, 7 co.).

[18] Commenting on this aspect of divine action, te Velde says: "The effect of being, *esse*, Thomas frequently says, belongs solely to God according to his own power. This is a well-known but often misinterpreted statement. Being is not simply poured in by God from above in all particular effects of natural causes as their common actualization. Although God's power is immediately related to the being of things, which is its formal effect, this immediacy does not mean that the divine gift of being remains extrinsic to the effects of the natural agents, as if being were exclusively God's effect; it is on the contrary by the immediacy (intimacy) of God's operation that every other agent is mediated with the being-in-act of its effect and thus constituted in its proper action. And it is by reflection on this mediation that it appears to us that being must be attributed to God as the effect proper to his universal power. This means that God gives being by causing every other agent to give being in a particular way, adapted to its particular power" (te Velde, *Participation and Substantiality*, 176–77).

[19] Silva speaks about "founding" (in his first paper on this topic from 2011, he uses the term "static") and "dynamic" "moments." I find it more appropriate to speak about "founding" and "dynamic" aspects of efficient divine action in the world.

Secondary Causation within Thomistic Circles

We know of enough cases where we meet a complex intertwined causality, and where a double efficiency does not simply stand beside each other, but works in a subordinated relationship. The classic doctrine of instrumentality has sufficiently studied the nature of such a causal subordination. Hence it is conceivable that, in the evolutionary process too, we must admit such a coordination of factors, in which a transcendent factor would cooperate not simply from without but from within with the evolutionary factors at work in the animal series. This means that the transcendent factor must at the same time be immanent so as to fuse innerly, as it were, with the purely immanent causality of the antecedent.[20]

A little bit more specific is the explanation provided by Jacques Maritain who, commenting on the passage from one ontological species to the next higher one, refers to the transcendent influence of the first cause, whose

existence-giving influx ... passing through created beings and using them as instrumental causes, was able – and is still able – to heighten the vital energies which proceed from the form in the organism it animates, so as to produce within matter, I mean within the germ-cells, dispositions beyond the limits of that organism's specificity. As a result, at the moment of generation a new substantial form, specifically "greater" or more elevated in being, would be educed from the potentiality of matter thus more perfectly disposed.[21]

Explanations offered by other Thomists – although generally correct and fitting within the orthodoxy of Aquinas's system of philosophy and theology (with some necessary revisions of its basic principles) – are sometimes even more general when it comes to a precise explanation of the exact nature of causal agency of God and creatures in an evolutionary change. They do address numerous questions concerning philosophies of evolution, randomness and order, design, species, intrinsic teleology, or creation and divine providence in evolutionary changes in general and in evolution of man in particular. They also provide, as I have shown in Chapter 1, a possible metaphysical "mechanism" of transformism. At the same time, however, they do not seem to clarify enough what exactly God does in an evolutionary transition and whether his causal power is entirely delegated to the secondary and instrumental causation of creatures. The purpose of this chapter is to fill this lacuna by developing a model explaining the relation and concurrence of divine action and the causality of creatures in evolutionary changes.

---

[20] N. Luyten, "Evolutionisme En Wijsbegeerte," *Tijdschrift Voor Philosophie* 16, no. 1 (1954), 30, after Donceel, "Causality and Evolution," 301–302.
[21] Jacques Maritain, *The Range of Reason* (New York: Scribner, 1952), 38.

CONCURRENCE OF DIVINE AND NATURAL
CAUSES IN BEGETTING OFFSPRING

Having in mind all principles of Aristotelian philosophy, Aquinas's definition of creation, and the principles of the Thomistic version of theistic evolutionism – presented in preceding chapters of this book – I should now offer my model of divine and natural causes concurrent in evolutionary transformation of species. I will describe it within the framework distinguishing between the two related, yet distinct orders of causation: the immanent and the transcendent. I will begin from a regular case of giving birth to an organism of the same species (see Figure 7.1).

In the immanent order of causation, looking at parental organisms (♀ and ♂) in the process of generating their offspring, we perceive them simply as proper causes of such an occurrence. We say it is due to their natural causal activity that a new exemplar of the same species comes into being.[22] Applying principles of the metaphysics and theology of Aristotle and Aquinas, however, we distinguish, first, between essence and existence of the newly born organism. Analyzing its essence, in recollection of what was said in Chapter 6 (in the section juxtaposing creation and eduction), we realize that the proper causal activity of the parents is not, in fact, a cause of PM and the SF as such of their offspring. Otherwise, they would be causes of themselves, since each of them is also an exemplar of the same species in virtue of that form. The first and ultimate cause of the essence of each contingent entity can only be God, the Creator of PM and all SSFF. Nothing prevents us, however, from attributing to parental organisms the role of instrumental causes of the essence of their offspring. Because their causal activity is accompanied by the instantiation of a new exemplar of their own species, it can be classified as instrumental for their offspring's essence taken as such. They make possible something which, strictly speaking, is beyond their own capacities to offer, *that is*, the fact of the actualization of PM by a right kind of SF of a given species (the principal cause of PM and SF is God).[23]

---

[22] Proper cause (*causa propria*) can be understood as an individual or particular cause, as distinguished from a general or universal cause. Aquinas uses the term *causa propria* in *ST* I, 2, 2, co. As such, it seems to belong to the most preliminary and intuitive causal description of the stability and change of things in nature.

[23] "[A]ll forms are potentially in prime matter, but they are not actually there, as those who held the 'hiddenness' doctrine said. The natural agent produces not the form but the composite, by bringing form from potentiality to actuality. This natural agent by its own action is, as it were, an instrument of God Himself who, as agent, both makes the matter and gives it the potency for form" (*Super II Sent.*, 1, 1, 4, ad 4).

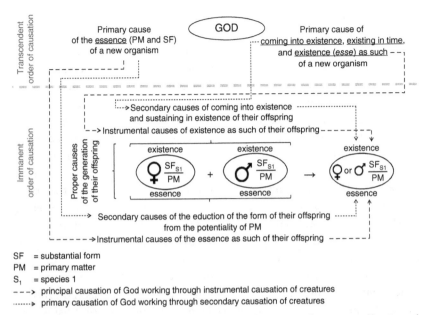

FIGURE 7.1 Concurrence of divine and natural causes in begetting offspring of the same species.

Moreover, the same parental organisms can be categorized as secondary causes of the eduction of the proper SF from the potentiality of PM, in the process of begetting their offspring, that is, secondary causes of the process of instantiation of a particular exemplar of the SF of their own species in a given "portion" of a signate matter, which is a principle of individuation.[24] As such, they give what is within their natural dispositions to offer, while being dependent in their action on the primary causality of God, the source of all efficient action leading to the actualization of PM by various types of SSFF and the ultimate end of natural teleology in all creatures.

As for the existence (*esse*) of a new organism, conceived by its parents, its first and principal cause can only be God. This fact concerns not only the existence of each contingent being in the ontological meaning of this term (existence as such) but also each contingent entity's coming into

[24] "Nature or quiddity [in substances composed of matter and form] is received in designated matter (*materia signata*). ... And because of the division of designated matter, the multiplication of individuals in one species is here possible" (*De ente*, 98). "Hence the form of the thing generated depends naturally on the generator in so far as it is educed from the potentiality of matter, but not as to its absolute existence" (*Q. de pot.* 5, 1, co.).

being (existence) and its further persistence in time (keeping in existence). God is the first and principal cause of creaturely *esse* in all three of these aspects. This is because *esse* has only one source, which is God, who bestows it on his creatures, or rather allows them to participate in his own *esse*, which is, nonetheless, predicated of them analogically.

At the same time, it seems right to say that the operation of efficient causes (parental organisms acting in the immanent order of causation) is accompanied or followed by coming into being of their offspring, even though they are not first and principal causes (sources) of *esse* as such. Therefore, they can be described as secondary causes of coming into existence of their offspring, acting with the power given them by God – the transcendent and first source of all *esse* in the immanent order of created world. Note that we are talking here about secondary causation, since the causality of parental organisms, which is followed by an instantiation (coming into being) of the *esse* of a new exemplar of their own species lies within their natural dispositions. Similarly, sustaining a contingent entity in being (*esse*) is also the work of God as the primary cause. At the same time, it seems right to say God does that using secondary causes that work in the immanent order of causation.[25] Hence, to give an example, parents of a newborn offspring taking care of its well-being should be considered as secondary causes of sustaining it in existence (*esse*). They realize their natural dispositions, while acting by the power of God, who is the first cause of *conservatio divina*. Moreover, even if *esse* as such has God as its principal cause, contingent creatures can be considered as causing it instrumentally. They cannot "give" *esse*, but their agency brings or is accompanied by an instantiation of a new organism, which has *esse* bestowed on it by God.

Consequently, we can say that parental organisms giving birth to a new exemplar of their own species are: (1) proper causes of its coming into being (in a most basic and pre-philosophical causal explanation); (2) secondary causes of the instantiation of its essence (i.e., the eduction of the appropriate form from the potentiality of PM) and of its coming into existence and keeping in existence (permanence in time) – dependent on the primary causality of God, the origin and source of all efficient causality effecting the actualization of PM by the variety of SSFF and the ultimate end of natural teleology in creatures; and (3) instrumental causes of the new organism's essence (*essentia*) and existence (*esse*)

---

[25] See *ST* I, 104, 2 sc.: "God gives being by means of certain intermediate causes," so too God "keeps things in being by means of certain causes."

as such – dependent on the principal causation of God, the Creator of PM and all SSFF, and the first and only source of *esse*. Note that creaturely *esse*, though having its primary and direct source in God (being *de facto* a participation in divine *esse*), is not the same as God's *esse*. It is *esse* that does come from God but is proportionate to the essence (*essentia*) of a creature and not identical with it. Hence, we predicate *esse* of creatures analogously (using both analogy of attribution and of proper proportionality).

In other words, the same action of parental organisms, which are considered as proper causes of their own descendant within the immanent order of causation, has the nature of secondary and instrumental causation from the point of view of the transcendent order of causation, in which God himself is the first and principal cause of the essence and existence of every contingent being.

The distinction between primary and principal causation of God and the secondary and instrumental causation of creatures seems to be crucial here. It helps us avoid the two extreme positions of deism (God who created the universe and the laws of nature is no longer actively engaged in its existence and the changes it is going through) and occasionalism (causation of creatures is not real but is merely an occasion for God to act). Creatures exercise causal action that is real and proper to their dispositions. Their agency, however, has the character of secondary causation in educing forms from the potentiality of PM and coming into existence of new contingent entities. Considering the essence and existence as such of these novel beings, other creatures can only be regarded as their instrumental causes, which emphasizes the depth of the involvement and causal activity of God as the primary and principal cause of creation.

Consequently, my analysis shows there is no opposition between the two already mentioned texts in Thomas' *Summa Theologiae* and *Summa Contra Gentiles*, the first stating "it is impossible for any creature to create, either by its own power or instrumentally – that is, ministerially" (*ST* I, 45, 5, co.), and the second asserting that "being is the proper product of the primary agent, that is, of God; and all things that give being do so because they act by God's power" (*SCG* III, 66, no. 4). To understand that they do not contradict each other, it suffices to realize (as mentioned in the section dedicated to the importance of *esse* of Chapter 4) that secondary agents (acting in the immanent causal order) can cause the eduction of a suitable SF from the potentiality of PM and the coming into existence of a new contingent entity (*causa fiendi*) but are never causes of its *essentia* and

216 *Concurrence of Divine and Created Causes*

esse as such (*causa essendi*). The principal cause of essence and existence of new entities is God. Even if other creatures can be regarded as instrumental causes of their essence and existence, they are not, strictly speaking, causing them. Their agency is simply providing suitable conditions for the instantiation of new entities of a given type (i.e., characterized by a particular essence and its proportionate act of existence).

CONCURRENCE OF DIVINE AND NATURAL CAUSES IN AN EVOLUTIONARY TRANSFORMATION

The description of causal relationships at the immanent and the transcendent levels of causation in begetting offspring turns our attention to a special case of such an occurrence, a begetting by parents belonging to the species S_1 of the first exemplar of a new species S_2 (i.e., coming to be of a new species in an evolutionary transformation). Remembering what was said in the section on virtual and eminent presence of perfections in Chapter 1, we must emphasize, once again, that the exact moment of the eduction of SF of a new species is an outcome of an extremely complex process that is extended in time and causally polygenic. It involves spontaneous chance mutations (affecting genes, chromosomes, or entire genomes), genetic recombination, gene transfer, genetic drift, and epigenetic changes, which affect genotype and phenotype of organisms that strive to survive and produce fertile offspring (natural teleology). Contribution of these changes to the benefit of the organism is verified by the mechanism of natural selection. All these factors, taken as a whole, can be regarded as proper causes (or one unified cause) of the first exemplar of a new species S_2 in the immanent order of causation. Looking at this process from the perspective of the transcendent order of causation, we can define and make a distinction between secondary and instrumental causes of the origin of the prototype of a new species S_2 (refer Figure 7.2).

If the explanation presented here is correct, then – as in the case of an ordinary begetting of an offspring belonging to the same species – our causal description of the instantiation of the first representative of the new species S_2 allows us to distinguish and name:

1. Proper cause of its origin in the immanent order of causation (in a most basic and prephilosophical causal explanation), that is, its parental organisms, within the complex system of immanent causes, involved in the polygenic causal matrix of an evolutionary change leading to the coming-to-be of the first exemplar of the species S_2.

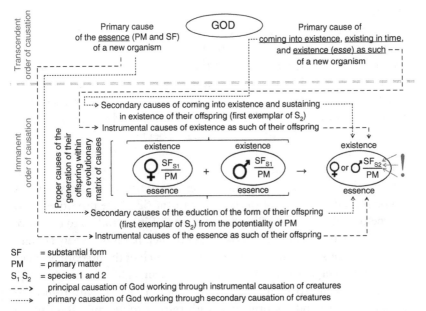

FIGURE 7.2 Concurrence of divine and natural causes in an evolutionary transition.

2. Secondary cause of the eduction of its proper SF from the potentiality of PM, that is, parental organisms, within the complex system of immanent causes, involved in the polygenic process of instantiation of the first exemplar of the SF of the new species S_2 in a given "portion" of a signate mater, which is its principle of individuation.
3. Instrumental cause of its essence (*essentia*) as such, that is, agency of the parental organisms, within the complex system of immanent causes, which is accompanied by the instantiation of the first exemplar of the new species S_2 (actualization of PM by a new kind of SF of the species S_2).
4. Secondary cause of its coming into existence (*esse*) and existence in time, that is, the operation of efficient causes (parental organisms acting within the evolutionary matrix of causes), which is accompanied or followed by coming into being (*esse*) of their offspring that happens to be the first exemplar of the new species S_2.
5. Instrumental cause of its existence (*esse*) as such, that is, the agency of parental organisms (within the evolutionary matrix of causes), which brings or is followed by an instantiation of the first exemplar of the new species S_2, which has *esse* bestowed on it by God.

218   *Concurrence of Divine and Created Causes*

In other words, similar to the begetting of a new exemplar of the same species, parental organisms of the species S_1, analyzed within the polygenic causal matrix of an evolutionary transition, can be regarded as proper causes of the prototype organism of the species S_2 within the immanent order of causation. The same causal agency has the nature of secondary and instrumental causation from the point of view of the transcendent order of causation, in which God himself is the first and principal cause of the essence and existence of every contingent being.

What seems to be crucial in this description is the distinction between secondary and instrumental causes. Even if it belongs to the natural dispositions of the parental organisms of the first exemplar of a new species S_2 to be secondary causes of the eduction of the SF of the prototype of S_2 from the potentiality of the PM (*essentia*) and of its coming into existence (*esse*) – their action in this process is proper to their natures – when it comes to the essence (*essentia*) and existence (*esse*) as such of the first organism of S_2, the parental organisms can only be their instrumental causes – "giving" something they in fact themselves cannot offer. The first (with respect to secondary causes) and the principal (with respect to instrumental causes) agent in an instantiation of the prototype of S_2 is God.

One might think this brings my description close to occasionalism, as it may seem that with respect to the essence (*essentia*) and existence (*esse*) of the first exemplar of S_2, the instrumental causation of its parents (within the evolutionary matrix of causes) provides merely an occasion for God to instantiate them. We must not forget, however, that the instrumental causation in question – which we can verify both within the methodology of science and the philosophical inquiry concerning causal dependencies in nature – is real and irreducible solely to the sort of divine action that a merely empirical inquiry might mistake for actions of creatures. This type of divine agency seems closest to a direct divine intervention in the natural order of the created world. Yet, it is neither miraculous nor occasionalist, since it is exercised in and through creatures, "giving" something they, in fact, do not themselves have to offer. This shows the depth of the involvement and the nature of the causal activity of God as the primary and principal cause of all things, and it effectively protects my analysis and explanation from falling into the pitfall of deism.[26]

---

[26] As I have already mentioned above (see Chapter 1, note 76 and Chapter 5, note 8), Aquinas's causal description of substantial changes also includes causation of separate substances (angels) and celestial bodies (the sun and the stars). If we want to follow his thought in all

THE QUESTION OF UNITY OF IMMANENT CAUSE(S)
IN AN EVOLUTIONARY TRANSFORMATION

One of the key questions concerning the explanation and model presented here is related to the complex system of immanent causes, involved in the polygenic causal origin of an evolutionary change. Is it plausible and justified to treat them as a unified causal principle of an evolutionary change? This question sends us back to the controversy around the PPC, discussed in the last section of Chapter 1, where I have referred to Feser's version of the medieval argument that perfections characteristic for a new species S_2 can be seen as present in a "total" cause of an evolutionary transition from S_1.

Now, the category of "total" cause, used in this context, seems to assert a unity to an evolutionary causal nexus. Hence, if such unity is a fact, we might consider introducing an important shift or twist to the causal scenario of evolutionary transitions presented here. If we assume there must be a cause of the unity of the polygenic matrix of causal agents engaged in an evolutionary transformation, we find it difficult, if not impossible, to trace it in the immanent order of causation. This might suggest that God, as the ultimate source of all causality, acting from the transcendent order of causation, brings unity to the evolutionary matrix of causes, causing thus directly the eduction of SF of the first exemplar of a new species from the potentiality of PM. All partial causes of this occurrence, including parental organisms, would act as secondary and instrumental causes of this new organism. Their unity, however, would be an outcome of a direct intervention of God in the created order of things.[27]

This scenario might look less attractive for theologians emphasizing "autonomy" of natural causes, as it suggests a direct interventionist divine action in the origin of the first exemplar of each new species. However, based on the research presented in Chapter 3 (especially in sections dedicated to Aristotle's and Aquinas's notion of teleology and chance, as well as the notion of their interplay in evolutionary transitions), one might suggest that God indeed brings the unity of the

---

details, we should list these agents among other secondary and instrumental causes entering a complex causal nexus, responsible for an evolutionary transition.

[27] My formulation of this scenario is partly inspired by a conversation on philosophical aspects of evolutionary transitions during the session of the Templeton grant on the Catholic and Thomistic approach to evolution, organized in the Spring of 2017 in Providence College, RI, USA.

220   *Concurrence of Divine and Created Causes*

evolutionary causal matrix, but he does that through the secondary quasi-causality of chance. I have said that Aristotle's and Aquinas's notion of chance occurrences relates them to *per se* causes of things and processes that "participate" in them. Hence, we might suggest that this is exactly what the nature of the unity of causally polygenetic evolutionary transitions is about. Grounded in numerous particular *per se* causes contributing to this evolutionary causal matrix, it comes about as a chance occurrence that remains, nonetheless, within God's providence.[28]

CONCLUSION

The proposed model of understanding divine concurrence with natural causes in evolutionary transitions has important theological advantages and consequences. First of all, it protects us from the fallacies of both deism and occasionalism. It does not see God as leaving the universe entirely to its own causal operations after creating it, which would suggest that the origin of new species is an autonomous mundane process with no need of God's involvement at any stage of its realization. Neither does it claim that God does everything, which would put into question the causal autonomy of creatures engaged in complex causal processes of evolutionary transitions.

Moreover, although I have suggested that God works in evolution through secondary and instrumental causation of his creatures rather than through his direct divine intervention, the latter (instrumental) type of causation puts an emphasis on the depth of God's involvement in evolutionary transitions. It reminds us that when it comes to the essence (*essentia*) and existence (*esse*) as such of the first exemplar of a new species (as well as all subsequent organisms of the same species), God is their principal cause, as it is beyond the capacity of contingent entities to be the source of essence and existence as such of any other created beings.

Finally, the proposed model of divine action in evolution offers an important explication of the seventh postulate of the Thomistic version of theistic evolutionism I developed in Chapter 5, as it specifies

---

[28] Alexander Pruss shares some thoughts on this topic – with important references to the Thomistic tradition – in "God, Chance and Evolution. In Memory of Benjamin Arbour," in *Neo-Aristotelian Metaphysics and the Theology of Nature*, ed. William M. R. Simpson, Robert C. Koons, and James Orr (New York: Routledge, 2022), 364–82.

Conclusion

the role of secondary and instrumental causes in evolutionary transitions, within the framework of the transcendent and immanent orders of causation. At the same time, there is one more topic that needs to be addressed in reference to the theory of evolution, that is, the account of the emergence of the human species. I will dedicate to it the remaining chapter of this book.

8

Theological Anthropogenesis and Evolution

In his message to the Pontifical Academy of Sciences on Evolution in 1996, Pope John Paul II states that if "there are apparent contradictions" between "the various scientific disciplines" and "those contained in the message of revelation. ... We know, in fact, that truth cannot contradict truth." He explains that it is remarkable how the theory of evolution "has been progressively accepted by researchers following a series of discoveries in various fields of knowledge." Moreover, "The convergence ... of the results of work that was conducted independently is in itself a significant argument in favor of this theory."[1] At the same time, John Paul II was aware of the fact that hominization introduces a particular challenge in the dialogue between theology and natural science, since "With man ... we find ourselves in the presence of an ontological difference, an ontological leap, one could say." Hence, he acknowledges that "posing of such ontological discontinuity" may be seen as running "counter to that physical continuity which seems to be the main thread of research into evolution in the field of physics and chemistry."[2]

Indeed, the encounter of theological and biological views on anthropogenesis inspired the most emotional reactions to evolutionary theory and posed a considerable challenge to both biblical exegesis and theological anthropology. The history of the conversation between scientific

---

[1] John Paul II, *Address to the Plenary Session on 'The Origins and Early Evolution of Life'*, www.pas.va/content/accademia/en/magisterium/johnpaulii/22october1996.html, nos. 2 and 4 (retrieved 14 June 2021) (Rome, 1996).
[2] *Ibid.*, no. 6.

Aristotelian–Thomistic Notion of Human Nature 223

and religious worldviews on the topic of hominization is thus long and complicated. However, what interests me in the final chapter of this book is the contemporary Thomistic approach to the question of the origin of our species. I believe it is theologically more accurate and precise than the most prevalent semi-naturalistic position that is favored and repeated by many theologians and accepted in the official statements of the Magisterium of the Catholic Church. I also believe it is preferable from the biological point of view.

The research presented in this chapter will proceed in the following order. First, I will concentrate on the Aristotelian–Thomistic notion of human nature, in reference to the biblical analysis emphasizing its unity. In the following section, I will develop a constructive Thomistic proposal of the evolutionary origin of the human species. I will also present an adjusted version of the model of the concurrence of divine and natural causes in evolutionary transitions, developed in Chapter 7, this time depicting their cooperation in the evolutionary emergence of the first human. The next section will be dedicated to alternative views on the origin of the human species. Naturalistic, semi-naturalistic, and antinaturalistic views will be presented and evaluated. In the last section, I will present the complexity of the debate concerning mono- *versus* polygenetic character of the human speciation. The chapter will end with a short conclusion.

ARISTOTELIAN–THOMISTIC NOTION OF HUMAN NATURE

One of the crucial topics in Christian philosophy and theology is human nature and a precise description of its foundational characteristics and dispositions. Emphasizing the integral unity of human nature, theology distinguishes material and spiritual aspects in it. Throughout the history of Western thought, we may speak about an ongoing tension between a more Platonic interpretation that tends to speak about human beings in terms of two separate substances – soul and body – coming together and forming a human person, and the Aristotelian notion of the substantial unity of a human being that has material (bodily) and spiritual aspects but is not a composite of two separable substances. Because the human soul can subsist after our death, the "two-substances" view of Plato is intuitively embraced even by those who otherwise want to see human nature through Aristotelian lenses. They also speak about the soul separated from the body after death. I think this assertion is, metaphysically speaking, fundamentally wrong.

224 *Theological Anthropogenesis and Evolution*

Human Nature in Biblical Theology

In the Old Testament, until the Hellenistic period, man was regarded as a unity with different aspects and functions of one and the same being. Early biblical texts do not specify in man a principle independent and distinct from the human body. Hence, although Hebrew *neshamah, nephesh,* and *ruah* are often translated as "soul," we must be careful not to impose on those texts a duality of soul and body, characteristic of Hellenistic thought and widespread in wisdom literature. The principle of life in the Old Testament is the conveyor of (1) thought and understanding, will and aspiration, feeling, and perception; (2) emotions; and (3) spiritual life. Most importantly, as says *Communion and Stewardship*:

> Among the basic Hebrew terms for man used in the Old Testament, *nèfèš* means the life of a concrete person who is alive (Gen 9:4; Lev. 24:17-18, Proverbs 8:35). But man does not have a *nèfèš*; he is a *nèfèš* (Gen 2:7; Lev 17:10). *Basar* refers to the flesh of animals and of men, and sometimes the body as a whole (Lev 4:11; 26:29). Again, one does not have a *basar*, but is a *basar*.[3]

Michael Schmaus notes that the unity of human being (defined later on in terms of the unity of soul and body) is expressed in the Old Testament as the "heart" of man. The heart is the living center in which the human self-possesses him/herself, the innermost "region" where we become aware of ourselves. From there originate our judgments and decisions. All emotions and states of our mind flow from the heart (e.g., courage, bravery, concern, parental feelings, joy, sorrow, pain, passions, desires, and longings – and above all love). It is the heart with which we reach out toward God and have a grasp of who he is. It is also with heart that we turn away from God. God transforms us by "giving us a new heart." Ratzinger further emphasizes Schmaus's point affirming that the biblical notion of "heart" denotes "the corporality of the spirit and the spirituality of the body."[4]

The authors of the New Testament, especially Saint Paul, certainly strived to continue some important theological traditions of Israel, including a deep conviction of the unity of a human being. Hence, Saint Paul's definition of human nature in relation to three categories: spirit, soul, and body (1 Thess 5:23), should be interpreted primarily in relation to how these terms were understood in the biblical texts. The term "spirit" (Hebrew *ruah*, Greek *pneuma*) refers to our consciousness and its key

---

[3] International Theological Commission, *Communion and Stewardship*, no. 28.
[4] Michael Schmaus, *Dogma: God and Creation* (London: Sheed and Ward, 1969), 141–42; Joseph Ratzinger, *Schöpfungslehre* (unpublished Freising lecture notes), 1958.

dispositions, that is, understanding (Ex 28:3; Is 11:2; Eph 4:22–24), character (Num 5:14; Is 57:15; 2Tim 1:7; 1 Peter 3: 3–4), and will (Judg 13:25; Prov 15:13; 1 Cor 2:11; Heb 9:14). It therefore refers to the reflective part of our psyche, which forms the matter of the body with its subconscious features, in analogy to God's Spirit shaping the primordial matter of the earth (Gen 1:2; Ps 104:29–30; analogously, the Spirit of Christ shapes the humanity of a Christian – Rom 8:9–10; 2 Cor 3:17; Gal 4:6; Phil 1:19).

The second term "body" (Hebrew *basar*, Greek *sarks*, *soma*), in addition to the material aspect of our nature (*soma*), describes also human subconsciousness (*sarks*) with its built-in patterns of behavior that require conscious formation. The ideal of the Christian life is therefore to work to form the body according to the spirit (Eph 4:20–24). Finally, "soul" (Hebrew *nephesh*, Greek *psyche*) defines primarily (1) the essence of human nature as a result of the cooperation of spirit and body (Dt 12:20; 1 Pet 3:20) but also (2) integrity of a human person (in reference to consciousness and subconsciousness – Prov 21:10; Matt 26:38; Acts 14:22) and (3) life (vital force – Gen 9:4–5; 1 Jn 3:16).

On the one hand, if one takes the category of soul in the writings of Saint Paul as expressing the cooperation of spirit and body, then it can be said that his theology is part of the biblical tradition that perceives man as an integral unity.[5] On the other hand, by adopting the Greek terms for soul (*psyche*) and body (*sarks*, *soma*), Saint Paul and other New Testament authors opened Christianity to the world of Greek philosophy with its understanding of human nature. This forged the way to dualism, not only existential – opposing sinful life according to the flesh (*sarx*) and the life of grace according to the spirit (*pneuma*) – but also ontological – considering body and soul as separate substances.

Human Nature in Speculative Theology

That the Platonic notion of human nature became dominant in Christian tradition for quite some time, including the thought of one

---

[5] If this is true then the International Theological Commission is right when – in reference to above-mentioned passage on *nephesh* and *basar* – it says "The New Testament term *sarx* (flesh) can denote the material corporality of man (2 Cor 12:7), but on the other hand also the whole person (Rom. 8:6). Another Greek term, *soma* (body) refers to the whole man with emphasis on his outward manifestation. Here too man does not have his body, but is his body. Biblical anthropology clearly presupposes the unity of man, and understands bodiliness to be essential to personal identity" (*Communion and Stewardship*, no. 28).

226 *Theological Anthropogenesis and Evolution*

of the most important Latin fathers of the Church – Augustine, is commonly acknowledged. Most importantly, even in the version that did not antagonize the body and the soul – and therefore free from heresies of Gnosticism and Manicheism – the early Christian interpretation of Platonism perpetuated the dualistic view of man (assuming the possibility of the separate existence of body and soul), thus departing significantly from the integral unity of human nature as defined in biblical theology. The spiritualism that characterizes it, even if it does not oppose the soul to the body, but only emphasizes its superiority, permeated the theory and practice of the Christian life (it was characteristic for some monastic movements, as well as the piety of many lay Christians).

It is in contrast to the Platonic notion of human nature that I want to emphasize the relevance of the Aristotelian–Thomistic anthropology with its insistence on the unity of a human person. According to the principles of hylomorphism and substantial and organic unity of a living being (presented in the opening sections of Chapter 1), we may say that the human soul is not so much connected with the body, but organizes matter in such a way that it becomes a body or – more precisely – a human being. In other words, the human body cannot exist without the soul. When the soul is missing, it ceases to be a body (a human person). For the proper correlate of the human soul – which is substantial form (SF) of a particular type, hence a metaphysical principle – is not a physical body (secondary matter) but primary matter (PM), that is, a complementary metaphysical principle of potentiality. Consequently, when we say that the human soul actualizes a human body, we must remember that this predication is analogical, that is, we say it in a derivative meaning.

Aristotle emphasizes this fact speaking about animals: "[W]hen the soul departs, what is left is no longer a living animal, and [...] none of the parts remain what they were before, excepting in configuration" (*De part. an.* I, 1 [641a 19–20]). Aquinas, on his part, although he uses the language of the unity of body and soul on numerous occasions, comes to a similar conclusion in his commentary to Aristotle's *On the Soul*:

"We must not think, therefore, of the soul and body as though the body had its own form making it a body, to which a soul is superadded, making it a living body; but rather that the body gets both its being and its life from the soul. This is not to deny, however, that bodily being as such is, in its imperfection, material with respect to life. Therefore, when life departs the body is not left specifically the same; the eyes and flesh of a dead man, as is shown in the *Metaphysics*, Book VII, are only improperly called eyes and flesh. When the soul leaves the body another substantial form takes its place; for a passing-away always involves a concomitant coming-to-be" (*In De an.* II, lect. 1 [§ 225–226]).

Similar is his short reflection on this topic in *Summa contra gentiles*:

[W]hen the soul departs, neither the whole body nor its part remain of the same species as before; the eye or flesh of a dead thing are so called only in an equivocal sense. (*SCG* II, 72, no. 3)

The same view is recalled by Aquinas one more time toward the end of his career, in his *Summa theologiae*:

Therefore, on the withdrawal of the soul, as we do not speak of an animal or a man unless equivocally, as we speak of a painted animal or a stone animal; so is it with the hand, the eye, the flesh and bones, as the Philosopher says (*De Anima* ii, 1). A proof of which is, that on the withdrawal of the soul, no part of the body retains its proper action; although that which retains its species, retains the action of the species. (*ST* I, 76, 8, co.)

Unfortunately, the Catholic Church, which repeatedly, throughout history, recommended Aquinas's theology as an important point of reference in theological reasoning and argumentation,[6] continues to speak about human nature in terms of the unity of body and soul (spirit), rather than in reference to the concept of one person (substance) that has both material and spiritual aspects to it. This restores Platonic dualism in the common understanding of our identity as human beings. To give some examples, we may first go back to the fourth Lateran Council in 1215, where we read:

They [Persons of the Trinity] are the one principle of the universe, the creator of all things, visible and invisible, spiritual and corporeal, who by his almighty power from the beginning of time made at once (*simul*) out of nothing both orders of creatures, the spiritual and the corporeal, that is, the angelic and the earthly, and then (*deinde*) the human creature, who as it were shares in both orders, being composed of spirit and body.[7]

Similar is the teaching of the synod of Vienne (1311–12), under pope Clement V, which uses the term "soul," defined as the form of the body:

---

[6] See Leo XIII, *Aeterni Patris: On the Restoration of Christian Philosophy* (Rome, 1879), www.vatican.va/content/leo-xiii/en/encyclicals/documents/hf_l-xiii_enc_04081879_aeterni-patris.html (retrieved 12 June 2021).

[7] Denzinger, *Enchiridion Symbolorum*, 43rd Ed., ed. Peter Hünermann (San Francisco: Ignatius Press, 2012), no. 428.

228   *Theological Anthropogenesis and Evolution*

We reject as erroneous and contrary to the truth of the Catholic faith any doctrine or opinion that rashly asserts that the substance of the rational and intellectual soul is not truly and of itself the form of the human body or that calls it into doubt.[8]

More recently, *Gaudium et spes* of the Second Vatican Council teaches that "Man, though made of body and soul, is a unity."[9] John Paul II, in his encyclical letter *Veritatis Splendor,* offers a more nuanced view:

Only in reference to the human person in his "unified totality", that is, as "a soul which expresses itself in a body and a body informed by an immortal spirit", can the specifically human meaning of the body be grasped.[10]

This subtle lack of terminological clarity does not escape the attention of Ratzinger, who in his *Eschatology* emphasizes that "[The soul is not] an addition to a being which really might subsist in an independent fashion. On the contrary, it constitutes what is deepest in man's being. It is nothing other than what we call 'soul'."[11] When saying this, Ratzinger confirms the teaching of the *Catechism* affirming that "spirit and matter, in man, are not two natures united, but rather their union forms a single nature."[12]

---

[8] *Ibid.,* no. 902. We know that the teaching of the synod of Vienne was directed against Peter John Olivi, who distinguished in man three principles-forms: a vegetative soul, a sensible soul, and a rational soul. He thought that only the first two of them were forms of the body, while the rational (spiritual) soul could only be related to the body indirectly. The synod, condemning the error of dividing human person into parts, defended the co-dependency and intertwined relation of soul and body. One might argue that it did not decide whether the material aspect of a human being should be defined in terms of PM or a body that is already in-formed, so the term "body" was used in the popular meaning. Others claim that the synod did not use the term PM because it did not want to raise hylomorphism to the level of an official dogmatic teaching of the Church.

[9] Second Vatican Council, *Gaudium et Spes* (Rome, 1965), www.vatican.va/archive/hist_councils/ii_vatican_council/documents/vat-ii_const_19651207_gaudium-et-spes_en.html (retrieved 15 may 2021), no. 14.

[10] John Paul II, *Veritatis splendor* (Rome, 1993), www.vatican.va/content/john-paul-ii/en/encyclicals/documents/hf_jp-ii_enc_06081993_veritatis-splendor.html (retrieved 15 July 2022.), no. 50.

[11] Joseph Ratzinger, *Eschatology: Death and Eternal Life* (Washington, DC: The Catholic University of America Press, 1988), 155. "The awakening of the dead (not of bodies!) of which Scripture speaks is thus concerned with the salvation of the one, undivided man, not just with the fate of one (perhaps secondary) half of man. It now also becomes clear that the real heart of the faith in resurrection does not consist at all in the idea of the restoration of bodies, to which we have reduced it in our thinking; such is the case even though this is the pictorial image used throughout the Bible. What, then, is the real content of the hope symbolically proclaimed in the Bible in the shape of the resurrection of the dead? I think that this can best be worked out by means of a comparison with the dualistic conception of ancient philosophy" (Joseph Ratzinger, *Introduction to Christianity* [San Francisco: Ignatius Press, 2004], 349–50).

[12] Catholic Church, *Catechism of the Catholic Church* (CCC), 2nd edition (Vatican City: Libreria Editrice Vaticana, 2000), no. 365.

Beginning and End of a Human Being

Having specified the Aristotelian–Thomistic understanding of human nature and its unity, we can now proceed to analyze a special case of speciation and generation, that is, the origin of the first human beings and the generation of their descendants. For as it turns out, according to the same classical Aristotelian–Thomistic tradition of philosophy and theology, human beings differ from all other living beings on account of the spiritual aspect of their nature. This difference finds an expression both in the way they come into existence and the way they cease to exist in this world.

First, when we think about the origin of all other creatures, we realize that they either came into existence as an outcome of the original divine act of *creatio ex nihilo* – at the beginning of the existence of the universe – or began/begin to exist in the course of its history, out of already existing matter. We already know that the former is neither movement nor change, while the latter is indeed characterized and defined in terms of movement and substantial changes, being part of God's governance of the created universe through the secondary and instrumental causality of the creatures. In the case of the origin of a human being, we are dealing with a situation or a phenomenon, which qualifies as both creation and change. God creates, *ex nihilo*, an immortal human soul which, in the substantial change accomapnying fertilization, actualizes a given "portion" of PM, which underlies ovum and sperm coming from parental organisms. As such, both gametes cease to exist giving rise to a new organism. This refers both to the origin of the first human being(s) and to the origin of each of their descendants. Hence, if the idea of God creating through evolution is meaningful at all, its unique application might be the case of speciation that effects the origin of the human species.

Catholic theology teaches that intellect, self-awareness, and free will are activities (dispositions of the soul) that allow humans to transcend the purely material world, thus making us similar to God himself. It is on this basis that we say that man carries/is created in the image and likeness of God. Moreover, even if the image and likeness of God are expressed in an integral human person – and not only in the intellectual and/or spiritual aspect of our nature – the independence of the agent intellect from the material aspect of a human person and its sense organs allows us to conclude that the human soul can exist after death – in a state in which it does not organize matter in an organic human body. All these confirm our belief that human souls do not have their cause in the world of passing and contingent beings. Their source can only be the omnipotent

230   *Theological Anthropogenesis and Evolution*

and immortal God, who creates them from nothingness (*ex nihilo*) at the moment of conception of every human being.[13]

Second, concerning the way in which human beings cease to exist in this world, their death, similar to their birth, is unlike death of any other sentient creature. For the SF actualizing a given "portion" of *materia signata* (designated matter) in a nonhuman animal does not survive through the dramatic substantial change accompanying death, as it cannot subsist in the state in which it does not actualize PM. The case of a human being is again radically different. At the moment of our death, the underlying PM, which is actualized by a particular SF (i.e., a particular human soul) in an organic human body, begins to be actualized by the SF of a cadaver, or rather by SSFF of numerous biomolecules, which are additionally characterized by a decreasing accidental unity of the corpse they form (belong to). At the same time, as mentioned in the previous paragraph, we have still many good reasons to believe that, unlike any other SF of animate and inanimate beings, the human soul survives death and is able to subsist, keeping its character of a metaphysical principle of substantiality (a SF) and the same individual identity that belonged to a deceased person it "came from."[14]

Consequently, it seems that human death is a separate category of change that falls somewhere in between substantial and accidental changes. What brings it close to the former type of change is the fact

[13] Theologians believe that the Magisterium of the Church confirmed indirectly the teaching on creation of human souls *ex nihilo* at the moment of conception in year 543, in its condemnation of the idea of the preexistence of souls. Even before the year 543, Augustine – who for most of his life supported traducianism – eventually changed his mind and embraced the idea of creation *ex nihilo* of human souls. The idea was further developed by Aquinas: "Now, it pertains to the human soul distinctively, in contrast to other forms, to be subsisting in its being, and to communicate to the body the being proper to itself. The human soul therefore enjoys, through itself, a mode of production beyond that of other forms, which come to be by accident through the making of the composites. But, since the human soul does not have matter as part of itself, it cannot be made from something as from matter. It therefore remains that the soul is made from nothing. And thus, it is created. And in view of the previously demonstrated fact that creation is the proper work of God, it follows that the soul is created immediately by God alone" (*SCG* II, 87, no. 3). "[S]ince it cannot be made of pre-existing matter – whether corporeal, which would render it a corporeal being – or spiritual, which would involve the transmutation of one spiritual substance into another, we must conclude that it cannot exist except by creation" (*ST* I, 90, 2, co.). CCC (no. 366) teaches that "The Church teaches that every spiritual soul is created immediately by God – it is not 'produced' by the parents – and also that it is immortal: it does not perish when it separates from the body at death, and it will be reunited with the body at the final Resurrection."

[14] I leave aside the opinion of those who favor the "resurrection-in-death" model of the human ultimate end (the position supported by Karl Rahner, Hans Urs von Balthasar, and Gisbert Greshake, and criticized by Ratzinger).

that the nature of the individual entity that enters it is radically changed. What keeps it closer to the latter type of change is that, at least in some way, the identity of the individual entity that enters it is preserved.

In other words, at the moment of our death, some essential aspects of who we are radically change. We cease to be fully human persons as we lose the ability to actualize the vegetative and sensory powers. Deprived of the material aspect, we do not move in time and space, we do not nourish ourselves, nor do we have sense perception. Consequently, our passive intellect (which depends on the data coming from the senses) is devoid of any cognitive material. On the other hand, we are not completely annihilated. Thanks to our agent intellect, self-awareness and free will, subsistent human souls that do not organize matter in the organic human body continue to exist and are capable of intellectual cognition. It is a strange state in which – due to certain powers (dispositions) inherent and characteristic of human nature – we still are and at the same time are not ourselves. We are the same individuals, the same beings, yet not fully human persons but subsistent human souls. This shows that human beings are indeed metaphysically distinct and peculiar.[15]

THOMISTIC VIEW OF THE EVOLUTIONARY ORIGIN OF THE HUMAN SPECIES

Based on the Aristotelian–Thomistic understanding of the human nature and the model of the concurrence of divine and creaturely causal agency in evolutionary transitions, developed in Chapter 7, we can now try to adapt the same model to depict the evolutionary origin of the human species.[16] Once again, we need to remember that for Aquinas God creates a new human soul (SF of a human being) *ex nihilo* at the moment when a new human being begins to exist. Thus, each human soul is not educed from the potentiality of PM, as are SSFF of all other natural beings. It is directly created by God. Parental organisms (together with other agents in an evolutionary matrix of causes) properly dispose PM to receive it.

[15] The unnatural character of the state in question becomes for Aquinas one of the crucial arguments in favor of the resurrection of human beings (see *SCG* IV, 79). The relation between human soul after death and the person it "belongs to" has become more recently a subject of a vivid debate among Thomists. A helpful introduction to its complexity can be found in Philip-Neri Reese, "The Separated Soul and the Human Person," *Nova et Vetera* (forthcoming).

[16] For a naturalist view of the philosophical aspects of human speciation see Michael Ruse, *The Philosophy of Human Evolution*, Cambridge Introductions to Philosophy and Biology (Cambridge: Cambridge University Press, 2012).

232   *Theological Anthropogenesis and Evolution*

Consequently, although they can still be regarded as secondary causes of the coming into existence, as well as instrumental causes of the existence (*esse*) as such of the first human being, when it comes to his/her essence (*essentia*), they can only be called secondary causes of the proper disposition of PM to be actualized by a human soul, which is not educed from the potentiality of PM but is directly created by God.[17] This refers to each subsequent begetting of a new human person. However, the direct divine action in creation of human souls is not miraculous. It belongs to the natural order of the universe, that human souls are not educed from the potentiality of PM but created by God *ex nihilo*.[18]

Moreover, as notes James Madden, the fact that the human soul(s) was(were) created *ex nihilo* does not introduce (or is an outcome of) an empirical gap. Quite contrary, due to the proper disposition of PM, biological material in the hominins' ovum(ova) and sperm(s) (*materia signata*) is ready to go through a substantial change that will give an origin to the first exemplar(s) of the human species. In other words, if there is a gap, it is ontological, not empirical.[19]

---

[17] Ratzinger argues that in conceiving a child "parents are co-workers of the Creator" (Ratzinger, *Schöpfungslehre* [1958], 76), who, acting as instrumental causes, outdo themselves in producing not just a human body but a complete human being: "God must be called the *causa prima et immediata* of every new human soul. Nevertheless, he cannot be considered as its *causa unica* in the strict sense, for in providing the body the parents are real co-causes (*reale Mitursache*) of new human souls. The matter provided by the parents is therefore already spirit-shaped matter" (Joseph Ratzinger, *Schöpfungslehre* [unpublished Freising lecture notes], 1964, 181). Similar is the view of Christopher Baglow: "Human souls, then, do come from parents; through the fertilization of the female ovum by the male sperm, human parents are the created causes acting according to their sexual natures. What makes human reproduction different is not that God disrupts this process but rather causes it to produce a life principle that transcends that of the other animals. The human soul, the very lifeprinciple that makes a human body to be a living body of a specific kind, is not a thing God makes separately" (Christopher Baglow, "Evolution and the Human Soul," *Church Life Journal*, https://churchlifejournal .nd.edu/articles/evolution-and-the-human-soul/ [retrieved 16 April 2022]). I remain skeptical about considering parents as instrumental causes of the souls (in themselves) of their children and uphold my position which sees them as secondary causes of disposing PM in a way that enables it to be actualized by particular souls of their children.

[18] In a somewhat dualistic manner, Ratzinger emphasizes the correspondence between properly disposed matter (PM) and the human soul that actualizes it: "Not only does the soul create the body, the body also creates the soul. Only when the soul becomes the soul of this body does it truly become a 'human' soul." He thinks Aquinas's formula "the soul is the form of the body" (*anima corporis forma*) should be now balanced with the complementary affirmation that "the body is in some sense the form of the soul" (*corpus quodammodo forma animae*)" (Ratzinger, *Schöpfungslehre* [1958], 76).

[19] "[W]hen I assert that the human soul has not evolved, I do not claim that there is some empirical gap that we expect to find in natural history" (James D. Madden, *Mind,*

Thomistic View of the Evolutionary Origin of the Human Species 233

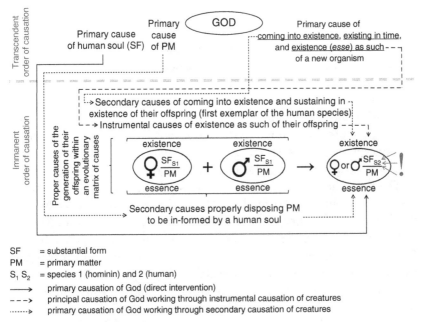

FIGURE 8.1 Concurrence of divine and natural causes in the evolution of man.

Hence, the variation of my model of causation applied to the evolution of man will look as depicted in Figure 8.1.

Note that I carefully avoid the claim which is popular among many theistic evolutionists who say that the formation of the human body came through the processes of evolution, while the first human soul was directly created by God.[20] Following Aristotle and Aquinas, I acknowledge that there cannot be a human body without a human soul nor a human body that can receive a human soul. Neither can a humanoid body receive a human soul. No already in-formed (actualized) entity (secondary matter) can receive another SF (it can only receive AAFF). The first human soul(s) was/were created *ex nihilo* at the moment of conception of the first human being(s). It/they actualized properly disposed PM, underlying gametes produced by male and female hominins at the

---

Matter, and Nature: A Thomistic Proposal for the Philosophy of Mind [Washington, DC: Catholic University of America Press, 2013], 273).

[20] This formula entered the official teaching of the Magisterium in 1950 in *Humani generis*, and was repeated in 1996 by John Paul II in his opening address at the symposium on evolution and the origins of life, sponsored by the Pontifical Academy of Sciences. I classify it as a semi-naturalistic view of anthropogenesis and discuss in more detail below.

moment of substantial change accompanying fertilization.[21] One could suggest that at the final step of hominization, a mature prehuman organism went through a very unusual substantial change in which the first human came into existence without considerable changes in its physical dispositions (the SF of a hominin was "replaced" by the SF of a human being). I argue that this scenario is both metaphysically and theologically dubious. It was much more fitting (argument *ex convenientia*) for God to bring the process of hominization to its conclusion at the moment of the conception of the first human being(s), that is, in a way, we assume speciation of sexually reproducing organisms regularly happens.

The first scholar who proposed a proper interpretation of evolutionary theory within the Aristotelian–Thomistic system of philosophy and theology, along the line proposed here, was French Dominican Marie–Dalmace Leroy, although his hypothesis was found unacceptable by the Congregation of the Index. Many Thomistic scholars claimed that the Church finds unacceptable only the claims that Adam's body came from lower entities by spontaneous transformation and that his soul was a product of evolution. That is, it did not condemn the theory of evolution as such but merely the position of those who believed that the processes of evolution in general or the processes of the origin of the human species proceeded without the assistance of divine causation. Hence, there should be no trouble with accepting the theory of evolution, which presupposes divine participation in evolutionary change, so that secondary causes can interact with continual divine action giving existence and activity to all organisms. All Catholics, however, should agree that a special act of divine causation is necessary for the origin of the soul, for it is only the beginning of the body that can be effected by evolutionary processes. In other words, concerning anthropogenesis, if God formed plants and animals by the action of secondary causes in evolution, nothing prevents us from recognizing that he formed the human body in a similar way, while the soul was created by God *ex nihilo*.[22]

---

[21] Following the most recent nomenclature I distinguish between hominids – the group consisting of all modern and extinct Great Apes (i.e., modern humans, chimpanzees, gorillas, and orangutans plus all their immediate ancestors) – and hominins – the group consisting of modern humans, extinct human species, and all our immediate ancestors (including members of the genera *Homo, Australopithecus, Paranthropus,* and *Ardipithecus*). In what follows, I concentrate on the transition from the last immediate human ancestor to modern humans.

[22] This early conviction of Thomistic theologians came as a reaction to the documents of the Provincial Synod of Cologne in 1860. In response to the Hegelian and pantheistic

Thomistic View of the Evolutionary Origin of the Human Species 235

What Marie–Dalmace Leroy did in his 1891 book was correcting the dualistic overtones of this view:

It is only after the infusion of the soul, and because of the infusion itself, that man is constituted a living being. Before infusing the spirit, there was nothing human, not even the body, inasmuch as human flesh cannot exist without the soul, which is its substantial form. ... Thus, the Bible – interpreted by theology – tells us that man's body cannot be derived from lower nature.[23]

A similar concern was more recently raised by Joseph Ratzinger, who, in one of his reflections on creation and evolution notes:

Now some have tried to get around this problem [of how to continue affirming man's special creation given what we know of evolution] by saying that the human body may be the product of evolution, but the soul is not by any means: God himself created it, since spirit cannot emerge from matter. This answer seems to have in its favor the fact that spirit cannot be examined by the same scientific method with which one studies the history of organisms, but only at first glance is this a satisfactory answer. We have to continue the line of questioning: Can we

---

overtones of German theology of the time, the synod dealt also with evolutionism in the first part of its decrees (although approved by the Holy See, the synod documents referred only to the diocese of Cologne). The first paragraph of Chapter XIV (*On the Beginning of the Human Race and the Nature of Man*) states: "The first parents were created [*conditi*] directly by God. Therefore, we declare as contrary to Sacred Scripture and to the faith the opinion of those who are not ashamed to assert that man, insofar as his body is concerned, came to be by a spontaneous change [*spontanea immutatione*] from imperfect nature to the most perfect and, in a continuous process, finally [became] human" (I quote after Artigas, et al., *Negotiating Darwin*, 23). The antievolutionist tone of the 1860 document is unambiguous.

[23] Marie-Dalmace Leroy, *L'évolution restreinte aux espèces organiques* (Paris: Delhomme et Briguet, 1891), 261, as cited in Mariano Artigas, Thomas F. Glick, and Rafael A. Martínez, *Negotiating Darwin: The Vatican Confronts Evolution, 1877–1902* (Baltimore: JHU Press, 2006), 59. Congregation of the Doctrine of the Faith made Leroy withdraw from supporting evolutionary theory. He commented on this fact saying: "Have I succeeded in making the theory of evolution less suspect? I hope so, but I have few illusions. Although it may be shown that certain objections are insubstantial, there will always be some who persist in repeating them. I expect, therefore, that I will still hear it repeated that evolution, even the limited form, is in opposition to the Bible and the teachings of the Church, that it is not supported by any scientific fact; and that to seek to explain, insofar as possible, the formation of the world without miracles, is to propose Creation without God. For this there is only one remedy: time. It is too much to expect that the problem could be discussed freely at this time. Thirty years ago one could not have done it without risk. Each generation needs to become accustomed to new ideas before being able to do them justice. This is the case of the system of limited evolution. ... I expect, nevertheless, that it will survive the test, and who can say if perhaps some day it will strike us as strange that it could have encountered such antipathy" (Leroy, *L'évolution restreinte*, 283, as cited in Artigas et al., *Negotiating*, 60).

236   *Theological Anthropogenesis and Evolution*

divide up man in this way between theologians and scientists – the soul for the former, the body for the latter?[24]

OTHER VIEWS ON THE ORIGIN OF THE HUMAN SPECIES

The Thomistic model of the evolutionary origin of the human species proposed here differs from other popular explanations, developed in Christian theology and beyond the Christian view of nature. I will contrast it with the (1) naturalistic, (2) semi-naturalistic, and (3) antinaturalistic approaches.

Naturalistic Position

The naturalistic position (inspired by Darwin's publication of *The Descent of Man, and Selection in Relation Sex*) assumes that the entire human being – including morphology, physiology, psychology, and spirituality – comes from the natural evolutionary development of lower living creatures. Humans are directly related to vertebrates, more specifically to primates. Spiritual aspect might be real, yet it is epiphenomenal. This position finds support among the proponents of materialistic monism. Many paleoanthropologists who classify themselves as naturalists support this position as well. The arguments in favor of this position come from comparative anatomy (morphological similarities among organisms and vestigial organs), paleoanthropology, and biochemistry (similarity of building blocks of living organisms: proteins, carbohydrates, lipids, and especially DNA).

This view is obviously not acceptable for Christians as it denies the reality of what John Paul II calls an "ontological discontinuity" between lower animals and humans. As distinctly human dispositions, he mentions "metaphysical knowledge, self-consciousness, moral conscience, freedom, and aesthetic and religious experience." They all, John Paul II goes on to say must be subjected to philosophical analysis. At their root, on the traditional Catholic analysis, is rationality, that is, the powers of intellect and will, and their acts (on the speculative side: concept-formation, judgment, and inference; and on the practical side: intention and choice).[25]

---

[24] Joseph Cardinal Ratzinger, "Belief in Creation and the Theory of Evolution," in *Dogma and Preaching* (San Francisco: Ignatius Press, 2011), 135. See also Terrence Ehrman, "Anthropogenesis and the Soul," *Scientia et Fides* 8, no. 2 (2020), 173–92; Giuseppe Tanzella-Nitti, "La questione antropologica in prospettiva teologica," in Centro di documentazione interdisciplinare di Scienza e fede, *Conversazioni su scienza e fede* (Torino: Edizioni Lindau, 2012), 192–95.

[25] See John Paul II, *Address to the Symposium 'Christian Faith and the Theory of Evolution'*, no. 6.

Other Views on the Origin of the Human Species   237

However, it needs to be added that a justified critical evaluation of the reductionist and monistic philosophical conclusions based on empirical research does not question the achievements of paleoanthropology and the plausibility of the anthropogenetic scenario it offers. The latter lists as the ancestors of the modern humans: *Australopithecinae* (3–1.4 million years ago), *Homo habilis* (2.4–1.5 million years ago), *Homo erectus* (1.9 million years ago), and prerational *Homo sapiens* (400 ka-approx. 150 ka years ago), together with *Homo neanderthalensis* (430 ± 25 ka) and Denisovans – understood to be unspecified archaic African hominins admixed into the *Homo sapiens* lineage.[26]

Semi-Naturalistic Position

The most popular, semi-naturalistic position assumes that God gave spiritual and immortal souls (created directly *ex nihilo*) to one or to a pair of animals whose bodies were properly prepared by evolution.[27] The proponents of this opinion do not specify exactly whether the union of the human soul with the body occurred in the embryonic (embryonic) stage or after birth. Among arguments in support of this opinion we find:

(1) Systematics and morphology of humans which indicate that in their bodily form, they belong to primates – hence, the conclusion that they evolved from them.

(2) Paleoanthropology which indicates the existence of human races morphologically similar to primates.

(3) The law of continuity in the development of new natural kinds, which should not be too easily questioned or bypassed, including the context of the interpretation of the revealed truth and theological reasoning.

(4) The lack of theological reasons directly rejecting this opinion, since:

---

[26] For a helpful summary of the most recent paleoanthropological views see Matthew Levering, *Engaging the Doctrine of Creation: Cosmos, Creatures, and the Wise and Good Creator* (Grand Rapids, Michigan: Baker Academic, 2017), 155–63; William Lane Craig, *In Quest of the Historical Adam: A Biblical and Scientific Exploration* (Grand Rapids, Michigan: Eerdmans, 2021), 245–329; and James P. Hurd, "Hominids in the Garden?," in *Perspectives on an Evolving Creation*, ed. Keith B. Miller (Grand Rapids, Mich: Eerdmans Publishing Co., 2003), 208–33.

[27] One might argue that calling this position "semi-naturalistic" is not entirely adequate, as its followers believe that the processes of evolution that "prepared" the human

238   *Theological Anthropogenesis and Evolution*

(a) *Humani generis* seems to accept it,
(b) contemporary biblical exegesis draws attention to the importance of the historical-critical method in the interpretation of the creation story in Genesis,
(c) the teaching about the direct formation of the body of Adam and the formation of the body of Eve was never solemnly proclaimed as a dogma.

This opinion was first formulated in the nineteenth century. It was proposed, among others, by Mivart, Zahm (I mentioned them already in Chapter 4), and the Italian naturalist Filippo De Filippi. The first one of them states:

Scripture ... says that 'God made man from the dust of the earth, and breathed into his nostrils the breath of life'. This is a plain and direct statement that man's body ... was evolved from preexisting material (symbolized by the term 'dust of the earth'), and was therefore [formed] by the operation of secondary laws.

The soul of every individual man is ... created ... produced by a direct or supernatural act, and, of course, ... by such an act the soul of the first man was similarly created.[28]

Concerning the human body Zahm adds:

Whatever may be the final proved verdict of science in respect of man's body, it cannot be at variance with Catholic dogma. Granting that future researches in paleontology, anthropology, and biology, shall demonstrate beyond doubt that man is genetically related to the inferior animals, and we have seen how far scientists are from such a demonstration, there will not be, even in such an improbable event, the slightest ground for imagining that then, at last, the conclusions of science are hopelessly at variance with the declarations of the sacred text, or the authorized teachings of the Church of Christ ... We should be obliged to revise the interpretation that has usually been given to the words of scripture which refer to the formation of Adam's body, and read these words in the sense which evolution demands, a sense which, as we have seen, may be attributed to the words of the inspired record, without either distorting the meaning of terms or in any way doing violence to the text.[29]

De Filippi, in his 1864 lecture "L'Uomo e le scimie" did much to launch the debate over Darwinism in Italy. He accepted a prominent role for

body are not outside of the workings of divine providence and God's action in created nature through secondary and instrumental causes – an aspect ignored or opposed by proponents of various forms of reductionist naturalism. Nevertheless, the category in question might be still acceptable on the assumption of the Christian notion of nature and the character of natural processes that take place in the contingent reality.

[28] Mivart, *On the Genesis of Species*, 300, 295.
[29] Zahm, *Evolution and Dogma*, 364–365.

Other Views on the Origin of the Human Species   239

natural selection.[30] Mivart, by contrast, did not, attributing evolutionary development rather to "natural laws, for the most part as yet unknown."[31] De Filippi deliberated also on common ancestry.[32] At one point he says:

The more we reduce the physical inequalities between man and ape, the more the inequalities that remain, the differences in powers, grow in importance. ... The place of man in nature must be determined not by the more or less of morphological characteristics subject to variation within the narrow confines of a species but by comparison of the powers proper to man with those of animals.[33]

More recently the semi-naturalistic position finds support in official documents of the Magisterium of the Catholic Church and in the official address to the Papal Academy of Sciences by John Paul II:

[T]he Teaching Authority of the Church does not forbid that, in conformity with the present state of human sciences and sacred theology, research and discussions, on the part of men experienced in both fields, take place with regard to the doctrine of evolution, in as far as it inquires into the origin of the human body as coming from pre-existent and living matter – for the Catholic faith obliges us to hold that souls are immediately created by God.[34]

Pius XII stressed this essential point: if the human body takes its origin from pre-existent living matter, the spiritual soul is immediately created by God.[35]

In light of what I have said in this chapter, it becomes clear that the main difficulty of the semi-naturalistic position is its dualistic flavor, as it speaks about the infusion of the human soul to an already existing human body. However, this does not seem to have a negative impact on its popularity, which I think might be an outcome of its intuitive character and simplicity.[36] The Thomistic model I propose requires much more elaborate explanation as it is grounded in some technical metaphysical

---

[30] See Filippo De Filippi, *L'uomo e Le Scimie: Lezione Pubblica Detta in Torino La Sera Dell'11 Gennaio 1864 Da Filippo De Filippi* (Milano: G. Daeli, 1864), 59–60.

[31] Mivart, *On the Genesis of Species*, 300, 295.

[32] De Filippi, *L'uomo e Le Scimie*, 43, 51.

[33] *Ibid.*, 45–46. I quote after Kenneth W. Kemp, "God, Evolution, and the Body of Adam," *Scientia et Fides* 8, no. 2 (2020), 152.

[34] Pius XII, *Humani generis* (Rome, 1950) www.vatican.va/content/pius-xii/en/encyclicals/documents/hf_p-xii_enc_12081950_humani-generis.html (retrieved 23 May 2021), no. 36.

[35] John Paul II, *Address to the Symposium 'Christian Faith and the Theory of Evolution,'* no. 5.

[36] The language of infusion of the human soul into a human body is partly grounded in medieval embryology, assumed by Aquinas in his philosophy and theology. It assumed that the human embryo has a human nature or essence because it is conceived via the human male seed which provides the sentient power, and the female matter which provides the nutritive power, potentially. Thus, the embryo necessarily has an intrinsic animating principle, but would not yet possess the rational soul which must be infused by

240 *Theological Anthropogenesis and Evolution*

definitions and categories. At the same time, it may be considered as closely related to the semi-naturalistic position. Its main advantage is the emphasis on the fact that it was not only the human body that arose through evolution but human being as such. This obviously does not contradict or neglect the conviction that human souls are created by God *ex nihilo*. The latter actualize PM, which is properly disposed within evolutionary processes. Thus, what comes into existence is – once again – not just human body but an integral human person.

Interestingly, some of the proponents of the same semi-naturalistic view developed an alternative version of its main premise saying that human body was formed partly by evolution, partly by a direct intervention of God. It was undoubtedly proposed as yet another attempt at reconciling evolutionism with a more literal interpretation of Genesis. Among Catholic theologians, this theory was suggested by Zeferino González, O.P. and Juan Arintero, O.P. González proposed a

juxtaposition of Mivart's hypothesis with a possibility noted by St. Thomas, regarding the possibility that causes or agents other than God intervened in the formation of Adam's body, that is to say, in its preliminary preparation up to an imperfect stage of development, reserving the final stages of its preparation to receive a rational soul to divine action. In this way, the essence of Mivart's hypothesis is preserved, with due regard to the direct and immediate action of God in the formation of the body of the first man, action which traditional Biblical exegesis seems to require.[37]

The same view was also considered by the French Jesuit entomologist and historian Robert de Sinéty. As notes Hofmann, de Sinéty held that it was

> God, at the later stage of its development. In *SCG* II, 89 no. 7 Aquinas speaks about the human soul becoming "rational through the infusion into it of a kind of light (*lumine intrinsecus inducto*)." Earlier on, in *SCG* II, 88 no. 13 we find him stating: "Moreover, if the soul did not, as we have shown, exist before the body, nor begin to exist with the separation of the semen, it follows that the formation of the body came first, the newly created soul being infused into it afterward (*et postea ei infundatur anima de novo creata*). Still earlier, in *SCG* II, 85 no. 15, this time in the mode of negation, Aquinas says that someone breathing into the face of someone (the image used metaphorically in Gen 2) "does not infuse part of his substance into him (*non autem aliquam suae substantiae partem in ipsum immittit*). Note that the English translation uses the same category of "infusion" for three different Latin terms: *inducere, infundere,* and *immittere.*

[37] Zeferino González, *La Biblia y La Ciencia*, 2nd ed. (Seville: Izquierdo, 1892), I:514–515. See also Juan Arintero, *La Evolución y la filosofía cristiana: Introducción general y Libro primero, La evolución y la mutabilidad de las especies orgánicas* (Gregorio del Amo, 1898). My account of the view presented by González and Arintero follows James R. Hofmann, "Catholicism and Evolution: Polygenism and Original Sin Part I," *Scientia et Fides* 8, no. 2 (2020): 95–138 and Kenneth W. Kemp, "*Humani Generis* & Evolution: A Report from the Archives" *Scientia et Fides* 11, no. 1 (2023), 9–27.

Other Views on the Origin of the Human Species 241

not theologically prudent to affirm that the natural evolution of the human body was complete prior to the introduction of a soul, although this opinion was not expressly forbidden; some physical transformation of the physical body prior to ensoulment should be reserved for divine intervention.[38]

In non-Catholic circles, the alternative variant of the semi-naturalistic position was supported by Russell Wallace who proposed the theory of natural selection at the same time as did Darwin. Concerning the human brain, he said that:

[Primitive peoples] possess a mental organ beyond their needs. Natural Selection could only have endowed savage man with a brain a little superior to that of an ape, whereas he actually possesses one very little inferior to that of a philosopher.[39]

Wallace argued that in order for such a brain to arise, evolutionary processes were not sufficient, a direct intervention of God was necessary.

Antinaturalistic Position

The followers of the traditional view among Christian theologians maintain that both the body and soul of man came through a direct divine intervention. Apart from a number of evangelical protestant thinkers, Reginald Garrigou-Lagrange is an example of a Catholic theologian who followed this line of reasoning. He was skeptical about any significant unmediated evolutionary progression that is, the descent of a "higher" species from a "lower" one. He thought such a transition would violate the PPC. He labeled evolution simply a hypothesis rather than an established fact and believed that the teaching about the direct formation of Adam's body out of dust is the common opinion of theologians (in terms of the grades of the dogmatic teaching of the Church) and that at least this qualification should also be given to the teaching about the origin of the body of Eve.[40]

A somewhat less evolutionary skeptical yet still critical response to the semi-naturalistic position was expressed more recently by José Morales, who in his textbook on creation theology states that:

[38] James R. Hofmann, "Catholicism and Evolution: Polygenism and Original Sin Part II," *Scientia et Fides* 9, no. 1 (2021), 111. He refers to Robert de Sinéty, "Les preuves et les limites du transformisme." *Études* 127(1911): 660–693.

[39] A. R. Wallace, *Contributions to the Theory of Natural Selection* (New York: MacMillan, 1870), 356.

[40] See Réginald Garrigou-Lagrange, "Le Monogénisme n'est-Il Nullement Révélé, Pas Même Implicitement?," *Doctor Communis* 2 (1948): 191–202. On page 202 of this article, we find him saying that "according to Scripture, Tradition, and theology, monogenism appears more and more to be a truth proxima fidei."

242   *Theological Anthropogenesis and Evolution*

The Church has left the way open for future doctrinal development and has established at least two basic principles: 1) One may posit that there is a physical line of descent linking the first human being to a lower animal, even though that link cannot be described as generation in the true sense; 2) one would have to think in terms of changes needing to be made in the new organism which would not make it in the proper sense a child or human progeny of the former living being "for only from man could another man come who can call him a father or progenitor."[41]

Even if he does not opt for a strictly literal interpretation of Genesis, Morals holds that evolution is a hypothesis, not a theory, and dismisses the semi-naturalistic position saying that it "would not hold up, because it would imply an artificial division between the elements which go to make up a human being, and it does not account properly for the unitary corporeal-spiritual being of man" – a criticism shared by other theologians, as noted above in this chapter.[42]

Among the Scriptural arguments in favor of the antinaturalistic position, we find references to Genesis 1:26; 2:7, 20–24 and to some other (literally interpreted) passages in the Bible: "Remember that you fashioned me from clay! Will you then bring me down to dust again?" (Job 10:9); "Your hands made me and fashioned me." (Ps 119:73); "All people are of clay, and from earth humankind was formed." (Sir 33:10); "The first man was from the earth, earthly; the second man, from heaven." (1 Cor 15:47).

Another set of arguments is grounded in the patristic tradition. Some say that the Church Fathers clearly teach about the direct formation of the body of the first humans by God. We may refer to Irenaeus: "[T]he Lord took dust from the earth and formed man."; Tertullian: "[Y]ou have both the clay made glorious by the hand of God, and the flesh more glorious still by His breathing upon it."; Basil the Great: "Creation of man goes beyond all other things. For he took (says Scripture) dust from the earth and shaped man"; or Ambrose: "... woman was made out of the rib of Adam. She was not made of the same earth with which he was formed ...".[43] Others make an exception

---

[41] José Morales, *Creation Theology* (Dublin: Four Courts Press, 2001), 167–68. Toward the end of this passage Morales quotes from Pius XII's *Message to the Pontifical Academy of Sciences*, delivered on 30 November 1941.

[42] Morales, *Creation Theology*, 168. One might argue that Morales's view remains closer to the alternative version of the semi-naturalistic position developed by González, Arintero, de Sinéty, and Wallace, which assumes direct divine intervention at the final stage of the evolutionary transition that gave origin to the human species.

[43] See respectively: Irenaeus, "Against Heresies," in *Ante-Nicene Fathers. Vol 1: The Apostolic Fathers, Justin Martyr, Irenaeus*, ed. Alexander Roberts and James Donaldson

Other Views on the Origin of the Human Species 243

for several Church Fathers, including Gregory of Nyssa, John Chrysostom, and Augustine, who supported gradualism in the actualization of *rationes seminales* (as noted in Chapter 4).

Scholastic theologians are also referred to as supporting the doctrine of a direct formation of the bodies of the first humans by God. However, there is no definitive and universal claim in medieval theology that this interpretation is an indispensable part of the Christian dogma. Concerning Aquinas's position, we have already seen him saying (in the opening section of Chapter 5) that the body of the first man must have been shaped by God because it could not arise from entities belonging to a different species: "The first formation of the human body could not be by the instrumentality of any created power but was immediately from God" (*ST* I, 91, 2, co.). In light of what was said about human nature, it becomes clear that this view of Aquinas requires reinterpretation, as it assumes a dualistic distinction between soul and body. One might say that the proper disposition of PM, preparing it to be actualized by the first human soul, required a direct divine intervention. This would bring it close to the alternative version of the semi-naturalistic position proposed by González, Arintero, de Sinéty, and Wallace (see the section on naturalistic and semi-naturalistic positions above).

The Thomistic model of the evolutionary origin of the human species I proposed differs considerably from the antinaturalistic view. While I remain open to further critical evaluation of the current status and important features of evolutionary theory, I do not share Garrigou-Lagrange's skepticism toward its explanatory power. Neither do I favor a literal interpretation of the Scripture advocated by Chaberek and others who support the antinaturalistic view. Moreover, I think they might be in danger of an unjustified identification of methodological and metaphysical versions of naturalism, which I have mentioned already in Chapter 5, in my response to an objection to the proposed version of the Thomistic version of theistic evolutionism.

(Grand Rapids, MI: Christian Classics Ethereal Library, 1885), Book III, Chapter 21, no. 10; Tertullian, "On the Resurrection of the Flesh," in *Ante-Nicene Fathers. Vol. 3: Latin Christianity – Its Founder, Tertullian,* ed. Philip Schaff and Alan Menzies (Grand Rapids, MI: Christian Classics Ethereal Library, 1885), VII, 962; Basil the Great, *De hominis structura,* In *Patrologia Graeca. Vol. 30* (Paris: Migne, 1888), 40; Ambrose, *Hexameron, Paradise, and Cain and Abel,* trans. John J. Savage (Washington, DC: Catholic University of America Press, 1961), Chapter X, 327.

244   *Theological Anthropogenesis and Evolution*

MONOGENISM *VERSUS* POLYGENISM

One more topic I would like to discuss is the complex contemporary debate concerning the monogenetic *versus* polygenetic origin of the first representative(s) of the human species. As commonly known, this controversy takes place in reference to the confrontation of the Genesis account and Saint Paul's theology of sin and redemption (i.e., the analogy of one Adam and one Christ) with the evolutionary worldview.[44] Aquinas unreservedly followed the classical (more literal) monogenetic interpretation of the Bible, assuming the creation of Adam from dust and Eve from Adam's rib (see *ST* I, 91–92). However, the contemporary conversation offers some more nuanced and viable options. James Hofmann

---

[44] Hans Madueme notes that scientific data in neuroscience, evolutionary psychology, and behavioral genetics, have "the cumulative effect of casting doubt on traditional formulations of original sin." Following an early voice in this debate, coming from F. R. Tennant, he adds that "Evolution offers the ingredients or 'material' of sin (e.g., fear, anger, emotion, appetite), but these are morally neutral as they are part of common human nature. They *become* sin when our individual free will acts on that inert material" (Hans Madueme, "'The Most Vulnerable Part of the Whole Christian Account': Original Sin and Modern Science," in *Adam, the Fall, and Original Sin: Theological, Biblical, and Scientific Perspectives*, ed. Hans Madueme and Michael Reeves [Grand Rapid, Michigan: Baker Academic, 2014], 226–27, 229). A detailed analysis of the challenges posed by evolutionary theory to the theological account of original sin (both *peccatum originale originans* and *peccatum originale originatum*) goes beyond the scope of my project. Madueme offers a helpful list of the most important attempts at resolving the conflict. He classifies them under three general categories: (1) developing theology without the fall, (2) incorporating biology in revised accounts of the fall, and (3) retaining the classical account of the fall, now framed in the paleoanthropological record (see *ibid.*, 229–38). See also R. J. Berry and T. A. Noble, eds., *Darwin, Creation and the Fall: Theological Challenges* (Nottingham: Intervarsity Press, 2009); William T. Cavanaugh and James K. A. Smith, eds., *Evolution and the Fall* (Grand Rapids, Michigan: Wm. B. Eerdmans Publishing, 2017); Andre-Marie Dubarle, *The Biblical Doctrine of Original Sin*, trans. E. M. Stewart (London: Geoffrey Chapman, 1964); Joseph Fitzpatrick, *The Fall and the Ascent of Man: How Genesis Supports Darwin* (Lanham, Md: University Press of America, 2012); Paul J. P. Flaman, "Evolution, the Origin of Human Persons, and Original Sin: Physical Continuity with an Ontological Leap," *The Heythrop Journal* 57, no. 3 (2016): 568–83; Richard Pendergast, "Evil, Original Sin, and Evolution," *The Heythrop Journal* 50, no. 5 (2009): 833–45; Raymund Schwager, *Banished from Eden: Original Sin and Evolutionary Theory in the Drama of Salvation* (Herefordshire: Gracewing Publishing, 2006); Antoine Suarez, "'Transmission at Generation': Could Original Sin Have Happened at the Time When Homo Sapiens Already Had a Large Population Size?," *Scientia et Fides* 4, no. 1 (April 26, 2016): 253–94; David L. Wilcox, "A Proposed Model for the Evolutionary Creation of Human Beings: From the Image of God to the Origin of Sin," *Perspectives on Science and Christian Faith* 68, no. 1 (2016): 22–43; Anthony Francis Zimmerman, *Evolution and the Sin in Eden: A New Christian Synthesis* (Lanham (Md.); New York; Oxford: University Press of America, 1998).

Monogenism versus Polygenism

has recently published an extended historical account of the debate on mono- and polygenism. My presentation, following the account provided by Paul Flaman, will take a more systematic approach.[45]

Terminology

In 1876 Haeckel introduced the distinction between mono- and polyphyletism. By 1866, he was already using the word "phylon," in the sense of "stem," as a root for both terms, which he used to differentiate the scenario in which all living things originate from one common ancestor from the one in which they are traced back to several independent places of origin:

The unitary, or monophyletic, hypothesis of descent will endeavor to trace the first origin of all individual groups of organisms, as well as their totality, to a single common species of Moneron which originated by spontaneous generation. The multiple, or polyphyletic, hypothesis of descent, on the other hand, will assume that several different species of Monera have arisen by spontaneous generation, and that these gave rise to several different main classes (tribes, or phyla).[46]

The distinction between mono- and polygenism entered the conversation within the context of evolutionary reinterpretation of anthropogenesis. At the beginning of the debate in the nineteenth century, "polygenism" was defined as the claim that there were multiple very ancient origins for distinct human races that should be classified as separate species. This inspired advocates of slavery, especially in the United States, who used polygenism ideologically to claim that humanity was indeed made up not only of distinct races but even of distinct species.[47] Monogenism was the

---

[45] See Hofmann, "Catholicism and Evolution I–II" and Flaman, "Evolution, the Origin of Human Persons, and Original Sin." In my presentation I will also refer to the material presented in Kemp, "God, Evolution, and the Body of Adam"; Kemp's upcoming extensive monograph on the history of the reaction of the Catholic Church to evolution; and Gaine, "The Teaching." I am indebted to all four authors.

[46] Ernst Haeckel, *The History of Creation*. Translated by E. Ray Lankester, (London: H. S. King and Company, 1876), 2: 45.

[47] See Hofmann, "Catholicism and Evolution I," 102–107. Some would even go as far as to disunite the species of distinguishable human races to no longer be compelled to submit to any principle of unity whatsoever. They saw the race of slaves as inferior by its very nature to the race of masters, and therefore justified the enslavement of the inferior race as some sort of an edict of the natural law. It is to these ideologically determined ideas that the terms "polygenism" and "monogenism" first came to be applied by a Harvard professor Louis Agassiz in 1840s, and Samuel A. Cartwright and Georges Gliddon in 1850s. In the modern debate they are distinguished as "racial polygenism" and "racial monogenism." See also, John S. Haller Jr., *Outcasts from*

246 Theological Anthropogenesis and Evolution

contrary view that racial distinctions are insignificant with respect to the unity that humanity owes to its singular origin, that is, single human lineage (rather than a single couple).

These definitions of poly- *versus* monogenism might be interpreted as referring, in fact, to poly- *versus* monophyletism. As notes Hofmann, it was in 1928 that de Sinéty introduced a terminological shift. It seems that independently from the ongoing discussion of racial origins, he proposed a new application of the terms "monogenism" and "polygenism" to the descent of humans from either a single couple or a larger population of our ancestors.[48]

Consequently, we may say that the appropriate list of terms in the debate on this particular aspect of evolutionary anthropogenesis includes:

(1) Polyphyletic origin – it assumes that the human species originates from several ancestor species. Human speciation is thus a result of convergent evolution in more than one region (ecological niche). Few scientists support this view as of today.[49]

(2) Monophyletic origin – it assumes that the human species originates from one common ancestral species. This theory is favored by contemporary comparative anatomy and paleoanthropology.

(3) Polygenetic origin – it assumes that the first humans came from many pairs of ancestors (within one population). In other words, the last step of speciation that gives rise to S_2 takes place in an entire group of organisms that belong to S_1.

Evolution: Scientific Attitudes of Racial Inferiority, 1859–1900 (Carbondale: Southern Illinois University Press, 1971); Stephen Jay Gould, *The Mismeasure of Man*, revised and expanded edition (New York: W. W. Norton & Company, 1996), and David N. Livingstone, *Adam's Ancestors*.

[48] See De Sinéty, Robert, "Transformisme," in *Dictionnaire Apologétique de la Foi Catholique*. 4, edited by D'Alès (Paris: Gabriel Beauchesne, 1922), col. 1793–1848. "Of course this sense of monogenism invoking Adam and Eve does imply the old sense of monogenism as the unity of the human race. However, the new sense of polygenism that attributes human origins to a population certainly does not imply the old sense of racial polygenism, the idea that human races are a plurality of deep evolutionary lineages that might even be distinct species" (Hofmann, "Catholicism and Evolution I," 120). Hofmann notes that experts were continually documenting accounts of fertile cross breeding, which made racial polygenism difficult to sustain. Stubborn racists, such as Karl Vogt, defended their position by arguing that different species evolved in parallel to a point where interbreeding became possible.

[49] This view was expressed already in 1655 by Isaac de la Peyrère, who suggested that this theory of origin (he called it "Pre-Adamitism") was necessary to explain the existence of remote families of humans (e.g., Greenlanders). His book was translated

Monogenism versus Polygenism

(4) Monogenetic origin – it assumes that the human species derives from one pair of hominins. In other words, the last step of speciation giving rise to S_2 takes place in just one or two organisms that belong to S_1.

Scientific Point of View

The modern synthetic theory of evolution supports monophyletism and polygenism. As notes Dobzhansky "[S]pecies arise not as single individuals but as diverging populations, breeding communities and races which do not reside at a geometric point, but occupy more or less extensive territories."[50] From a biological point of view, the classical monogenetic scenario would require a minimization of the genetic variation within the population, causing an effect similar to the so-called "bottleneck effect," that is, a sudden decrease in the size of the transitional and the newly emerged population, and then – after several generations of a minimal size – its increase to a considerable size. This scenario is highly improbable due to at least two reasons: (1) an extremely high level of inbreeding, which radically weakens the genetic material, and (2) minimal chances for the survival and the immense reproductive success of the first humans. Moreover, even if it possibly occurs, it does not assume a population of exactly two individuals, but rather a larger group of organisms, which does not fit into the strictly monogenetic version of anthropogenesis. As Dennis Venema and Scot McKnight note:

It is technically possible that a species could be founded by a single ancestral breeding pair, just as it is technically possible that a new language could be founded by

---

into English in 1656. For references see Kenneth W. Kemp, "Evolution, Adam, and the Catholic Church," *Logos: A Journal of Catholic Thought and Culture* 26, no. 1 (2023), 29–30, 42.

[50] Dobzhansky, *Mankind Evolving*, 180–81. Darwin had made the same point: "in the majority of cases, namely ... I believe that during the slow process of modification the individuals of the species will have been kept nearly uniform by intercrossing; so that many individuals will have gone on simultaneously changing, and the whole amount of modification will not have been due, at each stage, to descent from a single parent" (Darwin, *On the Origin of Species*, 356). On another occasion he concluded saying: "when the principles of evolution are generally accepted, as they surely will be before long, the dispute between the monogenists and the polygenists will die a silent and unobserved death" (Charles Darwin, *The Descent of Man, and Selection in Relation to Sex. In Two Volumes – Vol. 1.* [London: John Murray, 1871], 235). Concerning monophyletism we find Darwin saying that "those naturalists ... who admit the principle of evolution ... will feel no doubt that all the races of man are descended from a single primitive stock; whether or not they think fit to designate them as distinct species" (*ibid.*, 229). Although it was initially opposed by Vogt and Haeckel, his view on this issue became prevalent at the beginning of the twentieth century.

248   *Theological Anthropogenesis and Evolution*

two speakers. This is not what one would usually expect, however. ... Put most simply, DNA evidence indicates that humans descend from a large population because we, as a species, are so genetically diverse in the present day that a large ancestral population is needed to transmit that diversity to us.[51]

According to Nicholas Lombardo, the genetic evidence "not only challenges this view [strict monogenesis] but makes it completely unsustainable."[52] It does so on the account of our genetic variability, which requires a much larger group of ancestors to give an origin to our species. Kemp refers to the example of the DRB_1 gene (contributing to the immune system). It turns out that 32 of the 58 variants (alleles) of this gene are found in both humans and chimpanzees. Because it is highly unlikely that the same mutations occurred independently in both species, they must date back to before the lineages split. Since no individual can carry more than two alleles of one gene, a population bottleneck of a single couple is way too narrow to channel these many variants.[53]

Consequently, with regards to human evolution, our ancestral population size is estimated at about 7,000 – in the case of the African groups – and at least 3,000 in non-African groups. The new approach which is based not only on the comparison of humans with other primates but refers to the analysis of genetic diversity solely within our species (through mapping and cataloguing single nucleotide polymorphisms and analyzing linkage disequilibrium) continues to support the conclusion that

humans, as a species, are descended from an ancestral population of at least several thousand individuals. More importantly, the scalability of this approach reveals that there was no significant change in human population size at the time modern humans appeared in the fossil record (~200,000 years ago), or at the time of significant cultural and religious development at ~50,000 years ago.[54]

Naturally, all this becomes challenging for the theological interpretation of anthropogenesis within the camp of theistic evolutionism. I will now list and discuss arguments in favor of mono- and polygenism and the contemporary versions of both positions.

---

[51] Dennis R. Venema and Scot McKnight, *Adam and the Genome: Reading Scripture after Genetic Science* (Grand Rapids: Brazos Press, 2017), 46, 55.

[52] Nicholas E. Lombardo, "Evolutionary Genetics and Theological Narratives of Human Origins," *The Heythrop Journal* 59, no. 3 (2018), 523.

[53] See Kemp, "Evolution," 30.

[54] Dennis R Venema, "Genesis and the Genome: Genomics Evidence for Human-Ape Common Ancestry and Ancestral Hominid Population Sizes," *Perspectives on Science and Christian Faith* 62, no. 3 (2010), 175. A meaningful critical evaluation of this position can be found in S. Joshua Swamidass, "The Misunderstood Science of Genetic Bottlenecks," *Peaceful Science*, July 29, 2022, https://doi.org/10.54739/1w7j.

Monogenism versus Polygenism

Arguments in Favor of Monogenism

We can think about at least three theological arguments and one more scientifically grounded contention in favor of monogenism that have been proposed and are discussed in the context of the debate on biological, philosophical, and theological notions of anthropogenesis.

1. Scripture, Patrology, and Scholasticism. The first of those arguments builds upon the three foundational sources of the classical tradition in theology. It departs from Scripture passages that, at least indirectly, can be interpreted as supporting the position of monogenism. The standard points of reference include: (1) Genesis 2–4 – telling the story of the two first representatives of the human family – Adam and Eve; (2) Wis 10:1–2 – thus speaking about personified Wisdom: "She preserved the first-formed father of the world when he alone had been created; And she raised him up from his fall, and gave him power to rule all things."; (3) Acts 17:26a – where we read about God who "made from one the whole human race to dwell on the entire surface of the earth" (it is worth noting that the text does not contain the noun "human," hence some have suggested that it may refer to one hominin family); and (4) Rom 5:17 and 1 Cor 15:21-22 – Paul's analogical typology of one Adam and one Christ.[55]

Naturally, this raises the question of how literal our exegesis of the Scripture should be. But even if spiritual and metaphorical (allegorical) senses of the Bible were introduced already in early patristic literature, the proponents of monogenism assure us that the way in which the majority of the fathers of the Church commented on both accounts of the origins in Genesis leaves no doubt they believed that humanity began with one man and one woman.[56]

Building upon Scripture and the patristic tradition, scholastic theologians seem to share the same doctrine of the direct formation

---

[55] Concerning more recent scientifically informed theological defense of biblical monogenism see Craig, *In Quest of the Historical Adam* and S. Joshua Swamidass, *The Genealogical Adam and Eve: The Surprising Science of Universal Ancestry* (Downers Grove, IL: IVP, 2021). The former, in reference to paleoneurology and archaeology, makes a cumulative case to classify our species within the larger human family that includes Neanderthals and Denisovans, and argues that the "historical Adam" is to be located around 500,000 or more years ago within *Homo heidelbergensis*, the hominin population ancestral to Neanderthals, Denisovans and *Homo sapiens*. The latter suggests that Adam and Eve were a fresh creation by God some few thousand years ago who then interbred with an already existing population of hominins, leading eventually to the descent of every individual in the global population from this single couple.

[56] See my analysis of the anti-naturalistic view of anthropogenesis above.

250   *Theological Anthropogenesis and Evolution*

of the bodies of the first humans by God. As noted above, Aquinas thinks that the body of the first man must have been shaped by God, because it could not arise from entities belonging to a different species: "The first formation of the human body could not be by the instrumentality of any created power, but was immediately from God" (*ST* I, 91, 2, co.). Hence, the proponents of monogenism may suggest that if his theology can be reconciled with an evolutionary view of anthropogenesis, it has to embrace their position, which traces the history of the human species back to Adam and Eve.

2. Pius XII and *Humani generis.* A very important voice in the conversation on mono- *versus* polygenism came from Pius XII in his encyclical letter *Humani generis.* Opening the possibility for Catholic scholars and other faithful to think about some aspects of human origins in evolutionary terms, the pope expresses his skepticism about the polygenetic model of human speciation. Most importantly, he relates the question of mono- *versus* polygenism to the dogma of the original sin in Adam and the redemption in Christ:

> When, however, there is question of another conjectural opinion, namely polygenism, the children of the Church by no means enjoy such liberty. For the faithful cannot embrace that opinion which maintains that either after Adam there existed on this earth true men who did not take their origin through natural generation from him as from the first parent of all, or that Adam represents a certain number of first parents. Now it is in no way apparent how such an opinion can be reconciled with that which the sources of revealed truth and the documents of the Teaching Authority of the Church propose with regard to original sin, which proceeds from a sin actually committed by an individual Adam and which, through generation, is passed on to all and is in everyone as his own.[57]

As notes Gaine, theologians in the period before the encyclical had gone so far as to judge monogenism not only "certain," but even as "proximate to faith" or *de fide* by way of the ordinary and universal magisterium.[58] Nevertheless, despite such confidence

---

[57] Pius XII, *Humani generis*, no. 37.

[58] See Gaine, "The Teaching,"). The draft version of the canon condemning polygenism prepared for Vatican I stated: "Si quis universum genus humanum ab uno protoparente ortum esse negaverit: anathema sit" ("If anybody denies that the whole human race is descended from one first ancestor, let him be anathema"). The canon has never been promulgated (I quote its formulation after Piet Schoonenberg, *Man and Sin: A Theological View by Piet Schoonenberg,* trans. Joseph Donceel [Notre Dame, IN: University of Notre Dame Press, 1965], 175).

Monogenism versus *Polygenism* 251

on the part of those theologians, Pius XII did not solemnly define monogenism or even indicate that it was definitively taught. Rather, he left its proposal at the level of the ordinary magisterium. In itself this restraint was sufficient to suggest that theologians should restrict its theological note at the most to theologically certain. Gaine also mentions that as at Vatican I, a preparatory draft for Vatican II (1962–65) included a definition concerning monogenism, but the doctrine did not reach the final documents.[59]

Having said this, we must acknowledge that St. Paul's analogy between one Adam and one Christ, and soteriology built upon it, are deeply entrenched into the fabric of the Christian tradition. Hence, even if Pius XII did not solemnly define monogenism, he definitely did not see an acceptable reinterpretation of this tradition. At the same time, we might assume that if such an interpretation were worked out and widely accepted, it could significantly shift the mono- versus polygenism debate.

3. Paul VI's address to a symposium on original sin in 1966. The pope points out that some modern authors start "from the undemonstrated hypothesis of polygenism" and give "explanations of original sin" which are "irreconcilable with Catholic doctrine." They deny "that the sin from which" our many ills are derived "was first of all the disobedience of Adam, 'the first man,' a figure of the man to come – a sin that was committed at the beginning of history." He emphasizes that "The sin of the first man is transmitted to all his descendants not through imitation but through propagation." It "means privation and not just an absence of holiness and justice."[60]

4. Mitochondrial Eve and Y-Chromosomal Adam. An argument grounded, somewhat surprisingly, in evolutionary biology and

---

[59] Gaine, "The Teaching," forthcoming.

[60] Pope Paul VI, "Original Sin and Modern Science: Address to Participants in A Symposium on Original Sin," *The Pope Speaks*, Vol. 11 (1966), 229–35 (translated from the Italian *L'Osservatore Romano*, 11 July 1966, by Rev. Austin Vaughan). John Paul II quotes this passage in one of his 1986 catechizes, saying it is valid and should serve as "a stimulus for further research" for those who engage in "evaluating, with the wisdom of faith, the explanations offered by science about the origins of humanity" (John Paul II, "Consequences of Original Sin for All Humanity: Catechesis by Pope John Paul II on Jesus Christ," [October 1, 1986], http://totus2us.com/teaching/jpii-catechesis-on-god-the-son-jesus/ [retrieved 12 July 2021], no. 4).

Theological Anthropogenesis and Evolution

genetics. Based on the scientific research, it has been suggested – in the late 1980s for the "mitochondrial Eve" and in the early 1990s for the "Y-chromosomal Adam" – that human mitochondrial DNA coalesces leading to one common female ancestor in the recent past (170,000 years ago), while the human Y-chromosome sequences also coalesce to one common male ancestor even more recently (~50,000 years ago).[61]

Because the names alluding to the biblical narrative in Genesis were used by scientists, the theory of "mitochondrial Eve" and the "Y-chromosomal Adam" received considerable attention outside of the scientific community – where it was regarded by many as a scientific proof for monogenesis. However, it has been demonstrated that such conclusion is rather mistaken and ungrounded. As notes Venema, the reason for such rapid coalescence of mitochondrial and Y-chromosome sequences is that these particular sequences are inherited in a distinct way, compared with (non-Y) chromosomal DNA. The mitochondrial sequence is passed only through mothers (hence ends abruptly if a mother has only sons), while the Y-chromosome sequence is passed only through fathers to their sons (hence ends abruptly if a father has only daughters). However, Venema adds that, in both cases, non-Y chromosomal DNA lineages continue, that is, both fathers and mothers pass chromosomes to offspring of both genders. Consequently

> Though our mitochondrial DNA lineage coalesces to "Mitochondrial Eve" in the relatively recent past, present-day variation of human chromosomal DNA indicates that she was but one member of a substantial breeding population. The same logic, mutatis mutandis, applies to the inheritance of the Y-chromosome and the coalescence of human Y-chromosome variation to a single "Adam" in the recent past. While the rapid coalescence of these specially inherited DNA sequences is interesting in its own right, such sequences are not useful measures of ancestral human population sizes because of their unique modes of inheritance.[62]

---

[61] See Max Ingman et al., "Mitochondrial Genome Variation and the Origin of Modern Humans," *Nature* 408, no. 6813 (December 2000): 708–13; R. Thomson et al., "Recent Common Ancestry of Human Y Chromosomes: Evidence from DNA Sequence Data," *Proceedings of the National Academy of Sciences of the United States of America* 97, no. 13 (2000): 7360–65.

[62] Venema, "Genesis and the Genome," 176.

Monogenism versus *Polygenism* 253

Contemporary Version of the Monogenetic Scenario

Those who claim that strict theological monogenism requires just as strict biological monogenism face the challenge of evolutionary biology and biological anthropology, which – for the reasons mentioned above – favor the polygenetic scenario of the human speciation. One way of avoiding this difficulty is to assume special (miraculous) divine intervention(s) that enabled both evolutionary origin and extraordinary reproductive success of exactly one or two first human beings, eliminating all negative effects of the high level of inbreeding within the first generations of this new species.

This scenario, however, is not favored by those who envision human speciation as a natural process that needs to remain in agreement with the scientific data and refer to the classical theological argument emphasizing the dignity of creatures as secondary and instrumental causes "in the hand" of God. Consequently, most recent advocates of monogenism feel obliged to search for a more moderate and scientifically informed version of this model of human speciation, one that could be reconciled with a more traditional reading of Genesis and the doctrinal teaching of the Church.

The most prominent contemporary version of the mitigated monogenetic view of anthropogenesis was developed and defended by Kenneth Kemp. It is based on the trifold distinction of biological, philosophical, and theological notions of the human species.[63] In the delineation of his argument, Kemp refers to Andrew Alexander, who introduced this classification already in 1964, thus defining the three categories in question:

1. The biological species is the population of interbreeding individuals.
2. The philosophical species is the rational animal, that is, a natural kind characterized by the capacity for conceptual thought, judgment, reasoning, and free choice.
3. The theological species is, extensionally, the collection of individuals that have an eternal destiny. The *Catechism of the Catholic Church* says "God created man in his image and established him in his friendship."[64]

---

[63] See Kenneth W. Kemp, "Science, Theology, and Monogenesis," *American Catholic Philosophical Quarterly* 85, no. 2 (2011): 217–36. Similar to Kemp's are positions of Flaman ("Evolution," 573–575) and Austriaco, "The Historicity of Adam and Eve IV: A Theological Synthesis" in Austriaco, et al. *Thomistic Evolution*, 171–75.

[64] CCC, no. 396. Andrew Alexander, "Human Origins and Genetics," *Clergy Review* 49 (1964),350–51. See Kemp, "Science, Theology, and Monogenesis," 230. Approaching *imago Dei* from the personalist perspective, Ratzinger states: "The first Thou

254   *Theological Anthropogenesis and Evolution*

Camille Muller, a botanist at the University of Louvain, had already introduced a preliminary version of this idea in 1951. He assumed that Adam and Eve coexisted with a wider biologically human population (he did not identify this population with reference to a more precise scientific nomenclature). In his scenario, the conclusive step of the hominization hinges on God's elevating of the human soul through the gift of sanctifying grace, which developed in the first "theological humans" a disposition or receptivity to the divine will and thus raised them to the supernatural order. Offering his hypothetical "less strict" form of monogenism, he claimed that

Through the successive unions of the descendants of several primitive couples (including the initial couple of Genesis), a very limited number of generations would be enough for all men to be descended from the first man of which Genesis speaks (without requiring marriages between brothers and sisters), and, just as likely perhaps, for all modern humanity (the only ones the Fathers of the councils would have considered) to be tainted by original sin and saved by Christ. Would not this still be monogenism, less strict, but equally efficacious?"[65]

The main difficulty of Muller's position is his assumption that before God bestowed the gift of supernatural grace on the particular exemplar(s) of hominins, the wider population to which they belonged consisted of creatures, which both biologically and metaphysically speaking were "fully" human (*Homo sapiens sapiens*).[66] This would mean they had immortal human souls. If we assume (as classical theology does) that sanctifying grace is a supernatural gift, Muller's position appears to

that – however stammeringly – was said by human lips to God marks the moment in which spirit arose in the world. Here the Rubicon of anthropogenesis was crossed. For it is not the use of weapons or fire, not new methods of cruelty or of useful activity that constitutes man, but rather his ability to be immediately in relation to God" ("Belief in Creation and the Theory of Evolution," 142). On another occasion Ratzinger emphasizes the Christological aspect: "Man's full 'hominization' presupposes God's becoming man; only by this event is the Rubicon dividing the 'animal' from the 'logical' finally crossed for ever and the highest possible development accorded to the process that began when a creature of dust and earth looked out beyond itself and its environment and was able to address God as 'You'" (Ratzinger, *Introduction to Christianity*, 235). For an insightful elucidation of Ratzinger's contribution to the mono- *versus* polygenism debate see Matthew J. Ramage, *From the Dust of the Earth: Benedict XVI, the Bible, and the Theory of Evolution* (Washington, DC: The Catholic University of America Press, 2022), Chapter 7, 167–92.

[65] Camille Muller, "L'Encyclique 'Humani Generis' et Les Problèmes Scientifiques," *Synthèses; Revue mensuelle international* 5(57) 1951, 304.

[66] *Homo sapiens sapiens* is defined in paleoanthropology as the subspecies of *Homo sapiens* that consists of the only living members of the entire genus *Homo*, that is, modern human beings.

Monogenism versus *Polygenism*

suggest the existence of an entire population of human beings, in the state of pure nature (*natura pura*), before the bestowal of the gift of grace on some chosen representatives of this group. This would bring him back to polygenism, unless he assumed that supernatural grace is somehow constitutive for human nature, and only those who possessed it were truly humans. However, this proposition, which we might classify as theological monogenism within biological polygenism, puts into question the Christian understanding of divine grace as transcendent with respect to human nature, a free gift of God, which elevates and perfects it, but does not belong to its natural fabric.

Hence, leaving aside Muller's early formulation of the position he himself embraces and further develops, Kemp concentrates on its reformulation as offered by Alexander and says:

The distinction between the biological species concept and the theological one is important, since they are not necessarily co-extensive. Two individuals, one theologically human and the other not, would remain members of the same biological species as long as they were capable of producing fertile offspring. While it would certainly be a theological error to exclude any members of the biological species now living from the philosophical or theological species man (that is, to hold that they lacked rational souls, or that they were not among those to whom God had offered His friendship), there can be no theological objection to the claim that some one (or two) members of a prehistoric, biologically (that is, genetically) human species were made sufficiently different from the others that they constituted a new theological species, e.g., by being given a rational soul and an eternal destiny.[67]

Most importantly, on this account, the emergence of a "fully," that is, theological human species does not require the development of a barrier for sexual reproduction, which biologists assume takes at least around a thousand generations. To the contrary, a lack of sexual isolation allows the first "theological" human(s) to grow in number, through reproduction with hominins. According to Kemp, this assumption makes the monogenetic scenario plausible.

Note that Kemp speaks about the first human being(s) as "being given a rational soul." On another occasion, he uses the category of "infusion" (or "infusionism").[68] This suggests, once again, a dualistic anthropology and the notion of human soul as added to human body – an imprecise and confusing terminology that, regrettably, is still prevalent in Catholic philosophical and theological anthropology. That Kemp

---

[67] Kemp, "Science, Theology, and Monogenesis," 230–31.
[68] See Kemp, "Evolution," 33–34.

favors this explanation becomes clear from his alternative version of Alexander's scenario. Alexander saw the final step toward rationality in a particular and crucial genetic mutation, which nonetheless did not establish biological barriers to reproduction (i.e., did not give an origin to a new biological species).[69] He speculated that the new trait it introduced would manifest in the phenotype of the offspring, born as the first representative(s) of *Homo sapiens sapiens*, descending from an organism whose genome was changed. If the gene carrying the new trait were dominant, the trait would spread quickly.[70]

Kemp thinks Alexander's idea of the "crucial mutation" is misplaced as it would have to spontaneously affect two organisms, male and female. However, it remains unclear to me (1) why he presupposes that the mutation in the organism of one parent would not have been sufficient and (2) why the same mutation could not occur in two organisms (today we know that many mutations are very specific, targeting precise loci in particular parts of genomes). Nevertheless, having criticized Alexander's position, Kemp offers a new variant of the same view:

[69] It is important to remember that Alexander seems to speak about the last step of an evolutionary transition, which might include only one mutation while being preceded by numerous genetic changes at the former stages of the same process. The question concerning the number of mutations necessary for speciation, is continually debated. On the one extreme we find those who claim that even one mutation can be sufficient (see, e.g., H. Allen Orr, "Is Single-Gene Speciation Possible?," *Evolution* 45, no. 3 [1991]: 764–69). A more prevalent view suggests that speciation in more complex plants and animals involves differentiation across many genetic regions (see, e.g., Patrik Nosil, Jeffrey L. Feder, and Zachariah Gompert, "How Many Genetic Changes Create New Species?," *Science* 371, no. 6531 [2021]: 777–79).

[70] Benedict Ashley proposes a similar hypothesis. He claims that "In current evolutionary theory, it is not individuals but populations which evolve from one species to another" and considers truly human intelligence to be a unitary, "all or none" trait. He speculates how this could have come into a population by a mutation in a subhuman individual, who then had a child that was the first human being. This human interbred with other members of the population, producing more human children. Ashley speculates that "the origin of that final genetic trait responsible to produce a human brain capable of functioning at the human level depended on the mutation of one dominant gene that occurred in the germ-cells of a primate ancestor, which was not itself human but which then bred with another primate of its own kind to produce a male and female child who were genotypically the first human beings having fully human brains, and who by interbreeding became the ancestors of the entire human race. Either this or the former explanation is consistent with the interpretation of *Genesis* which is not concerned with the exact way in which the human species came into existence and began as a single interbreeding and intercommunicating species to have a history determined by a primordial act of human choice [that is, original sin]" (Benedict M. Ashley, *Theologies of the Body: Humanist and Christian* [St. Louis: Pope John Center, 1985], 377). Flaman classifies Ashley's position as punctiliar monogenism occurring within a gradual polygenism.

Monogenism versus Polygenism

There is an alternative use of Alexander's distinction which does the work of reconciliation without entailing the problems that his view faces. That account can begin with a population of about 5,000 hominids, beings which are in many respects like human beings, but which lack the capacity for intellectual thought. Out of this population, God selects two and endows them with intellects by creating for them rational souls, giving them at the same time those preternatural gifts the possession of which constitutes original justice. Only beings with rational souls (with or without the preternatural gifts) are truly human. The first two theologically human beings misuse their free will, however, by choosing to commit a (the original) sin, thereby losing the preternatural gifts, though not the offer of divine friendship by virtue of which they remain theologically (not just philosophically) distinct from their merely biologically human ancestors and cousins.[71]

In his more recent publication, Kemp once again delineates his position as follows:

Stage 1 – The Foundation: The evolutionary emergence of a biological species having perceptual powers sufficiently complex to *allow* the infusion of a created human (rational) soul, but able to live an ordinary animal life (with perceptions and emotions, but no intellect) without it. This I will call merely biological man.

Stage 2 – Anthropogenesis: Divine creation of rational souls and their infusion into exactly two of those merely biologically human beings, without thereby affecting their interfertility with the rest of the biological species. This produced beings that are philosophically human because they are rational beings, and theologically human because they are, in a conceptually distinguishable sense, beneficiaries of God's special grace. They are, that is to say, fully human beings.

Stage 3 – Succeeding Generations: (1) A certain amount of interbreeding between the fully human beings and their merely biologically human "cousins," and (2) infusion of rational souls into all (or at least most) of the beings that have even one fully human parent, so that, within a few centuries, the entire biological population will, as a matter of practical, if not mathematical, certainty, be fully human.

The resultant population will be biologically (genetically) polygenetic (because there was never a population bottleneck of just two individuals) but theologically (or, genealogically) monogenetic (in the sense that all of the fully human beings who ever lived will be genealogically descended, though not exclusively, from one single first human couple).[72]

---

[71] Kemp, "Science, Theology, and Monogenesis," 231–32. Note that on Kemp's account one and the same transition becomes a threshold to both philosophical (rational or intellectual) and theological (spiritual) human.

[72] Kemp, "Evolution," 33. Note that Kemp departs not only from Alexander, but also from Muller who claimed that most likely "biological," and certainly "philosophical humans" (to use Kemp's categories), would already have had human souls, yet not elevated by the gift of the sanctifying grace (which would leave them in the state of

Theological Anthropogenesis and Evolution

The scenario proposed by Kemp finds further grounding in the evidence of early *Homo sapiens* being able to interbreed with Neanderthals and Denisovans. As notes Austriaco:

This replacement [of Neanderthals in Europe and western Asia as well as other more ancient human-like species] was accompanied by interbreeding among these human-like species such that all non-African populations today inherited roughly 1.5–4 percent of their genomes from their Neanderthal ancestors, and all Melanesians today inherited between 1.9–3.4 percent of their genome from another extinct species of archaic humans called Denisovans. Clearly, our history as a biological species is shaped by migration, interbreeding, and unrelenting adaptation that has generated much diversity within the human population.[73]

Contemporary Version of the Monogenetic Scenario – Critical Evaluation

The model developed by Kemp is perceived by many as a viable and consistent version of monogenetic anthropogenesis that remains in line with the most recent paleoanthropology and human genetics. While sharing this opinion, I would like to raise some critical questions and offer some suggestions, that are grounded in the Aristotelian–Thomistic framework of philosophy and theology.

---

mortality). On Kemp's account "truly" human, that is, immortal souls are created and bestowed on selected hominins.

Ramage notes that Kemp's position finds support in the thought of young Ratzinger who already in 1964 stated that "[E]ven if it is highly probable that hominization occurred within a biological population in a polygenic manner, it is possible that the brilliant flash of transcendence occurred for the first time in one or two individuals. Biological polygenism and theological monogenism are therefore not necessarily mutually exclusive antitheses, because the level of their questions does not fully coincide. ... [I]t is clear that biological polygenism is largely a theologically neutral theme because it does not overlap directly with the theological poly- or monogenism" (Ratzinger, *Schöpfungslehre* [1964], 194).

More recently, Kemp's proposal is followed by Lombardo. Having rejected strict monogenism, he states: "Since new genetic traits do not usually appear in more than one individual in the same place at the same time, the genetic traits necessary for ensoulment probably appear in a single individual and then spread by reproduction. (It is theoretically possible that the genetic traits could have appeared in two or more individuals at the same time by purely natural processes. Statistically, however, such an occurrence would have been extremely improbable.)" (Lombardo, "Evolutionary Genetics," 526).

[73] Nicanor Pier Giorgio Austriaco, "Defending Adam After Darwin: On the Origin of Sapiens as a Natural Kind," *American Catholic Philosophical Quarterly* 92, no. 2 (2018), 345. Moreover, states Ramage, "there is now strong evidence that these other two archaic humans [Neanderthals and Denisovans] were rational and that bona fide intelligence dates as far back as two million years ago with *Homo erectus*, for this species

Monogenism versus *Polygenism*   259

What seems to be crucial in Kemp's scenario is that God arbitrarily and without reference to any biological change selects two hominins and "endows them with intellects by creating for them rational souls." Moreover, he also endows them with gifts that constitute original justice (Kemp does not specify them, but he most likely means supernatural grace and praeternatural gifts). I claim that this proposition, correct in its basic presuppositions, is nonetheless: (1) voluntaristic – as it depends on God's arbitrary decision without a particular natural condition that enables the final step of hominization to occur, (2) dualistic – since human souls are added to otherwise almost rational human beings, which is not acceptable from the Aristotelian–Thomistic point of view, and (3) metaphysically dubious – as it suggests a very unusual case of substantial change of an already existing (biologically) human organism into a different living being that belongs to a new natural kind *Homo sapiens* (philosophical and theological human) – without considerable changes in its physical dispositions (the soul of a hominin is "replaced" by the soul of the first representative of *Homo sapiens*).

My impression is that, concerning (2) and (3), Kemp's position is not so much in a direct opposition to the classical thought but rather suffers from a lack of terminological precision. While in his most recent article, he once again speaks about the "infusion [of human souls] into exactly two of ... merely biologically human beings,"[74] he would most likely agree that, technically (metaphysically) speaking, the first human soul(s) actualized properly disposed PM in the substantial change that accompanied (or simply can be identified with) fertilization. Hence, the final step of human speciation did not involve an unusual (and metaphysically dubious) substantial change. Rather – from a biological point of view – it came as an unusual effect of a regular process of generation (and substantial change that accompanies it).

However, my criticism raised under (1) is more problematic as it seems to question the core of Kemp's proposal. Divine voluntarism, typical of William of Ockham and some strains of post-Reformation theology, is

---

made sophisticated stone tools and possibly also possessed a capacity for symbolic thought and language that enabled its members to sail across large bodies of water" (Ramage, *From the Dust of the Earth*, 188). Kemp suggests that already *Homo heidelbergensis* (a common ancestor of Neanderthals and *Homo sapiens*) might have been rational. He says our classification depends on the definition of the species we accept and concludes stating that "The *homo factus est* of the Nicene Creed refers to the natural species, rational animals; any attempt to restrict it to *H. sapiens* as currently defined would be anachronistic" (Kemp, "Evolution," 38).

[74] Kemp, "Evolution," 33.

260   *Theological Anthropogenesis and Evolution*

rather foreign to the Thomistic understanding of divine action. According to this tradition, God's agency takes into account the nature of things and works through them as secondary and instrumental causes.

Hence, I consider it crucial to assume that God's direct creation of the first human soul(s), corresponded to the proper disposition of PM within the complex process of speciation, as well as the procreative action of hominins, which enabled their gametes to meet and merge in fertilization. The latter, being a substantial change that gave origin to the first modern human being(s), was possible – once again – because of some decisive natural change in the biological material that prepared (disposed) it, and the PM that underlaid it, to enter such a change. Consequently, in trying to distance my own position on this matter from both occasionalism and deism, as well as divine voluntarism, I am inclined to follow Alexander's position, which seems to go along with the model presented in the opening of this chapter.[75]

There is one more issue that needs needs to be considered, in reference to the contemporary monogenetic account of anthropogenesis. Even if we assume that the first rational human being(s) was(were) able to procreate with nonrational, yet biologically human beings, producing new representatives of *Homo sapiens sapiens*, we still face the difficulty of the extremely low probability of a new species of "theological humans" beginning from just one or two organisms (a challenge similar to the one that refers to the classical version of the monogenetic scenario). In other words, the first exemplar(s) of "theological humans" was(were) also biological organism(s) that had to survive and achieve reproductive success. And here, the possibility to interbreed with hominins might not have been enough. There must have been something – be it a psychological, mental, or a spiritual feature – that helped them succeed, while various other species of hominins went into extinction.

---

[75] My view finds support in the – somewhat more dualistic – account of evolutionary anthropogenesis proposed by Nicholas Lombardo: "[If we] hold that the human body is intrinsically oriented toward the human soul and vice versa, it follows that the bodies of the first humans must have been different from the bodies of their nonhuman ancestors. The bodies of the first humans could not have been identical to the bodies of their immediate ancestors. There must have been something about their bodies fitted to their souls. And if there was something about their bodies fitted to their souls, there must have been something new and different about their genetic traits. If we accept this conclusion – if we accept the idea that the human body and the human soul are intrinsically fitted to each other, and that this intrinsic orientation implies that human bodies are different from all nonhuman bodies – then we must also conclude that the genomes of the first humans were different from the genomes of their immediate ancestors" (Lombardo, "Evolutionary Genetics," 525).

Monogenism versus Polygenism

One could speculate that the crucial change which completed hominization – even if physiologically and phenotypically insignificant – gave the first rational human being, or a pair of the first rational humans beings, a significant advantage and tools – most likely intellectual dispositions – that enabled them to enhance their perception of reality. Another possible explanation refers to the praeternatural gifts bestowed by God on the first human being(s). In any case, whatever the nature of the advantageous feature(s) characterizing the first human beings, it(they) must have provided them with considerable superiority and prevalence, possibly a strong supremacy over the entire population, which helped them to survive and grow in number. They would have then achieved evolutionary success descending from just one organism or one pair of parental organisms – something that according to population genetics is on the verge of being impossible.

Those who do not find this argument convincing might suggest that, at the end of the day, the monogenetic scenario of hominization seems to require a direct divine intervention, not only in creating human souls specifically for only one or two first human beings but also in providing for their reproductive success. This scenario might be considered plausible and need not stand in opposition to science. God is omnipotent, and he might have directly intervened in this particular and unique evolutionary transition. At the same time, the argument emphasizing the dignity of natural causes and the notion of God's primary and principal action in nature through secondary and instrumental causation of his creatures (mentioned above) might speak against it, which inspires a number of contemporary theologians to embrace some version of the polygenetic model of human speciation.

Arguments in Favor of Polygenism I: Interpretation of the Bible

An entire group of arguments that polygenism does not stand in opposition with the Church's teaching on the origin of man departs from the historical-critical exegesis of the Scripture. Concerning the account of Genesis, one could argue, as does Peter Enns, that since Gen 1:27–28 does not specify the number of humans (*'adam*) – males (*zakar*) and females (*neqevah*) – "the editor may be signaling that the individual man, Adam, in Chapter 2 is a subset of humanity, *'adam*, in Chapter 1."[76] This interpretation

---

[76] Peter Enns, *The Evolution of Adam: What the Bible Does and Doesn't Say about Human Origins* (Grand Rapids, MI: Brazos Press, 2012), 100–101, 81. In other words, "There is *'adam* in the universal sense outside Eden, but inside Eden, God's garden, there

262   *Theological Anthropogenesis and Evolution*

answers the difficulty of Cain – the only surviving offspring of Adam and Eve after he has killed Abel – being afraid of retaliation (on the side of other human beings) for murdering his brother (Gen 4:14).

Concerning original sin, we read in Genesis that it was both Eve and Adam that transgressed against God. Hence, the proponents of polygenism claim that we may speak about a "fellowship" in turning away from God. According to them, the original sin has a communal aspect already in Genesis.[77] However, the truth is that in the biblical account, it is Eve who sins first and then leads Adam to join her in turning away from God. The act of sin is individual in reference to each one of them. The reason why in later tradition, it is referred only to Adam (except for 1 Tim 2:14, where Saint Paul states that "Adam was not deceived, but the woman was deceived and transgressed.") is the patriarchal character of ancient cultures.

From a biological point of view, one might suggest that Adam was an Alpha-male head of the entire group of first human beings. Hence, Rahner speculates, "it is possible, even in an originally polygenetic mankind, that *one* man decided the issue whether human descendance coincided with a communication of grace or not." His suggestion is grounded in an emphasis on the freedom of each individual human being understood as situated (contextualized, co-determined) within the moral condition of the community. Based on this presupposition, Rahner assumes that "only a *whole* sinless original group can transmit grace to its descendants." Consequently, "the personal guilt of one individual within the original group of human beings can be thought of as blocking the grace-transmitting function which accompanied human descent from this group."[78]

---

is Adam – who has a unique relationship with God and represents God's chosen people, Israel" (*ibid.*, 101). One could refer this interpretation to the notion of first (philosophical and theological) human being(s) emerging among hominins (biological humans), discussed in the preceding section on monogenism.

[77] "Even present-day evolutionary monogenism accepts a 'group' (namely, two) that sinned" (Karl Rahner, "Evolution and Original Sin" *Concilium* 26 [1967], 72).

[78] *Ibid.*, 68, 70, 69. Rahner suggests this scenario is also valid with one couple (not just one man) playing the central role. His category of the "grace transmitting function" of a human population might be considered in sacramental terms (human nature transmitting supernatural grace). Also, it is important to remember that even if this scenario (at least to some extent) goes along the traditional interpretation of original sin – it is Adam's individual decision that affects the "grace transmitting function" of the group – Rahner clearly states that it departs from the strict definition of the physical (biological) transmission of original sin. In his understanding, sin is inherited not from Adam but from all members of the population that has lost its "grace transmitting function," and is inherited not merely biologically but multidimensionally, as the phenomenon of situating every individual's freedom by guilt, which becomes an intrinsic aspect of human nature. "[W]e must ... eliminate that misunderstanding which treats original sin as if the specifically and strictly

Monogenism versus Polygenism

Following Rahner's suggestion, Pierre Grelot proposed a "mitigated polygenism" in which, even if Adam and Eve are assumed to have initiated sin, they would have done so within a tightly integrated population in which the effects of sin were actualized.

Would not strict monogenism, which would eliminate any social group from the initial human lineage, condemn the first couple to a *solipsism* hardly compatible with an important aspect of revealed anthropology? On the contrary, in making of this couple the point of crystallization of a society, one discovers in the human stock all the characteristics of a complete social experience.[79]

An alternative scenario assumes that it was the community that rebelled (sinned) first (as Eve did in the biblical account) and was eventually joined by the Alpha-male leader, whose decision was crucial for the future of the species as a whole. The wound of the original sin (*peccatum originale originatum*) would then be passed (through inheritance) by him and all other human beings onto their children. Rahner considers a variation of this model, which does not assume any leading figure:

Can one think of original sin as the sin of the whole original group of human beings, polygenetically one, and that this whole group, historically united and the vanguard of mankind, committed collectively what is called *peccatum originale originans*, original sin at the start, and that this group can be personified as "Adam" because it represents a genuine unit?[80]

Rahner answers positively to this question, which enables those who are willing to follow his suggestion to speak about one collective act of sin within a biologically polygenetic population of first humans.[81]

Concerning the New Testament, one might try to apply the same interpretation to the exegesis of Saint Paul's teaching on sin in the letter to the Romans. As early as 1935, Jean and Amédée Bouyssonie wrote:

subjective guilt element were passed on to those that 'inherit' because they are *physically* descended from the one who committed this subjective sin" (*ibid.*, 68–69). "The notion that the personal deed of 'Adam' or of the first group of people is imputed to us in such a way that it has been transmitted on to us biologically, as it were, has absolutely nothing to do with the Christian dogma of original sin" (Karl Rahner, *Foundations of Christian Faith: An Introduction to the Idea of Christianity* [New York: Crossroad, 1978], 110).

[79] Pierre Grelot, *Réflexions sur le Problème du Péché Originel* (Tournai: Casterman, 1968), 105.

[80] Rahner, "Evolution and Original Sin," 68. It is worth noting that both models proposed by Rahner in this article stand in a stark contrast to his former position, which strongly supported monogenism. See Karl Rahner, "Theological Reflections on Monogenism," in *Theological Investigations. Vol. I*, trans. Cornelius Ernst (Baltimore: Helicon, 1961), 229–96.

[81] In addition, Rahner lists several aspects which he believes confirm that "*mankind remains a biological–historical unity, even in terms of polygenism:*" (a) the real unity of physical

264 *Theological Anthropogenesis and Evolution*

Might it be that original sin is due to a more or less large collectivity rather than a single couple, and, if this is the case, might not all humanity still be descended from these first sinners? Secondly, might the analogies drawn by Saint Paul between the first Adam, father of the human race, and the new Adam, Jesus Christ, be more relevant to the universal and hereditary culpability of humanity and its redemption rather than to its community of origin?[82]

Following this proposal, one might suggest that the collective interpretation of *ādām* in Genesis can be seen as showing the universality of sin – both in the fact that it was a common act of the entire primordial human family (a collective act of individual, conscious, and free human beings), and in the fact that it is inherited by all future members of the same human species (family). Christ, as the new Adam, focuses (concentrates) in himself the entire history of humanity (a shared experience of all human beings), which he saves through his cross and resurrection. This shows the universality of the redemption in Christ. In this reinterpretation, one might argue to be holding on to Saint Paul's parallel of Adam and Christ, while showing that both terms of this parallel (analogy) can be, in a way, interpreted collectively.[83]

This interpretation seems to find support in the modern translation and interpretation of Rom 5:12. In the *Vetus Latina* version of the New Testament, available to Augustine whose notion of original sin had a strong (if not decisive) impact on the shape of this doctrine, we learn that "Sin passed to all in whom [Adam] all have sinned." The new and more accurate translation says about "Death [that] passed to all because all have sinned." It becomes clear that the latter version might be seen as opening a way to a polygenetic reinterpretation of the doctrine of original sin.[84]

---

existence in an ambiance; (b) the real unity of the animal population from which mankind descended; (c) the unity of the concrete biotype within which alone mankind can endure and procreate; (d) the actual human and personal intercommunication; and (e) the unity of man's destiny toward a supernatural aim and Christ (this is not merely related to mankind as one but makes this oneness even more radically one). See *ibid.*, 67.

[82] Jean and Amédée Bouyssonie, "Polygénisme" *Dictionnaire de théologie catholique* 12(2), 1935: col. 2536 (transl. Hofmann, "Catholicism and Evolution I," 124).

[83] Hence, Schoonenberg suggests we should see "the sins of Israel itself, [as] committed 'in similitude with Adam's transgression' (Rom. v. 14), the 'many transgressions' which preceded the justification by One. (Rom. v. 16.) In this manner Christ's death on the cross clearly brings out the sin of those who brought about his rejection. This gives the redeeming influence of Christ's death and resurrection a much more paradoxical aspect than when, as is practically the case, it finds its counterimage only in the sin of the first human couple. It pulls not only Adam's sin out of its isolated position but also original sin itself, which follows from it" (Schoonenberg, *Man and Sin*, 178–79).

[84] See Thomas R. Schreiner, "Original Sin and Original Death: Romans 5:12–19," in *Adam, the Fall, and Original Sin: Theological, Biblical, And Scientific Perspectives*, ed. Hans

Monogenism versus Polygenism

The collective interpretation of the biblical term *ādām* as human species in general, inspired further and more progressive reflection. A number of exegetes argued that the entire account of the first chapters of Genesis could be interpreted in a communal sense, as a general description of people in their nature, in reference to supernatural and praeternatural gifts they received, and the account of their fall into sin. Hence, Rahner speaks critically about "the tendency of the Oriental mind to think in concrete and personalistic terms and to see the foundation of every sociological unit in a single king or ancestor."[85] While the unity of a biological species is expressed in terms of the gene pool it shares, in the case of humans, it is expressed in culture and language, and these can exist only in a human group.

Following this train of thought, a Dutch Jesuit Piet Schoonenberg inspired a school of thought in which he proposed to redefine original sin (*peccatum originale originans*) as a collective state of sin of the human family, the "sin of the world." He suggested that the phrase used by John the Baptist in John 1:29, "Behold, the Lamb of God, who takes away the sin of the world," could be interpreted as referring to the sin of the world, not the sin of Adam. As Hofmann notes, he characterized original sin of each individual person as being situated within a spiritually hostile environment.[86] Inspired by Schoonenberg, Edward Yarnold, among others, defends this interpretation of the doctrine of original sin, arguing that "The sin of the

---

Madueme and Michael Reeves (Grand Rapid, Michigan: Baker Academic, 2014), 271–88. However, it seems to me that this argument should be confronted with Paul's statement in 1 Cor 15,22, where we read: "For just as in Adam all die, so too in Christ shall all be brought to life." It is evident that in this passage Paul does see Adam as a "universal particular."

[85] Karl Rahner, "Theological Reflections on Monogenism," 229–96.

[86] See Hofmann, "Catholicism and Evolution II," 93. He refers to Piet Schoonenberg, "Erbsünde und 'Sünde der Welt'" *Orientierung: Katholische Blätter für weltanschauliche Information* 6 (1962), 65–69. Schoonenberg speaks about our freedom as "situated," that is, affected by its "field of action" where the latter is shaped by (1) being deprived of good examples (which exercises pressure on us, making evil appealing), and (2) an obscuration of values and norms (in its radical version it precedes our existence and encompasses it). This may lead to a partial "death of the soul," with which we begin our existence. Consequently, "When the human race starts to organize its existence and to express it in culture – that is, at that important threshold of human history which is the start of the Neolithic era – the sins against fellow man and against God come to the fore. The great agricultural cultures especially show us war, plunder, exploitation of the vanquished, slavery, and oppression of the lower classes connected with their political and social organization. Their organized religion is paired with idolatry" (Schoonenberg, *Man and Sin*, 108, see also *ibid.*, entire Chapter 3 and Section 5 of Chapter 4, 98–123; 177–91). Schoonenberg's position had later on a great influence on Giovanni Blandino.

266   *Theological Anthropogenesis and Evolution*

world is a collective will in which I am a partner, a pressure on the individual in which I share and to which I contribute. The sin of the world is original sin."[87]

Kemp reminds us that the Council of Trent teaches that original sin is spread by propagation not imitation. This requires that a line be drawn between the two concepts. The traditional interpretation of the canon understands "propagation" to mean "biological descent" and "imitation" to mean "learned through social contact with other human beings." Some revisionists have proposed to redefine these terms, restricting the concept of imitation to voluntary acts and extending the concept of propagation to include habits or attitudes that are spread from one generation to the next by socialization.[88] Hence, Stephen Duffy writes:

> Being situated in and participating in the "sin of the world" is not in the first instance a conscious decision. It is "non imitatione." For sin works its shaping influence before one is capable of moral decision.[89]

Some theologians go as far as to question the importance or even the very notion of the *peccatum originale originans*. Alfred Vanneste says that "Original sin is the need of every man for redemption by Christ."[90] Approaching the same topic on another occasion, he states "It is our opinion that the *peccatum originale originans* has only a symbolical significance left."[91] Duffy says that "it is difficult to imagine a world created for development and the becoming of freedom where evil is not a structural component."[92] Being aware of the pressure this statement puts on Genesis 2–4,

---

[87] Edward Yarnold, *The Theology of Original Sin* (Notre Dame: Fides, 1971), 77. Similar is the notion of original sin as the universality of personal sin, offered by Henri Rondet: "From all eternity, God sees all men in his well-loved Son, leader of a mystical body whose head, purpose and reason for existence he is. But he also sees them to be sinners, as the result at once of a personal and a collective sin which constitutes the sin of Adam" (Henri Rondet, *Original Sin: The Patristic and Theological Background* [Staten Island, N.Y: Alba House, 1972], 263).

[88] Kemp, "Science, Theology, and Monogenesis," 228.

[89] Stephen J. Duffy, "Our Hearts of Darkness: Original Sin Revisited," *Theological Studies* 49, no. 4 (1988), 615–16.

[90] Alfred Vanneste, "Toward a Theology of Original Sin" *Theology Digest* 15(1967), 209. "First, our aim is to free the theology of original sin from the insurmountable difficulties of the traditional historical framework. How many hypotheses have tried to explain how a sin can be inherited! Nor should the explanation of original sin be tied to some other scientific or pseudo-scientific theory – monogenism, polygenism, even evolution. Original sin is concerned only with salvation history" (*ibid.*, 213).

[91] Alfred Vanneste, *The Dogma of Original Sin*, translated by Edward Callens (Louvain: Vander, 1975), 180.

[92] Duffy, "Our Hearts of Darkness," 619.

Monogenism versus Polygenism

Duffy replies "The garden is the dream, not memory."[93] Those who follow him add that the idea of the inheritance of guilt is implausible. To give an example, Zoltán Alszeghy and Maurice Flick, Jesuits at the Gregorian University in Rome, did not accept the necessity of the doctrine that the effects of Adam's sin always propagate through procreation. Instead, they considered the initial solidarity and unity of humanity to be such that all members would be affected by Adam acting as their "corporate personality," a concept they appropriated from H. Wheeler Robinson.[94]

In the same vein, already in 1920 (published only in 1969), Teilhard de Chardin proposed "an extensive metamorphosis of the notion of original sin," emphasizing its universal scope, yet untethered to one historical event.

[...] original sin, taken in its widest sense, is not a malady specific to the earth, nor is it bound up with human generation. It simply symbolizes the inevitable chance of evil (*Necesse est ut eveniant scandala*) which accompanies the existence of all participated being. Wherever being *in fieri* is produced, suffering and wrong immediately appear as its shadow: not only as a result of the tendency towards inaction and selfishness found in creatures, but also (which is more disturbing) as an inevitable concomitant of their effort to progress.

Original sin is the essential reaction of the finite to the creative act. Inevitably it insinuates itself into existence through the medium of all creation. It is the reverse side of all creation. By the very fact that he creates, God commits himself to a fight against evil and in consequence to, in one way or another, effecting a redemption.[95]

While teaching in Paris, de Chardin found the rejection of both monogenism and any idyllic prehistoric world without evil to be scientifically unavoidable.

As far as the mind can reach, looking backwards, we find the world dominated by physical evil, impregnated with moral evil (sin is manifestly 'in potency' close

---

[93] *Ibid.* This interpretation finds support in the approach of Enns, who emphasizes that the first chapters of Genesis offer a cosmic backdrop to the story of Israel as a nation (rather than teaching about human origins), and in the thought of Schwager, who builds an analogy between the biblical projection of Israel's covenantal sin to primordial origins and the Christian interpretation of the primordial history in light of Christ. See Enns, *The Evolution of Adam*, Part 1; Schwager, *Banished from Eden*, 105–11. Similar is the suggestion made by Rahner who says that Genesis 2–3 should be conceived as a "historical aetiology, that is, as statements which man made from the standpoint of his latter experience of the history of salvation and perdition in his relations with God" (Karl Rahner, *Hominisation: The Evolutionary Origin of Man as a Theological Problem* [New York: Herder and Herder, 1965], 37–38).

[94] Zoltán Alszeghy and Maurice Flick, "Il peccato originale in prospettiva evoluzionistica" *Gregorianum* 47 (1966), 223–24.

[95] Pierre Teilhard de Chardin, "Fall, Redemption, and Geocentrism." Translated by René Hague in *Christianity and Evolution*, 36–44 (New York: Harcourt, 1971), 40.

268 *Theological Anthropogenesis and Evolution*

to actuality as soon as the least spontaneity appears) – we find it in a state of original sin. The truth is that it is so impossible to include Adam and the earthly paradise (taken literally) in our scientific outlook, that I wonder whether a single person today can at the same time focus his mind on the geological world presented by science, and on the world commonly described by sacred history.[96]

Arguments in Favor of Polygenism II: Interpretation of *Humani generis*

While proponents of monogenism claim that Pius XII in *Humani generis*, no. 37 stands clearly in support of their view, the advocates of polygenism argue this is not necessarily the case. What is at stake is a proper interpretation of the text. First, the pope states that "For the faithful cannot embrace that opinion which maintains that either after Adam there existed on this earth true men who did not take their origin through natural generation from him as from the first parent of all, or that Adam represents a certain number of first parents." Some claim that while writing it, Pius XII was thinking in terms of the first ("racial") definition of poly- *versus* monogenism, that is, more in terms of the later distinction between poly- and monophyletism. I think that while the first scenario mentioned by the pope refers indeed to polyphyletism, the latter refers to monophyletic polygenism. Pius XII continues in the same point 37, sharing the reason for his reservation toward polygenism:

Now it is in no way apparent how such an opinion can be reconciled with that which the sources of revealed truth and the documents of the Teaching Authority of the Church propose with regard to original sin, which proceeds from a sin actually committed by an individual Adam and which, through generation, is passed on to all and is in everyone as his own (Rom 5:12–19, *Council of Trent* V, can. 1–4).

Does this formula close the conversation? Crucial here is the expression "Now it is in no way apparent how such an opinion can be reconciled with ..." ("cum nequaquam appareat quomodo huiusmodi sententia componi queat cum ..."). Some claim it is a final statement of the Magisterium in favor of monogenism. Others claim it leaves the issue for further discussion (it is not apparent today how to reconcile polygenism with Saint Paul's teaching on sin – but it may be possible tomorrow).

---

[96] Pierre Teilhard de Chardin, "Note on Some Possible Historical Representations of Original Sin." Translated by René Hague in *Christianity and Evolution*, 45–55 (New York: Harcourt, 1971), 47.

Monogenism versus Polygenism

Ernest Messenger stated that "the Pope has carefully given the reason why the polygenism in question is to be rejected: he says, not that 'it is altogether clear that such a theory cannot be reconciled with' the doctrine of original sin, but 'it is in no wise clear how such a doctrine can be reconciled with', etc."[97] Kemp's research in the archives of the Vatican shows that less than two weeks before the publication of the encyclical, the Secretariate responsible for the final stylistic editing of the document received two versions of the passage in question, (1) one approved by the theologians of the commission working on the encyclical and (2) the other proposed by one of the two informal consultants, Édouard Dhanis.[98] The commission's draft read: "One cannot hold the view that ... since it cannot be reconciled with the Catholic dogma according to which ..." ["Non enim teneri potest sententia iuxta quam, etc. ... cum huiusmodi opinio componi nequeat cum dogmate catholico, secundum quod, etc. ..."]. Dhanis had proposed a "less rigid" alternative: "... since it is not [non] apparent how such an opinion can be reconciled with that which the fonts of revealed truth and the acts of the Magisterium of the Church propose..." As notes Kemp in the end, the Pope replaced the wording suggesting the impossibility of reconciliation with what it would be best to call a mere *presumption* of inconsistency, though strengthening slightly the formulation proposed by Dhanis: "it is in no way [nequaquam] apparent, etc."[99]

Others point toward the motivation of the teaching of Trent that the Pope alludes to. Our point of reference is the beginning of the third canon on original sin saying that "in its origin [it] is one [origine unum], and by propagation, not by imitation, [it is] transfused [transfusum] into all."[100] The text was directed back then against a Catholic theologian Albert Pighi (1490–1542) who argued that hereditary sin is nothing else but Adam's own sin, which God attributes to his offspring ever since it was committed by Adam. According to Pighi, there was only one hereditary sin that is not internal and proper to every human being. A child is born with a guilt (reatus) for which he/she did not perform any act (actus).

The expression origine unum is therefore a concession to Pighi. This sin is one in origin only, but it multiplies in the descendants of Adam, which

---

[97] Ernest Messenger, *Theology and Evolution* (London: Sands & Co., 1951), 214.

[98] Dhanis was newly appointed to the faculty of the Gregorian University after having taught for a number of years at Louvain.

[99] See Kemp, "*Humani Generis* & Evolution," 23.

[100] Denzinger, *Enchiridion Symbolorum*, no. 790.

270 *Theological Anthropogenesis and Evolution*

Pighi denied. Commentators engaged in the mono- *versus* polygenism debate claim that these historical refinements are not without significance for a proper understanding of the intentions of the canon. It would be an anachronism to read the confirmation of theological monogenism in it. The Council of Trent does not take a position in a conversation concerning the possible communal character of the original sin, which was already discussed at the time. In other words, the point of emphasis at Trent was that all humans acquired the effects of original sin through *propagatione* from the initial perpetrators, traditionally referred to as Adam and Eve (hence, it had been concerned predominantly with existing humanity). This form of monogenism is assumed without argumentation. But this does not make polygenetic interpretation impossible or unacceptable in general.

Most importantly, Kemp documents (based on his research in Vatican archives) that the Holly Office showed interest in revisiting the question of polygenism in 1955. After gaining approval from Pius XII, Augustin Bea (a Jesuit who worked on the original text of the encyclical) prepared a draft of the document offering a fairly restrictive interpretation of *Humani generis* on polygenism:

A provision in this regard seems to be necessary since the assertion of the reformability of the decrees of the Council of Trent is becoming more and more common. As early as September 1950, some Catholic authors said that the words of the encyclical allow the possibility of interpreting it in the sense that the intent of the decrees of the Council are not yet entirely certain. That interpretation is finding more and more adherents. Fr. Rahner [then dogmatic theologian at the University of Innsbruck] is only one of the representatives of that opinion, and not the only one. Since he has discussed this idea theologically in a highly-respected review, there is a danger that this tendency will only become more emphasized from now on.

There is no doubt that the intent of the Holy Father was to assert that polygenism, as described in the encyclical, *cannot be reconciled* with Catholic doctrine on original sin.[101]

The controversy and debate among the members of the Holly Office raised by the draft and its proposed corrections most likely inspired the pope to say at the papal audience held on 4 July of 1955 that

there was no need for any clarification of the quoted passage from the encyclical, the formulation of which was deliberately cautious and it is good for it to remain as it is, without any further clarifications, except – of course – the absolute "irreformability" of the dogma of original sin in the descendants of Adam. The two

---

[101] I quote after Kemp: "Voto del Rev.mo P. Agostino Bea, SJ, Consultore" (HG Box-4, fol. 44–5).

Monogenism versus Polygenism 271

cardinals (Ciriaci and Ottaviani) rightly observed that "one needs to be very careful in the matter, as the words of the encyclical are."[102]

Difficulties of the Polygenetic Scenario

Those who are in favor of the polygenetic scenario of the origin of the human species face some serious theological difficulties, which become a general challenge for this view. Taking into account the mechanics of population genetics and excluding a scenario in which God arbitrarily decides to directly intervene to bring into existence a larger group of the first human beings in just one generation, we need to acknowledge that the formation of the entire group of human beings would have required at least several generations. We would then have a number of human beings that lived and died without sin. This would mean, in turn, that Christ's redemption does not refer to them.

A possible answer to this challenge might be suggested in reference to the reflection developed already by Giovanni Blandino (who was trained both in philosophy and theology, and in biology). Anticipating Alexander's threefold typology of the human species, and to some extent the position of Muller, he speculated about a longer time period that the first members of the primordial human species (i.e., already ensouled human beings, pre-Adamites) required for their mental capacity to develop. As an outcome of this process, he saw human capability of understanding revealed truth and moral command. He claimed that salvation in Christ would not refer to them. At the moment this took place, in Adam and Eve, they would have existed within a larger human population of co-Adamites. As notes Hofmann, "Although the Genesis text does not distinguish between the initial production of humans and a subsequent infusion of sanctifying grace, Blandino argued that the conflation of separate events for expository purposes is not uncommon in biblical literature."[103] However, although this explanation might sound plausible, it becomes apparent that

---

[102] I quote after ... "Ex Audientia Sanctissimi," 4 July 1955 (HG Box-4, fol. 70v). The passage quoted is from a summary approved by the Pope (fol. 72).

[103] Hofmann, Catholicism and Evolution II," 77. "Perhaps the human couple that was the first to receive sanctifying grace from God, as well as other preternatural gifts, and that committed the original sin and from which the entire human race descends, was not the first human couple to live on earth, but was engendered by pre-existing humans" (Giovanni Blandino, *Deux hypotheses sur l'origine de l'homme, Observations theologiquese et scientifiques* [Bologna: Assoguidi, 1962], 1). Note that, similar to Camille Muller, Blandino seems to suggest that the final step of hominization hinges on God's elevating human soul through the gift of sanctifying grace.

272   *Theological Anthropogenesis and Evolution*

in fact it takes us back to monogenism (theological monogenism within biological polygenism). Hence, the difficulty remains.

Another difficulty on this scenario is that the collective act of sin would take place in a community, which included small children. We would then have to specify their relation to *peccatum originale originans*. As notes Kemp:

> [A]nother problem that confronts theories of a collective original sin is the problem of the small children. A group of any significant size will contain children below the age of reason, who are not capable of committing any sin. What would be their relation to original sin? Original sin is in all human beings. These children could not have participated in the commission of the original sin.[104]

In answer to this puzzle, one might argue that presumably, on a polygenetic account, the small children would lose their state of grace when the Alpha-male did, since their grace was dependent on the Alpha's grace as the head of the community. However, one might question this solution claiming that the free gift of grace, given to a particular human being (including little children), does not depend on other human beings.

Finally, there remains the challenge concerning the way in which humans grew in number. It seems that it had to include bestiality (procreative activity with hominins) and incest or at least one of these. This difficulty refers to polygenetic and monogenetic scenarios alike. Austriaco claims that while the parent-sibling incest was a taboo most likely even among hominins, an incest among siblings might have been accepted at the early development of the human species. Moreover, taking into account biological, psychological, and cultural closeness of the first humans and hominins, we might reasonably ask whether we should classify sexual relationships among them as cases of bestiality.[105]

Contemporary Versions of the Polygenetic Scenario[106]

1. Germain Grisez – he claims that neither Pius XII nor Paul VI "proposed monogenism as the position to be held definitively." He affirms that free choice and the spiritual reality of persons either are present or not. Their emergence in the world had to be a sudden event. For the sake of argument, he speculates how polygenism might be reconciled with Catholic teaching on original sin:

---

[104] Kemp, "Science," 229.
[105] See Austriaco *Thomistic Evolution*, 175.
[106] This section is based on Flaman, "Evolution," 570–73.

Monogenism versus *Polygenism* 273

[T]heology must assume that the spiritual capacity for free choice was given initially by a special divine intervention, which completed hominization, to a group of individuals small and cohesive enough to function socially as a single body. In this way, solidarity in sin by the whole of humankind was possible at the beginning.[107]

God may then have hominized additional groups which "emerged into an already-given existential situation, and so shared prior to any personal act in the moral condition of humankind. In this sense, they shared 'by propagation not by imitation' ... even if not all humans were lineal descendants of a single couple." Therefore, "there is no obstacle to thinking the original human community had a single leader whose action was decisive for its action as such."[108] Grisez's view might be classified as punctiliar polygenism. The sin is committed by a community.

2. Denis Lamoureux, mentioned already in Chapter 6, distinguishes five views with regard to evolution and creation: young earth creation, progressive creation, evolutionary creation, deistic evolution and dysteleological evolution. He supports evolutionary creation. With regard to human evolution in particular, he speaks of two options: a punctiliar event, involving either monogenism or polygenism, and gradual polygenism. He supports the latter:

[T]he Image of God and human sinfulness were gradually and mysteriously manifested through many generations of evolving ancestors. The origin of spiritual characteristics that define and distinguish humanity is not marked by a single punctiliar event in history. Rather, these metaphysical realities arose slowly and in a way that cannot be fully comprehended. Their manifestation during human evolution is similar to that in embryological development. Consequently, there never was an Adam/s or Eve/s.[109]

Lamoureux believes the view of gradual polygenism "is free from the assumption that the first chapters of the Bible feature scientific and historical concordism. In contrast, evolutionary monogenism and punctiliar polygenism are concordist models, in varying degrees."[110]

---

[107] Germain Grisez, *The Way of the Lord Jesus, Volume One: Christian Moral Principles* (Chicago: Franciscan Herald Press, 1983), 342–43.

[108] *Ibid.*

[109] Denis O. Lamoureux, *Evolutionary Creation: A Christian Approach to Evolution* (Eugene, OR: Wipf & Stock, 2008), 290–91.

[110] *Ibid.*

274   *Theological Anthropogenesis and Evolution*

3. Earl Muller – he suggests that "the transformation of an animal species into fit dialogue partners with God – with the implications for full personhood this requires for individuals of that species – surely calls for more than material causality, and to many it makes no sense apart from a specific divine initiative."[111] He continues, "The question of original sin derives less from a reading of Chapter 3 of Genesis than it does from acceptance of the Pauline perspective (and of the New Testament in general) on the person and mission of Jesus Christ." Muller thinks that faith requires that,

> [T]here is a single human race. ... [T]he sin that disrupted human solidarity must have truly been sin. This in itself requires a spiritual dimension of human reality that simply transcends all other forms of life: monkeys ... do not sin. ... Furthermore, disrupted spiritual solidarity ... and the universality of that condition require a disruption "in the beginning" – that is (as the Council of TRENT insisted), transmitted by propagation rather than merely by imitation. ... But sin is a moral action, and this requires moral individuals.[112]

He then adds:

> Christians have tended to prefer monogenetic evolutionary accounts. In point of fact, all that is strictly required by Christian faith is the universal solidarity in sin that is traced back "to the beginning." ... There has been an implicit tendency to identify the human race (which is to say, rationally ensouled simians) with *Homo sapiens* and, accordingly, for many Christians to want to argue that *Homo sapiens* originated with a single couple. There is no necessary theological reason to do this. Rational ensoulment could have taken place prior to the achievement of the final physical form of the human race, or even after this had been achieved. Ensoulment would not, in principle, preclude ongoing interbreeding with non-"human" animal relatives until the present material solidarity of the human race had been achieved. In any event, the sketchiness of the material evidence precludes answering these sorts of questions with any precision.[113]

4. Alan Porter – he argues that biological gradualism is incompatible with "sudden ensoulment," better to say a saltational character of the final stage of hominization:

---

[111] Earl Muller, "Evolution," *New Catholic Encyclopedia, Supplement 2009, A-I* (Detroit: Gale in association with The Catholic University of America, Washington, DC, 2010), 321.

[112] *Ibid.*

[113] *Ibid.*, 322.

Monogenism versus Polygenism

The premise that evolution was gradual but ensoulment was discontinuous predicates the irrational conclusion that for one generation the parents were animals without souls and their children humans, made in the image of God, and with souls. Biological gradualism is incompatible with a sudden ensoulment dichotomy both in the evolutionary history of humans and for a maturing fetus, human or animal.

At some point ... there must have existed a strange family. The parents are hominid "animals" without souls, incapable of the knowledge of good and evil and of the experience of God after death and thus devoid of any of the theological interpretations of "imago Dei". John and Jenny their children by contrast, have been ensouled by an arbitrary gift of God and possess all the physical, cognitive, behavioural and spiritual attributes of a human. This implies a speciation event involving one generation only which is an evolutionary, anthropological and spiritual absurdity.[114]

Status Quaestionis

My analysis of the debate on mono- *versus* polygenism clearly shows that it is unresolved. It might be legitimate to think that the Church deliberately leaves it open for further research and conversation. In the document on the understanding of the theological notion of *imago dei* in the context of contemporary culture and science *Communion and Stewardship* – issued in 2004 by the International Theological Commission chaired by then Cardinal Joseph Ratzinger – we read what follows:

While the story of human origins is complex and subject to revision, physical anthropology and molecular biology combine to make a convincing case for the origin of the human species in Africa about 150,000 years ago in a humanoid population of common genetic lineage.[115]

Many interpret this claim as – at least indirectly – supportive of polygenism. But this interpretation is rather too hasty. Nothing precludes a different reading, according to which philosophically monogenetic transition from a hominin to a human being took place within biologically polygenic processes typical of larger populations. In fact, the document made only a passing and noncommittal reference to the distinction between monogenism and polygenism:

Catholic theology affirms that the emergence of the first members of the human species (whether as individuals or in populations) represents an event that is

---

[114] Alan N.W. Porter, "Do Animals Have Souls? An Evolutionary Perspective," *The Heythrop Journal* (2013), 533, 538.
[115] International Theological Commission, *Communion and Stewardship*, no. 63.

276   *Theological Anthropogenesis and Evolution*

not susceptible of a purely natural explanation and which can appropriately be attributed to divine intervention.[116]

While this pronouncement of the International Theological Commission appears to make space for future contributions to the debate concerning mono- *versus* polygenism, the lack of a more precise and univocal statement in this matter on the side of the Magisterium might become a considerable challenge for the contemporary theologians engaged in the dialogue between science and theology. Hence, Kevin MacMahon, in his entry on "Monogenism and Polygenism" states:

The present situation amounts to a quandary for theologians. On the one hand, even though it has not been formally addressed by the magisterium since *Humani generis*, monogenism continues to be accepted as a basic premise in Church teaching, as is shown by the relevant sections of the *The Catechism of the Catholic Church* (nn. 374–379, 390, 399–407). On the other hand, to deny the polygenistic origin of the human species places the theologian in clear opposition with science, and conjures up the image of an obscurantist faith combating the truth of reason.[117]

However, I believe that a more conciliatory and optimistic interpretation of the *status questionis* is possible as well. An attempt at formulating it was recently offered by Gaine, who – in the conclusion of his chapter on the Magisterial teaching of the Church on anthropogenesis in the light of the evolutionary worldview – states what follows:

I suggest that, while the ordinary magisterium has not given up monogenism, it has effectively tolerated polygenism since the late 1960s. In other words, like immediate formation of Adam's body to the exclusion of evolution, it is now a tolerated opinion. However, there is a significant difference between the magisterium's toleration of each of these. Each is tolerated for a quite different reason. Immediate formation, as with denial of the Immaculate Conception in the seventeenth century, though no longer regarded as theologically probable, is treated with a measure of respect in view of a venerable past when it was commonly held. Polygenism, however, has no such venerable past, but at least some form of it is tolerated for the sake of theological progress in the light of and out of respect for advances in scientific reason. ... In any case, theological progress may eventually mature either way, with a choice ultimately

---

[116] *Communion and Stewardship*, no. 70. This statement remains in agreement with the opinion of Ratzinger, dating back to 1964, when he stated that *Humani generis* was "carefully and cautiously worded" on the question of polygenism so that it "clearly opens the door in principle" (Ratzinger, *Schöpfungslehre* [1964], 190–91).

[117] McMahon, Kevin. 2003. "Monogenism and Polygenism." *New Catholic Encyclopedia*. www.encyclopedia.com/religion/encyclopedias-almanacs-transcripts-and-maps/monogenism-and-polygenism (retrieved 21 June 2021).

Conclusion 277

made in favour of monogenism or polygenism. So for the present the ordinary magisterium continues to teach monogenism, but at the same time tolerates at least certain forms of polygenism, in order, one way or another, to benefit the advance of our understanding of the Catholic faith and the teaching of the Church.[118]

CONCLUSION

The most important and lasting contribution of the Aristotelian–Thomistic philosophy and theology with regards to the understanding of human nature is undoubtedly its strong and persistent emphasis on its unity. The notion of the human soul as informing PM rather than secondary matter of the human body and the logical conclusion that can be drawn from this hylomorphic understanding of the human being, namely that there cannot be a human body without a human soul actualizing it, are probably the most significant theses of the Aristotelian–Thomistic anthropology. The value and explanatory power of the evolutionary model of human speciation built on these principles are apparent, especially in comparison with naturalistic, semi-naturalistic, and antinaturalistic scenarios discussed in this chapter.

The debate on mono- *versus* polygenism continues. As I have mentioned in the last point of my constructive proposal of the TVTE (presented in the central section of Chapter 5), I suggest contemporary followers of classical philosophy and theology should remain open-minded, searching for the ways in which the tradition they come from and follow may contribute to the ongoing research and speculative reasoning on this topic.

[118] Gaine, "The Teaching," forthcoming.

General Conclusion

"When it comes to the topic of evolution, nearly any point that can be disputed is disputed," claim Fowler and Kuebler, as it "touches so many fundamental questions, issues, attitudes, and subjects."[1] The points of contention refer not only to the reality and the mechanisms of evolutionary transitions but also to the multiple areas of research in natural and human sciences, where the notion of evolvability of things, processes, individuals, groups, and communities seem to matter. From astrophysics to physics and chemistry, from geology to paleontology, from biochemistry to physiology, from systematics to ecology, from anthropology to psychology and political science, from the study of culture to art and architecture, and from computer algorithms to artificial intelligence, in all these and many other divisions of human knowledge, we speak about gradual, and possibly directional, change over time. Applying the theory of evolution in these areas requires a careful confirmation and substantiation. In addition, as indicated in the Introduction, Darwin's original idea and its further developments are also subject to a continual critical verification, where experts do not hesitate to question claims and intuitions that were once considered as forming the core of evolutionary dogma. Awaiting the formulation of an updated evolutionary synthesis, we may be sure it will not be the ultimate one. This further complicates a conclusive evaluation of the evolutionary "research program."

Naturally, it was not my aim in this book to verify the validity of the theory of evolution nor to determine the adequacy of its extrapolation to other areas of scientific research. This remains the task for those who

[1] Fowler and Kuebler, *The Evolution Controversy*, 113, 360.

General Conclusion 279

engage in the scientific endeavor. Rather, aware of the particular status of the theory of evolution at the current stage of the development of the science of biology, I aimed in this book to show that, if true, evolution does not oppose or contradict the classical Aristotelian–Thomistic philosophical and theological view of reality.

At the same time, my approach was not only defensive. In the process of exploring various aspects of the encounter of classical thought with evolutionary theory, I argued that the initial act of creation should be restricted to the *creatio ex nihilo* of the most basic physical matter, which then entered into the incessant processes of multidimensional accidental and substantial transformations that give origin to new entities (elements, mixtures, chemical, and biochemical compounds, living systems, etc.).[2] I also offered a constructive proposal of the metaphysics of evolutionary transitions, of understanding the interplay of chance and teleological order in evolutionary changes, and of the concurrence of divine and contingent causes in speciation (including hominization). Finally, engaging in a critical evaluation of theistic evolutionism, I refuted the concept of "evolutionary creation" and argued that we should classify evolutionary changes and newly emerged species as an integral aspect of divine governance rather than divine creation. In doing all these, I believe I have managed to develop an up-to-date Thomistic version of theistic evolution. Grounding it in Aquinas's theology, I nonetheless pointed toward some necessary changes that need to be introduced in his theological reasoning for it to be relevant with respect to the evolutionary theory.

In doing so, I also wanted to show that, despite a certain dose of skepticism toward classical philosophy and theology, the longstanding legacy of the Aristotelian–Thomistic tradition remains vigorous and ready to enter a vivid and fruitful conversation with contemporary philosophy and science. Both Aristotle and Thomas present systems of thought that are not only coherent and consistent but also flexible and open to the new data and current ways of understanding the universe, its structures, and processes. Moreover, in the light of the research presented in this volume, Aristotelian metaphysics presents itself not as an aged doctrine that is limited to humble listening and adjusting of its principles to the new scientific theories, but, quite to the contrary, as a voice that has much to

---

[2] It is worth noting that this idea might serve as an inspiration for developing a separate research project (within the context of the Aristotelian–Thomistic philosophy and theology) on the plausibility of the hypothesis of the origin of life through a transition from inanimate matter that does not require direct divine intervention. See Mariusz Tabaczek, "Aristotelian-Thomistic Contribution to the Contemporary Studies on Biological Life and Its Origin," *Religions* 14, no. 2 (February 2023): 214, https://doi.org/10.3390/rel14020214.

280   *General Conclusion*

offer. In the debate on the concepts of species, natural selection, teleology, and the role of chance in evolutionary processes, the Aristotelian philosophical tradition brings an essential contribution to the results achieved by science – a contribution that has considerable explanatory power, which must not be neglected. A similar point can be made in reference to Aquinas's longstanding notion of creation and God's providential governance of the universe, as well as his understanding of divine action. The categories introduced in his theology prove to serve as remarkably precise and useful conceptual tools, helpful in delineating the contemporary framework of theistic evolutionism.

Naturally, all that was said in this book does not exhaust the subject.[3] Both the theory of evolution and its philosophical and theological interpretations are subject to an ongoing critical verification and actualization. These processes take place through the exchange of ideas among various members of academic circles and beyond them. It remains my hope that this book will inspire many such conversations.

---

[3] One of the important topics that were not addressed in this volume (due to the lack of space) goes to the question about theodicy, asked in the context of animal suffering in evolutionary processes. On this topic see: Michael Anthony Corey, *Evolution and the Problem of Natural Evil* (Lanham (Md.); New York; Oxford: University Press of America, 2000). B. Kyle Keltz, *Thomism and the Problem of Animal Suffering* (Eugene, OR: Wipf and Stock, 2020). Bethany N. Sollereder, God, *Evolution, and Animal Suffering: Theodicy without a Fall* (New York: Routledge, 2019). Christopher Southgate, *The Groaning of Creation: God, Evolution, and the Problem of Evil* (Louisville: Westminster John Knox Press, 2008).

Bibliography

Adler, Mortimer J. "Problems for Thomists: I. – The Problem of Species (Part One)." *The Thomist* 1, no. 1 (1939): 80–122.

"Problems for Thomists: I. – The Problem of Species (Part Two)." *The Thomist* 1, no. 2 (1939): 237–70.

"Problems for Thomists: I. – The Problem of Species (Part Three)." *The Thomist* 1, no. 3 (1939): 381–443.

"Problems for Thomists: I. – The Problem of Species (Part Four)." *The Thomist* 2, no. 1 (1940): 88–155.

"Problems for Thomists: I. – The Problem of Species (Part Five)." *The Thomist* 2, no. 2 (1940): 237–300.

Albert the Great. *Questions Concerning Aristotle's On Animals.* Translated by Irven M Resnick and Kenneth F Kitchell. Washington, DC: Catholic University of America Press, 2008.

Alexander, Andrew. "Human Origins and Genetics." *Clergy Review* 49, no. 6 (1964): 344–53.

Alexander, Denis. *Creation or Evolution: Do We Have to Choose?* Oxford: Monarch Books, 2008.

Allen, Colin, Marc Bekoff, and George Lauder, eds. *Nature's Purposes: Analyses of Function and Design in Biology.* Cambridge, MA: A Bradford Book, 1998.

Allen, Colin, and Jacob Neal. "Teleological Notions in Biology." In *Stanford Encyclopedia of Philosophy*, edited by Edward N. Zalta. Stanford University, 2020. https://plato.stanford.edu/archives/spr2020/entries/teleology-biology/. Retrieved 20 July 2022.

Allis, C. David, Marie-Laure Caparros, Thomas Jenuwein, and Danny Reinberg, eds. *Epigenetics, Second Edition.* Cold Spring Harbor, NY: Cold Spring Harbor Laboratory Press, 2015.

Alszeghy, Zoltan, and Maurizio Flick. "Il Peccato Originale in Prospettiva Personalistica." *Gregorianum* 46, no. 4 (1965): 705–32.

Ambrose. *Hexameron, Paradise, and Cain and Abel.* Translated by John J. Savage. Washington, DC: Catholic University of America Press, 1961.

282 Bibliography

Amundson, Ron. *The Changing Role of the Embryo in Evolutionary Thought: Roots of Evo-Devo*. Cambridge Studies in Philosophy and Biology. Cambridge: Cambridge University Press, 2005.

Aquinas, Thomas. *Aquinas on Creation: Writings on the "Sentences" of Peter Lombard Book 2, Distinction 1, Question 1*. Translated by William E. Carroll and Steven E. Baldner. Toronto: Pontifical Institute of Mediaeval Studies, 1997.

Aquinas: Selected Writings. Translated by Robert P. Goodwin. New York: Bobbs-Merrill, 1965.

Compendium theologiae seu brevis compilation theologiae ad fratrem Raynaldum. In *Opera omnia iussu Leonis XIII P. M. edita*, Vol. 42. Rome: Editori di San Tommaso, 1979, 83–191. [English translation: *Compendium of Theology*, tr. C. Vollert. St. Louis: B. Herder Book Co., 1947.]

De ente et essentia. In *Opera omnia iussu Leonis XIII P. M. edita*, Vol. 43. Rome: Editori di San Tommaso, 1976, 131–57. [English translation: *Aquinas on Being and Essence: A translation and Interpretation*, tr. Joseph Bobik. Notre Dame: University of Notre Dame Press, 1965.]

De mixtione elementorum ad magistrum Philippum de Castro Caeli. In *Opera omnia iussu Leonis XIII P. M. edita*, Vol. 43. Rome: Typographia polyglotta, 1976, 315–81. [English translation: *Aquinas on Matter and Form and the Elements: A Translation and Interpretation of the* De Principiis Naturae *and the* De Mixtione Elementorum *of St. Thomas Aquinas*, tr. Joseph Bobik. Notre Dame: University of Notre Dame Press, 1998.]

De principiis naturae. Vol. 43 of *Opera Omnia iussu Leonis XIII P. M. edita*. Rome. Typographia polyglotta, 1976, 39–47. [English translation: *The Principles of Nature*. In *Selected Writings of St. Thomas Aquinas*. Edited and translated by Robert P. Goodwin. New York: Bobbs-Merrill, 1965, 7–28.]

In Aristotelis librum De anima commentarium. Vol. 45/1 of *Opera Omnia*. Rome: Typographia polyglotta, 1984. [English translation: *Aristotle's De Anima in the Version of William of Moerbeke and the Commentary of St. Thomas Aquinas*. Translated by Kenelm Foster and Silvester Humphries. London: Routledge and Kegan Paul, 1951.]

In Librum Boethii de Trinitate, Quaestiones Quinta et Sexta, ed. Paul Wyser. Fribourg: Societe Philosophique and Louvain: Nauwelaerts, 1948. [English translation: *The Division and Methods of the Sciences. Quaestions V and VI of his Commentary on the* De Trinitate *of Boethius* translated with Introduction and Notes, Third Revised Edition by Armand Maurer. Toronto: The Pontifical Institute of Mediaeval Studies, 1963.]

In Metaphysicam Aristotelis commentaria. Turin and Rome: Marietti, 1926. [English translation: *Commentary on The Metaphysics of Aristotle*. 2 vols. Translated by John Rowan. Chicago: Regnery Press, 1961.]

In octo libros Physicorum Aristotelis expositio. Turin and Rome: Marietti, 1965. [English translation: *Commentary on Aristotle's Physics*. Translated by Richard J. Blackwell, Richard J. Spath, and W. Edmund Thirlkel. Notre Dame, IN: Dumb Ox Books, 1999.]

Quaestio disputata de anima. Edited by James H. Robb. Toronto: Pontifical Institute of Medieval Studies, 1968. [English translation: *Quaestions on the*

Bibliography

Soul. Translated by James H. Robb. Milwaukee, Wis.: Marquette University Press, 1984.]

Quaestiones disputatae de malo. Vol. 23 of *Opera Omnia.* Rome: Typographia polyglotta, 1982. [English translation: *On Evil.* Translated by John A. Oesterle and Jean T. Oesterle. South Bend, IN: University of Notre Dame Press, 1995.]

Quaestiones disputatae de potentia Dei. Turin and Rome: Marietti, 1965. [English translation: *On the Power of God.* Translated by English Dominican Fathers. Westminster, MD: Newman Press, 1952.]

Quaestiones disputatae de veritate. Vol. 22/1–3 of *Opera Omnia.* Rome: Typographia polyglotta, 1972–1976. [English translation: *Truth.* 3 vols. Translated by Robert W. Mulligan S.J. et al. Albany, New York: Preserving Christian Publications, 1993.]

Quaestiones disputatae de virtutibus. In *Quaestionis disputatae* vol. 2, 10th ed. Edited by E. Odetto. Turin: Marietti, 1965, 707–828. [English Translation: *Disputed Questions on Virtue:* Quaestio Disputata de Virtutibus in Communi *and* Quaestio Disputata de Virtutibus Cardinalibus. Translated by Ralph McInerny. South Bend, IN: St. Augustines Press, 2009.]

Quaestiones quodlibetales. Turin and Rome: Marietti, 1949.

Scriptum super Libros Sententiarum. Edited by S. E. Fretté and P. Maré. Vols. 7–11 of *Opera omnia.* Paris: Vivès, 1882–1889.

Summa contra gentiles. 3 vols. Turin and Rome: Marietti, 1961–1967. [English translation: *On the Truth of the Catholic Faith: Summa Contra Gentiles.* 4 vols. Translated by Anton C. Pegis et al. Garden City, New York: Image Books, 1955–1957.]

Summa theologiae. Rome: Editiones Paulinae, 1962. [English translation: *Summa Theologica.* 3 vols. Translated by the Fathers of the English Dominican Province. New York: Benzinger Bros., 1946.]

Super librum De causis expositio. Edited by H. D. Saffrey, Fribourg and Louven: Société Philosophique, 1954. [English translation: *Commentary on the Book of Causes.* Translated and annotated by Vincent A. Guagliardo, O.P., Charles R. Hess, O.P., and Richard C. Taylor. Washington, DC: Catholic University of America Press, 1996.]

Arintero, Juan. *La Evolución y la filosofía cristiana: Introducción general y Libro primero, La evolución y la mutabilidad de las especies orgánicas.* Madrid: Gregorio del Amo, 1898.

Aristotle. *De anima (On the Soul),* translated by J. A. Smith. In *The Basic Works of Aristotle,* edited by Richard McKeon, 533–603. New York: The Modern Library, 2001.

De generatione animalium (On the Generation of Animals), translated by Arthur Platt. In *The Basic Works of Aristotle,* edited by Richard McKeon, 665–80. New York: The Modern Library, 2001.

De generatione et corruptione (On Generation and Corruption), translated by Harold H. Joachim. In *The Basic Works of Aristotle,* edited by Richard McKeon, 465–531. New York: The Modern Library, 2001.

De partibus animalium (On the Parts of Animals), translated by William Ogle. In *The Basic Works of Aristotle,* edited by Richard McKeon, 641–61. New York: The Modern Library, 2001.

Bibliography

Historia animalium (*The History of Animals*), translated by D'Arcy Wentworth Thompson. In *The Complete Works of Aristotle: The Revised Oxford Translation*, vol. 1, edited by Jonathan Barnes, 774–993. Princeton: Princeton University Press, 1984.

Metaphysica (*The Metaphysics*), translated by W. D. Ross. In *The Basic Works of Aristotle*, edited by Richard McKeon, 681–926. New York: The Modern Library, 2001.

Meteorologica (*The Meteorology*), translated by W. Webster. In *The Complete Works of Aristotle: The Revised Oxford Translation*, vol. 1, edited by Jonathan Barnes, 555–625. Princeton: Princeton University Press, 1984.

Physica (*The Physics*), translated by R. K Gaye. In *The Basic Works of Aristotle*, edited by Richard McKeon, 213–394. New York: The Modern Library, 2001.

Artigas, Mariano. *The Mind of the Universe: Understanding Science and Religion.* Philadelphia: Templeton Foundation Press, 2000.

Artigas, Mariano, Thomas F. Glick, and Rafael A. Martínez. *Negotiating Darwin: The Vatican Confronts Evolution, 1877–1902.* Baltimore: Johns Hopkins University Press, 2006.

Artmann, Stefan. "Biological Information." In *A Companion to the Philosophy of Biology*, edited by Sahotra Sarkar and Anya Plutynski, 22–39. Chichester: Wiley-Blackwell, 2010.

Ashley, Benedict M. "Causality and Evolution." *The Thomist* 36, no. 2 (1972): 199–230.

Theologies of the Body: *Humanist and Christian*. St. Louis: Pope John Center, 1985.

Attfield, Robin. *Creation, Evolution and Meaning*. Aldershot, England; Burlington, VT: Ashgate, 2006.

Augustine. *The Literal Meaning of Genesis*. Vol. 1–2. Translated by John Hammond Taylor. New York: Newman Press, 1982.

Austin, Christopher J. "Aristotelian Essentialism: Essence in the Age of Evolution." *Synthese* 194, no. 7 (2017): 2539–56.

"Contemporary Hylomorphisms: On the Matter of Form." *Ancient Philosophy Today* 2, no. 2 (2020): 113–44.

Essence in the Age of Evolution: *A New Theory of Natural Kinds*. New York: Routledge, 2018.

Austriaco, Nicanor Pier Giorgio. "Defending Adam After Darwin: On the Origin of Sapiens as a Natural Kind." *American Catholic Philosophical Quarterly* 92, no. 2 (2018): 337–52.

"The Fittingness of Evolutionary Creation." In *Thomistic Evolution: A Catholic Approach to Understanding Evolution in the Light of Faith*, edited by Nicanor Pier Giorgio Austriaco, James Brent, Thomas Davenport, and John Baptist Ku. 182–91. Tacoma, WA: Cluny Media, 2016.

"The Historicity of Adam and Eve IV: A Theological Synthesis." In *Thomistic Evolution: A Catholic Approach to Understanding Evolution in the Light of Faith*, edited by Nicanor Pier Giorgio Austriaco, James Brent, Thomas Davenport, and John Baptist Ku. 171–75. Tacoma, WA: Cluny Media, 2016.

Bibliography

Austriaco, Nicanor Pier Giorgio, James Brent, Thomas Davenport, and John Baptist Ku. *Thomistic Evolution: A Catholic Approach to Understanding Evolution in the Light of Faith*. Tacoma, WA: Cluny Media, 2016.

Ayala, Francisco J. "Teleological Explanations." In *Philosophy of Biology*, edited by Michael Ruse, 187–95. New York: Macmillan Publishing Company, 1989.

———. "Teleological Explanations in Evolutionary Biology." In *Nature's Purposes: Analyses of Function and Design in Biology*, edited by Colin Allen, Marc Bekoff, and George Lauder, 29–49. Cambridge, MA: A Bradford Book, 1998.

Bacon, Francis. *The Dignity and Advancement of Learning*. London and New York: The Colonial Press, 1900.

Baglow, Christopher. "Evolution and the Human Soul." *Church Life Journal*. https://churchlifejournal.nd.edu/articles/evolution-and-the-human-soul/. Retrieved 16 April 2022.

Balme, David M. "Aristotle's Biology Was Not Essentialist." In *Philosophical Issues in Aristotle's Biology*, edited by Allan Gotthelf and James G. Lennox, 287–312. Cambridge: Cambridge University Press, 1987.

Balsas, Álvaro. *Divine Action and the Laws of Nature: An Approach Based on the Concept of Causality Consonant with Contemporary Science*. Braga: Axioma, 2018.

Barrett, Paul H., ed. *The Collected Papers of Charles Darwin: Two Volume Set*. 1st ed. Chicago, IL: The University of Chicago Press, 1977.

Basil the Great. *De hominis structura*. In *Patrologia Graeca*. Vol. 30. Paris: Migne, 1888.

Baedke, Jan, and Scott F. Gilbert. "Evolution and Development." In *The Stanford Encyclopedia of Philosophy*, edited by Edward N. Zalta, Fall 2021. Metaphysics Research Lab, Stanford University, 2021. https://plato.stanford.edu/archives/fall2021/entries/evolution-development/. Retrieved 20 July 2022.

Beatty, John. "Speaking of Species: Darwin's Strategy." In *The Darwinian Heritage*, edited by David Kohn, 265–82. Princeton: Princeton University Press, 1985.

Bedau, Mark. "Where's the Good in Teleology?" *Philosophy and Phenomenological Research* 52, no. 4 (1992): 781–806.

Beebee, Helen, and Nigel Sabbarton-Leary, eds. *The Semantics and Metaphysics of Natural Kinds*. New York: Routledge, 2010.

Benzinger. *Enchiridion Symbolorum, 43rd Ed.* Edited by Peter Hünermann. San Francisco: Ignatius Press, 2012.

Bergson, Henri. *Creative Evolution*. Translated by Arthur Mitchel. New York: Henry Holt and Company, 1911.

Berry, R. J., and T. A. Noble, eds. *Darwin, Creation and the Fall: Theological Challenges*. Nottingham: Intervarsity Press, 2009.

Bethell, Tom. "Darwin's Mistake." *Harper's* 252, no. 1509 (1976): 70–75.

Binswanger, Harry. *The Biological Basis of Teleological Concepts*. Los Angeles, CA: TOF Publications, Inc., 1990.

Blanchette, Oliva. *The Perfection of the Universe According to Aquinas: A Teleological Cosmology*. University Park, PA: Penn State University Press, 1992.

Blandino, Giovanni S. *Deux Hypotheses Sur L'Origine De L'Homme. Observations Theologiquese Et Scientifiques*. Bologna: Assoguidi, 1962.

Bostock, David. *Space, Time, Matter, and Form: Essays on Aristotle's "Physics"*. Oxford: Clarendon Press, 2006.

Boulter, Stephen J. "Can Evolutionary Biology Do Without Aristotelian Essentialism?" *Royal Institute of Philosophy Supplements* 70 and 71 (2012): 83–103.

"Evolution and the Principle of Proportionality." In *Neo-Aristotelian Metaphysics and the Theology of Nature*, edited by William M. R. Simpson, Robert C. Koons, and James Orr, 125–48. New York: Routledge, 2021.

Bouyssonie, Jean and Amédée Bouyssonie. "Polygénisme." *Dictionnaire de théologie catholique* 12, no. 2 (1935): col. 2536.

Bowler, Peter J. *Evolution: The History of an Idea, 25th Anniversary Edition, With a New Preface*. Berkeley, CA: University of California Press, 2009.

Bowler, Peter J., and John Henry. "Evolution." In *Science and Religion: A Historical Introduction*, edited by Gary B. Ferngren, 2nd ed., 204–19. Baltimore: Johns Hopkins University Press, 2017.

Boyd, Richard. "Homeostasis, Species, and Higher Taxa." In *Species: New Interdisciplinary Essays*, edited by Robert A. Wilson, 141–85. Cambridge, MA: A Bradford Book, 1999.

Braillard, Pierre-Alain, and Christophe Malaterre, eds. *Explanation in Biology: An Enquiry into the Diversity of Explanatory Patterns in the Life Sciences*. Dordrecht: Springer, 2015.

Brandon, Robert N. *Adaptation and Environment*. Princeton, NJ and Chichester: Princeton University Press, 1995.

"Biological Teleology: Questions and Explanations." *Studies in History and Philosophy of Science Part A* 12, no. 2 (June 1, 1981): 91–105.

Brandon, Robert N., and Grant Ramsey. "What's Wrong with the Emergentist Statistical Interpretation of Natural Selection and Random Drift." In *The Cambridge Companion to the Philosophy of Biology*, edited by David L. Hull and Michael Ruse, 66–84. Cambridge University Press, 2007.

Brower, Jeffrey E. *Aquinas's Ontology of the Material World: Change, Hylomorphism, and Material Objects*. New York: Oxford University Press, 2014.

Brown, Christopher. *Aquinas and the Ship of Theseus: Solving Puzzles about Material Objects*. London: Continuum, 2005.

Brown, David O. "St. George Jackson Mivart: Evo-Devo, Epigenetics and Thomism." *Theology and Science* 20, no. 4 (2022): 474–92.

Butler, Samuel. *Evolution: Old and New*. London: Boque, 1882.

Byl, Simon. "Le Jugement de Darwin Sur Aristote." *L'Antiquité Classique* 42, no. 2 (1973): 519–21.

Campbell, Joseph Keim, Michael O'Rourke, and Matthew H. Slater, eds. *Carving Nature at Its Joints: Natural Kinds in Metaphysics and Science*. Cambridge, MA: Bradford Books, 2011.

Campbell, Richard. *The Metaphysics of Emergence*. New York: Palgrave Macmillan, 2015.

Carl, Brian T. "Thomas Aquinas on the Proportionate Causes of Living Species." *Scientia et Fides* 8, no. 2 (2020): 223–48.

Bibliography

Carroll, William E. "At the Mercy of Chance? Evolution and the Catholic Tradition." *Revue Des Questions Scientifiques* 177, no. 2 (2006): 179–204.

Caruana, Louis, ed. *Darwin and Catholicism: The Past and Present Dynamics of a Cultural Encounter.* London and New York: T&T Clark, 2009.

Catholic Church. *Catechism of the Catholic Church,* 2nd edition. Vatican City: Libreria Editrice Vaticana, 2000.

Catholic News Agency. "Francis Inaugurates Bust of Benedict, Emphasizes Unity of Faith, Science," www.catholicnewsagency.com/news/francis-inaugurates-bust-of-benedict-emphasizes-stewardship-43494. Retrieved 9 January 2021.

Cavanaugh, William T., and James K. A. Smith, eds. *Evolution and the Fall.* Grand Rapids, MI: William. B. Eerdmans Publishing, 2017.

Centore, Floyd. F. "Darwin on Evolution: A Re-Estimation." *The Thomist* 33, no. 3 (1969): 456–96.

"Evolution after Darwin." *The Thomist* 33, no. 4 (1969): 718–36.

Chaberek, Michael. *Aquinas and Evolution.* Lexington: The Chartwell Press, 2017.

"Classical Metaphysics and Theistic Evolution: Why Are They Incompatible?" *Studia Gilsoniana* 8, no. 1 (2019): 47–81.

Knowledge and Evolution: How Theology, Philosophy, and Science Converge in the Question of Origins. Eugene, OR: Resource Publications, 2021.

"The Metaphysical Problem for Theistic Evolution: Accidental Change Does Not Generate Substantial Change." *Forum Philosophicum* 26, no. 1 (2021): 35–49.

"Where Do Substantial Forms Come From? – A Polemic with the Theistic Evolution of Mariusz Tabaczek." *Nova et Vetera* 21, no. 2 (2023): forthcoming.

Chardin, Pierre Teilhard de. "Fall, Redemption, and Geocentrism." In *Christianity and Evolution,* edited by Pierre Teilhard de Chardin, translated by René Hague, 36–44. New York: Harcourt, 1971.

"Note on Some Possible Historical Representations of Original Sin." In *Christianity and Evolution,* edited by Pierre Teilhard de Chardin, translated by René Hague, 45–55. New York: Harcourt, 1971.

The Phenomenon of Man. New York: Harper, 1959.

Charlton, William. "Did Aristotle Believe in Prime Matter?" In *Physics: Books I and II, by Aristotle, Translated with Introduction and Notes by W. Charlton,* 129–45. Oxford: Clarendon Press, 1983.

Chiu, Lynn. *Extended Evolutionary Synthesis: A Review of the Latest Scientific Research,* www.templeton.org/wp-content/uploads/2022/08/EES_Review_FINAL_.pdf. Retrieved 12 January 2023.

Clayton, Philip. *God and Contemporary Science.* Grand Rapids, MI: Eerdmans, 1997.

"Kenotic Trinitarian Panentheism." *Dialog* 44, no. 3 (2005): 250–55.

Coffey, Peter. *Ontology or the Theory of Being.* Gloucester, MA: Peter Smith, 1970.

Collins, Francis S. *The Language of God: A Scientist Presents Evidence for Belief.* New York: Free Press, 2006.

Bibliography

Corey, Michael Anthony. *Evolution and the Problem of Natural Evil*. Lanham (Md.) ; New York ; Oxford: University Press of America, 2000.

Corning, Peter A. "Beyond the Modern Synthesis: A Framework for a More Inclusive Biological Synthesis." *Progress in Biophysics and Molecular Biology* 153 (July 1, 2020): 5–12.

Craig, William Lane. *In Quest of the Historical Adam: A Biblical and Scientific Exploration*. Grand Rapids, MI: Eerdmans, 2021.

Craver, Carl F. "Functions and Mechanisms: A Perspectivalist View." In *Functions: Selection and Mechanisms*, edited by Philippe Huneman, 133–58. Dordrecht: Springer, 2013.

Cummins, Robert. "Functional Analysis." *Journal of Philosophy* 72, no. 20 (1975): 741–64.

Darwin, Charles. "Letter no. 2534." In *Correspondence Project*, www.darwinproject.ac.uk/letter/DCP-LETT-2534.xml. Retrieved 20 July 2021.

"Letter no. 7273." In *Correspondence Project*, www.darwinproject.ac.uk/letter/DCP-LETT-7273.xml. Retrieved 20 July 2021.

On the Origin of Species by Means of Natural Selection, or the Preservation of Favoured Races in the Struggle for Life. London: John Murray, 1859.

The Descent of Man, and Selection in Relation to Sex. In two volumes – Vol. 1. London: John Murray, 1871.

The Autobiography of Charles Darwin, 1809–1882. Edited by Nora Barlow. London: Collins, 1958.

Darwin, Charles, and Ernst Mayr. *On the Origin of Species: A Facsimile of the First Edition*. Facsimile ed. Cambridge, MA: Harvard University Press, 2001.

Darwin, Francis. *The Life and Letters of Charles Darwin. Vols. 1–3*. London: John Murray, 1887.

Davies, Paul. "Teleology without Teleology: Purpose through Emergent Complexity." In *In Whom We Live and Move and Have Our Being: Panentheistic Reflections on God's Presence in a Scientific World*, edited by Philip Clayton and Arthur Robert Peacocke, 95–108. Grand Rapids, MI / Cambridge, UK: William. B. Eerdmans Publishing, 2004.

Dawes, Gregory W., and Tiddy Smith. "The Naturalism of the Sciences." *Studies in History and Philosophy of Science Part A* 67 (2018): 22–31.

Dawkins, Richard. *River Out of Eden: A Darwinian View of Life*. New York: Basic Books/Harper Collins, 1995.

Deane-Drummond, Celia. "In Adam All Die?: Questions at the Boundary of Niche Construction, Community Evolution, and Original Sin." In *Evolution and the Fall*, edited by William T. Cavanaugh and James K. A. Smith, 23–47. Grand Rapids, MI: William B. Eerdmans Publishing, 2017.

De Filippi, Filippo. *L'uomo e Le Scimie: Lezione Pubblica Detta in Torino La Sera Dell'11 Gennaio 1864 Da Filippo De Filippi*. Milano: G. Daeli, 1864.

De Haan, Daniel. "*Nihil dat quod non habet*: Thomist Naturalism Contra Supernaturalism on the Origin of Species." In *A Catholic View on Evolution: New Perspectives in Thomistic Philosophy and Theology*, ed. by Nicanor Austriaco (Washington, DC: Catholic University of America Press, 2023).

Delbrück, Max. "Aristotle-Totle-Totle." In *Of Microbes and Life*, edited by Jacques Monod and Ernest Borek, 50–55. New York: Columbia University Press, 1971.

Bibliography

Depew, David J. "Aristotelian Teleology and Philosophy of Biology in the Darwinian Era." In *The Cambridge Companion to Aristotle's Biology*, edited by Sophia M. Connell, New ed., 261–79. Cambridge: Cambridge University Press, 2021.

"Consequence Etiology and Biological Teleology in Aristotle and Darwin." *Studies in History and Philosophy of Biological and Biomedical Sciences* 39, no. 4 (December 2008): 379–90.

Depew, David J., and Bruce H. Weber. "Challenging Darwinism: Expanding, Extending, Replacing." In *The Cambridge Encyclopedia of Darwin and Evolutionary Thought*, edited by Michael Ruse, 405–11. Cambridge; New York: Cambridge University Press, 2013.

"The Fate of Darwinism: Evolution After the Modern Synthesis." *Biological Theory* 6, no. 1 (December 1, 2011): 89–102.

de Queiroz, Kevin. "Different Species Problems and Their Resolution." *BioEssays* 27, no. 12 (December 2005): 1263–69.

"Species Concepts and Species Delimitation." *Systematic Biology* 56, no. 6 (2007): 879–86.

"Systematics and the Darwinian Revolution." *Philosophy of Science* 55, no. 2 (1988): 238–59.

"The General Lineage Concept of Species and the Defining Properties of the Species Category." In *Species: New Interdisciplinary Essays*, edited by Robert A. Wilson, 49–90. Cambridge, MA: MIT Press, 1999.

de Sinéty, Robert. "Les Preuves et Les Limites Du Transformisme." *Études* 127 (1911): 660–93.

"Transformisme." In *Dictionnaire Apologétique de La Foi Catholique*, edited by D'Alès. Paris: Gabriel Beauchesne, col. 1793–1848.

Deacon, Terrence W. *Incomplete Nature: How Mind Emerged from Matter*. New York: W. W. Norton, 2012.

Decaen, Christopher. "Elemental Virtual Presence in St. Thomas." *The Thomist* 64, no. 2 (2000): 271–300.

Deely, John N. "The Philosophical Dimensions of the Origin of Species. Part I." *The Thomist* 33, no. 1 (1969): 75–149.

"The Philosophical Dimensions of the Origin of Species. Part II." *The Thomist* 33, no. 2 (1969): 251–335.

DeKoninck, Charles. "Darwin's Dilemma." *The Thomist* 24, no. 2 (1961): 367–82.

Dembski, William A., and Jonathan Witt. *Intelligent Design Uncensored: An Easy-to-Understand Guide to the Controversy*. Downers Grove, IL: IVP Books, 2010.

Dembski, William A., and Michael Ruse, eds. *Debating Design: From Darwin to DNA*. Cambridge: Cambridge University Press, 2004.

Descartes, René. *The Philosophical Writings of Descartes: Volume 2*. Translated by John Cottingham, Robert Stoothoff, and Dugald Murdoch. Cambridge: Cambridge University Press, 1984.

Devitt, Michael. *Biological Essentialism*. Oxford: Oxford University Press, 2023.

"Defending Intrinsic Biological Essentialism." *Philosophy of Science* 88, no. 1 (2021): 67–82.

Bibliography

"Historical Biological Essentialism." *Studies in History and Philosophy of Biological and Biomedical Sciences* 71 (2018): 1–7.

"Individual Essentialism in Biology." *Biology & Philosophy* 33, no. 5 (2018): 1–22.

"Resurrecting Biological Essentialism." *Philosophy of Science* 75, no. 3 (2008): 344–82.

Dewan, Lawrence. "The Importance of Substance," https://maritain.nd.edu/jmc/ti/dewan.htm. Retrieved 19 August 2022.

DeYoung, Rebecca Konyndyk, Colleen McCluskey, and Christina Van Dyke. *Aquinas's Ethics: Metaphysical Foundations, Moral Theory, and Theological Context*. Notre Dame, IN: University of Notre Dame Press, 2009.

Dobzhansky, Theodosius. *Genetics of the Evolutionary Process*. New York: Columbia University Press, 1970.

The Biology of Ultimate Concern. Later Printing edition. New York: The New American Library, 1967.

Dodds, Michael J. "Science, Causality and Divine Action: Classical Principles for Contemporary Challenges." *CTNS Bulletin* 21, no. 1 (2001): 3–12.

The Philosophy of Nature. Oakland, CA: Western Dominican Province, 2010.

Unlocking Divine Action: Contemporary Science and Thomas Aquinas. Washington, DC: Catholic University of America Press, 2012.

Donceel, Joseph. "Causality and Evolution: A Survey of Some Neo-Scholastic Theories." *New Scholasticism* 39, no. 3 (1965): 295–315.

Dorlodot, Henry de. *Darwinism and Catholic Thought*. New York: Benziger, 1922.

Le Darwinisme Au Point de Vue de l'Orthodoxie Catholique. Brussels: Lovanium, 1921.

Dudley, John. *Aristotle's Concept of Chance: Accidents, Cause, Necessity, and Determinism*. Albany: State University of New York Press, 2012.

Duffy, Stephen J. "Our Hearts of Darkness: Original Sin Revisited." *Theological Studies* 49, no. 4 (1988): 597–622.

Dulles, Avrey Robert. "God and Evolution." *First Things* 176 (2007): 19–24.

Dumsday, Travis. "A New Argument for Intrinsic Biological Essentialism." *Philosophical Quarterly* 62, no. 248 (2012): 486–504.

"Is There Still Hope for a Scholastic Ontology of Biological Species?" *The Thomist* 76, no. 3 (2012): 371–95.

Dupré, John. *Humans and Other Animals*. Oxford: Clarendon, 2002.

"On the Impossibility of a Monistic Account of Species." In *Species: New Interdisciplinary Essays*, edited by Robert A. Wilson, 3–22. Cambridge, MA: A Bradford Book, 1999.

Processes of Life: Essays in the Philosophy of Biology. Oxford: Oxford University Press, 2012.

The Disorder of Things: Metaphysical Foundations of the Disunity of Science. Cambridge, MA: Harvard University Press, 1993.

Dubarle, Andre-Marie. *The Biblical Doctrine of Original Sin*. Translated by E. M. Stewart. London: Geoffrey Chapman, 1964.

Edwards, Denis. *How God Acts: Creation, Redemption, And Special Divine Action*. Minneapolis: Fortress Press, 2010.

The God of Evolution: A Trinitarian Theology. New York: Paulist Press, 1999.

Bibliography

Ehrman, Terrence. "Anthropogenesis and the Soul." *Scientia et Fides* 8, no. 2 (2020): 173–92.

Elder, Crawford L. "Biological Species Are Natural Kinds." *The Southern Journal of Philosophy* 46, no. 3 (2008): 339–62.

Elders, Leo J. "The Philosophical and Religious Background of Charles Darwin's Theory of Evolution." *Doctor Communis* 37 (1984): 32–67.

Eldredge, Niles, and Stephen Jay Gould. "Punctuated Equilibria: An Alternative to Phyletic Gradualism." In *Models in Paleobiology*, edited by T. J. M. Schopf, 82–115. San Francisco: Freeman, Cooper & Co., 1972.

Ellis, Brian D. *Scientific Essentialism*. Cambridge and New York: Cambridge University Press, 2001.

The Philosophy of Nature: A Guide to the New Essentialism. Montreal and Ithaca, NY: McGill-Queen's University Press, 2002.

Ereshefsky, Marc. "Darwin's Solution to the Species Problem." *Synthese* 175, no. 3 (2010): 405–25.

"Microbiology and the Species Problem." *Biology & Philosophy* 25, no. 4 (2010): 553–68.

Poverty of the Linnaean Hierarchy: A Philosophical Study of Biological Taxonomy. Cambridge New York: Cambridge University Press, 2001.

"Species." In *The Stanford Encyclopedia of Philosophy*, edited by Edward N. Zalta, Fall 2017. Metaphysics Research Lab, Stanford University, 2017. https://plato.stanford.edu/archives/fall2017/entries/species/. Retrieved 20 July 2022.

"Species and the Linnean Hierarchy." In *Species: New Interdisciplinary Essays*, edited by Robert A. Wilson, 285–305. Cambridge, MA: A Bradford Book, 1999.

"Species Pluralism and Anti-Realism." *Philosophy of Science* 65, no. 1 (1998): 103–20.

"Systematics and Taxonomy." In *A Companion to the Philosophy of Biology*, edited by Sahotra Sarkar and Anya Plutynski, 99–118. Chichester: Wiley-Blackwell, 2010.

Ereshefsky, Marc, and Mohan Matthen. "Taxonomy, Polymorphism, and History: An Introduction to Population Structure Theory." *Philosophy of Science* 72, no. 1 (2005): 1–21.

Facchini, Fiorenzo. "Man, Origin and Nature." In Interdisciplinary Encyclopedia of Religion and Science, 2002. http://inters.org/origin-nature-of-man. Retrieved 17 April 2020.

Fáinche, Ryan. "Aquinas and Darwin." In *Darwin and Catholicism: The Past and Present Dynamics of a Cultural Encounter*, edited by Louis Caruana, 43–59. London; New York: T&T Clark, 2009.

Feser, Edward. *Scholastic Metaphysics: A Contemporary Introduction*. Heusenstamm: Editiones Scholasticae, 2014.

Fitzpatrick, Joseph. *The Fall and the Ascent of Man: How Genesis Supports Darwin*. Lanham, MD: University Press of America, 2012.

Flaman, Paul J. P. "Evolution, the Origin of Human Persons, and Original Sin: Physical Continuity with an Ontological Leap." *The Heythrop Journal* 57, no. 3 (2016): 568–83.

Fowler, Thomas B., and Daniel Kuebler. *The Evolution Controversy: A Survey of Competing Theories*. Grand Rapids, MI: Baker Academic, 2007.

Francis, Pope. *Laudato Si': On Care for Our Common Home*. Huntington, IN: Our Sunday Visitor, 2015.

Franklin, Laura R. "Bacteria, Sex, and Systematics." *Philosophy of Science* 74, no. 1 (2007): 69–95.

Frost, Gloria. *Aquinas on Efficient Causation and Causal Powers*. New York: Cambridge University Press, 2022.

Gaine, Simon F. "The Teaching of the Catholic Church and the Evolution of Humanity." In *A Catholic View on Evolution: New Perspectives in Thomistic Philosophy and Theology*, edited by Nicanor Austriaco (Washington, DC: Catholic University of America Press, 2023).

Gage, Logan Paul. "Can a Thomist Be a Darwinist?" In *God and Evolution*, edited by Jay W. Richards, 187–202. Seattle: Discovery Institute Press, 2010.

Garrigou-Lagrange, Réginald. "Le Monogénisme n'est-Il Nullement Révélé, Pas Même Implicitement?" *Doctor Communis* 2 (1948): 191–202.

Ghiselin, Michael T. "A Radical Solution to the Species Problem." *Systematic Zoology* 23, no. 4 (1974): 536–44.

"Introduction." In Charles Darwin, *The Various Contrivances by Which Orchids Are Fertilized by Insects*, 2nd rev. ed. Chicago: University of Chicago Press, 1984.

"Species Concepts, Individuality, and Objectivity." *Biology and Philosophy* 2, no. 2 (1987): 127–43.

The Triumph of the Darwinian Method. Chicago: University of Chicago Press, 1969.

Giberson, Karl W., ed. *Abraham's Dice: Chance and Providence in the Monotheistic Traditions*. New York: Oxford University Press, 2016.

Gilbert, S. F., J. M. Opitz, and R. A. Raff. "Resynthesizing Evolutionary and Developmental Biology." *Developmental Biology* 173, no. 2 (1996): 357–72.

Gilson, Étienne. *From Aristotle to Darwin and Back Again: A Journey in Final Causality, Species, and Evolution*. Notre Dame, IN: Notre Dame Press, 1984.

The Christian Philosophy of St. Thomas Aquinas. Translated by L. K. Shook. New York: Random House, 1956.

Godfrey-Smith, Peter. "A Modern History Theory of Functions." In *Philosophy of Biology: An Anthology*, edited by Alex Rosenberg and Robert Arp, 175–88. Oxford: Blackwell, 2010.

Godfrey-Smith, Peter, and Kim Sterelny. "Biological Information." In *The Stanford Encyclopedia of Philosophy*, edited by Edward N. Zalta, Summer 2016. Metaphysics Research Lab, Stanford University, 2016. https://plato.stanford.edu/archives/sum2016/entries/information-biological/. Retrieved 20 July 2022.

"Information in Biology." In *The Cambridge Companion to the Philosophy of Biology*, edited by David L. Hull and Michael Ruse, 103–19. Cambridge; New York: Cambridge University Press, 2007.

González, Zeferino. *La Biblia y La Ciencia*. 2nd ed. Seville: Izquierdo, 1892.

Goodwin, Brian. *How the Leopard Changed Its Spots: The Evolution of Complexity*. New York: Charles Scribner's Sons, 1994.

Gorman, Michael. "Essentiality as Foundationality." In *Neo-Aristotelian Perspectives in Metaphysics*, edited by Daniel D. Novotný and Lukáš Novák, 119–37. New York: Routledge, 2014.

Bibliography

Gotthelf, Allan. "Aristotle's Conception of Final Causality." *Review of Metaphysics* 30, no. 2 (1976): 226–54.

"Darwin on Aristotle." *Journal of the History of Biology* 32, no. 1 (1999): 3–30.

Teleology, First Principles, and Scientific Method in Aristotle's Biology. Oxford: Oxford University Press, 2012.

Gotthelf, Allan, and James G. Lennox, eds. *Philosophical Issues in Aristotle's Biology.* Cambridge: Cambridge University Press, 1987.

Gould, Stephen Jay. *The Mismeasure of Man.* Revised and Expanded edition. New York: W. W. Norton & Company, 1996.

Gould, S. J., and R. C. Lewontin. "The Spandrels of San Marco and the Panglossian Paradigm: A Critique of the Adaptationist Programme." *Proceedings of the Royal Society of London. Series B. Biological Sciences* 205, no. 1161 (September 21, 1979): 581–98.

Graham, William. *The Creed of Science: Religious, Moral, and Social.* London: Kegan Paul, 1881.

Gray, Asa. "Scientific Worthies." *Nature* 10 (1874): 79–81.

Gregersen, Niels Henrik. "Deep Incarnation and Kenosis: In, With, Under, and As: A Response to Ted Peters." *Dialog* 52, no. 3 (2013): 251–62.

Grelot, Pierre. *Réflexions sur le Problème du Péché Originel.* Tournai: Casterman, 1968.

Grene, Marjorie, and David J. Depew. *The Philosophy of Biology: An Episodic History.* Cambridge and New York: Cambridge University Press, 2004.

Griesemer, James. "Origins of Life Studies." In *The Oxford Handbook of Philosophy of Biology*, edited by Michael Ruse, 263–90. Oxford, New York: Oxford University Press, 2008.

Griffiths, Paul E. "Squaring the Circle: Natural Kinds with Historical Essences." In *Species: New Interdisciplinary Essays*, edited by Robert A. Wilson, 209–28. Cambridge, MA: A Bradford Book, 1999.

"What Is Innateness?" *The Monist* 85, no. 1 (2001): 70–85.

Grisez, Germain Gabriel. *Christian Moral Principles: Way of the Lord Jesus: 1.* Chicago: Franciscan Herald Press, 1983.

Guthrie, William Keith Chambers. *A History of Greek Philosophy: Volume 6, Aristotle: An Encounter.* New York and Cambridge: Cambridge University Press, 1981.

Haeckel, Ernst. *The History of Creation.* Translated by E. Ray Lankester. London: H. S. King and Company, 1876.

Haller Jr., John S. *Outcasts from Evolution: Scientific Attitudes of Racial Inferiority, 1859 – 1900.* Carbondale: Southern Illinois University Press, 1971.

Haught, John F. *God After Darwin: A Theology of Evolution.* Boulder, CO: Westview Press, 2000.

Hayward, Alan. *Creation and Evolution: Rethinking the Evidence from Science and the Bible.* Ada, Ml: Bethany House Publishers, 1985.

Hefner, Philip J. *The Human Factor: Evolution, Culture, and Religion.* Minneapolis: Fortress Press, 1993.

Hempel, Carl G., and Paul Oppenheim. "Studies in the Logic of Explanation." *Philosophy of Science* 15, no. 2 (1948): 135–75.

Henry, John, and Mariusz Tabaczek. "Causation." In *Science and Religion: A Historical Introduction*, edited by Gary B. Ferngren, 377–94. Baltimore: Johns Hopkins University Press, 2017.

Hey, Jody. *Genes, Categories, and Species: The Evolutionary and Cognitive Cause of the Species Problem*. New York: Oxford University Press, 2001.

Hofmann, James R. "Catholicism and Evolution: Polygenism and Original Sin Part I." *Scientia et Fides* 8, no. 2 (2020): 95–138.

——— "Catholicism and Evolution: Polygenism and Original Sin Part II." *Scientia et Fides* 9, no. 1 (2021): 63–129.

——— "Erich Wasmann, S.J.: Natural Species and Catholic Polyphyletic Evolution during the Modernist Crisis." *Journal of Jesuit Studies* 7 (2020): 244–62.

——— "Some Thomistic Encounters with Evolution." *Theology and Science* 18, no. 2 (2020): 325–46.

——— "The Evolving Taxonomy of Progressive Creation." *Scientia et Fides* 11, no. 1 (2023): 199–214.

——— "Thomistic Hylomorphism and Theistic Evolution." *Scientia et Fides* 11, no. 2 (2023): forthcoming.

Howerth, I. W. "Natural Selection and the Survival of the Fittest." *The Scientific Monthly* 5, no. 3 (1917): 253–57.

Hull, David L. "A Matter of Individuality." *Philosophy of Science* 45, no. 3 (1978): 335–60.

——— "Genealogical Actors in Ecological Roles." *Biology and Philosophy* 2, no. 2 (April 1, 1987): 168–84.

——— "On the Plurality of Species: Questioning the Party Line." In *Species: New Interdisciplinary Essays*, edited by Robert A. Wilson, 23–48. Cambridge, MA: A Bradford Book, 1999.

——— "The Effect of Essentialism on Taxonomy – Two Thousand Years of Stasis (I-II)." *The British Journal for the Philosophy of Science* 15–16, no. 60–61 (1965): 314–26, 1–18.

——— "What Philosophy of Biology Is Not." *Synthese* 20, no. 2 (1969): 157–84.

Hunt, Tam. "Reconsidering the Logical Structure of the Theory of Natural Selection." *Communicative & Integrative Biology* 7, no. 6 (2014): e972848.

International Theological Commission. *Communion and Stewardship: Human Persons Created in the Image of God*. Vatican City: Libreria Editrice Vaticana, 2004.

Ingman, Max, Henrik Kaessmann, Svante Pääbo, and Ulf Gyllensten. "Mitochondrial Genome Variation and the Origin of Modern Humans." *Nature* 408, no. 6813 (December 2000): 708–13.

Irenaeus. "Against Heresies." In *Ante-Nicene Fathers. Vol 1: The Apostolic Fathers, Justin Martyr, Irenaeus*, edited by Alexander Roberts and James Donaldson, 834–1391. Grand Rapids, MI: Christian Classics Ethereal Library, 1885.

Irwin, Terence. *Aristotle's First Principles*. Oxford: Clarendon Press, 1988.

Jablonka, Eva, and Marion J. Lamb. *Evolution in Four Dimensions: Genetic, Epigenetic, Behavioral, and Symbolic Variation in the History of Life*. Cambridge, MA: MIT Press, 2014.

Bibliography

John Paul II. *Address to the Plenary Session on 'The Origins and Early Evolution of Life.'* Rome: Pontifical Academy of Sciences, 1996. www.pas.va/content/accademia/en/magisterium/johnpaulii/22october1996.html. Retrieved 14 June 2021.

Address to the Symposium 'Christian Faith and the Theory of Evolution.' Translated by Paolo Zanna. Rome, 1985, http://inters.org/John-Paul-II-Faith-Evolution-1985. Retrieved 15 May 2021.

"Consequences of Original Sin for All Humanity: Catechesis by Pope John Paul II on Jesus Christ." October 1, 1986, http://totus2us.com/teaching/jpii-catechesis-on-god-the-son-jesus/. Retrieved 12 July 2021.

Veritatis Splendor. Rome, 1993. www.vatican.va/content/john-paul-ii/en/encyclicals/documents/hf_jp-ii_enc_06081993_veritatis-splendor.html. Retrieved 15 July 2022.

Kaiser, Christopher B. "Early Christian Belief in Creation and the Beliefs Sustaining the Modern Scientific Endeavor." In *The Blackwell Companion to Science and Christianity*, edited by J. B. Stump and Alan G. Padgett, 3–13. Malden, MA: Wiley-Blackwell, 2012.

Kampourakis, Kostas, and Alessandro Minelli. "Understanding Evolution: Why Evo-Devo Matters." *BioScience* 64, no. 5 (May 1, 2014): 381–82.

Kant, Immanuel. *Critique of the Power of Judgment.* Edited by Paul Guyer. Translated by Eric Matthews and Paul Guyer. Cambridge: Cambridge University Press, 2002.

Kauffman, Stuart. *At Home in the Universe: The Search for the Laws of Self-Organization and Complexity.* New York: Oxford University Press, 1995.

Kellert, Stephen H., Helen E. Longino, and C. Kenneth Waters, eds. *Scientific Pluralism.* Minneapolis, MN: University of Minnesota Press, 2006.

Keltz, B. Kyle. *Thomism and the Problem of Animal Suffering.* Eugene, OR: Wipf and Stock, 2020.

Kemp, Kenneth W. "God, Evolution, and the Body of Adam." *Scientia et Fides* 8, no. 2 (2020): 139–72.

"Humani Generis & Evolution: A Report from the Archives." *Scintia ef Fides* 11, no. 1 (2023): 9–27.

"Science, Theology, and Monogenesis." *American Catholic Philosophical Quarterly* 85, no. 2 (2011): 217–36.

Kendal, Jeremy, Jamshid J. Tehrani, and John Odling-Smee. "Human Niche Construction in Interdisciplinary Focus." *Philosophical Transactions of the Royal Society B: Biological Sciences* 366, no. 1566 (2011): 785–92.

Kerr, Gaven. *Aquinas and the Metaphysics of Creation.* New York: Oxford University Press, 2019.

Kimura, Motoo. *The Neutral Theory of Molecular Evolution.* Cambridge: Cambridge University Press, 1983.

King, Hugh R. "Aristotle without Prima Materia." *Journal of the History of Ideas* 17, no. 1/4 (1956): 370–89.

Kitcher, Philip. *In Mendel's Mirror: Philosophical Reflections on Biology.* Oxford and New York: Oxford University Press, 2003.

"Species." *Philosophy of Science* 51, no. 2 (1984): 308–33.

Kitts, David B., and David J. Kitts. "Biological Species as Natural Kinds." *Philosophy of Science* 46, no. 4 (1979): 613–22.

Bibliography

Klubertanz, George P. "Causality and Evolution." *Modern Schoolman* 19, no. 1 (1941): 11–14.

Kohn, David. "Darwin's Keystone: The Principle of Divergence." In *The Cambridge Companion to the "Origin of Species"*, edited by Michael Ruse and Robert J. Richards, 87–108. Cambridge: Cambridge University Press, 2008.

Kopf, Simon Maria. *Reframing Providence: New Perspectives from Aquinas on the Divine Action Debate.* New York: Oxford University Press, 2023.

Kretzmann, Norman. *The Metaphysics of Creation: Aquinas's Natural Theology in Summa Contra Gentiles II.* Oxford: Clarendon Press, 1998.

Kripke, Saul A. *Naming and Necessity.* Cambridge, MA: Harvard University Press, 1980.

Lamoureux, Denis O. *Evolutionary Creation: A Christian Approach to Evolution.* Eugene, OR: Wipf and Stock, 2008.

——— "Evolutionary Creation: Moving Beyond the Evolution Versus Creation Debate." *Christian Higher Education* 9, no. 1 (2009): 28–48.

Lang, David P. "The Thomistic Doctrine of Prime Matter." *Laval Théologique et Philosophique* 54, no. 2 (1998): 367–85.

LaPorte, Joseph. *Natural Kinds and Conceptual Change.* Cambridge: Cambridge University Press, 2004.

Lawlor, Leonard, and Valentine Moulard Leonard. "Henri Bergson." In *The Stanford Encyclopedia of Philosophy*, edited by Edward N. Zalta, Summer 2016. Metaphysics Research Lab, Stanford University, 2016. https://plato.stanford.edu/archives/sum2016/entries/bergson/. Retrieved 17 April 2020.

Lennox, James G. *Aristotle's Philosophy of Biology: Studies in the Origins of Life Science.* Cambridge: Cambridge University Press, 2001.

——— "Darwin Was a Teleologist." *Biology and Philosophy* 8 (1993): 409–21.

Leo XIII. *Aeterni Patris: On the Restoration of Christian Philosophy.* Rome, 1879. www.vatican.va/content/leo-xiii/en/encyclicals/documents/hf_l-xiii_enc_04081879_aeterni-patris.html. Retrieved 12 June 2021.

Leroy, Marie-Dalmace. *L'évolution Restreinte Aux Espèces Organiques.* Paris: Delhomme et Briguet, 1891.

Levada, William Joseph, Gennaro Auletta, Marc Leclerc, and Rafael A. Martínez, eds. *Biological Evolution: Facts and Theories: A Critical Appraisal 150 Years after "The Origin of Species".* Analecta Gregoriana 312. Roma: Gregorian & Biblical Press, 2011.

Lickliter, Robert. "Developmental Evolution." *Wiley Interdisciplinary Reviews. Cognitive Science* 8, no. 1–2 (2017).

Livingstone, David N. *Adam's Ancestors: Race, Religion, and the Politics of Human Origins.* Baltimore: Johns Hopkins University Press, 2011.

——— *Dealing with Darwin: Place, Politics, and Rhetoric in Religious Engagements with Evolution.* Baltimore: Johns Hopkins University Press, 2014.

Lombardo, Nicholas E. "Evolutionary Genetics and Theological Narratives of Human Origins." *The Heythrop Journal* 59, no. 3 (2018): 523–33.

Luyten, N. "Evolutionisme En Wijsbegeerte." *Tijdschrift Voor Philosophie* 16, no. 1 (1954): 3–36.

Bibliography

"The Philosophical Implications of Evolution." *The New Scholasticism* 25 (1951): 290–312.

Macbeth, Norman. *Darwin Retried: An Appeal to Reason.* Boston: Gambit, 1971.

Mackie, John Leslie. "Evil and Omnipotence." *Mind* 64, no. 254 (1955): 200–12.

Madden, James D. *Mind, Matter, and Nature: A Thomistic Proposal for the Philosophy of Mind.* Washington, DC: Catholic University of America Press, 2013.

Madueme, Hans. "'The Most Vulnerable Part of the Whole Christian Account': Original Sin and Modern Science." In *Adam, the Fall, and Original Sin: Theological, Biblical, and Scientific Perspectives*, edited by Hans Madueme and Michael Reeves, 225–49. Grand Rapid, MI: Baker Academic, 2014.

Magnus, P. D. *Scientific Enquiry and Natural Kinds: From Planets to Mallards.* London: Palgrave Macmillan, 2012.

Mallet, James. "Mayr's View of Darwin: Was Darwin Wrong about Speciation?" *Biological Journal of the Linnean Society* 95, no. 1 (2008): 3–16.

Maritain, Jacques. "On the Philosophy of Nature (I): Toward a Thomist Idea of Evolution." In *Untrammeled Approaches*, 85–131. Notre Dame, IN: University of Notre Dame Press, 1997.

The Range of Reason. New York: Scribner, 1952.

Massie, Pascal. "The Irony of Chance: On Aristotle's Physics B, 4–6." *International Philosophical Quarterly* 43, no. 1 (2003): 15–28.

Matthen, Mohan. "Biological Universals and the Nature of Fear." *The Journal of Philosophy* 95, no. 3 (1998): 105–32.

Mayden, Richard L. "A Hierarchy of Species Concepts: The Denouement in the Saga of the Species Problem." In *Species: The Units of Biodiversity*, edited by M. F. Claridge, A. H. Dawah, and M. R. Wilson, 381–424. London and New York: Springer, 1997.

Mayr, Ernst. *Evolution and the Diversity of Life: Selected Essays.* Cambridge, MA: Harvard University Press, 1976.

Populations, Species, and Evolution, An Abridgment of Animal Species and Evolution. Abridged ed. Cambridge, MA: Harvard University Press, 1963.

"Teleological and Teleonomic: A New Analysis." In *Evolution and the Diversity of Life: Selected Essays*, 383–404. Cambridge, MA, and London: Harvard University Press, 1976.

The Growth of Biological Thought: Diversity, Evolution, and Inheritance. Cambridge, MA: Harvard University Press, 1982.

"The Multiple Meanings of Teleological." In *Toward a New Philosophy of Biology: Observations of an Evolutionist*, 38–66. Cambridge, MA: Harvard University Press, 1989.

This Is Biology: The Science of the Living World. Cambridge, MA: Harvard University Press, 1997.

Toward a New Philosophy of Biology: Observations of an Evolutionist. Cambridge, MA: Harvard University Press, 1989.

"Typological Versus Population Thinking." In *Evolution and Anthropology: A Centennial Appraisal*, edited by Betty J. Meggers, 409–12. Washington, DC: Anthropological Society of Washington, 1959.

What Evolution Is. London: Phoenix, 2002.

McIver, Tom. "Formless and Void: Gap Theory Creationism." *Creation/Evolution Journal* 8, no. 3 (1988): 1–24.

McMahon, Kevin. "Monogenism and Polygenism." In *New Catholic Encyclopedia*, 2003. www.encyclopedia.com/religion/encyclopedias-almanacs-transcripts-and-maps/monogenism-and-polygenism. Retrieved 21 June 2021.

McMullin, Ernan. "Introduction: Evolution and Creation." In *Evolution and Creation*, edited by Ernan McMullin, 1–56. Notre Dame, IN: University of Notre Dame Press, 1986.

Melsen, Andreas Gerardus Maria van. *The Philosophy of Nature*. 3rd ed. Pittsburgh: Duquesne University Press, 1961.

Messenger, Ernest C. *Evolution and Theology: The Problem of Man's Origin*. New York: Macmillan, 1932.

Theology and Evolution. London: Sands & Co., 1951.

Miller, Kenneth R. *Finding Darwin's God: A Scientist's Search for Common Ground Between God and Evolution*. New York: Cliff Street Books, 1999.

Millikan, Ruth Garrett. *Language, Thought, and Other Biological Categories: New Foundations for Realism*. Cambridge, MA: MIT Press, 1984.

On Clear and Confused Ideas: An Essay about Substance Concepts. Cambridge: Cambridge University Press, 2000.

Mishler, Brent D. "Getting Rid of Species?" In *Species: New Interdisciplinary Essays*, edited by Robert A. Wilson, 307–15. Cambridge, MA: A Bradford Book, 1999.

Mivart, St George Jackson. "Darwin's Brilliant Fallacy." *The Forum* 7 (1889): 99–105.

On the Genesis of Species. New York: D. Appleton & Company, 1871.

Molnar, George. *Powers: A Study in Metaphysics*. Edited by Stephen Mumford. New York: Oxford University Press, 2003.

Monod, Jacques. *Chance and Necessity: An Essay on the Natural Philosophy of Modern Biology*. Translated by Austryn Wainhouse. New York: Vintage Books, 1970.

Morales, José. *Creation Theology*. Dublin: Four Courts Press, 2001.

Morange, Michel. "Is There an Explanation for ... the Diversity of Explanations in Biological Studies?" In *Explanation in Biology: An Enquiry into the Diversity of Explanatory Patterns in the Life Sciences*, edited by Pierre-Alain Braillard and Christophe Malaterre, 31–46. Dordrecht: Springer, 2015.

Moreno, Alvaro, and Matteo Mossio. *Biological Autonomy: A Philosophical and Theoretical Enquiry*. Dordrecht: Springer, 2015.

Moreno, Antonio. "Finality and Intelligibility in Biological Evolution." *The Thomist* 54, no. 1 (1990): 1–31.

"Some Philosophical Considerations on Biological Evolution." *The Thomist* 37, no. 3 (1973): 417–54.

Moss, Lenny, and Daniel J. Nicholson. "On Nature and Normativity: Normativity, Teleology, and Mechanism in Biological Explanation." *Studies in History and Philosophy of Science Part C: Studies in History and Philosophy of Biological and Biomedical Sciences* 43, no. 1 (2012): 88–91.

Muller, Camille. "L'Encyclique 'Humani Generis' et Les Problèmes Scientifiques." *Synthèses; Revue Mensuelle International* 5, no. 57 (1951): 296–312.

Bibliography

Muller, Earl. "Evolution." In *New Catholic Encyclopedia, Supplement 2009, A-I*. Detroit: Gale in association with The Catholic University of America, 2010.

NABRE: New American Bible Revised Edition. Charlottesville, VA: Saint Benedict Press, 2011.

Nagel, Ernst. "Types of Causal Explanation in Science." In *Cause and Effect*, edited by Daniel Lerner, 11–32. New York: Free Press, 1965.

Neander, Karen. "Functions as Selected Effects: The Conceptual Analyst's Defense." *Philosophy of Science* 58, no. 2 (1991): 168–84.

Nicholson, Daniel J., and John Dupré. *Everything Flows: Towards a Processual Philosophy of Biology*. Oxford: Oxford University Press, 2018.

Nicolas, M. J. *Evolution et Christianisme. De Teilhard de Chardin à Saint Thomas d'Aquin*. Paris: Fayard, 1973.

Nogar, Raymond J. "From the Fact of Evolution to the Philosophy of Evolutionism." *The Thomist* 24, no. 2 (1961): 463–501.

The Wisdom of Evolution. New York: Doubleday, 1963.

Nosil, Patrik, Jeffrey L. Feder, and Zachariah Gompert. "How Many Genetic Changes Create New Species?" *Science* 371, no. 6531 (2021): 777–79.

Novo, Francisco J. "The Theory of Evolution in the Writings of Joseph Ratzinger." *Scientia et Fides* 8, no. 2 (2020): 323–49.

Numbers, Ronald L. *The Creationists: From Scientific Creationism to Intelligent Design, Expanded Edition*. Cambridge, MA: Harvard University Press, 2006.

Oakes, Edward T. "Dominican Darwinism: Evolution in Thomist Philosophy After Darwin." *The Thomist* 77, no. 3 (2013): 333–65.

Oderberg, David S. *Real Essentialism*. New York: Routledge, 2007.

O'Hara, Robert J. "Systematic Generalization, Historical Fate, and the Species Problem." *Systematic Biology* 42, no. 3 (1993): 231–46.

Okasha, Samir. "Darwinian Metaphysics: Species and the Question of Essentialism." *Synthese* 131, no. 2 (2002): 191–213.

O'Leary, Don. *Roman Catholicism and Modern Science: A History*. New York: Continuum, 2006.

Olson, Richard G. *Science and Religion, 1450–1900: From Copernicus to Darwin*. Westport, CT: Greenwood Press, 2004.

O'Malley, Maureen. *Philosophy of Microbiology*. Cambridge: Cambridge University Press, 2014.

O'Malley, Maureen, and John Dupré. "Size Doesn't Matter: Towards a More Inclusive Philosophy of Biology." *Biology and Philosophy* 22, no. 2 (2007): 155–91.

O'Rourke, Fran. "Aristotle and the Metaphysics of Evolution." *The Review of Metaphysics* 58, no. 1 (2004): 3–59.

Orr, H. Allen. "Is Single-Gene Speciation Possible?" *Evolution* 45, no. 3 (1991): 764–69.

Paley, William. *Natural Theology: Or, Evidences of the Existence and Attributes of the Deity, Collected from the Appearances of Nature*. London: R. Faulder, 1802.

Paro, Renato, Ueli Grossniklaus, Raffaella Santoro, and Anton Wutz. *Introduction to Epigenetics*. Berlin: Springer, 2021.

Bibliography

Pasnau. *Thomas Aquinas on Human Nature*. Cambridge and New York: Cambridge University Press, 2002.

Paul VI, Pope. "Original Sin and Modern Science: Address to Participants in A Symposium on Original Sin," *The Pope Speaks 11, no. 3* (1966): 229–35 (translated from the Italian *L'Osservatore Romano*, 11 July 1966, by Rev. Austin Vaughan).

Peacocke, Arthur. "Articulating God's Presence in and to the World Unveiled by the Sciences." In *In Whom We Live and Move and Have Our Being: Panentheistic Reflections on God's Presence in a Scientific World*, edited by Philip Clayton and Arthur Robert Peacocke, 137–54. Grand Rapids, MI / Cambridge, UK: William. B. Eerdmans Publishing, 2004.

"Biological Evolution – A Positive Theological Appraisal." In *Evolutionary and Molecular Biology: Scientific Perspectives on Divine Action*, edited by Robert J. Russell, William R. Stoeger, and Francisco José Ayala, 357–76. Berkeley, CA: Vatican Observatory & Center for Theology and the Natural Sciences, 1998.

Theology for a Scientific Age: Being and Becoming – Natural, Divine, and Human. Minneapolis: Fortress, 1993.

Pendergast, Richard. "Evil, Original Sin, and Evolution." *The Heythrop Journal* 50, no. 5 (2009): 833–45.

Pennisi, Elizabeth. "Evo-Devo Enthusiasts Get Down to Details." *Science* 298, no. 5595 (November 1, 2002): 953–55.

Pennock, Robert T. *Intelligent Design Creationism and Its Critics: Philosophical, Theological, and Scientific Perspectives*. Cambridge, MA: A Bradford Book, 2001.

Perlman, Mark. "The Modern Philosophical Resurrection of Teleology." In *Philosophy of Biology: An Anthology*, edited by Alex Rosenberg and Robert Arp, 149–63. Oxford: Blackwell, 2010.

Peters, Ted, and Martin Hewlett. *Evolution from Creation to New Creation: Conflict, Conversation, and Convergence*. Nashville: Abingdon Press, 2003.

Peterson, Daniel J. "The Kenosis of the Father: Affirming God's Action at the Higher Levels of Nature." *Theology and Science* 11, no. 4 (2013): 451–54.

Phillips, Richard Percival. *Modern Thomistic Philosophy: An Explanation for Students. Volume 1: The Philosophy of Nature*. Reprint of the second reprinted edition (1962). Heusenstamm: Editiones Scholasticae, 2013.

Pittendrigh, Colin S. "Adaptation, Natural Selection and Behavior." In *Behavior and Evolution*, edited by Anne Roe and George Gaylord Simpson, 390–419. New Haven, CT: Yale University Press, 1958.

Pius XII. *Humani Generis*. Rome, 1950. www.vatican.va/content/pius-xii/en/encyclicals/documents/hf_p-xii_enc_12081950_humani-generis.html. Retrieved 23 May 2021.

Plantinga, Alvin. *God, Freedom, and Evil*. Grand Rapids, MI: Eerdmans, 1977.

Polkinghorne, John C. "Kenotic Creation and Divine Action." In *The Work of Love: Creation as Kenosis*, edited by J. C. Polkinghorne, 90–106. Grand Rapids, MI / Cambridge, UK: Eerdmans, 2001.

Pontifical Academy of Sciences. "Statement by the Pontifical Academy of Sciences on Current Scientific Knowledge on Cosmic Evolution and Biological

Bibliography

Evolution." In *Scientific Insights into the Evolution of the Universe and of Life*, edited by Werner Arber, Nicola Cabibbo, and Marcelo Sanchez Sorondo, 583–86. Vatican City: Pontificia Academia Scientiarum, 2009.

Portalié, Eugène. *A Guide to the Thought of St. Augustine*. Chicago, IL: Regnery Publishing 1960.

Porter, Alan M. W. "Do Animals Have Souls? An Evolutionary Perspective." *The Heythrop Journal* 54, no. 4 (2013): 533–42.

Pruss, Alexander R. "God, Chance and Evolution. In Memory of Benjamin Arbour." In *Neo-Aristotelian Metaphysics and the Theology of Nature*, edited by William M. R. Simpson, Robert C. Koons, and James Orr, 364–82. New York: Routledge, 2022.

Pušić, Bruno, Pavel Gregorić, and Damjan Franjević. "What Do Biologists Make of the Species Problem?" *Acta Biotheoretica* 65, no. 3 (2017): 179–209.

Putnam, Hilary. "The Meaning of 'Meaning.'" In *Mind, Language, and Reality: Philosophical Papers, Vol. 2*, edited by Hilary Putnam, 215–71. Cambridge: Cambridge University Press, 1975.

Quine, Willard Van Orman. "Two Dogmas of Empiricism." In *From a Logical Point of View*, edited by Willard Van Orman Quine, 20–46. Cambridge, MA: Harvard University Press, 1953.

Rahner, Karl. "Evolution and Original Sin." *Concilium* 26, no. 6 (1967): 61–73.

Foundations of Christian Faith: An Introduction to the Idea of Christianity. New York: Crossroad, 1978.

"Theological Reflections on Monogenism." In *Theological Investigations. Vol. I*, translated by Cornelius Ernst, 229–96. Baltimore: Helicon, 1961.

Ramage, Matthew J. *From the Dust of the Earth: Benedict XVI, the Bible, and the Theory of Evolution*. Washington, DC: The Catholic University of America Press, 2022.

Ramsey, Ian T. *Models for Divine Activity*. Eugene, OR: Wipf and Stock, 2011.

Ratzinger, Joseph Cardinal. "Belief in Creation and the Theory of Evolution." In *Dogma and Preaching*, edited by Joseph Ratzinger, 131–42. San Francisco: Ignatius Press, 2011.

Eschatology: Death and Eternal Life. Washington, DC: The Catholic University of America Press, 1988.

Introduction to Christianity. San Francisco: Ignatius Press, 2004.

Schöpfungslehre [unpublished Freising lecture notes], 1958.

Schöpfungslehre [unpublished Freising lecture notes], 1964.

The Spirit of the Liturgy. San Francisco, CA: Ignatius Press, 2000.

Rescher, Nicholas. *Process Metaphysics: An Introduction to Process Philosophy*. Albany: State University of New York Press, 1996.

Revol, Fabien. "The Concept of Continuous Creation Part I: History and Contemporary Use." *Zygon* 55, no. 1 (2020): 229–50.

Richards, Richard A. "Species and Taxonomy." In *The Oxford Handbook of Philosophy of Biology*, edited by Michael Ruse, 161–88. Oxford, New York: Oxford University Press, 2008.

The Species Problem: A Philosophical Analysis. Cambridge: Cambridge University Press, 2010.

Rieppel, Olivier. "New Essentialism in Biology." *Philosophy of Science* 77, no. 5 (2010): 662–73.

Robert, Jason Scott. "Evo-Devo." In *The Oxford Handbook of Philosophy of Biology*, edited by Michael Ruse, 291–309. Oxford, New York: Oxford University Press, 2008.

Robinson, H. M. "Prime Matter in Aristotle." *Phronesis* 19, no. 2 (1974): 168–88.

Rondet, Henri. *Original Sin: The Patristic and Theological Background*. Staten Island, NY: Alba House, 1972.

Rosen, Robert. *Life Itself: A Comprehensive Inquiry into the Nature, Origin, and Fabrication of Life*. New York: Columbia University Press, 1991.

Rosenberg, Alexander. *Instrumental Biology, or The Disunity of Science*. Chicago: University of Chicago Press, 1994.

The Structure of Biological Science. Cambridge: Cambridge University Press, 1985.

Rosenberg, Alexander, and Frederic Bouchard. "Fitness." In *The Stanford Encyclopedia of Philosophy*, (Spring 2020 Edition), 2020. https://plato.stanford .edu/cgi-bin/encyclopedia/archinfo.cgi?entry=fitness&archive=spr2020. Retrieved 20 July 2022.

Rosenberg, Alex, and Daniel W. McShea. *Philosophy of Biology: A Contemporary Introduction*. New York, NY: Routledge, 2008.

Ross, Hugh. *A Matter of Days: Resolving a Creation Controversy*. Colorado Springs: NavPress, 2004.

Ruse, Michael. "Biological Species: Natural Kinds, Individuals, or What?" In *The Units of Evolution: Essays on the Nature of Species*, edited by Marc Ereshefsky, 343–62. Cambridge, MA: A Bradford Book, 1992.

Darwin and Design: Does Evolution Have a Purpose? Cambridge, MA: Harvard University Press, 2003.

Taking Darwin Seriously: A Naturalistic Approach to Philosophy. Amherst, NY: Prometheus Books, 1998.

The Philosophy of Human Evolution. Cambridge Introductions to Philosophy and Biology. Cambridge: Cambridge University Press, 2012.

Russell, Robert John. *Cosmology from Alpha to Omega: The Creative Mutual Interaction of Theology and Science*. Minneapolis: Fortress, 2008.

"Special Providence and Genetic Mutation: A New Defense of Theistic Evolution." In *Evolutionary and Molecular Biology: Scientific Perspectives on Divine Action*, edited by Robert J. Russell, William R. Stoeger, and Francisco José Ayala, 191–223. Berkeley, CA: Vatican Observatory & CTNS, 1998.

Russell, Robert J., Nancey C. Murphy, and C.J. Isham, eds. *Quantum Cosmology and the Laws of Nature: Scientific Perspectives on Divine Action*. Berkeley, CA: Vatican Observatory & CTNS, 1993.

Russell, Robert J., Nancey C. Murphy, Theo C. Meyering, and Michael A. Arbib, eds. *Neuroscience and the Person: Scientific Perspectives on Divine Action*. Berkeley, CA: Vatican Observatory & CTNS, 1999.

Russell, Robert J., Nancey C. Murphy, and Arthur Robert Peacocke, eds. *Chaos and Complexity: Scientific Perspectives on Divine Action*. Berkeley, CA: Vatican Observatory & CTNS, 2000.

Bibliography

Russell, Robert J., Nancey C. Murphy, and William R. Stoeger, eds. *Scientific Perspectives on Divine Action: Twenty Years of Challenge and Progress*. Berkeley, CA: Vatican Observatory & CTNS, 2008.

Russell, Robert J., Philip Clayton, Kirk Wegter-McNelly, and John Polkinghorne, eds. *Quantum Mechanics: Scientific Perspectives on Divine Action*. Berkeley, CA: Vatican Observatory & Center for Theology and the Natural Sciences, 2001.

Russell, Robert J., William R. Stoeger, and Francisco José Ayala, eds. *Evolutionary and Molecular Biology: Scientific Perspectives on Divine Action*. Berkeley, CA: Vatican Observatory & CTNS, 1998.

Sanz Sánchez, Santiago. "La Dottrina Della Creazione Nelle Lezioni Del Professor Joseph Ratzinger: Gli Appunti Di Freising (1958)." *Annales Theologici* 30, no. 1 (2016): 11–44.

Saunders, Nicholas. *Divine Action and Modern Science*. Cambridge and New York: Cambridge University Press, 2002.

Scheffczyk, Leo. *Schwerpunkte des Glaubens: Gesammelte Schriften zur Theologie*. Einsiedeln: Johannes-Verlag [Auslfg. Benziger], 1977.

Schmaus, Michael. *Dogma: God and Creation*. London: Sheed and Ward, 1969.

Schoonenberg, Piet. "Erbsünde und 'Sünde der Welt'." *Orientierung: Katholische Blätter für weltanschauliche Information* 6, no. 6 (1962): 65–69.

Man and Sin: A Theological View by Piet Schoonenberg. Translated by Joseph Donceel. Notre Dame, IN: University of Notre Dame Press, 1965.

Schönborn, Christoph Cardinal. *Chance or Purpose? Creation, Evolution and a Rational Faith*. San Francisco, CA: Ignatius Press, 2007.

Schreiner, Thomas R. "Original Sin and Original Death: Romans 5:12–19." In *Adam, the Fall, and Original Sin: Theological, Biblical, And Scientific Perspectives*, edited by Hans Madueme and Michael Reeves, 271–88. Grand Rapid, MI: Baker Academic, 2014.

Schroeder, Gerald. *Genesis and the Big Bang Theory: The Discovery of Harmony Between Modern Science and The Bible*. New York: Bantam Books, 1990.

Schrödinger, Erwin. *What Is Life? The Physical Aspect of the Living Cell*. Cambridge: Cambridge University Press, 1944.

Schwager, Raymund. *Banished from Eden: Original Sin and Evolutionary Theory in the Drama of Salvation*. Herefordshire: Gracewing Publishing, 2006.

Scott, Eugenie Carol. *Evolution Vs. Creationism: An Introduction*. Berkeley, CA: University of California Press, 2005.

"The Creation/Evolution Continuum." In *National Center for Science Education*, 2016. https://ncse.ngo/creationevolution-continuum. Retrieved 17 April 2020.

Second Vatican Council, *Gaudium et Spes* (Rome, 1965), www.vatican.va/archive/hist_councils/ii_vatican_council/documents/vat-ii_const_19651207_gaudium-et-spes_en.html. Retrieved 15 may 2021.

Seibt, Johanna, ed. *Process Theories: Crossdisciplinary Studies in Dynamic Categories*. Dordrecht/Boston/London: Kluwer Academic, 2003.

Silva, Ignacio. "A Cause Among Causes? God Acting in the Natural World." *European Journal for Philosophy of Religion* 7, no. 4 (2015): 99–114.

"Divine Action and Thomism: Why Thomas Aquinas's Thought Is Attractive Today." *Acta Philosophica* 25, no. 1 (2016): 65–84.

Providence and Science in a World of Contingency: Thomas Aquinas' Metaphysics of Divine Action. New York: Routledge, 2021.

"Revisiting Aquinas on Providence and Rising to the Challenge of Divine Action in Nature." *Journal of Religion* 94, no. 3 (2014): 277–91.

"Thomas Aquinas Holds Fast: Objections to Aquinas within Today's Debate on Divine Action." *Heythrop Journal* 48, no. 1 (2011): 1–10.

Simpson, George Gaylord. *Principles of Animal Taxonomy.* New York: Columbia University Press, 1961.

Skrzypek, Jeremy. "Three Concerns for Structural Hylomorphism." *Analytic Philosophy* 58, no. 4 (2017): 360–408.

Smit, Harry. "Darwin's Rehabilitation of Teleology Versus Williams' Replacement of Teleology by Natural Selection." *Biological Theory* 5, no. 4 (2010): 357–65.

Smith, John Maynard, and Eors Szathmary. *The Origins of Life: From the Birth of Life to the Origin of Language.* Oxford: Oxford University Press, 2000.

Snyder, Steven. "Evolution and the Origin of Species: Aristotelian Reflections." https://maritain.nd.edu/jmc/ti/snyder.htm. Retrieved 19 August 2022.

Sober, Elliott. "Evolution, Population Thinking and Essentialism." *Philosophy of Science* 47, no. 3 (1980): 350–83.

Philosophy of Biology. Boulder, CO: Westview Press, 1993.

"Sets, Species, and Evolution: Comments on Philip Kitcher's 'Species.'" *Philosophy of Science* 51, no. 2 (1984): 334–41.

Solinas, M. *From Aristotle's Teleology to Darwin's Genealogy: The Stamp of Inutility.* Translated by James Douglas. London: Palgrave Macmillan UK, 2015.

Sollereder, Bethany N. *God, Evolution, and Animal Suffering: Theodicy without a Fall.* New York: Routledge, 2019.

Solmsen, Friedrich. "Aristotle and Prime Matter: A Reply to Hugh R. King." *Journal of the History of Ideas* 19, no. 2 (1958): 243–52.

Southgate, Christopher, ed. *God, Humanity and the Cosmos – 3rd Edition: A Textbook in Science and Religion.* London and New York: T & T Clark, 2011.

The Groaning of Creation: God, Evolution, and the Problem of Evil. Louisville: Westminster John Knox Press, 2008.

Spinoza, Benedict. "Ethics." In *The Chief Works of Benedict de Spinoza. Vol. 2,* translated by Robert Harvey Monro Elwes, 43–271. New York: Dover Publications, 1951.

Stamos, David N. *The Species Problem, Biological Species, Ontology, and the Metaphysics of Biology.* Lanham: Lexington Books, 2004.

Sterelny, Kim. "Species as Ecological Mosaics." In *Species: New Interdisciplinary Essays,* edited by Robert A. Wilson, 119–38. Cambridge, MA: A Bradford Book, 1999.

Sterelny, Kim, and Paul E. Griffiths. *Sex and Death: An Introduction to Philosophy of Biology.* Chicago and London: University of Chicago Press, 1999.

Stipe, Claude E. "Scientific Creationism and Evangelical Christianity." *American Anthropologist* 87, no. 1 (1985): 148–50.

Bibliography

Stoeger, William R. "Contemporary Physics and the Ontological Status of the Laws of Nature." In *Quantum Mechanics: Scientific Perspectives on Divine Action*, edited by Robert J. Russell, Philip Clayton, Kirk Wegter-McNelly, and John Polkinghorne, 207–31. Berkeley, CA: Vatican Observatory & Center for Theology and the Natural Sciences, 2001.

Storck, Michael Hector. "Parts, Wholes, and Presence by Power: A Response to Gordon P. Barnes." *The Review of Metaphysics* 62, no. 1 (2008): 45–59.

Stump, Eleonore. *Aquinas.* New York: Routledge, 2003.

Suarez, Antoine. "'Transmission at Generation': Could Original Sin Have Happened at the Time When Homo Sapiens Already Had a Large Population Size?" *Scientia et Fides* 4, no. 1 (April 26, 2016): 253–94.

Suarez, Francisco. *Opera Omnia, Vol. 25.* Edited by Carolo Berton. Paris: Louis Vivès, 1861.

Swamidass, S. Joshua. *The Genealogical Adam and Eve: The Surprising Science of Universal Ancestry.* Downers Grove, IL: IVP, 2021.

"The Misunderstood Science of Genetic Bottlenecks." *Peaceful Science*, July 29, 2022. https://doi.org/10.54739/1w7j.

Tabaczek, Mariusz. "Afterword to the Polish Edition of *Thomistic Evolution: A Catholic Approach to Understanding Evolution in the Light of Faith* by Nicanor Pier Giorgio Austriaco, O.P., James Brent, O.P., Thomas Davenport, O.P., and John Baptist Ku, O.P." *Nova et Vetera* 21, no. 2 (2023): forthcoming.

"An Aristotelian Account of Evolution and the Contemporary Philosophy of Biology." In *The 1st Virtual International Conference on the Dialogue between Science and Theology. Dialogo Conf 2014: Cosmology, Life & Anthropology*, edited by Cosmin Tudor Ciocan and Anton Lieskovský, 57–69. Zilina: Publishing Institution of the University of Zilina, 2014.

"Aristotelian-Thomistic Contribution to the Contemporary Studies on Biological Life and Its Origin." *Religions* 14, no. 2 (February 2023): 214. https://doi.org/10.3390/rel14020214.

"Contemporary Version of the Monogenetic Model of Anthropogenesis: Some Critical Remarks from the Thomistic Perspective." *Religions* 14, no. 4 (2023): 523. https://doi.org/10.3390/rel14040528.

Divine Action and Emergence: An Alternative to Panentheism. Notre Dame: University of Notre Dame Press, 2021.

"Does God Create Through Evolution? A Thomistic Perspective." *Theology and Science* 20, no. 1 (January 2, 2022): 46–68.

Emergence: Towards A New Metaphysics and Philosophy of Science. Notre Dame, IN: University of Notre Dame Press, 2019.

"Essentialist and Hylomorphic Notion of Species and Species Transformation," in *A Catholic View on Evolution: New Perspectives in Thomistic Philosophy and Theology*, edited by Nicanor Austriaco (forthcoming). Washington D.C.: Catholic University of America Press, 2023.

"Evolution and Creation – A Response to Michael Chaberek's Polemic with Theistic Evolution." *Nova et Vetera* 21, no. 2 (2023): forthcoming.

"Hegel and Whitehead: In Search for Sources of Contemporary Versions of Panentheism in the Science–Theology Dialogue." *Theology and Science* 11 (2013): 143–61.

"The Metaphysics of Evolution: From Aquinas's Interpretation of Augustine's Concept of Rationes Seminales to the Contemporary Thomistic Account of Species Transformism." *Nova et Vetera* 18, no. 3 (2020).

"Thomistic Response to the Theory of Evolution: Aquinas on Natural Selection and the Perfection of the Universe." *Theology and Science* 13, no. 3 (2015): 325–44.

"What Do God and Creatures Really Do in an Evolutionary Change? Divine Concurrence and Transformism from the Thomistic Perspective." *American Catholic Philosophical Quarterly* 93, no. 3 (2019): 445–82.

Tanzella-Nitti, Giuseppe. "La questione antropologica in prospettiva teologica." In Centro di documentazione interdisciplinare di Scienza e fede, *Conversazioni su scienza e fede*, 192–95. Torino: Edizioni Lindau, 2012.

Tertullian. "On the Resurrection of the Flesh." In *Ante-Nicene Fathers. Vol. 3: Latin Christianity – Its Founder, Tertullian*, edited by Philip Schaff and Alan Menzies, 1202–316. Grand Rapids, MI: Christian Classics Ethereal Library, 1885.

Thomas, Owen C., ed. *God's Activity in the World: The Contemporary Problem*. Chico, CA: Scholars Press, 1983.

Thomson, Russell, Jonathan K. Pritchard, Peidong Shen, Peter J. Oefner, and Marcus W. Feldman. "Recent Common Ancestry of Human Y Chromosomes: Evidence from DNA Sequence Data." *Proceedings of the National Academy of Sciences of the United States of America* 97, no. 13 (2000): 7360–65.

Torrell, Jean-Pierre. *Saint Thomas Aquinas, Vol. 1. The Person and His Work*. Translated by Robert Royal. Washington, DC: The Catholic University of America Press, 1996.

Valen, Leigh Van. "Ecological Species, Multispecies, and Oaks." *Taxon* 25, no. 2/3 (1976): 233–39.

Vander Laan, David. "Creation and Conservation." In *The Stanford Encyclopedia of Philosophy*, edited by Edward N. Zalta, Winter 2017. Metaphysics Research Lab, Stanford University, 2017. https://plato.stanford.edu/archives/win2017/entries/creation-conservation/. Retrieved 20 July 2022.

Vanneste, Alfred. *The Dogma of Original Sin*. Translated by Edward Callens. Louvain: Vander, 1975.

"Toward a Theology of Original Sin." *Theology Digest* 15 (1967): 209–14.

Varela, Francisco J. *Principles of Biological Autonomy*. New York: North Holland, 1979.

Velde, Rudi A. *Aquinas on God: The "Divine Science" of the Summa Theologiae*. Aldershot: Ashgate, 2006.

Participation and Substantiality in Thomas Aquinas. Cologne: Brill, 1995.

Venema, Dennis R. "Genesis and the Genome: Genomics Evidence for Human-Ape Common Ancestry and Ancestral Hominid Population Sizes." *Perspectives on Science and Christian Faith* 62, no. 3 (2010): 166–78.

Venema, Dennis R., and Scot McKnight. *Adam and the Genome: Reading Scripture after Genetic Science*. Grand Rapids: Brazos Press, 2017.

Verschuuren, Gerard M. *Aquinas and Modern Science: A New Synthesis of Faith and Reason*. Kettering, OH: Angelico Press, 2016.

Waddington, C. H. *Evolution after Darwin*. Chicago: University of Chicago Press, 1960.

Bibliography

Walsh, Denis. "Evolutionary Essentialism." *The British Journal for the Philosophy of Science* 57, no. 2 (2006): 425–48.

Walsh, Denis. "Teleology." In *The Oxford Handbook of Philosophy of Biology*, edited by Michael Ruse, 113–37. Oxford and New York: Oxford University Press, 2008.

Wallace, Alfred Russel. *Contributions to the Theory of Natural Selection: A Series of Essays*. New York: Macmillan, 1870.

Wallace, Stan W. "In Defense of Biological Essentialism," *Philosophia Christi* 4, no. 1 (2002), 34–35.

Wallace, William A. *The Modeling of Nature: Philosophy of Science and Philosophy of Nature in Synthesis*. Washington, DC: Catholic University of America Press, 1996.

Warfield, Benjamin Breckinridge. *Evolution, Scripture, and Science: Selected Writings*. Edited by Mark A. Noll and David N. Livingstone. Grand Rapids: Baker Books, 2000.

Wasmann, Erich. *Modern Biology and the Theory of Evolution*. London: Kegan Paul, Trench, Trübner, & Company, 1910.

Webster, Gerry, and Brian Goodwin. *Form and Transformation: Generative and Relational Principles in Biology*. Cambridge: Cambridge University Press, 1996.

West-Eberhard, Mary Jane. *Developmental Plasticity and Evolution*. New York: Oxford University Press, 2003.

Whitehead, Alfred North. *Process and Reality*. New York: Free Press, 1979.

Wilcox, David L. "A Proposed Model for the Evolutionary Creation of Human Beings: From the Image of God to the Origin of Sin." *Perspectives on Science and Christian Faith* 68, no. 1 (2016): 22–43.

Wilkins, John S. *Species: A History of the Idea*. Berkeley: University of California Press, 2009.

Williams, George Ch. *Adaptation and Natural Selection*. Princeton, NJ: Princeton University Press, 2018.

Wilson, Robert A. "Realism, Essence, and Kind: Resuscitating Species Essentialism." In *Species: New Interdisciplinary Essays*, 187–207. Cambridge, MA: A Bradford Book, 1999.

Wimsatt, William C. "Teleology and the Logical Structure of Function Statements." *Studies in History and Philosophy of Science Part A* 3, no. 1 (1972): 1–80.

Wippel, John F. *The Metaphysical Thought of Thomas Aquinas: From Finite Being to Uncreated Being*. Washington, DC: Catholic University of America Press, 2000.

Wright, Larry. "Functions." *Philosophical Review* 82, no. 2 (1973): 139–68.

Teleological Explanations: An Etiological Analysis of Goals and Functions. Berkeley: University of California Press, 1976.

Wuellner, Bernard J. *Summary of Scholastic Principles*. Chicago: Loyola University Press, 1956.

Yarnold, Edward. *The Theology of Original Sin*. Notre Dame: Fides, 1971.

Zahm, John Augustine. *Evolution and Dogma*. Chicago, IL: McBride, 1896.

Zimmerman, Anthony Francis. *Evolution and the Sin in Eden: A New Christian Synthesis*. Lanham, MD; New York; Oxford: University Press of America, 1998.

Index

accidental change, 37n35–36, 85n90
accidental form (AF, accident), 23–25,
    25n14, 100
  inseparable (proper), 24–25
  separable (not proper, non-essential),
    24–25
accidental property, 24, 35, 79n70, 80–81,
    87, 153, 162, 172
actuality, 22n5, 41, 139, 144, 145, 268
  principle of, 22, 28, 81, 172
actuality and potentiality, 11, 25n13, 41,
    47n63, 80, 156, 199, 212n23
  actualization of primary matter, 29,
    41, 104, 141n34, 193, 194,
    212–214, 217
  actualizing principle, 30, 85, 154, 230.
    See also substantial form (SF)
adaptation, 10, 79, 108, 109, 116, 258
Alexander, Andrew, 253, 255–256, 260
Alexander, Denis, 183, 188
anthropogenesis
  antinaturalistic view of, 223, 236,
    241–243, 277
  biological (evolutionary), 17, 245–248,
    260n75
  dualistic view of, 232n18, 237–241, 259
  monogenetic. See monogenism
  naturalistic view of, 223, 236–237, 277
  polygenetic. See polygenism
  semi-naturalistic view of, 17, 223,
    236–243, 277
  theological, 17, 222–223. See also
    origin of the human species
  Thomistic view of, 231–236

Aquinas
  on emergence of new species, 157–160
    in general, 161–163
    through transformism, 164–165
  on the importance of esse, 139–141
  and natural selection, 105–107
  on primary matter (PM), 20
  on teleology and chance, 99–104
  on the work of the six days, 148
Aristotle
  and natural selection, 105–107
  on primary matter (PM), 19–20
  on species, 79–81, 85
    compatibility with evolution, 83–88
  on substantial form (SF), 22–26
  on teleology and chance, 99–104
Ashley, Benedict, 49–50, 186, 200,
    256n70
Augustine
  on creation, 128–134
  on Hexameron, 134
  on rationes seminales, 134
  his theology of creation as evolutionary,
    135–137
Austin, Christopher, 73, 74n56, 75n57,
    77, 78n67
Austriaco, Nicanor Pier Giorgio, 1n1, 186,
    188, 199, 258, 272
Ayala, Francisco, J., 3, 10, 111–114,
    118

baramins (biblical kinds), 173
Bergson, Henri, 187–188
bottleneck effect, 247, 248, 257

308

Index

Boulter, Stephen, 43–47, 51n73, 52–54, 59n3, 78
Brower, Jeffrey, 20, 24n11, 25n13, 28n19

Carroll, William, E., 1n1, 13n26, 37n34, 143n40, 165n9, 169n14
causation
  immanent order of, 178, 201, 203, 212, 214–219, 221
  transcendent order of, 188, 201, 203, 212, 214–218, 221
cause
  accidental, 103n30
  causal matrix, 48, 55, 88, 198, 217–220
  efficient. *See* efficient cause
  final. *See* final cause; teleology; goal-directedness
  formal. *See* formal cause
  hierarchy of causes, 54–55
  immanent (intrinsic) *versus* transeunt (extrinsic), 96
  material. *See* matter
  per accidens (accidental, incidental), 80, 100–102, 104, 105, 124, 144, 146
  per se, 100, 101, 102n27, 103, 104n33, 105, 107, 124, 146, 220
  supernatural, 42, 51, 123, 167, 238
  total, 43, 48
central dogma of molecular biology, 120n71
Chaberek, Michael, 16, 37n35, 45n57, 157, 169–176
chance, 105, 106, 118n66, 126, 131, 144, 146–147, 181, 182n5, 206, 216, 219–220
  epistemological *versus* ontological, 99, 104, 124
  God as the source of, 146
  and order (teleology), 9, 106, 123–125, 168, 183n12, 279
  Aquinas on, 104–105
  Aristotle on, 99–104
  Darwin on, 92, 123–124
change
  accidental, 22, 23, 28, 30, 33n26, 34–35, 37, 49, 95, 124, 155, 178, 191, 193, 196, 230, 279
  epigenetic, 4, 6, 34, 36, 49, 216
  genetic, 5, 122, 256n69
  substantial, 23, 33n26, 34, 155, 179, 191, 193, 196, 279
Clayton, Philip, 183, 184
Collins, Francis, 166, 167

Communion and Stewardship, 125n82, 208n13, 224n3, 225n5, 275
conservatio a nihilo, 143, 191, 194
conservatio rerum, 16, 140, 142, 143n39, 168, 180, 199
continual creation, 142, 180n1, 199
creatio continua, 140n33, 142, 180, 181n3, 182–184, 191, 199, 214
creatio ex creatione, 184
creatio versus productio (formatio), 189–191
creation
  Aquinas on, 141–154
  Augustine on, 128–134
  as dependence of creatures on God, 144–147
  emanationist view of, 140n34, 142
  and evolution, 187, 188, 198–200, 235
  ex nihilo (out of nothing), 13, 16, 42n47, 127, 134, 136, 140n33, 142, 143n38, 144n40, 147, 148, 154, 156, 164, 168, 178, 180, 183, 187, 189–194, 196, 197, 199, 229–235, 237, 240, 279
  progressive, 129n4, 170, 175, 191, 273
  through evolution. *See* evolutionary creation
  versus eduction, 194–198
  versus governance, 191–194
  versus transformism, 189–191
creationism, 129n4, 166n11, 175
creative evolution, 178, 187–188, 200. *See also* evolutionary creation
creatures as co-creators (with God), 16, 178, 179, 183–184, 186n25, 189, 198, 199
crossbreeding, 156, 157, 163
Cummins, Robert, 115

Darwin, Charles
  and Aristotelian essentialism, 85n90
  on chance, 123–124
  The Descent of Man, and Selection in Relation to Sex, 247n50
  on independent and direct creation of each species, 137n28
  on inheritance, 2n2
  as nominalist about species, 58–60
  On the Origin of Species by Means of Natural Selection, 12, 58n2, 59n4, 109n44, 121n73, 124n79, 136n27, 247n50

Index

Darwin, Charles (cont.)
  on secondary causation in evolution, 58n2
  on species, 58–60, 60n6, 72
  on teleology, 92–93, 107–111
  theory of evolution, 58
Davies, Paul, 184
Dawkins, Richard, 3, 94
de Queiroz, Kevin, 66, 71, 72
Deane-Drummond, Celia, 6
deism, 167, 205n3, 215, 218, 220, 260
Depew, David J., 8n17, 106n36, 110n47, 116n62
Descartes, René, 43, 93
determinism (necessity), 93n4, 103, 106, 204
  suppositional, 103, 106
development, 2n2, 8n18, 73, 77, 78n67, 117, 132n12, 134, 194, 195, 204, 236, 237, 239, 273
developmental biology, 4–5, 7n16, 10, 49, 78–79, 122, 123n76, 204
developmental program, 75n58, 81, 82, 91, 172
Devitt, Michael, 68, 74n54, 75, 76n59, 76n60, 86n34
disposition of (primary) matter, 14, 28–31, 33–37, 42, 54n76, 55, 85n90, 154, 168, 211, 231, 232n18, 233, 240, 243, 259, 260
  remote and proximate, 29
dispositions (dispositionalism), 9, 11, 27, 38, 41, 43, 47, 51, 57, 72, 77, 78, 81, 87, 91, 104, 134, 208, 213, 231, 234, 236, 259
divine action, 1, 13, 123, 131n10, 147n45, 164n8, 186n24, 191n38, 202–207, 234, 240, 260, 280
  anthropo-theological compatibilism versus anthropo-theological incompatibilism, 203
  concurrent (concurrence of), 17, 200, 212–218, 220, 223, 231, 233, 279
  direct, 167, 188, 193, 201, 219, 232
  efficient – four aspects of, 209–210
  in evolutionary transitions.
    See evolutionary transition
  kinds of, 204
  primary versus secondary, 17, 54, 145, 155, 167, 178, 179, 192, 200, 202–218, 261
  principal versus instrumental, 17, 35, 54, 141, 145, 147, 155, 167, 178, 179, 192, 200, 202–218, 261

  secondary in theistic evolution
    outside of Thomistic circles, 204–207
    within Thomistic circles, 207–211
  univocal predication of, 167, 203, 206, 207
divine and natural causes (concurrence of)
  in an evolutionary transition, 216–218
divine and natural causes (concurrence of)
  in begetting offspring, 212–216
divine governance (government), 13, 16, 177–179, 185, 191–194, 198, 200, 229, 279, 280
divine providence, 13, 54, 125n82, 141, 146, 150n55, 186, 193, 211, 220, 238n27
divine self-limitation (kenosis), 184n18, 199, 206, 206n5, 208
Dobzhansky, Theodosius, 2, 10, 112, 192n38, 247
Dodds, Michael, 13n26, 23n8, 169n14, 202n1
Donceel, Joseph, 1n1, 169n14, 186, 200
dualism, 25
dualistic view of the human being, 224–227, 228n10, 235, 243, 255
Dudley, John, 99n21, 101n23, 103n30, 107n38
Duffy, Stephen, 266
Dumsday, Travis, 73n51, 79, 86, 91
Dupré, John, 9n20, 48n66, 67, 68n33, 70, 72n47, 77n62

efficient causation
  God as the source of, 145
efficient cause
  passive obediential capacity of, 51
Eldredge, Niles, 3
electromagnetic field, 21
Ellis, Brian D., 11n24, 73n52
entelechy (entelecheia), 45, 46, 106
epigenetics (epigenesis), 4, 6n11, 7n16, 8n17, 35, 49, 123
Ereshefsky, Marc, 60n6, 61n10, 64n17, 65n20, 66n24, 67, 68n33, 71n41, 72n48, 82n78, 88, 91
esse, 42n46, 44, 127, 128, 139n31, 155, 164, 191, 193, 197, 203, 213, 215, 216
  Aquinas on the importance of esse, 139–141
  creation as dependence on God in esse, 15, 143

Index

creatures as causes of, 213–214, 216–217
divine and creaturely causation in the
origin of, 196–198
God as *ipsum esse subsistens*, 139
essentia
creation as dependence on God in
essentia, 15, 128, 144–147,
191, 193
creatures as secondary causes of,
212–218
essentialism, 9–11, 14, 57, 59n3, 69n36,
71–79, 83, 84n82, 85–88, 91, 173
antiessentialism, 57, 71–72, 91
evo-devo, 4–5, 8n17, 10, 49, 77, 78,
122. *See also* development,
developmental biology
evolution
adaptive (progressive), 4n6, 60, 78,
112, 117, 126
and development. *See* evo-devo
historical account of the debate on,
12n25
neutral theory of, 4
theistic. *See* theistic evolution
evolutionary biology, 1, 2–8, 12n25,
14, 16, 43, 52, 56, 58, 59n3, 80,
83, 116, 117, 126, 153, 169,
171, 251, 253
philosophy of, 10, 11, 15
theological repercussions of, 13, 17
evolutionary creation, 16, 178–179, 184,
185n20, 187–189, 198, 200,
273, 279
critical evaluation of, 198–200
outside of Thomistic circles, 180–185
within Thomistic circles, 185–187
evolutionary essentialism, 78–79
evolutionary synthesis, 2–3, 8, 15, 57, 59,
60, 83, 94, 111, 118, 123, 278
extended (EES), 8n18, 122n74
evolutionary transition, 34, 35, 38, 42,
47, 50n69, 54, 124, 156, 177, 178,
200, 204, 219, 221, 256n69, 261
complexity of, 37, 49, 51, 218, 220
divine action in, 201, 211, 220
divine and natural causes in, 17, 220,
223, 231
mechanism of, 2, 9, 278
metaphysics of, 11, 14, 18, 28, 36n34,
48, 56, 167, 279
model of, 10
saltational, 5

teleology and chance in, 10, 111, 121, 219
units of, 3, 64
unity of immanent cause(s) of, 219–220
exaptation, 4

Feser, Edward, 48, 51, 219
final cause. *See* teleology
fitness, 112, 118, 119
expected, 120
form
accidental. *See* accidental form
(AF, accident)
substantial. *See* substantial form (SF)
formal cause, 9, 70, 93n4, 95, 107, 145,
145n42, 197
fortune. *See* luck (fortune)
fossil record, 38, 248
Francis (Pope), 182
free-will defense argument, 201, 205n5
Frost, Gloria, 37n36, 40, 51n72, 120n71
function (functionality), 4, 10, 70, 77,
97, 109n46, 110–112, 115n62,
116–118, 262
functional explanation, 114, 115
fundamentalism (biblical), 174

Gaine, Simon, 245n45, 250, 276
Garrigou-Lagrange, Réginald, 241, 243
gene transfer, 2, 49, 75n57, 216
genetic drift, 2, 4, 49, 216
genetic inheritance, 7
genetic recombination, 2, 49, 68n33, 216
genetic trait, 256n70, 258n72, 260n75
genetic variation, 8, 59n3, 70, 117, 122,
123, 125n82, 247
Ghiselin, Michael T., 60n6, 64n19, 71n40,
72, 108
Gilson, Étienne, 1n1, 37n34, 136n27,
169n14, 207n10
goal-directedness, 10, 15, 78, 85, 95, 98,
109–111, 113, 115, 116, 118, 126.
See also teleology
Godfrey-Smith, Peter, 50n70
Goodwin, Brian, 5n10, 82n79
Gotthelf, Allan, 97n16, 98n17, 110n49,
111n50, 116n62, 117n65
Gould, Stephen, J., 3–5
grace. *See* supernatural grace (gift)
Gray, Asa, 92, 108, 109
Griffiths, Paul E., 72, 76n60, 77n62,
84n83
Grisez, Germain, 272

Index

Haught, John, 184, 205, 206n7
heredity, 2n2, 6. *See also* inheritance
  hereditary culpability, 264
  hereditary relations, 64
  hereditary sin, 269
  hereditary units, 2
Hewlett, Marty, 12n25, 204, 206
Hofmann, James, R., 1n1, 170, 171n17,
  175, 176n27, 240, 244n45, 245,
  246n48, 265
hominid, 234n21, 257, 275
hominin, 232–233, 234n21, 237, 247,
  249n55, 254, 255, 258n73,
  259–260, 262n76, 272, 275
Hull, David L., 64, 65n21, 72, 93
human being, 156, 168, 173, 203,
  206, 223, 224, 226, 227, 253,
  255, 257–264, 266, 269, 271,
  275, 277
  beginning of existence, 229–230
  end of existence, 230–231
  origin of the first. *See* anthropogenesis
human nature, 223, 229, 231, 239n36,
  243, 244n44, 255, 262n78, 277
  Aristotelian–Thomistic view of, 223
  in biblical theology, 224–225
  in speculative theology, 225–228
human species, 13, 136n25, 168, 221, 223,
  229, 231, 234, 236, 242n42, 243,
  246, 250, 253, 255, 256n70, 264,
  271, 275
  origin of. *See* anthropogenesis
Humani generis, 233n20, 238, 239n34,
  250n57, 268, 270, 276n114
Huxley, Thomas, 92n1, 108, 109n46
hylomorphism, 9–11, 14, 18–26, 28, 33,
  79, 83, 91, 95, 102, 139, 153, 167,
  172, 173, 226, 277
  contemporary versions of, 11n24

individuation (principle of), 213
information, 50n69, 53
  biological, 50n70, 120n71
  genetic, 27
infusion (of soul), 235, 239n36, 255,
  257, 259
infusion of sanctifying grace, 271
inheritance, 252
  Darwin on, 2n2
  epigenetic, 6
  mechanisms of, 2n2, 6, 49
  of sin (guilt), 263, 267

Jablonka, Eva, 6
John Paul II, 181, 222, 228, 233n20, 236,
  239, 251n60

Kauffman, Stuart, 7
Kemp, Kenneth W., 245n45, 248, 253,
  255–261, 269, 270, 272
kenosis (divine), 16, 179, 184. *See also*
  divine self-limitation (kenosis)
Kimura, Motoo, 4
Kitcher, Philip, 61n10, 67, 71n40, 76n60
Klubertanz, George P., 169n14

Lamb, Mary, 6, 123n75
Lamoureux, Denis O., 187, 273
Lennox, James G., 85n90, 108, 109n46,
  110, 116n62
Leroy, Marie-Dalmace, 170, 234, 235n23
living being, 14, 25n14, 68, 81, 82, 87,
  93n5, 125, 167, 170, 187, 195,
  226, 229, 235, 242, 259
  hylomorphic notion of, 18, 19
  substantial unity of, 14, 18, 26
Lombardo, Nicholas, 248, 258n72,
  260n75
luck (fortune), 80, 101n23, 103n29, 104,
  106, 146, 147
Luyten, Norbert, 1n1, 50n68, 169n14,
  186n25, 210

Maritain, Jacques, 1n1, 169n14, 186n25,
  211
material cause, 19, 47, 144
matter
  disposition of. *See* disposition of
    (primary) matter
  primary (prime) (PM). *See* primary
    matter (PM)
Mayr, Ernst, 3, 10, 60, 63, 72, 75, 84n83,
  85, 112–114
McMullin, Ernan, 1n1, 128n1, 128n3,
  129n5, 131, 133n18, 151n59,
  169n14
mechanicism, 57, 93n3, 94n8, 111
meromorphism (mereology), 28
meta-Darwinian theories, 3
Mivart, St. George Jackson, 8n17, 123,
  135, 136, 186n24, 238–240
monogenism, 241n40, 245n47, 246n48,
  47, 249n55, 256n70, 258n72,
  262n77, 263n80, 266n90, 267–268,
  272, 273, 276

Index

arguments in favor of, 252
contemporary version of, 258
critical evaluation of, 261
and polygenism - *status quaestionis*,
275–277
science on, 248
theological, 258n72, 270, 272
monophyletism, 246, 247n50, 268
Morales, José, 242n42
Moreno, Antonio, 1n1, 33n23, 36n34,
121
morphogenetic field, 5n10, 79
morphology, 35, 70, 73, 77, 78n67, 81,
83, 84n82, 88, 92n1, 108, 109n46,
236, 237, 239
Muller, Camille, 253–255, 257n72,
271n103
Muller, Earl, 274
mutation, 2n2, 4, 5, 36, 49, 75n57, 79,
88, 112, 117, 118n66, 124, 162,
216, 248, 255, 256n69–270

natural selection, 2, 5n9, 7, 8, 15, 49,
57, 60n6, 83, 94, 108, 109, 111,
118n66, 121n73, 125n82, 166,
176, 192n38, 205, 216, 239,
241, 280
in Aristotle and Aquinas, 105–107
as tautological, 118–120
as teleological, 112, 118–123
natural species, 86, 129n4, 170–171,
174, 175
naturalism
methodological *versus* ontological,
175–176, 243
necessity, 95, 102–106, 111, 121, 137,
146, 151, 152, 159. *See also*
determinism
hypothetical (suppositional), 103n31,
117
neo-Darwinism, 2, 3, 77, 93, 113, 125n82,
184
niche construction, 4, 6, 49
nominalism (about species), 14, 57
Darwin on, 58–60

O'Rourke, Fran, 1n1, 32, 34, 37n34
occasionalism, 203, 215, 218, 220, 260
Oderberg, David, 11n23–24, 59n3, 69, 70,
80n74–75, 83, 87, 90
Okasha, Samir, 62n11, 63, 72, 76n60,
84n82

opus creationis, 148, 155, 164, 177, 190
opus distinctionis, 148n47, 150, 155, 193
opus ornatus, 52n74, 148n51, 155, 157,
163, 164, 168, 177, 190, 193
original sin, 244n44, 250, 251, 254,
262n78, 263–270, 272, 274

Paley, William, 108, 123
Paul VI, 251, 272
Peacocke, Arthur, 183, 205, 206
perfection, 18, 43, 117n66, 145n43, 159,
160, 163, 185, 210, 219
of being (*esse*), 139, 147
matter as striving for, 31–34, 168
Plato and Aristotle on, 45–47
of the universe, 52–54, 157, 158,
161–162, 168
versus adequacy, 43–45
virtual and eminent presence of, 47–52
phenotypic plasticity, 10, 77, 78, 117, 126
Pius XII, 239, 242n41, 250, 251, 268,
270, 272
polygenism, 168, 244–246
and biblical exegesis, 261–268
contemporary versions of, 272–275
difficulties of, 271–272
and interpretation of *Humani generis*,
268–271
and monogenism - *status quaestionis*,
275–277
science on, 247–248
polyphyletism, 245, 246, 268
Pontifical Academy of Sciences, 180n2,
182, 222, 233n20, 242n41
population genetics, 2, 5n9, 57, 123, 171,
261, 271
population thinking, 59, 64n18, 70,
84n84
Porter, Alan, 274
potentiality, 33, 52n74, 137, 156, 159,
164n8, 186n24, 193, 199. *See also*
actuality and potentiality
and actuality, 80, 212n23
levels of, 14, 18, 28–30, 85, 153, 154,
168
pure (primary matter), 19–23, 25n13,
34, 36, 37, 41n43, 42, 49, 80, 81,
141n34, 144, 147, 179, 194–196,
211, 213n24, 214–215, 217–219,
226, 231
and *rationes seminales*, 131–134, 150,
152

Index

powers, 26, 27, 34, 36, 37n36, 40, 41,
43, 44, 49n66, 51n73, 52–53,
54n76, 102, 103n28, 145n43,
146, 150, 158, 159, 209, 231,
236, 239, 257
praeternatural gifts, 259, 261, 265
pre-established harmony, 93n4, 137
primary matter (PM), 19–22
Aquinas on, 20
Aristotle on, 19–20
as created, 145
metaphysical status of, 22n5
principle of proportionate (accurate,
commensurate) causation (PPC),
42–45, 47–49, 51n73, 52, 54,
219, 241
Aquinas on, 38–40
privation, 20
progressive creation, 129n4, 170, 175,
192n38, 273
punctuated equilibrium, 3
purpose, 92–95, 96n11, 97, 99, 108n41,
109, 113, 114, 183, 202, 203,
266n87
putrefaction, 152n62, 156–158, 160, 163

quantum field (quantum vacuum), 21

Rahner, Karl, 186n25, 230n14, 262n77,
263n81, 265, 267n93, 270
rationes seminales, 15, 127, 128, 130n6,
135–138, 155, 156, 163, 164, 168,
193, 195, 204, 243
Aquinas on, 149–153
Augustine on, 128–134
evolutionary redefinition of, 154
Ratzinger, Joseph, 181n5, 224, 228n10,
230n14, 232n17, 232n18, 235,
253n64, 258n72, 275, 276n114
realism (about species), 14, 57, 60n9, 67,
121, 153, 163, 173n18, 174n19
reproduction, 36, 121, 122n74, 158, 163,
232n17, 256, 258n72
asexual, 38, 68
differential, 112, 118, 119
sexual, 195, 255
Rosenberg, Alexander, 65n22, 72, 116n62,
119n68
Ruse, Michael, 65, 113, 119, 231n16
Russell, Robert John, 144n40, 184, 205,
206
NIODA, 207

scala naturae, 31–33
Schoonenberg, Piet, 186n25, 250n58,
264n83, 265n86
scientific revolution, 57, 126
secondary (proximate) matter (*materia
secunda*), 22, 30, 41, 85, 154, 168,
226, 233, 277
self-organizing systems, 7
Silva, Ignacio, 13n26, 202n1, 209, 210
Simpson, George Gaylord, 63n15, 114n58
Sober, Elliott, 63n12, 71n40, 72, 84n84,
84n86, 116n62
species
Aquinas on emergence of
in general, 161–163
through transformism, 164–165
biological, 14, 56, 57, 60, 61, 69, 72,
73, 78, 82, 84, 171, 172, 174, 253,
255, 257, 258, 265
Darwin on, 58–60
definition (concept, notion) of
biological species concept (BSC), 63,
68, 69n37
ecological species concept (ESC), 63,
68n33, 69n37, 71
essentialist species concept (EssSC),
71, 73–88, 91, 171
homeostatic property cluster species
concept (HPCSC), 82, 86, 173n18
intrinsic species concepts (ISCs), 14, 58,
64, 67, 71, 73, 80n75, 82, 83, 153
microbiological, 68n33
morphology species concept (MSC).
See phenetic species concept (PSC)
phenetic species concept (PSC), 82–83,
88
phylogenetic-cladistic species concept
(P-CSC), 63, 66, 69–72
pluralism of species concepts, 65–67,
68n33, 70
population structure species concept
(PSSC), 63–64, 70
relational species concepts (RSCs),
62–67, 68n33, 70–72, 76n60,
80n75, 83, 86
fixism, 30, 83, 85–86, 132, 137, 154, 156
human. *See* human species
hylomorphic approach (definition of),
79–81
as individuals, 64–65
intermediate, 32, 35
metaphysical, 171, 172, 174

Index

315

natural. *See* natural species
as natural kinds, 62, 73, 74n54, 82
nominalism *versus* realism about, 58–60
transitional, 38. *See also* species:
intermediate
species transformism, 1, 164, 165. *See also*
evolutionary transition
Sterelny, Kim, 50n70, 63n16, 72, 76n60,
77n62
substantial changes, 230
substantial form (SF), 14, 22n5, 37n35,
40, 87, 101, 150n55, 170, 172,
194, 211, 227, 235
Aristotle on, 22–26
eduction of (educed), 23, 29, 30, 34–37,
40–42, 49, 54n76, 86, 141n34,
147, 152, 154, 164, 194–198, 200,
211, 213n24, 214–219, 231, 232
divine action in, 194–198
induction of (induced), 36, 41, 51,
240n36
introduction of (introduced), 41
source of, 40–42
substantial unity, 25
of a human being, 223
of living beings, 14, 18, 26, 27
sun (as causal agent), 39n38, 54n76,
143n39, 164n8, 165n9, 218n26
supernatural grace (gift), 225, 254–255,
257, 259, 262n78, 265, 271, 272
survival of the fittest, 106, 112, 118n66,
118, 119, 121n73, 247

Tabaczek, Mariusz, xiii, 11n22, 28n18,
58n1, 174n20, 200n47, 206n7
taxon - mono- and paraphyletic, 89
taxonomy, 57, 61, 77, 81, 88
cladistic school of (CST), 89
evolutionary school of (EST), 88–89
phenetic school of (PST), 88
Porphyrian school of (PorST), 89–90
Teilhard de Chardin, Pierre, 186n25, 187,
204, 205n3, 267
teleology, 10, 11, 14, 15, 92–95, 105, 106,
125–126, 147, 205, 211, 213, 216.
See also goal-directedness

antiteleological approach, 1, 2, 94, 111
and chance, 15, 123–125, 168, 219,
280
classical notion of, 95–97
current status of, 114–118
God as the source of, 145–146, 214
and natural selection. *See* natural
selection: as teleological
normative aspect of, 97–98
twentieth-century evolutionary synthesis
on, 111–114
teleology and chance
Aquinas on, 104–105
Aristotle on, 99–104
Darwin on, 92, 123–124
teleomatics, 113
teleonomy, 113–114
theistic evolution, 15–16, 129n4, 135–136,
157, 169, 171, 172, 174, 175,
178–180, 183, 187–189, 200–202,
204, 206–208, 210, 248, 279, 280
Thomistic version of (TVTE), 13, 15,
128, 157, 166–169, 176, 177, 212,
220, 243, 279
versus evolutionary creation, 187–189
traducianism, 134n22
transformation *versus* creation, 189–191
Trent (on original sin), 266, 269, 270, 274

unity. *See* substantial unity

Vanneste, Alfred, 266
Venema, Dennis R., 247, 248n54, 252
virtual presence, 14, 18, 26–28, 47–50,
51n73, 151, 154
vitalism, 93, 113
voluntarism, 259, 260

Walsh, Denis, 59n3, 78, 85n90, 86,
114n59, 116n62
on teleology, 116–117, 126
Whitehead, Alfred, North, 9n20

Yarnold, Edward, 265

Zahm, John A., 135, 170, 238

Printed in the USA
CPSIA information can be obtained
at www.ICGtesting.com
LVHW041555160324
774517LV00002B/167